Technical Innovation in Financial Economics:

Advanced Theory, Practice, and Policy

Haojun Chen
Guangzhou Huali College, China

IGI Global
Scientific Publishing
Publishing Tomorrow's Research Today

Published in the United States of America by
IGI Global Scientific Publishing
701 East Chocolate Avenue
Hershey, PA, 17033, USA
Tel: 717-533-8845
Fax: 717-533-7115
Website: https://www.igi-global.com E-mail: cust@igi-global.com

Library of Congress Cataloging-in-Publication Data

Names: Chen, Haojun, 1980- editor http://id.loc.gov/vocabulary/relators/edt http://id.loc.gov/authorities/names/n2025000965 http://id.loc.gov/rwo/agents/n2025000965
Title: Technical innovation in financial economics : advanced theory, practice, and policy / [edited by] Haojun Chen.
Description: Hershey, PA : IGI Global Scientific Publishing, [2026] | Includes bibliographical references and index.
Identifiers: LCCN 2025018916 (print) | LCCN 2025018917 (ebook) | ISBN 9798337328409 ebook | ISBN 9798337328386 hardcover | ISBN 9798337328393 paperback
Subjects: LCSH: Finance--Technological innovations | Finance--Econometric models http://id.loc.gov/authorities/subjects/sh2008120472 | Economics http://id.loc.gov/authorities/subjects/sh85040850
Classification: LCC HG173 (ebook) | LCC HG173 .T375 2025 (print) | DDC 332 23/eng/20250--dc26
LC record available at https://lccn.loc.gov/2025018916

British Cataloguing in Publication Data
A Cataloguing in Publication record for this book is available from the British Library.

Table of Contents

Detailed Table of Contents

Section 2
AI and Advanced Analytics in Finance

This paper reviews recent advancements in applying reinforcement learning (RL) to financial markets, highlighting key algorithms such as DQN, PPO, SAC, and A3C. It examines their use in trading equities, managing portfolios, executing trades, and making markets. We discuss both value-based and policy-based methods, as well as hybrid and emerging approaches like meta-RL. Real-world applications and case studies from institutions like JPMorgan and Man Group are included to illustrate practical adoption. The paper also addresses challenges such as overfitting, non-stationarity, and interpretability, offering insights into the future of RL in finance.

This paper investigates hierarchical reinforcement learning (HRL) for multi-asset portfolio management using equities, bonds, commodities, and gold. We propose a two-level RL system where a high-level policy dynamically allocates capital across asset classes, while a low-level policy executes trades cost-efficiently. Using representative ETFs and training on historical data, the model is tested from July 2023 to June 2025. The HRL portfolio achieved an annualized return of 45.5%, volatility of 12.5%, Sharpe ratio of 3.6, and max drawdown of 6.2%, outperforming all individual assets and traditional strategies. We compare performance against static benchmarks and explore the agent's asset allocation dynamics, highlighting how the model adjusts exposures in response to market shifts. This study demonstrates HRL's potential to deliver high returns with controlled risk, offering a robust AI-driven solution for adaptive asset allocation.

Deep learning architectures have advanced global equity forecasting by capturing nonlinear and long-range dependencies across major markets. This study empirically assesses their predictive power on international indices (S&P 500, FTSE 100, Nikkei 225, Hang Seng, DAX 30) from 2010 to 2023, benchmarking against ARIMA and GARCH models. Results show that deep learning models outperform traditional econometrics in forecast accuracy, directional prediction, and Sharpe ratios, especially under volatile or regime-switching conditions. However, their "black-box" nature limits interpretability, raising concerns for financial decision-making and regulation. Techniques like SHAP, LIME, and Transformer attention help bridge this gap. We further explore applications in algorithmic trading, portfolio optimization, and market stress testing, while addressing ethical risks and regulatory challenges. Our findings underline deep learning's potential in finance, contingent on explainability and governance.

This study investigates the periodic behavior of U.S. residential heating oil prices (1990–2025) using three analytical techniques: wavelet multiresolution decomposition, analogue pattern retrieval, and spectral analysis via FFT. Wavelet analysis disentangles price dynamics into long-term trends, seasonal cycles, and high-frequency noise, identifying a dominant annual seasonality alongside irregular multi-year cycles. Analogue retrieval finds historical winters (2003–04, 2017–18, 2013–14) with similar price patterns to the 2024–25 winter, aiding scenario-based forecasting. Spectral analysis confirms the strength of the 1-year cycle and highlights significant low-frequency variability. The integrated approach provides a comprehensive understanding of price formation driven by seasonal demand, macro trends, and episodic shocks. Findings support hybrid forecasting strategies combining

Preface

SUBJECT MATTER

In the past decade, Artificial Intelligence (AI) and broader financial technology (FinTech) innovations have had a profound and transformative impact on the financial industry. AI is no longer a niche experiment; it has rapidly become central to how financial institutions operate, how investments are managed, and how risks are assessed. Global surveys show that organizational AI adoption has surged dramatically – rising from roughly 50% of firms to 72% in early 2024 – with generative AI fueling much of this recent growth (Singla et al., 2024). At the same time, FinTech services have moved mainstream. The global FinTech adoption rate (Ernst & Young, 2019) among consumers climbed from just 16% in 2015 to about 64% by 2019, led by emerging markets such as China and India where adoption reaches 80–90%. This dual revolution of AI and FinTech is reshaping financial services at every level: from algorithmic trading desks at hedge funds to mobile banking apps on smartphones.

AI technologies are driving unprecedented efficiencies and capabilities in finance. In banking, for example, AI-powered solutions are optimizing customer service, improving credit decisioning, and automating back-office operations. Banks adopting an "AI-first" strategy report significant gains in productivity and customer engagement (Fares et al., 2022). On the investment front, AI-driven tools are democratizing asset management. One clear example is the rise of robo-advisors in wealth management, which leverage machine learning to provide automated portfolio advice. Advances in deep learning have enabled robo-advisors to continuously learn from market data and adjust strategies in real-time (Abbas, 2024). This has lowered barriers to entry for individual investors, giving retail clients access to diversified portfolios and sophisticated risk management that were once the preserve of high-net-worth or institutional investors (Baek et al., 2020). Studies have found that these AI-fueled platforms can offer personalized financial advice at low cost, making financial planning more accessible and affordable than traditional human advisory models (Snihovyi et al., 2018). The democratization of financial services through AI and FinTech is a recurring theme of this book, with examples ranging from algorithmic micro-investing apps to peer-to-peer lending platforms.

AI and data-driven methods have also greatly enhanced the analytical power available to financial practitioners. In the realm of investment and trading, numerous studies have shown that machine learning techniques can detect complex patterns and generate predictive insights beyond the reach of traditional models. For example, researchers using tree-based classifiers and neural networks have achieved impressive accuracy in predicting stock index movements, in some cases challenging the notion of market efficiency by beating passive benchmarks (Borovkova & Tsiamas, 2019; Siami-Namini & Namin, 2018). Advanced AI models such as Long Short-Term Memory (LSTM) networks and ensemble methods (e.g. XGBoost) have demonstrated the ability to exploit subtle inefficiencies in capital markets. One study found that hedge funds employing algorithmic trading strategies significantly outperformed those relying on human discretion – earning at least a 50-basis point higher monthly return on average (Grobys et al., 2022). These outcomes suggest that AI-driven strategies, when properly implemented, can enhance investment performance and risk management. At the same time, the growing reliance on algorithmic systems raises questions about new forms of systemic risk – an issue explored in chapters on market dynamics and AI ethics. For instance, automated high-frequency trading has been linked to episodic market disruptions (flash crashes), highlighting the need for safeguards as human oversight diminishes.

Beyond prediction tasks, AI is broadening the scope of information that financial analysis can incorporate. Natural Language Processing (NLP) techniques now enable analysis of unstructured textual data – news articles, social media posts, earnings call transcripts – alongside numerical data. Financial institutions are using NLP-based sentiment analysis to gauge market mood and to detect early warning signals of corporate distress (Pejić Bach et al., 2019). In credit risk management, AI models can process alternative data to evaluate borrowers who lack extensive credit histories (Bhatore et al., 2020). Fraud detection systems leverage machine learning to identify anomalous transaction patterns in real time, significantly reducing losses. These applications illustrate how AI can uncover insights and relationships that were previously hidden, leading to more informed and timely decision-making. They also illustrate why interpretability is crucial: as financial decisions become increasingly data-driven, stakeholders demand clarity on why an AI model made a given recommendation (Fisher et al., 2016; Ghosh et al., 2024). Throughout the chapters of this book, the tension between performance and explainability emerges as a central theme – one that financial firms must navigate carefully to maintain trust.

It is also important to recognize that FinTech is not limited to AI and data analytics; it encompasses a broader wave of digital innovation in finance. Blockchain and cryptocurrencies have introduced decentralized alternatives to traditional finance, enabling new products like crypto-assets, stablecoins, and decentralized finance (DeFi) protocols. These innovations promise greater inclusivity and disintermediation – anyone with an internet connection can participate in blockchain networks – but they also pose novel risks from cybersecurity to monetary stability. Governments and regulators worldwide are grappling with how to integrate crypto and DeFi into the financial system, a topic addressed in this volume through comparative studies and analyses of crypto's role in illicit finance. FinTech advancements have also driven the growth of digital payment platforms and super-apps, particularly in Asia, transforming how consumers save, borrow, and invest. By 2025, China's leading mobile payment networks each boast over a billion users, showcasing how quickly financial behavior can shift given the right technological infrastructure. This book examines such shifts in detail – from how decentralized finance (DeFi) is reshaping virtual economies, to the strategic implications of stablecoins on global monetary sovereignty. It further explores the cutting-edge application of AI techniques including reinforcement learning and deep neural networks to transform investment strategies and financial forecasting across global markets.

TARGET AUDIENCE

This book is designed to meet the needs of a diverse audience, including graduate students, academic researchers, industry professionals, and policymakers. For graduate students – especially those in fields like financial data science, finance, or information technology – the book serves as an invaluable introduction to cutting-edge topics at the intersection of AI and finance. It provides a fast-track to understanding contemporary research problems and methodologies. For instance, one chapter (Chapter 7) provides a comprehensive review of deep reinforcement learning in financial applications, offering students both a conceptual foundation and practical insights into how autonomous learning agents are being applied to trading, portfolio optimization, and risk management problems. Such overviews can help aspiring scholars identify knowledge gaps and formulate new research questions. Importantly, the collection bridges theory and practice in a way that textbooks often do not. This is increasingly crucial as employers demand tech-savvy finance graduates: a recent survey found that only about half of finance leaders feel new graduates are adequately prepared for the technology-driven finance roles of today. By studying the successes and challenges documented here – from implementing AI algorithms to managing digital transformation – students can acquire a well-rounded foundation that improves their job readiness. In short, the book can be viewed as both a state-of-the-art academic reference and a professional training resource for the next generation of financial experts.

For academic audiences, the chapters offer a rigorous exploration of the theories, models, and empirical evidence surrounding AI and FinTech applications in finance. The contributors to this volume include esteemed professors and experienced practitioners from around the world, ensuring that each chapter provides both deep technical insight and contextual expertise. Researchers will find detailed expositions of advanced methodologies – from reinforcement learning techniques and wavelet analyses to NLP and blockchain architectures – all grounded in the financial domain. Many chapters blend quantitative results with conceptual discussion, which is ideal for academics looking to understand not just how a technique works, but why it matters for financial research. The scholarly thoroughness allows researchers to delve into the primary literature on topics such as algorithmic bias, DeFi regulation, or green finance innovation. By bringing together diverse topics under the unifying theme of AI/FinTech in finance, the book also encourages a cross-pollination of ideas across subfields. An academic reader in finance, for example, can see how techniques from computer science are being applied to financial problems, while a computer scientist can appreciate the unique challenges and datasets of the finance world. This interdisciplinary perspective reflects the growing recognition that complex financial issues – be it predicting markets or ensuring fair AI – require a multidisciplinary approach. Academics will thus find this volume useful for both reference and inspiration, possibly spurring new lines of inquiry that build on the comprehensive coverage presented.

For professionals in the financial sector, this book offers timely insights and practical knowledge drawn from real-world implementations. The rapid pace of AI and FinTech adoption in industry means practitioners must constantly update their skills and understanding. Indeed, 91% of asset managers are now using or planning to use AI in their investment processes, and two-thirds of finance leaders say they already rely on AI tools in some form at work (Mercer Investments, 2024). This widespread integration of technology has created a pressing need for financial professionals to stay abreast of best practices, regulatory expectations, and emerging risks. The book directly addresses this need: several chapters are written with a practitioner lens, including case studies, industry surveys, and implementation frameworks. For example, Chapter 3 examines how institutional investors are securing Bitcoin assets and complying with evolving regulations, drawing on interviews with bank executives and compliance officers. Chapter 7 presents a comparative study of deep learning vs. traditional models in equity forecasting, complete with performance metrics that a portfolio manager could apply to their own strategy evaluation. Readers will find actionable takeaways such as guidelines for deploying AI in trading, strategies for mitigating cybersecurity threats in FinTech applications, and checklists for ethical AI governance. The inclusion of concrete examples – like the analysis of high-profile ransomware cases or the discussion of Hong Kong's new stablecoin regulations – provides professionals with analogies and lessons that can inform their decision-making. In essence, the book functions as a knowledge transfer from the frontiers of research to the front lines of practice, equipping financiers, technologists, and regulators with insights to navigate the ongoing digital transformation of finance.

Finally, the book's cross-disciplinary approach means it will also appeal to readers beyond the traditional finance community. Professionals and students in computer science, data analytics, economics, and public policy will find value in its pages. A data scientist can learn about the unique challenges of applying AI in a high-stakes, regulated environment like finance. An economist or policymaker can gain a better understanding of how technological innovations are reshaping economic systems and what new regulatory frameworks might be required. By covering topics from monetary sovereignty and digital currencies to green finance and financial inclusion, the book provides a front view that can inform policy debates and strategy discussions in both the public and private sectors.

ORGANIZATION OF THE BOOK

The book includes 8 chapters grouped into 2 parts, each part focusing on a major thematic area of technical innovation in finance. Below, we outline the organization and provide a brief summary of each chapter:

Part I: Digital Assets and Decentralized Finance – The first part explores innovations in cryptocurrency, blockchain, and financial decentralization, along with their implications for traditional finance and regulation.

- **Chapter 1, *Revealing the Overlooked Financial Value of Cryptocurrency in the Ransomware Economy*,** examines the controversial valuation of cryptocurrencies by emphasizing their utility in illicit markets such as ransomware. It introduces a hybrid valuation model incorporating legitimate utility and illicit demand, offering a fresh lens for understanding crypto price dynamics. By analyzing real-world cases like Travelex and CNA Financial, the chapter underscores how anonymity and decentralized structures shape both regulatory challenges and asset valuation.
- **Chapter 2, *The Stablecoins Race in Monetary Sovereignty between China and the US*,** explores the geopolitical and monetary implications of stablecoins, contrasting China's e-CNY initiative with the U.S. market-driven stablecoin ecosystem. This chapter reveals how stablecoins have become a

new arena for global monetary power and discusses the potential for RMB internationalization. It highlights risks such as financial stability and digital dollarization, while also considering global regulatory coordination.

- **Chapter 3, *Securing Bitcoin in Financial Services: New Risks, Evolving Regulations, and Institutional Strategies*,** delves into the intersection of cybersecurity, institutional adoption, and regulatory compliance. By addressing issues ranging from consensus attacks to quantum computing threats, the chapter highlights the importance of multi-layered security and compliance strategies. It also introduces the concept of "compliance by design," emphasizing how institutions can integrate technical and regulatory frameworks for long-term resilience.
- **Chapter 4, *Financial Innovation in Virtual Economies: The Role of DeFi in Metaverse Integration*,** explores the convergence of decentralized finance and the Metaverse. Through platforms like Decentraland and Sandbox, it illustrates how lending, staking, and asset tokenization create self-sustaining virtual economies. The chapter emphasizes both the opportunities and the regulatory and security challenges of this emerging financial landscape.

Part II: AI and Advanced Analytics in Finance – The second part of the book delves into the applications of artificial intelligence, machine learning, and other analytical techniques for financial modeling, trading, and forecasting.

- **Chapter 5, *Recent Developments in Financial Reinforcement Learning*,** provides a systematic review of state-of-the-art RL algorithms like DQN, PPO, and A3C, applied across trading, portfolio optimization, and market-making. It discusses real-world case studies from leading institutions and highlights both the performance advantages and risks associated with RL in volatile markets. Future trends, including hybrid RL and meta-learning, are explored as next-generation solutions.
- **Chapter 6, *Adaptive Asset Allocation with Hierarchical Reinforcement Learning: A Multi-Class Investment Strategy*,** introduces a multi-layered AI approach that dynamically allocates capital across multiple asset classes. By integrating high-level allocation policies with low-level trading strategies, this chapter demonstrates the superiority of HRL in adapting to market shifts. Its empirical findings show exceptional returns compared to traditional strategies, providing a blueprint for AI-driven portfolio management.
- **Chapter 7, *Deep Learning for Global Equity Forecasting: New Evidence Across Major Markets*,** investigates how deep learning models like LSTM and Transformers outperform classical econometric approaches. By analyzing international indices under volatile conditions, this chapter showcases

the predictive accuracy of AI while also addressing interpretability issues. It highlights explainable AI techniques such as SHAP and LIME as tools for building trust in AI-driven forecasting.

- **Chapter 8,** ***Multi-Scale Decomposition and Analogue Modeling of Heating Oil Prices: A Wavelet, Spectral, and Pattern Retrieval Approach to Seasonal and Cyclical Forecasting*****,** applies wavelet decomposition, spectral analysis, and analogue pattern retrieval to forecast seasonal and cyclical price patterns. This chapter demonstrates how integrating time-frequency techniques yields more accurate energy price forecasts. The approach is particularly valuable for risk management, hedging, and energy policy planning.

Each chapter in this volume builds on the central theme of AI and financial innovation transforming finance, while highlighting different facets – from technical breakthroughs and business applications to regulatory frameworks and social implications. The organization of the book reflects an intentional progression: starting with disruptive innovations (crypto, DeFi), moving through advanced AI techniques in practice, then examining how we govern and mitigate the risks of these technologies, and finally considering how they can serve broader societal goals. Readers can approach the chapters sequentially for a holistic understanding, or selectively focus on sections most relevant to their interests, whether it be algorithmic trading, digital banking policy, or sustainable finance.

CONCLUSION

This book makes a significant contribution to the rapidly evolving field of AI and FinTech in finance, providing a comprehensive and up-to-date perspective on the intersection of technology, financial markets, and societal change. By bringing together a diverse range of chapters authored by experts across academia and industry, the book offers both deep theoretical insights and practical case studies. Collectively, these chapters illustrate how innovations such as machine learning, blockchain, and digital platforms are not abstract concepts but real forces reshaping financial services – from the way banks grant loans and investors trade, to how individuals save and governments regulate. The volume not only documents the current landscape of financial technology applications but also presents forward-looking discussions of emerging trends like quantum computing in finance, central bank digital currencies, and the integration of sustainability considerations into fintech.

Several unifying themes emerge from the book's two parts. One is the transformative potential of AI and data analytics in finance – we see clear evidence of improved performance and efficiency in areas like forecasting, trading, and risk management when advanced algorithms are applied. But another theme is the necessity of marrying technological innovation with responsibility and governance. Encouragingly, many chapters offer solutions – from technical fixes to policy interventions – suggesting that the challenges, while significant, are manageable with informed action.

Ultimately, this book is both a knowledge repository and a call to action. It equips readers with a broad and deep understanding of how AI and FinTech are rewriting the rules of finance. But it also encourages readers – whether they are students, seasoned professionals, or regulators – to actively engage with this transformation. The insights here can inform the development of more robust algorithms, the drafting of smarter regulations, the design of more user-friendly financial apps, and the pursuit of research that drives the field further. Finance is often described as the lifeblood of the economy; what we are witnessing through the developments chronicled in this book is a bold transfusion of new technology into that bloodstream, promising great vitality if done right. We hope that the knowledge consolidated in these chapters will inspire innovation that is not only cutting-edge but also responsible and inclusive. By bridging theory and practice, highlighting successes and pitfalls, and drawing connections between disparate topics, this book positions itself as an essential resource for anyone looking to navigate – or shape – the future of financial innovation in an AI-driven world.

REFERENCES

Abbas, S. K. (2024). AI meets finance: The rise of AI-powered robo-advisors. *Journal of Electrical Systems*, *20*(11), 1011–1016.

Baek, S., Lee, K. Y., Uctum, M., & Oh, S. H. (2020). Robo-advisors: Machine learning in trend-following ETF investments. *Sustainability (Basel)*, *12*(16), 6399. DOI: 10.3390/su12166399

Bhatore, S., Mohan, L., & Reddy, Y. R. (2020). Machine learning techniques for credit risk evaluation: A systematic literature review. *Journal of Banking and Financial Technology*, *4*(1), 111–138. DOI: 10.1007/s42786-020-00020-3

Borovkova, S., & Tsiamas, I. (2019). An ensemble of LSTM neural networks for high-frequency stock market classification. *Journal of Forecasting*, *38*(6), 600–619. DOI: 10.1002/for.2585

Ernst & Young. (2019). *Global FinTech adoption index 2019*. https://eyfinancialservicesthoughtgallery.ie/global-fintech-adoption-index-2019

Fares, O. H., Butt, I., & Lee, S. H. M. (2022). Utilization of artificial intelligence in the banking sector: A systematic literature review. *Journal of Financial Services Marketing*, *27*(4), 299–315.

Fisher, I. E., Garnsey, M. R., & Hughes, M. E. (2016). Natural language processing in accounting, auditing and finance: A synthesis of the literature with a roadmap for future research. *Intelligent Systems in Accounting, Finance & Management*, *23*(3), 157–214. DOI: 10.1002/isaf.1386

Ghosh, J., Maiti, B., Bhaduri, A., Das, A., Patra, J., Gupta, S., & Hazra, S. (2024). NLP and ML for real-time sentiment analysis in finance. In *2024 IEEE International Conference on Communication, Computing and Signal Processing (IICCCS)* (pp. 1–6). IEEE. DOI: 10.1109/IICCCS61609.2024.10763733

Grobys, K., Kolari, J. W., & Niang, J. (2022). Man versus machine: On artificial intelligence and hedge fund performance. *Applied Economics*, *54*(40), 4632–4646. DOI: 10.1080/00036846.2022.2032585

Mercer Investments. (2024, March 21). AI integration in investment management: 2024 global manager survey. *Mercer*. https://www.mercer.com/insights/investments/portfolio-strategies/ai-in-investment-management-survey/

Pejić Bach, M., Krstić, Ž., Seljan, S., & Turulja, L. (2019). Text mining for big data analysis in the financial sector: A literature review. *Sustainability (Basel), 11*(5), 1277. DOI: 10.3390/su11051277

Siami-Namini, S., & Namin, A. S. (2018). Forecasting economics and financial time series: ARIMA vs. LSTM [Preprint]. arXiv. https://arxiv.org/abs/1803.06386

Singla, A., Sukharevsky, A., Yee, L., & Chui, M. (2024, May 30). The state of AI in early 2024: Generative AI adoption spikes and starts to generate value. *McKinsey & Company.* https://www.mckinsey.com/capabilities/quantumblack/our-insights/the-state-of-ai-2024

Snihovyi, O., Kobets, V., & Ivanov, O. (2018, May). Implementation of robo-advisor services for different risk attitude investment decisions using machine learning techniques. In *International Conference on Information and Communication Technologies in Education, Research, and Industrial Applications* (pp. 298–321). Cham: Springer International Publishing.

Section 1
Digital Assets and Decentralized Finance

Chapter 1

Revealing the Overlooked Financial Value of Cryptocurrency in the Ransomware Economy

Chee Hon Lew
https://orcid.org/0000-0003-1986-7977
Guangzhou Huali College, China

ABSTRACT

This paper challenges conventional perspectives on cryptocurrency valuation by examining their indispensable role in illicit economies, particularly ransomware. While mainstream analyses emphasize speculative demand, scarcity, or decentralized innovation, we argue that a significant and persistent source of value stems from cryptocurrencies' utility in facilitating untraceable payments, laundering illicit gains, and evading financial sanctions. Through detailed case studies, we demonstrate how features like pseudonymity, borderless transferability, and irreversible settlement make cryptocurrencies integral to cyber extortion. We propose a hybrid valuation model incorporating legitimate utility, illicit utility premium, and regulatory friction discount, offering a more nuanced framework for pricing. The paper concludes by discussing regulatory and ethical implications, urging policymakers to target transactional chokepoints without stifling legitimate innovation.

1. INTRODUCTION

Warren Buffett, the legendary investor and the oracle of Omaha, has famously dismissed Bitcoin as "probably rat poison squared" (Franck, 2018), arguing that it

DOI: 10.4018/979-8-3373-2838-6.ch001

produces nothing, has no intrinsic value, and is fundamentally a speculative gamble rather than a sound investment. He has repeatedly expressed skepticism toward cryptocurrencies, asserting that they lack the earnings power, productive capacity, or cash flow characteristics that define a truly valuable asset (Folkinshteyn et al, 2015). If even the most revered authority on value investing struggles to identify the intrinsic worth of Bitcoin or any other cryptocurrency, what then, if any, is the source of their value? This conundrum-why cryptocurrencies continue to command market attention and significant capital flows despite such criticisms-forms the intellectual provocation that this paper seeks to address. In doing so, we diverge from mainstream economic perspectives that focus narrowly on legitimate use cases and instead turn to the darker realities of the digital economy, where cryptocurrencies serve indispensable roles.

The reality is that value is not merely a function of productive output or traditional economic utility. An asset can derive substantial value from its functional indispensability in particular systems, whether those systems operate within the boundaries of the law or beyond them. In the case of cryptocurrencies, their architecture-marked by pseudonymity, decentralization, and resistance to censorship-renders them uniquely suitable for transactions in shadow economies. Chief among these is the ecosystem of ransomware, where malicious actors encrypt victims' data and demand payment in digital currencies to restore access or prevent sensitive information from being publicly disclosed. Here, cryptocurrencies exhibit a form of utility that transcends the moral valuation of their application: they function seamlessly where conventional finance cannot, specifically in facilitating ransom payments, laundering illicit gains, and circumventing economic sanctions.

This paper therefore aims to unpack the paradox of cryptocurrency value by shifting the analytical focus away from speculative enthusiasm and technological optimism, and toward the pragmatic demands of illicit economies. In particular, we explore how cryptocurrencies have become not merely tools, but integral components of ransomware operations. The demand generated by these actors is not incidental-it is structural, shaping the liquidity, infrastructure, and even the innovation trajectory of cryptocurrencies themselves. By examining this shadow-side of digital finance, we gain insights into why certain coins, particularly Bitcoin and Monero, have proven resilient and even appreciated in value despite-or perhaps because of-their controversial roles in cybercrime.

Ransomware has emerged as a major adopter of cryptocurrencies, inadvertently stress-testing their scalability, anonymity features, and transaction efficiency under high-stakes conditions. What began as opportunistic attacks for modest sums has evolved into a professionalized, globalized criminal enterprise, often facilitated by Ransomware-as-a-Service (RaaS) platforms that democratize access to hacking tools for less technically skilled criminals. These operations demand cryptocurrency payments for the same reasons that legitimate actors appreciate crypto's appeal: borderless transferability, the ability to transact without intermediaries, and irreversible settlements that mitigate the risk of chargebacks or asset freezes. The parallels between these illicit imperatives and the promises of financial innovation are both striking and instructive. As shown in Figure 1 below, according to Chainalysis (2025), ransomware criminals have collected roughly $813.55 million through victim payments in 2024, marking a 35% drop from the previous year's record of $1.25 billion. This dip signifies, for the first time since 2022, a decline in ransomware earnings.

Figure 1. Annual Ransomware Payment by Chainalysis (2025)

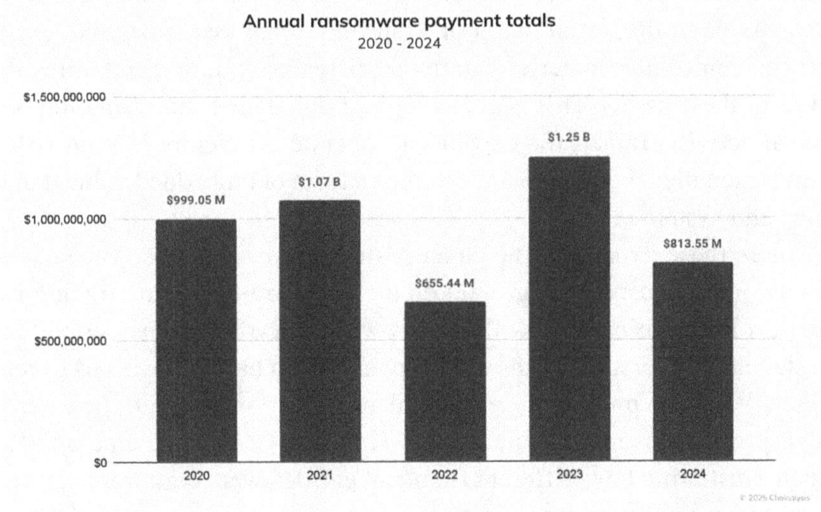

Moreover, the role of cryptocurrencies in ransomware extends beyond mere payments. Cryptocurrencies sustain complex financial ecosystems that enable laundering, obfuscation, and reintegration of illicit funds into legitimate markets. Mixers and tumblers anonymize transaction flows, while privacy coins like Monero enhance untraceability. Chain hopping-converting one cryptocurrency into another across different blockchains-further complicates tracking efforts by law enforcement. These laundering mechanisms not only highlight the technological sophistication underpinning the ransomware economy but also drive ongoing demand for specific crypto technologies and services, ensuring their continued development and market relevance.

Additionally, the geopolitical dimension of cryptocurrency valuation is increasingly evident. Entities subjected to international sanctions, such as those imposed by the United States on certain state actors and their affiliates, have also turned to cryptocurrencies as a means of evading financial exclusion (Pantin, 2023). These sanctioned actors engage in cyber operations, including ransomware, as both an economic strategy and a form of asymmetric warfare. In these contexts, cryptocurrencies provide a financial lifeline where conventional banking avenues are closed, further embedding their relevance in global financial flows - even if those flows are illicit. This connection between ransomware, sanctions evasion, and cryptocurrency usage adds a geopolitical layer to the valuation discourse, suggesting that the worth of digital currencies is in part sustained by their geopolitical indispensability (Trouble, 2020).

This paper is therefore an inquiry into the functional value of cryptocurrencies, derived from their utility in ransomware and related illicit activities. We argue that this shadow-side utility, often overlooked in traditional assessments of cryptocurrency worth, contributes materially to the persistence, liquidity, and infrastructural robustness of these assets. This is not to suggest that their entire valuation is driven by criminal activity; rather, the capacity to operate efficiently in high-risk, high-stakes, and often illegal domains underscores a form of embedded value that is both functional and systemic.

To explore these dynamics, the paper is structured as follows. The next section provides a comprehensive background on the rise of ransomware, tracing its technological evolution in parallel with the growth of cryptocurrency adoption. This sets the stage for understanding how both phenomena have co-evolved to reinforce each other. We then present an empirical examination through case studies of three high-profile ransomware incidents - Travelex, CNA Financial, and Flagstar Bank-each illustrating how different financial entities were compromised and how cryptocurrencies facilitated these crimes. These cases help to concretize the abstract notions of value and utility by showcasing real-world applications of crypto assets under criminal pressures.

Following the case studies, the analysis section dissects the technical mechanisms that make cryptocurrencies effective within ransomware ecosystems, including the use of mixers, privacy coins, and cross-chain transactions. This section also connects these mechanisms to broader market effects, such as increased liquidity and market confidence in certain cryptocurrencies, despite regulatory crackdowns. We further explore the financial, operational, and reputational risks faced by institutions that fall victim to crypto-enabled ransomware, linking these to the dual-use nature of cryptocurrencies as both innovative financial tools and instruments of crime.

The paper also introduces a forward-looking discussion on AI-enhanced ransomware and emerging laundering techniques across decentralized finance (DeFi) platforms, highlighting how technological convergence is shaping the next generation of ransomware threats and crypto adaptations. This is followed by a policy-oriented section proposing regulatory and strategic frameworks to mitigate the negative externalities of cryptocurrency's illicit utility, without stifling their legitimate potential for innovation and financial democratization.

Finally, the paper concludes by synthesizing these insights to offer a revised understanding of cryptocurrency valuation, one that accounts not only for speculative and legitimate use cases but also for the undeniable value cryptocurrencies hold in the global shadow economy. By illuminating these dimensions, the paper aims to contribute to more comprehensive policy, investment, and academic dialogues on the future of digital finance in an increasingly complex and contested global landscape.

2. TECHNICAL AND THEORETICAL BACKGROUND: CRYPTOCURRENCIES AND RANSOMWARE

Understanding the symbiotic relationship between cryptocurrencies and ransomware requires a grasp of the fundamental technologies that underpin both domains. Cryptocurrencies emerged as a novel solution to the problem of decentralized trust and digital value transfer, while ransomware evolved as a particularly effective form of cyber extortion powered by encryption technologies. Together, these technologies have enabled a new paradigm of cyber-enabled crime, where financial extortion is seamlessly integrated with anonymous, borderless payment infrastructures. This section offers a comprehensive technical and theoretical background on cryptocurrencies and ransomware, providing essential context for understanding their intersection in illicit economies.

2.1 Cryptocurrencies: Technical Foundations and Economic Theory

Cryptocurrencies are digital or virtual currencies that rely on cryptography for security and function on decentralized networks, typically maintained via blockchain technology (Tredinnick, 2019). Bitcoin, proposed by the pseudonymous Satoshi Nakamoto in 2008, was the first cryptocurrency to solve the double-spending problem without the need for a trusted third party (Nakamoto, 2008). The core innovation lies in the blockchain, a distributed ledger that records transactions in a transparent and immutable manner, verified by consensus mechanisms such as proof-of-work (PoW).

2.1.1 Blockchain Technology

A blockchain is a sequential chain of blocks, each containing a list of transactions, a timestamp, and a cryptographic hash of the previous block (Komalavalli et al, 2020). This structure ensures that altering any past transaction would require re-mining all subsequent blocks, an endeavor that is computationally infeasible under the PoW system (Narayanan et al., 2016). In Bitcoin, miners expend computational power to solve complex mathematical problems, a process that secures the network and validates transactions. Alternative consensus mechanisms such as proof-of-stake (PoS) have been developed to address the energy inefficiencies of PoW. In PoS systems, validators are chosen to confirm transactions based on the amount of cryptocurrency they hold and are willing to "stake" as collateral (Saleh, 2021). These innovations have broadened the landscape of cryptocurrencies beyond Bitcoin to include Ethereum, Cardano, and Solana, among others.

2.1.2 Anonymity and Pseudonymity

While all transactions on blockchains like Bitcoin are publicly visible, they are pseudonymous: users interact via alphanumeric addresses rather than personal identities. This pseudonymity offers a degree of privacy but is not foolproof, as blockchain analysis can sometimes deanonymize users through transaction patterns and off-chain data (Conti et al., 2018). In response to these traceability concerns, privacy-centric cryptocurrencies such as Monero and Zcash have emerged. Monero employs technologies such as ring signatures, stealth addresses, and confidential transactions to obfuscate sender, receiver, and transaction amounts (Noether, 2016). Similarly, Zcash offers optional privacy through zk-SNARKs (zero-knowledge succinct non-interactive arguments of knowledge), allowing transaction data to be shielded while still verifiable (Banerjee et al., 2020). These privacy features have made such cryptocurrencies particularly attractive in illicit markets.

2.1.3 Cryptocurrency Market Dynamics

Economically, the value of cryptocurrencies is influenced by factors such as scarcity, network effects, security, and perceived utility (Catalini & Gans, 2016). Bitcoin's capped supply of 21 million coins introduces a scarcity akin to digital gold, while network effects-where the utility of a network grows with the number of users-enhance adoption and valuation. However, beyond speculative investment, cryptocurrencies derive functional value from their utility in financial transactions that require privacy, censorship resistance, and cross-border transferability. These attributes are particularly salient in use cases that operate outside the bounds of regulated finance, including ransomware payments, sanctions evasion, and black-market commerce (Foley et al., 2019).

2.2 Ransomware: Technical Mechanisms and Operational Models

Ransomware is a form of malware designed to encrypt a victim's data or system, rendering it inaccessible until a ransom is paid, typically in cryptocurrency. Its potency arises from the combination of strong cryptography, social engineering, and the anonymity afforded by digital currencies (Kshetri & Voas, 2017). Ransomware leverages robust cryptographic algorithms to lock victims' data (Berrueta et al, 2019). Most modern ransomware employs hybrid encryption, combining symmetric encryption (e.g., AES-256) for data encryption due to its speed, with asymmetric encryption (e.g., RSA-2048) to encrypt the symmetric key itself (Kharraz et al., 2015). This dual-layer approach ensures that even if victims can access their systems, the decryption key remains inaccessible without paying the ransom.

Variants like WannaCry exploited vulnerabilities in network protocols (such as SMBv1 on Windows systems) to propagate automatically across networks, demonstrating the devastating potential of ransomware with worm-like capabilities (Akbanov et al., 2019).

2.2.1 Ransomware-as-a-Service (RaaS)

RaaS models have professionalized the ransomware ecosystem by separating development and deployment roles. In RaaS, developers create and maintain ransomware software, which is then leased to affiliates who execute attacks. Profits, paid in cryptocurrency, are split between developers and affiliates (Alwashali et al., 2021). This model lowers barriers to entry, allowing even technically unsophisticated actors to participate in ransomware campaigns. RaaS platforms often provide customer support for affiliates, updates to malware to evade detection, and even negotiation services with victims, mirroring legitimate software-as-a-service (SaaS) businesses in operational sophistication.

2.2.2 Double and Triple Extortion

Contemporary ransomware attacks frequently employ double extortion tactics, where attackers not only encrypt data but also exfiltrate it, threatening to leak sensitive information if the ransom is not paid (Fitzgerald, 2022). Some groups have advanced to triple extortion by also pressuring victims' customers, partners, or stakeholders, further amplifying the coercive leverage (Payne & Mienie, 2021). The evolution of extortion techniques underscores the strategic thinking behind ransomware operations, transforming them from simple technical exploits into complex socio-technical attacks.

2.3 The Convergence of Cryptocurrencies and Ransomware

The convergence of cryptocurrencies and ransomware is not coincidental but a result of aligned technological affordances. Cryptocurrencies provide the financial infrastructure necessary for ransomware's business model to scale globally. Without cryptocurrencies, the anonymity, speed, and reach required for effective extortion would be severely compromised. Moreover, the innovation in crypto-laundering techniques parallels advancements in ransomware. Tools such as mixers, decentralized exchanges, and cross-chain bridges enable cybercriminals to obfuscate financial trails (Conti et al., 2018; Sanders, 2025). The use of "chain hopping," moving funds between different cryptocurrencies, complicates forensic analysis and frustrates law enforcement efforts (Bartoletti et al., 2021). Blockchain analytics firms such as Chainalysis, Elliptic, and CipherTrace have developed sophisticated tracking methods to follow illicit crypto flows. Yet, the emergence of privacy coins and increasingly decentralized financial infrastructures presents ongoing challenges to these efforts.

2.4 Theoretical Perspectives on Value and Illicit Economies

From a theoretical standpoint, the integration of cryptocurrencies into ransomware economies can be examined through the lens of economic sociology and criminology. Theories of value in shadow economies suggest that assets gain value not only from legitimate market functions but also from their indispensability in illegal or semi-legal transactions (Naylor, 2004). Cryptocurrencies, in this view, serve as functional substitutes for cash in digital black markets. Additionally, routine activity theory in criminology posits that crime occurs when a motivated offender, a suitable target, and the absence of capable guardians converge (Cohen & Felson, 1979). Cryptocurrencies reduce the role of "capable guardians" by bypassing regulated financial systems, thus facilitating the commission of ransomware crimes. Network theory also provides insights: as more ransomware operators adopt certain cryptocurrencies, the network effects strengthen the position of these assets within both legal and illicit financial systems, contributing to their market resilience and speculative value (Gandal, 2018).

2.5 Regulatory and Policy Responses

Recognizing the challenge, regulators have intensified efforts to curb the misuse of cryptocurrencies in ransomware. The Financial Action Task Force (FATF) has mandated that virtual asset service providers (VASPs) implement stringent KYC and anti-money laundering (AML) measures. The OFAC has issued advisories emphasizing that ransom payments to sanctioned entities may violate U.S. law[2]. Despite these efforts, the decentralized and pseudonymous nature of cryptocurrencies continues to offer significant barriers to enforcement. The emergence of decentralized finance (DeFi) platforms, which often operate without centralized intermediaries, further complicates regulatory oversight (Zetzsche et al., 2020).

3. METHODOLOGY

This paper adopts a qualitative case study methodology to explore how ransomware operations contribute to the functional and perceived value of cryptocurrencies. Rather than approaching cryptocurrencies purely as speculative financial instruments or technological curiosities, this study investigates their demonstrated utility in facilitating illicit financial flows-specifically in the context of ransomware attacks. By examining real-world incidents where cryptocurrencies have played an indispensable role, this paper aims to empirically anchor the argument that the value of cryptocurrencies is, in part, sustained by their capacity to serve as critical enablers of cybercrime economies. Through this lens, the paper seeks to provide both empirical and analytical insights into the symbiotic relationship between digital currencies and ransomware, a nexus that is often acknowledged but insufficiently analyzed in discussions of cryptocurrency valuation.

3.1 Research Design

The research design is structured around a tripartite analytical approach that examines the technical, financial, and institutional dimensions of ransomware cases involving cryptocurrency payments. The first dimension focuses on the technical mechanisms through which cryptocurrencies are operationalized in ransomware attacks. This involves an examination of the specific cryptocurrencies demanded, the technological features that make them attractive to cybercriminals, and the laundering tactics employed to obscure illicit gains post-payment.

The second dimension investigates financial flows, assessing how the payment of ransoms in digital currencies shapes the liquidity, demand, and fungibility of those assets. Here, the analysis considers not only the direct movement of funds but also the broader market implications, such as increased transactional volume and the development of auxiliary services like mixers and chain-hopping protocols that enhance the usability of cryptocurrencies in illicit markets.

The third dimension explores the institutional impacts of ransomware attacks; particularly how financial sector entities respond to these incidents. This includes examining the regulatory, reputational, and operational consequences for targeted organizations, as well as the policy responses these incidents provoke. By analyzing these three dimensions across selected cases, the study provides a multi-faceted understanding of how ransomware both exploits and amplifies the functional value of cryptocurrencies.

3.2 Data Sources

The research relies on a diverse array of data sources to construct a comprehensive and reliable analytical foundation. Peer-reviewed academic literature provides theoretical frameworks and empirical findings on both ransomware and cryptocurrency usage in illicit finance. This is supplemented by industry reports from blockchain analytics firms such as Chainalysis, Elliptic, and CipherTrace, which offer up-to-date insights into crypto transaction flows and laundering methodologies.

Official documents from regulatory and governmental bodies, including reports from the U.S. Senate Homeland Security and Governmental Affairs Committee, the Office of Foreign Assets Control (OFAC), and the Financial Crimes Enforcement Network (FinCEN), contribute authoritative perspectives on policy, compliance, and enforcement. News reports from reputable financial journalism sources like Reuters, Bloomberg, and the American Banker provide contemporaneous accounts of ransomware incidents and institutional responses. Additionally, forensic analyses and publicly available incident reports enrich the data corpus, ensuring that each case study is grounded in verifiable and multi-sourced information.

3.3 Case Study Selection

To elucidate the intersection of ransomware and cryptocurrency, the study examines three high-profile ransomware incidents involving significant cryptocurrency payments within the financial sector. These cases were selected based on their public documentation, the substantial size of ransom payments, and the diversity they represent in terms of institutional targets and ransomware tactics. The first case is Travelex, the international currency exchange service provider that suffered a crippling ransomware attack by the REvil gang in late 2019, leading to a $2.3 million ransom payment in Bitcoin. The second case is CNA Financial, a major U.S. insurance firm that in 2021 paid a record-setting $40 million ransom in Bitcoin after a devastating attack by the Phoenix CryptoLocker group. The third case involves Flagstar Bank, a mid-sized U.S. financial institution targeted in 2021, which paid approximately $1 million in Bitcoin to prevent the public disclosure of exfiltrated customer data. Collectively, these cases span different financial sector subsectors-currency exchange, insurance, and banking-offering a rich comparative perspective on the deployment of cryptocurrencies in ransomware contexts. The selected cases also vary in the scale of ransom payments and the operational tactics employed by attackers, allowing for a nuanced analysis of cryptocurrency's functional role across different extortion strategies.

3.4 Analytical Framework

Each case is analyzed through a consistent framework that addresses key dimensions of cryptocurrency utilization in ransomware attacks. First, the study identifies the specific cryptocurrencies involved, examining why certain coins-most frequently Bitcoin and Monero-are preferred by attackers. The analysis then traces the payment processes, including negotiation dynamics, payment execution, and the subsequent laundering of funds through mixers, privacy coins, and cross-chain transactions. Next, the analysis evaluates how these ransom payments and laundering activities influence the liquidity and visibility of the cryptocurrencies involved. This includes examining the effects on transaction volumes, price fluctuations, and the development of ancillary services that support the anonymity and usability of these digital assets in illicit economies. The institutional response is also a critical component of the analysis. For each case, the paper investigates how the affected financial institution managed the incident, including interactions with law enforcement, regulatory disclosures, crisis communication strategies, and cybersecurity remediations. This dimension offers insights into the broader economic and policy implications of ransomware-facilitated cryptocurrency usage. Through this structured analytical approach, the paper not only demonstrates the indispensable role of cryptocurrencies in ransomware but also contextualizes their value within a broader socio-economic and regulatory landscape.

3.5 Limitations

Several methodological limitations are acknowledged in this study. First, comprehensive data on ransomware payments and subsequent laundering is inherently difficult to obtain, as many transactions remain confidential or unreported. Victim institutions often avoid public disclosure to minimize reputational damage, and attackers operate in secrecy to evade law enforcement. Second, while the study draws connections between ransomware payments and cryptocurrency valuation, establishing direct causal links is challenging due to the multitude of factors influencing cryptocurrency markets, including speculation, regulatory developments, and technological innovation. Third, the analysis is based on data available up to early 2025. The rapidly evolving nature of both ransomware tactics-especially with the advent of AI-driven malware-and cryptocurrency technologies may introduce new dynamics not captured in this study. Future research could extend this work by incorporating real-time blockchain analytics and machine learning-based detection of laundering patterns. Despite these limitations, the methodology employed in this paper provides a robust framework for understanding how ransomware operations contribute to the functional value of cryptocurrencies. By grounding the analysis in empirical case studies and a multi-dimensional framework, the study offers valuable insights into the dark yet illuminating nexus between digital finance and cybercrime.

4. CASE STUDY

4.1 Travelex – Cryptocurrency's Central Role in Enabling Global Extortion

The ransomware attack on Travelex in late 2019 and early 2020 marked one of the most significant financial-sector breaches where cryptocurrency demonstrated its critical value to ransomware operators. Travelex, a London-based global foreign exchange service provider with operations spanning over 25 countries, was paralyzed by the Sodinokibi (also known as REvil) ransomware group. The attackers encrypted Travelex's systems worldwide, severely disrupting services at airports, banks, and partner institutions. The demand: a ransom of $6 million, exclusively payable in Bitcoin.

This incident highlights the indispensable role of cryptocurrency in operationalizing large-scale cyber extortion (Nish et al.,2022). Bitcoin was not chosen arbitrarily; its unique properties made it the optimal medium for attackers and a feasible payment mechanism for the victim under duress. For the attackers, Bitcoin provided pseudonymity, high liquidity, and global acceptability. The Bitcoin blockchain's transparency paradoxically offers visibility without identity-wallet addresses are public, but without direct ties to real-world names unless voluntarily revealed or discovered through forensic blockchain analysis (Conti et al., 2018). This allowed REvil to confidently solicit payments without disclosing their identities, leveraging Bitcoin's decentralized architecture to stay beyond the reach of any single legal authority (Jun et al, 2024).

The attackers further benefited from Bitcoin's global infrastructure. Because Bitcoin transactions can be executed across borders instantly and without intermediaries, REvil could operate transnationally with ease. This borderless capacity is invaluable to ransomware groups operating in jurisdictions that are hostile or indifferent to Western law enforcement, such as Russia. The absence of centralized control ensured that no government or financial intermediary could freeze or intercept the ransom payment mid-transfer (Harwick, 2016).

For Travelex, the use of Bitcoin by the attackers presented a grim yet clear pathway to potential resolution. Facing operational paralysis during a peak travel season and mounting reputational damage, Travelex's executives negotiated the ransom down to approximately $2.3 million, ultimately paying around 285 BTC at the time. The transaction was facilitated via intermediaries specialized in ransomware payment negotiations and crypto transfers-an emergent service industry that reflects cryptocurrency's growing role in managing cyber extortion crises (Kalinaki, 2024).

For the victim, paying in Bitcoin offered the advantage of transaction speed and certainty. Unlike traditional financial transfers that may involve scrutiny, clearance times, and reversibility, Bitcoin payments are settled rapidly and irreversibly. This immediacy is critical in ransomware scenarios where delays may provoke further data destruction, leak threats, or permanent loss of access. Moreover, using Bitcoin allowed Travelex to meet the attackers' non-negotiable demand without complicating factors such as currency controls, bank reporting thresholds, or cross-border payment restrictions.

Once the ransom was paid, REvil provided Travelex with decryption tools to restore their systems. However, the company's recovery was neither swift nor complete; weeks of downtime and cascading disruptions ensued. The technical transaction of Bitcoin, while enabling resolution, did not guarantee operational recovery without substantial additional remediation. Nevertheless, Bitcoin functioned effectively as the medium that unlocked the immediate crisis-a stark demonstration of its utilitarian value in the ransomware economy (Zimba & Chishimba, 2019).

On the attackers' side, the received Bitcoin was swiftly laundered to evade tracking. Blockchain analysis revealed that ransom payments were dispersed through multiple wallet addresses, mixed with other transactions, and sometimes converted into privacy coins like Monero, which further obscures the trail (Sanders, 2025). This process, often involving chain-hopping across cryptocurrencies and the use of mixers, exploits the fragmented regulatory oversight in global crypto markets, enhancing the fungibility of illicitly obtained digital assets.

Importantly, the Travelex case illuminates how cryptocurrencies like Bitcoin are not merely passive tools but active enablers of ransomware's business model. The characteristics of Bitcoin-decentralization, pseudonymity, high market liquidity, and global acceptance-make it uniquely suited for criminal enterprises that require untraceable, secure, and rapid financial settlement across borders. Furthermore, the victim's ability to procure Bitcoin and remit payment through legitimate exchanges and brokers indicates that the infrastructure supporting Bitcoin's legal economy inadvertently serves the needs of the illegal economy as well.

For cybercriminals, cryptocurrencies reduce transaction risk while maximizing operational security and revenue extraction capabilities (Shanmugam et al, 2017). For victims, despite the moral and legal complexities, the practicality of Bitcoin payments often presents the fastest route to business recovery, especially when critical services are at stake. This dual-sided value reinforces Bitcoin's standing not just as a speculative asset but as a functional currency within illicit economic systems (Reddy & Minnaar, 2018).

4.2 CNA Financial – Scaling Extortion with Cryptocurrency Liquidity

The 2021 ransomware attack on CNA Financial, one of the largest commercial insurance firms in the United States, stands as a landmark case in the scale and operational sophistication of cryptocurrency-enabled extortion. This incident, executed by a group associated with the Phoenix CryptoLocker ransomware strain, culminated in a staggering $40 million ransom paid in Bitcoin-one of the largest confirmed ransomware payments in history (Falco et al, 2023). The CNA case epitomizes how the features of cryptocurrency ecosystems-liquidity, pseudonymity, and global accessibility-not only facilitate massive financial crimes but also render such attacks operationally viable and commercially appealing for cybercriminals.

CNA Financial provides a compelling example of how attackers strategically exploit cryptocurrency to scale their operations to corporate targets capable of meeting extraordinary ransom demands. The attackers infiltrated CNA's network, deploying ransomware that encrypted over 15,000 devices, including employee systems critical to the company's insurance operations. The attackers demanded payment exclusively in Bitcoin, leveraging the cryptocurrency's ability to handle large-value transfers without the constraints of traditional financial scrutiny or regulatory gatekeeping (Khantamonthon & Chimmanee, 2022).

For the Phoenix CryptoLocker group, Bitcoin's liquidity was crucial. The ability to receive tens of millions of dollars in a single, unmediated transaction, settled within minutes, exemplifies the unmatched capacity of cryptocurrencies to facilitate high-stakes extortion without reliance on banks or payment processors. This financial infrastructure made it conceivable for attackers to demand sums equivalent to the annual profits of mid-sized firms, knowing that such transactions could be executed discreetly and irreversibly.

Bitcoin's mature market ecosystem further emboldened attackers. By 2021, a wide array of services, including over-the-counter (OTC) trading desks, cryptocurrency mixers, and privacy coins, were readily accessible to launder large crypto holdings. The attackers could confidently anticipate that even an unprecedented $40 million payment could be processed through these layers without immediate detection or asset seizure. This confidence in the post-payment laundering pathway enhances Bitcoin's strategic value to ransomware groups-not merely as a payment method, but as a critical component of the monetization pipeline.

From CNA's perspective, the use of Bitcoin presented both a constraint and a solution. On one hand, the exclusive demand for Bitcoin meant that the company could not negotiate alternative, more traceable or reversible payment forms. On the other hand, Bitcoin enabled CNA to transfer an immense ransom amount swiftly once negotiations concluded. The company's decision-making process involved careful legal and compliance considerations, particularly given the U.S. Treasury's Office of Foreign Assets Control (OFAC) guidance on the risks of paying ransoms to sanctioned entities. CNA engaged law enforcement and sought confirmation that the Phoenix group was not under direct sanctions, highlighting the compliance complexities in handling crypto payments in the context of U.S. regulations.

For CNA, Bitcoin's irreversibility was both a benefit and a risk. Once the payment was made, there was no transactional recourse, but it also ensured that the attackers had no incentive to default on delivering the decryption tool-a foundational logic underpinning the trust dynamics in ransomware economies. This transactional finality, intrinsic to Bitcoin's protocol (Das, et al, 2019), guarantees that attackers receive their payment in full without third-party interference, while victims gain assurance that paying the ransom is not rendered futile by potential clawbacks or freezes common in traditional banking.

Following the payment, blockchain analytics firms tracked portions of the $40 million through various laundering channels. Some of the funds were reportedly funneled through crypto exchanges operating in regions with lax AML controls, and some were potentially converted into privacy-enhanced cryptocurrencies such as Monero to further mask origins (Chainalysis, 2025). The ability to perform chain-hopping and utilize decentralized exchanges with minimal regulatory oversight reveals how the cryptocurrency ecosystem empowers attackers to evade financial surveillance even after such high-profile transactions (Gürses et al, 2016).

CNA's case also illustrates how the availability and acceptance of Bitcoin among both criminal networks and legitimate financial intermediaries (such as OTC brokers) have made it a de facto currency in ransomware dealings. Its dominance in ransom payments is not solely due to anonymity features, which are limited compared to privacy coins, but because of its deep liquidity, global recognition, and the mature infrastructure surrounding its exchange and storage. For attackers, this means a reliable, scalable, and secure method to receive and launder payments. For victims, Bitcoin offers a pathway to resolution that aligns with the attackers' operational preferences, albeit at significant financial and reputational cost.

The CNA Financial incident further cemented Bitcoin's role in the ransomware ecosystem. It validated that multi-million-dollar ransoms could be paid and processed without collapsing the financial pathways necessary for laundering and eventual cash-out. This success likely incentivized other ransomware groups to escalate their demands, knowing that the infrastructure supporting Bitcoin transactions could accommodate such sums without immediate interdiction.

Moreover, CNA's payment indirectly reinforced Bitcoin's market demand. Large transactions like these not only inject significant liquidity into the market but also stimulate ancillary services that support transaction obfuscation and asset conversion, thereby deepening the crypto economy's capacity to serve both legal and illegal participants (Gronwald, 2019; Ilk, et al, 2021).

4.3 Flagstar Bank – Cryptocurrency and the Business of Data Extortion

The ransomware-related data breach at Flagstar Bank in late 2021 exemplifies how cryptocurrencies extend their value beyond simple ransom payment channels to enable more complex extortion models, such as double extortion. Flagstar, a mid-sized U.S. bank with substantial operations in mortgage servicing, was compromised by a ransomware group that not only encrypted some of the bank's data but primarily stole sensitive customer information, including Social Security numbers and other personally identifiable data. Unlike classic ransomware attacks where decryption of data is the primary leverage, this incident focused on the threat of publicly exposing or selling the stolen data-a form of extortion made viable and efficient by cryptocurrency payment mechanisms.

The attackers demanded payment in Bitcoin to prevent the publication of the stolen data on leak sites or dark web marketplaces. Reports later revealed that Flagstar paid approximately $1 million in Bitcoin to suppress the data's release (Baisley & Cherrat, 2023). This transaction was critical to the attackers' business model: the anonymity, liquidity, and non-reversibility of Bitcoin made it possible to monetize the threat without exposing their identities or locations. For attackers, cryptocurrencies function not just as a payment mechanism but as a safeguard against transactional risks. Without Bitcoin or comparable digital assets, executing such extortion schemes would require more traceable and logistically burdensome methods, such as cash drops or traditional wire transfers, which are more susceptible to law enforcement interception.

Bitcoin's value to attackers in the Flagstar case lay in its immediate convertibility and global acceptance. Despite regulatory efforts, Bitcoin remains readily exchangeable for fiat currencies, often via intermediaries that operate in jurisdictions with weak anti-money laundering enforcement. The attackers, therefore, could efficiently liquidate the $1 million ransom without fear of seizure, especially if routed through privacy-preserving techniques like mixers or by converting Bitcoin into privacy coins like Monero. This ease of post-payment laundering directly contributes to the functional value of cryptocurrencies in cybercrime economies (Fanusie & Robinson, 2018).

For Flagstar, paying in Bitcoin was a strategic decision aimed at crisis containment. The irreversibility of Bitcoin payments gave the bank a mechanism to settle the extortion swiftly, minimizing the risk of data exposure that could lead to regulatory penalties, reputational harm, and customer lawsuits. Indeed, despite the payment, Flagstar still faced significant legal and regulatory consequences, including class action lawsuits from affected customers. However, the bank's leadership likely assessed that paying the ransom, despite its moral and strategic complexities, was less damaging than the fallout from a mass data leak.

The utility of Bitcoin to the victim in this context is paradoxical: while it is the very tool that enables the attack, it is also the fastest available solution to mitigate its impact. Traditional payment systems would require longer processing times, trigger regulatory scrutiny, and introduce the possibility of asset freezes, all of which are impractical in a time-sensitive extortion scenario. Bitcoin's pseudonymous nature also provides plausible deniability and discretion for the payer; Flagstar could execute the transaction without immediate public disclosure, although the payment details eventually surfaced through legal proceedings.

Additionally, the attackers' insistence on Bitcoin underscores its role as a trust mechanism in criminal dealings. In double extortion scenarios, victims need assurance that paying will prevent data leakage. Bitcoin's visibility on the blockchain allows victims to verify that the payment has been made, while its irreversibility ensures that attackers receive funds securely, creating a crude but effective trust dynamic in illicit transactions.

From a broader perspective, the Flagstar Bank incident demonstrates the entrenchment of cryptocurrencies within evolving ransomware strategies. Double extortion and pure data-theft blackmail have become increasingly common, driven in part by the scalability that cryptocurrency payments afford. Attackers can target a broader range of institutions, not just for locking systems but for data privacy violations, confident that cryptocurrency payments facilitate monetization even when decryption is not involved (Payne & Mienie, 2021).

This case also reflects how the infrastructure around Bitcoin supports both criminal and defensive services. Flagstar reportedly engaged professional negotiators and cybersecurity firms specialized in ransomware response-many of which maintain operational capabilities in cryptocurrency transactions, including secure wallets and rapid access to liquidity. The existence of such intermediaries further embeds Bitcoin within the ecosystem of ransomware response, enhancing its practical value to both sides of the transaction.

Figure 2. Ransomware payments vs. data leak site victims

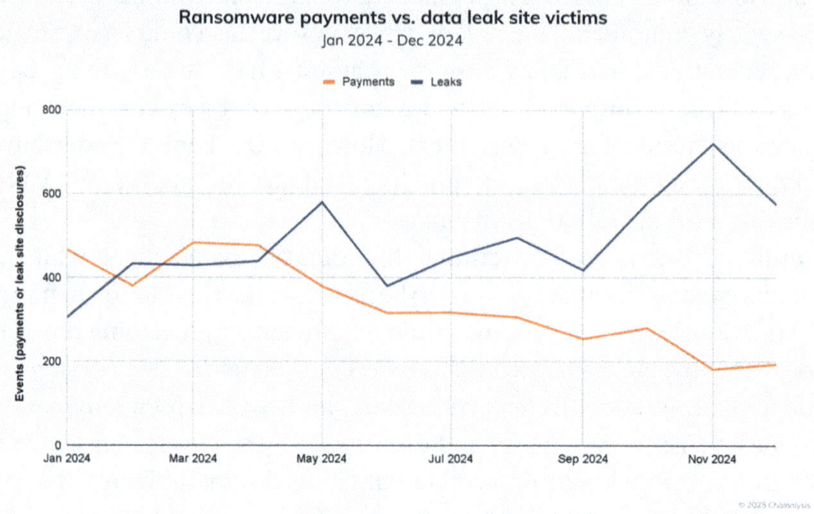

5. ANALYSIS: THE FINANCIAL VALUE OF CRYPTOCURRENCIES BEYOND RANSOMWARE

The preceding case studies-Travelex, CNA Financial, and Flagstar Bank-collectively illustrate the indispensable role that cryptocurrencies play in enabling and sustaining ransomware operations. Across these diverse incidents, one theme remains consistent: the ability of attackers to demand, receive, and launder large sums of money is inseparable from the unique financial attributes of cryptocurrencies, especially Bitcoin. Travelex's $2.3 million ransom, CNA Financial's unprecedented $40 million payout, and Flagstar Bank's strategic $1 million payment to prevent a data leak all converged on the same medium of exchange: cryptocurrency. In each case, the attackers relied on the transactional fluidity, borderless nature, and irreversibility of crypto assets to execute and profit from extortion schemes. The victims, in turn, had little choice but to comply within the operational constraints dictated by their adversaries-constraints shaped fundamentally by the properties of the cryptocurrency ecosystem.

These examples highlight that the financial value of cryptocurrencies extends far beyond their speculative appeal or technological innovation. Instead, their utility in facilitating unregulated, pseudonymous financial flows endows them with a form of shadow-market credibility. This credibility not only sustains demand among criminal enterprises but also offers a parallel financial infrastructure for actors seeking to bypass legal, regulatory, or geopolitical restrictions. The cases analyzed demonstrate that Bitcoin remains dominant in this realm due to its liquidity and widespread recognition, but they also foreshadow the growing use of privacy-centric alternatives like Monero and Zcash when higher levels of anonymity are needed (Biryukov & Tikhomirov, 2019). Against this backdrop, the broader financial value of cryptocurrencies can be comprehensively understood through their applications in ransomware, untraceable transactions, sanction evasion, tax avoidance, and participation in broader shadow economies.

The financial architecture of cryptocurrencies-characterized by decentralization, pseudonymity, and a lack of centralized oversight-provides the backbone for these illicit applications. In ransomware, as shown in the previous cases, cryptocurrencies serve not just as a transactional medium but as an enabling technology that underwrites the profitability and operational security of criminal schemes. Yet, the utility of cryptocurrencies does not end with ransomware. In fact, the same features that make them suitable for extortion payments also facilitate a range of other financial behaviors designed to circumvent traditional regulatory frameworks.

One of the most significant dimensions of cryptocurrency's financial value is its role in untraceable or semi-traceable transactions. Bitcoin, while pseudonymous, still leaves a public ledger that can be analyzed by law enforcement and blockchain analytics firms. However, privacy-focused cryptocurrencies such as Monero, Zcash, and Dash have been specifically engineered to thwart such analysis. Monero uses advanced cryptographic techniques like ring signatures and stealth addresses to ensure that neither the sender, receiver, nor the transaction amount is visible on the public ledger (Liu et al, 2019). This degree of privacy is not just a technical achievement; it represents a financial service to users who prioritize secrecy, whether for personal privacy, illicit trade, or political reasons.

In practice, Monero has become the cryptocurrency of choice for those engaged in drug trafficking, illicit arms trade, and other dark web transactions (Bahamazava & Nanda, 2022). Its mandatory privacy features make it difficult for authorities to trace, enhancing its attractiveness in markets where opacity is a competitive advantage. Zcash offers similar privacy through its shielded transactions, although its optional nature means that only a subset of transactions achieves full privacy. Dash, while offering a privacy option, is less commonly used in criminal enterprises due to its lower levels of anonymity compared to Monero and its declining market prominence. The existence and continued development of these privacy coins underscore the market demand for financial instruments that can facilitate secretive transactions without reliance on the traditional banking system.

Another critical financial application of cryptocurrencies lies in the evasion of international sanctions. Countries like North Korea and Iran have reportedly turned to cryptocurrencies to bypass economic restrictions imposed by the United States and its allies (Kim et al, 2022). North Korea's Lazarus Group, for example, has been implicated in numerous cyberattacks on cryptocurrency exchanges, funneling the proceeds into the country's nuclear weapons program3. Iran has legalized and promoted domestic Bitcoin mining as a way to monetize its energy surplus, converting mined Bitcoin into foreign currency to circumvent sanctions (Ismael, 2021). These state-level strategies highlight how cryptocurrencies provide a mechanism for sanctioned entities to access global financial markets from which they would otherwise be excluded. The borderless nature of digital assets effectively neutralizes the geographic constraints that underpin traditional financial sanctions.

On a more individual level, sanctioned persons and organizations have also exploited cryptocurrencies to preserve and move wealth discreetly. Russian oligarchs, particularly after the sanctions following the 2022 invasion of Ukraine, have increasingly been linked to crypto transactions intended to shield assets from asset freezes and seizures[4]. Although precise quantification is challenging, the pattern of wealth migration into crypto assets during sanction regimes points to a persistent and growing use case that reinforces the demand for these digital instruments.

Wealth concealment for the purpose of tax avoidance is another area where cryptocurrencies demonstrate significant financial value. The opacity afforded by privacy coins and the decentralized nature of blockchain networks allow high-net-worth individuals to obscure ownership and evade tax reporting obligations. Unlike bank accounts, which are subject to Know Your Customer (KYC) and Anti-Money Laundering (AML) regulations, self-custodied cryptocurrency wallets can store and transfer wealth without triggering immediate regulatory scrutiny. Offshore exchanges and peer-to-peer platforms further facilitate this concealment, allowing users to convert between fiat and crypto without clear oversight. This aspect of financial opacity is exacerbated by decentralized finance (DeFi) platforms, where users can lend, borrow, and earn yields on crypto assets without revealing their identities.

Tax authorities are increasingly aware of these challenges. The U.S. Internal Revenue Service has expanded efforts to track and tax cryptocurrency holdings, but enforcement remains limited by the technical capabilities of tax agencies compared to the rapid innovation in the crypto space. Foley et al. (2019) estimate that a significant portion of cryptocurrency transactions-up to 46%-are linked to illegal activities, including tax evasion, money laundering, and unregulated trading. This not only inflates the transactional volume on blockchains but also adds speculative demand, as users seek to acquire assets that can facilitate discreet wealth management.

The broader shadow economy, encompassing drug trade, human trafficking, illegal gambling, and counterfeit goods, also relies on cryptocurrencies. Dark web marketplaces like Silk Road and Hydra Market utilized Bitcoin and later Monero as standard currencies for illicit commerce (Christin, 2013; Kermitsis et al, 2021). Even as law enforcement continues to dismantle such platforms, new markets emerge, perpetuating the demand for cryptocurrencies that enable anonymous trade. These markets collectively drive significant transactional volume, which in turn supports liquidity and market depth for the associated cryptocurrencies. As liquidity grows, these assets become more attractive to both legitimate investors and criminals, creating a self-reinforcing cycle of adoption and valuation.

The financial value of cryptocurrencies is also evident in their role as hedging instruments against financial surveillance and capital controls. In countries with unstable currencies or authoritarian regimes, individuals often turn to cryptocurrencies to safeguard their wealth from inflation, expropriation, or restrictive banking policies. For example, during periods of economic crisis in Venezuela and Argentina, Bitcoin and stablecoins like Tether (USDT) have seen surges in demand as citizens seek to preserve the value of their savings in more stable or liquid forms (Yermack, 2024). Although these use cases are not inherently illicit, they leverage the same attributes-decentralization, privacy, and cross-border mobility-that make cryptocurrencies valuable in criminal and semi-legal contexts.

Beyond Bitcoin, other cryptocurrencies are playing increasingly important roles in this shadow financial system. Ethereum, while not a privacy coin, facilitates a vast ecosystem of DeFi applications that can be used to obscure the origins of funds through complex financial operations (Garg, 2022). Smart contracts enable services like decentralized exchanges, automated market makers, and yield farming, all of which can be exploited to layer transactions in ways that complicate tracing efforts. The sanctioned Ethereum-based mixer Tornado Cash exemplifies how Ethereum's flexibility can be harnessed to anonymize funds (Brownworth et al., 2024). Stablecoins like Tether are similarly entrenched in gray markets, providing a means of value transfer that avoids the volatility of other cryptocurrencies while maintaining the borderless and low-friction characteristics of digital assets.

The interplay between these various cryptocurrencies-Bitcoin for liquidity, Monero for privacy, Ethereum for financial engineering, and Tether for stability-creates a diversified toolkit for financial actors operating both within and outside the law. This toolkit enhances the overall resilience and attractiveness of the cryptocurrency market, ensuring that even as specific coins face regulatory headwinds, the ecosystem as a whole continues to thrive.

6. TOWARDS A NEW PRICING MODEL FOR CRYPTOCURRENCIES: INTEGRATING ILLICIT UTILITY AND SHADOW DEMAND

The findings of this paper suggest that the conventional models for valuing cryptocurrencies, which often emphasize network effects, scarcity, technological innovation, or investor sentiment, are insufficient to capture the full scope of value drivers that sustain and elevate these digital assets. Standard frameworks, such as Metcalfe's Law-based models or stock-to-flow ratios, tend to overlook a critical but often unspoken dimension of cryptocurrency demand: their indispensable role in facilitating illicit, opaque, and extralegal financial activities. As this paper has demonstrated through the analysis of ransomware cases, untraceable transactions, sanctions evasion, and wealth concealment, the shadow financial utility of cryptocurrencies constitutes a significant and persistent source of demand that is largely uncaptured by traditional valuation methodologies.

A revised pricing model for cryptocurrencies must, therefore, incorporate both observable market factors and latent demand stemming from their value in shadow economies. We propose a hybrid valuation model that integrates three core components:

Legitimate Utility Value (LUV): This dimension captures traditional use cases such as investment vehicles, payments, decentralized finance (DeFi) applications, and hedging against fiat currency devaluation. It is influenced by network adoption rates, transaction volumes in regulated markets, technological upgrades, and macroeconomic conditions like inflation and interest rates.

Illicit Utility Premium (IUP): This component reflects the embedded value derived from criminal, extralegal, and privacy-seeking uses of cryptocurrencies. As shown in the ransomware case studies, the ability of Bitcoin, Monero, and other privacy coins to facilitate untraceable payments commands a premium that is often realized in heightened transactional demand during periods of regulatory stress, geopolitical conflict, or heightened enforcement against traditional financial channels.

Regulatory Friction Discount (RFD): Cryptocurrencies also carry a pricing penalty or discount based on regulatory risks. Announcements of stricter KYC/AML enforcement, bans on privacy coins, or sanctions against specific protocols (e.g., Tornado Cash) negatively affect the market value by increasing the friction and legal risk associated with certain forms of usage.

The hybrid pricing model can be expressed conceptually as:

Crypto Valuation = LUV + IUP - RFD

Each of these factors is dynamic and context-dependent. For example, during periods of intensified geopolitical sanctions, such as those imposed on Russia post-2022, the IUP component rises as demand for privacy-centric and censorship-resistant assets like Bitcoin or Monero increases. Similarly, regulatory announcements or successful law enforcement actions, such as the takedown of Hydra Market or the sanctioning of Tornado Cash, increase the RFD, depressing prices or at least muting speculative growth.

To operationalize this model, empirical proxies can be constructed. The LUV can be measured via network metrics like active addresses, transaction counts, and total value locked in DeFi platforms. The IUP could be estimated through blockchain analytics data on the volume of transactions associated with known dark markets, ransomware payments, and mixer usage, as firms like Chainalysis and Elliptic provide (Aidoo et al., 2024). The RFD might be proxied by tracking regulatory announcements, sanctions, or the global trend in cryptocurrency-related legal actions. This enhanced model not only offers a more comprehensive lens through which to understand cryptocurrency pricing but also acknowledges that part of crypto's resilience and valuation is anchored in demand that policymakers often seek to suppress but which remains structurally persistent. It reframes the discussion around crypto value as not merely a function of innovation or speculation, but as an artifact of its utility in the full spectrum of financial activities-licit and illicit alike.

7. POLICY AND ETHICAL IMPLICATIONS

Recognizing that a substantial portion of cryptocurrency's market value is underpinned by illicit and opaque financial activities presents both policy and ethical dilemmas. If cryptocurrencies derive part of their valuation from facilitating ransomware, sanctions evasion, tax avoidance, and other shadow transactions, regulators face the challenge of curbing these uses without stifling legitimate innovation or punishing lawful users.

From a policy perspective, targeted regulation is essential. Rather than broad bans on cryptocurrency usage, which often prove ineffective and counterproductive, authorities should focus on chokepoints within the crypto ecosystem-such as exchanges, mixing services, and OTC brokers. Imposing stringent KYC/AML requirements, mandating transaction monitoring, and sanctioning privacy-preserving services when directly linked to criminal activity can reduce illicit flows without eliminating privacy protections entirely. Cross-border cooperation is also necessary, given the inherently global nature of crypto networks.

Ethically, regulators must balance the right to financial privacy with the societal need to combat crime and enforce tax compliance. Privacy-enhancing technologies are not inherently unethical; they serve legitimate users in oppressive regimes or those protecting personal privacy. However, the deliberate use of these technologies for illicit enrichment imposes social costs, such as weakened law enforcement and increased risks to financial integrity. In essence, a nuanced regulatory framework-one that differentiates between privacy for personal freedom and anonymity for crime-is vital. This approach would sustain the benefits of cryptocurrency innovation while minimizing its exploitation by bad actors, aligning financial integrity with ethical governance.

8. CONCLUSION AND DIRECTIONS FOR FUTURE RESEARCH

This paper has explored a critical but often overlooked dimension of cryptocurrency valuation-its functional utility in illicit economies, particularly in ransomware ecosystems. Contrary to mainstream narratives that tether cryptocurrency value to network growth, technological innovation, or speculative sentiment, we argue that part of this value is embedded in the digital assets' capacity to serve as indispensable tools in ransomware attacks, cyber laundering, sanctions evasion, and untraceable wealth transfer. Through three detailed case studies-Travelex, CNA Financial, and Flagstar Bank-we demonstrated how cryptocurrencies, especially Bitcoin and Monero, have become integral to modern extortion operations. The attributes that make them appealing in legitimate contexts-pseudonymity, decentralization, global liquidity-are the same features that facilitate criminal enterprise, reinforcing their demand and consequently their market valuation.

Our proposed hybrid pricing model, incorporating Legitimate Utility Value (LUV), Illicit Utility Premium (IUP), and Regulatory Friction Discount (RFD), offers a more complete framework for understanding the real drivers of cryptocurrency prices. It acknowledges that shadow demand-though morally and legally problematic-is structurally persistent, technologically evolving, and economically significant. As long as cryptocurrencies remain uniquely suited to high-risk, censorship-averse, or extralegal environments, this demand will not only sustain but potentially grow, especially amid geopolitical volatility and fragmented regulatory oversight.

This recognition, however, poses urgent policy and ethical questions. Financial authorities must craft regulations that suppress malicious uses without crippling the privacy and innovation that legitimate users value. Strategies must target transactional chokepoints-such as mixers, OTC desks, and privacy wallets-while promoting transparency and accountability among virtual asset service providers (VASPs). The balance between preserving financial freedom and preventing criminal exploitation will define the future trajectory of digital finance governance.

Looking ahead, several avenues warrant deeper academic and empirical inquiry. First, future research should develop quantitative proxies for the Illicit Utility Premium using blockchain forensic data, enabling time-series modeling of how criminal demand impacts cryptocurrency volatility, liquidity, and long-term price trends. Second, interdisciplinary studies integrating criminology, network science, and behavioral finance could shed light on how criminal actors make strategic choices among different cryptocurrencies, especially under evolving law enforcement pressures. Third, as ransomware becomes increasingly AI-driven and decentralized finance (DeFi) platforms grow more complex, future studies must assess how smart contracts, decentralized exchanges, and synthetic assets are repurposed for laundering and extortion. The role of AI-enhanced malware in adapting to countermeasures and automating illicit crypto usage is a critical frontier. Finally, comparative studies of regulatory regimes and their unintended consequences on illicit crypto activity would help policymakers better calibrate their interventions.

REFERENCES

Aidoo, S. AML, I. D., Officer, M. S. A. C., & Certified, I. C. A. (2024, Dec 18). *Cryptocurrency and sanctions evasion: Stablecoins, mixers, and the role of blockchain forensics* [Unpublished manuscript]. ResearchGate. https://www.researchgate.net/publication/393687826_Cryptocurrency_and_Sanctions_Evasion_Stablecoins_Mixers_and_the_Role_of_Blockchain_Forensics

Akbanov, M., Vassilakis, V. G., & Logothetis, M. D. (2019). Ransomware detection and mitigation using software-defined networking: The case of WannaCry. *Computers & Electrical Engineering*, *76*, 111–121. DOI: 10.1016/j.compeleceng.2019.03.012

Alwashali, A. A. M. A., Abd Rahman, N. A., & Ismail, N. (2021, December). A survey of ransomware as a service (RaaS) and methods to mitigate the attack. In *2021 14th International Conference on Developments in eSystems Engineering (DeSE)* (pp. 92-96). IEEE.

Bahamazava, K., & Nanda, R. (2022). The shift of DarkNet illegal drug trade preferences in cryptocurrency: The question of traceability and deterrence. *Forensic Science International Digital Investigation*, *40*, 301377. DOI: 10.1016/j.fsidi.2022.301377

Baisley, T., & Cherrat, Y. (2023). *Cyber threats and engagements in 2022* (Publication No. AD1208002) [Government technical report]. Defense Technical Information Center. https://apps.dtic.mil/sti/html/trecms/AD1208002/

Banerjee, A., Clear, M., & Tewari, H. (2020, Nov). Demystifying the role of zk-SNARKs in Zcash. In *2020 IEEE Conference on Application, Information and Network Security* (pp. 12–19). IEEE. DOI: 10.1109/AINS50155.2020.9315064

Bartoletti, M., Lande, S., Loddo, A., Pompianu, L., & Serusi, S. (2021). Cryptocurrency scams: Analysis and perspectives. *IEEE Access : Practical Innovations, Open Solutions*, *9*, 148353–148373. DOI: 10.1109/ACCESS.2021.3123894

Berrueta, E., Morato, D., Magaña, E., & Izal, M. (2019). A survey on detection techniques for cryptographic ransomware. *IEEE Access : Practical Innovations, Open Solutions*, *7*, 144925–144944. DOI: 10.1109/ACCESS.2019.2945839

Biryukov, A., & Tikhomirov, S. (2019). Security and privacy of mobile wallet users in Bitcoin, Dash, Monero, and Zcash. *Pervasive and Mobile Computing*, *59*, 101030. DOI: 10.1016/j.pmcj.2019.101030

Brownworth, A., Durfee, J., Lee, M. J., & Martin, A. (2024, August). *Regulating decentralized systems: Evidence from sanctions on Tornado Cash* (Staff Report No. 1112). Federal Reserve Bank of New York. DOI: 10.59576/sr.1112

Catalini, C., & Gans, J. S. (2018). *Initial coin offerings and the value of crypto tokens* (NBER Working Paper No. 24418). National Bureau of Economic Research. https://www.nber.org/papers/w24418

Chainalysis Team. (2025, Feb 5). *35% year-over-year decrease in ransomware payments, less than half of recorded incidents resulted in victim payments*. Chainalysis Blog. https://www.chainalysis.com/blog/crypto-crime-ransomware-victim-extortion-2025/

Christin, N. (2013, May). Traveling the Silk Road: A measurement analysis of a large anonymous online marketplace. In *Proceedings of the 22nd International Conference on World Wide Web* (pp. 213–224). DOI: 10.1145/2488388.2488408

Cohen, L. E., & Felson, M. (1979). Social change and crime rate trends: A routine activity approach. *American Sociological Review*, *44*(4), 588–608. DOI: 10.2307/2094589

Conti, M., Kumar, E. S., Lal, C., & Ruj, S. (2018). A survey on security and privacy issues of bitcoin. *IEEE Communications Surveys and Tutorials*, *20*(4), 3416–3452. DOI: 10.1109/COMST.2018.2842460

Das, R. A., Pahalovi, M. M. S., & Yanhaona, M. N. (2019, Dec). Transaction finality through ledger checkpoints. In *2019 IEEE 25th International Conference on Parallel and Distributed Systems* (pp. 183–192). IEEE.

Falco, G., Thummala, R., & Kubadia, A. (2023, Jul). Wannafly: An approach to satellite ransomware. In *2023 IEEE 9th International Conference on Space Mission Challenges for Information Technology* (pp. 84–93). IEEE.

Fanusie, Y., & Robinson, T. (2018). *Bitcoin laundering: An analysis of illicit flows into digital currency services* [PDF]. Center on Sanctions and Illicit Finance, Foundation for Defense of Democracies. https://www.fdd.org/wp-content/uploads/2018/01/MEMO_Bitcoin_Laundering.pdf

Fitzgerald, M. (2022). *Tactics, techniques, and procedures (TTPs) of ransomware groups and the threats posed to United States national security* (Master's thesis, Utica University). https://www.proquest.com/openview/a1c2c2ab19921b6dbd43cf2ba343ecba/1?pq-origsite=gscholar&cbl=18750&diss=y

Foley, S., Karlsen, J. R., & Putniņš, T. J. (2019). Sex, drugs, and bitcoin: How much illegal activity is financed through cryptocurrencies? *Review of Financial Studies*, *32*(5), 1798–1853. DOI: 10.1093/rfs/hhz015

Folkinshteyn, D., Lennon, M. M., & Reilly, T. (2015). *The Bitcoin mirage: An oasis of financial remittance* [Manuscript submitted for publication]. *Journal of Strategic and International Studies*.

Franck, T. (2018, May 5). *Warren Buffett says bitcoin is 'probably rat poison squared'*. CNBC. https://www.cnbc.com/2018/05/05/warren-buffett-says-bitcoin-is-probably-rat-poison-squared.html

Gandal, N. (2018). Network goods (empirical studies). In *The New Palgrave Dictionary of Economics* (pp. 9432–9436). Palgrave Macmillan. DOI: 10.1057/978-1-349-95189-5_2036

Garg, R. (2022). Ethereum-based smart contracts for trade and finance. *International Journal of Economics and Management Engineering*, *16*(11), 619–629.

Gronwald, M. (2019). Is Bitcoin a commodity? On price jumps, demand shocks, and certainty of supply. *Journal of International Money and Finance*, *97*, 86–92. DOI: 10.1016/j.jimonfin.2019.06.006

Gürses, S., Kundnani, A., & Van Hoboken, J. (2016). Crypto and empire: The contradictions of counter-surveillance advocacy. *Media Culture & Society*, *38*(4), 576–590. DOI: 10.1177/0163443716643006

Harwick, C. (2016). Cryptocurrency and the problem of intermediation. *The Independent Review, 20*(4), 569–588.

Ilk, N., Shang, G., Fan, S., & Zhao, J. L. (2021). Stability of transaction fees in Bitcoin: A supply and demand perspective. *Management Information Systems Quarterly*, *45*(2), 563–692. DOI: 10.25300/MISQ/2021/15718

Ismael, R. (2021). Challenges and opportunities cryptocurrency in Iran economy & e-businesses. *Вестник Российского университета дружбы народов. Серия. Ekonomika (Nis)*, *29*(4), 689–698.

Jun, A. Y. M., Jinu, B. A., Seng, L. K., Maharaiq, M. H. F. B. Z., Khongsuwan, W., Junn, B. T. K., . . . Sindiramutty, S. R. (2024). *Exploring the Impact of Crypto-Ransomware on Critical Industries: Case Studies and Solutions. Preprint PDF:* https://www.preprints.org/frontend/manuscript/f0bbffef9dcc633cd52819e93336aeda/download_pub

Kalinaki, K. (2024). Ransomware threat mitigation strategies for protecting critical infrastructure assets. In *Ransomware Evolution* (pp. 120–143). CRC Press. DOI: 10.1201/9781003469506-10

Kermitsis, E., Kavallieros, D., Myttas, D., Lissaris, E., & Giataganas, G. (2021). Dark web markets. In *Dark Web Investigation* (pp. 85–118). Springer. DOI: 10.1007/978-3-030-55343-2_4

Khantamonthon, N., & Chimmanee, K. (2022, Nov). Digital forensic analysis of ransomware attacks on virtual private networks: A case study in factories. In *2022 6th International Conference on Information Technology (InCIT)* (pp. 410-415). IEEE. DOI: 10.1109/InCIT56086.2022.10067674

Kharraz, A., Robertson, W., Balzarotti, D., Bilge, L., & Kirda, E. (2015, Jun). Cutting the gordian knot: A look under the hood of ransomware attacks. In *International Conference on Detection of Intrusions and Malware, and Vulnerability Assessment* (pp. 3–24). Springer. DOI: 10.1007/978-3-319-20550-2_1

Kim, H. M., Lee, J., & Paik, R. (2022). *North Korean cryptocurrency operations: An alternative revenue stream*. Belfer Center for Science and International Affairs. https://www.belfercenter.org/publication/north-korean-cryptocurrency-operations-alternative-revenue-stream

Komalavalli, C., Saxena, D., & Laroiya, C. (2020). Overview of blockchain technology concepts. In *Handbook of Research on Blockchain Technology* (pp. 349–371). Academic Press. DOI: 10.1016/B978-0-12-819816-2.00014-9

Kshetri, N., & Voas, J. (2017). Do crypto-currencies fuel ransomware? *IT Professional, 19*(5), 11–15. DOI: 10.1109/MITP.2017.3680961

Liu, Z., Nguyen, K., Yang, G., Wang, H., & Wong, D. S. (2019, Sep). A lattice-based linkable ring signature supporting stealth addresses. In *European Symposium on Research in Computer Security* (pp. 726–746). Springer. DOI: 10.1007/978-3-030-29959-0_35

Nakamoto, S. (2008). *Bitcoin: A peer-to-peer electronic cash system* [PDF]. U.S. Sentencing Commission. https://www.ussc.gov/sites/default/files/pdf/training/annual-national-training-seminar/2018/Emerging_Tech_Bitcoin_Crypto.pdf

Narayanan, A., Bonneau, J., Felten, E., Miller, A., & Goldfeder, S. (2016). *Bitcoin and cryptocurrency technologies: A comprehensive introduction.* Princeton University Press.

Naylor, R. T. (2004). *Wages of crime: Black markets, illegal finance, and the underworld economy.* Cornell University Press.

Nish, A., Naumann, S., & Muir, J. (2022). *Enduring cyber threats and emerging challenges to the financial sector.* Carnegie Endowment for International Peace.

Noether, S., Mackenzie, A., & Research Lab, T. M. (2016). Ring confidential transactions. *Ledger*, *1*, 1–18. DOI: 10.5195/ledger.2016.34

Pantin, L. P. (2023). Financial inclusion, cryptocurrency, and Afrofuturism. *Northwestern University Law Review*, *118*, 621.

Payne, B., & Mienie, E. (2021, Jun). Multiple-extortion ransomware: The case for active cyber threat intelligence. In *ECCWS 2021 20th European Conference on Cyber Warfare and Security* (Vol. 6, pp. 331–336). Academic Conferences Inter Ltd.

Reddy, E., & Minnaar, A. (2018). Cryptocurrency: A tool and target for cybercrime. *Acta Criminologica: African Journal of Criminology & Victimology*, *31*(3), 71–92.

Saleh, F. (2021). Blockchain without waste: Proof-of-stake. *Review of Financial Studies*, *34*(3), 1156–1190. DOI: 10.1093/rfs/hhaa075

Sanders, A. (2025, May 21). *How do cybercriminals launder cryptocurrency?* Barracuda Networks Blog. https://blog.barracuda.com/2025/05/21/cybercriminals-launder-cryptocurrency

Shanmugam, B., Azam, S., Yeo, K. C., Jose, J., & Kannoorpatti, K. (2017, Jan). A critical review of Bitcoins usage by cybercriminals. In *2017 International Conference on Computer Communication and Informatics (ICCCI)* (pp. 1-7). IEEE. https://ieeexplore.ieee.org/abstract/document/8117693

Tredinnick, L. (2019). Cryptocurrencies and the blockchain. *Business Information Review*, *36*(1), 39–44. DOI: 10.1177/0266382119836314

Trouble, R. C. I. (2020). *Is the world's reserve currency in trouble? International Economy*. https://williamwhite.ca/wp-content/uploads/2020/04/InternationalEconomyDollarSurvivalWinter2020.pdf

Yermack, D. (2024). Is Bitcoin a real currency? An economic appraisal. In *Handbook of Digital Currency* (pp. 29–40). Academic Press. DOI: 10.1016/B978-0-323-98973-2.00014-9

Zetzsche, D. A., Arner, D. W., & Buckley, R. P. (2020). Decentralized finance. *Journal of Financial Regulation*, *6*(2), 172–203. DOI: 10.1093/jfr/fjaa010

Zimba, A., & Chishimba, M. (2019). On the economic impact of crypto-ransomware attacks: The state of the art on enterprise systems. *European Journal for Security Research*, *4*(1), 3–31. DOI: 10.1007/s41125-019-00039-8

ENDNOTES

1 Corresponding Author: lewcheehon@qq.com

2 See https://ofac.treasury.gov/

3 https://www.justice.gov/archives/opa/pr/three-north-korean-military-hackers-indicted-wide-ranging-scheme-commit-cyberattacks-and

4 See https://www.ecb.europa.eu/press/economic-bulletin/articles/2019/html/ecb.ebart201905_03~c83aeaa44c.en.html

Chapter 2
The Stablecoins Race in Monetary Sovereignty Between China and the US

Shawn Li
https://orcid.org/0009-0005-6180-5130
McGill University, Canada

Peng Liu
CFA, China

ABSTRACT

This study compares stablecoin and CBDC approaches in China (state-controlled e-CNY), Hong Kong (regulated private stablecoins), and the U.S. (market-driven USD stablecoins), analyzing their implications for monetary sovereignty and dollar dominance. China's e-CNY aims to supplant private crypto while advancing RMB internationalization, whereas Hong Kong's hybrid model fosters innovation under strict oversight. The U.S. leverages private USD stablecoins, now dominant globally, reinforcing dollar hegemony. Findings suggest USD stablecoins currently extend U.S. monetary power, but China's e-CNY and Hong Kong's regulatory experiments may gradually challenge this. The paper highlights risks (financial stability, digital dollarization) and recommends tailored policies—U.S. regulation, China's adoption incentives, and Hong Kong's interoperability—to navigate this evolving landscape.

DOI: 10.4018/979-8-3373-2838-6.ch002

1. INTRODUCTION

Stablecoins have rapidly moved from the fringes of cryptocurrency into the mainstream of global finance. These digital tokens – typically pegged 1:1 to a fiat currency or other assets – promise the speed and programmability of crypto with the relative price stability of traditional money. Since the introduction of Tether (USDT) and other early stablecoins in the mid-2010s, the sector has seen explosive growth, reaching a global market capitalization in the hundreds of billions of dollars (CoinMarketCap, 2024; FSB, 2023). Stablecoins now play a pivotal role in crypto markets, accounting for a majority of trading volume and functioning as a critical bridge between crypto-assets and fiat currencies. As of mid-2024, U.S. dollar-pegged stablecoins dominate the sector, comprising roughly 99% of total stablecoin value in circulation (U.S. Department of the Treasury, 2025). This overwhelming dominance of USD-backed tokens (such as USDT and USDC) has effectively extended the reach of the U.S. dollar into the digital asset realm, prompting observers to note that stablecoins may serve to reinforce "dollar hegemony" on the blockchain (Prasad, 2021; Eichengreen, 2019).

Yet, the rise of stablecoins has also sparked monetary competition and strategic responses from major economies. China has eschewed privately issued stablecoins entirely, instead pioneering a state-run central bank digital currency (CBDC) known as the e-CNY (digital yuan). This reflects China's focus on monetary sovereignty, surveillance, and control, as well as its strategic ambition to internationalize the renminbi (RMB) as an alternative to the dollar in the long run (PBOC, 2023; IMF, 2024). Hong Kong, as a global financial hub under a "one country, two systems" special economic zone of China, is positioning itself as a regulated stablecoin center. Hong Kong's monetary authorities are crafting a comprehensive licensing regime for stablecoin issuers, seeking to attract fintech activity and serve as a bridge between mainland China's digital yuan experiments and Western crypto markets (Hong Kong Monetary Authority, 2022). Hong Kong's approach balances openness to innovation with safeguards to maintain financial stability in a dollar-pegged economy (Arner et al., 2020).

United States, home to the largest stablecoin issuers and markets, has so far taken a market-driven approach. Private companies have issued USD stablecoins that now underpin much of the crypto economy. U.S. regulators and legislators, after some delay, are moving toward clearer rules – such as proposed federal stablecoin legislation – aiming to address risks without stifling innovation. The U.S. also views stablecoins through the lens of preserving the dollar's global role and the integrity of its financial system (Board of Governors of the Federal Reserve System, 2022).

The challenge to dollar dominance posed by these developments is a central theme of this study. The U.S. dollar has been the world's primary reserve and settlement currency for decades, conferring what economists call an "exorbitant privilege" to the United States (Eichengreen, 2019). Over 58% of global foreign exchange reserves are held in USD, whereas China's renminbi accounts for only around 2–3% (International Monetary Fund, 2025). This disparity underlies China's and others' efforts toward "de-dollarization" – reducing reliance on the dollar-centric system. Stablecoins and CBDCs introduce new instruments through which such currency competition could play out. If, for example, digital yuan usage expands in cross-border trade or if HKD or RMB-pegged stablecoins gain traction in international markets, they might gradually chip away at the dollar's ubiquity (Prasad, 2021). Conversely, if USD-backed stablecoins remain dominant and become integrated into global payment networks, they could further cement the dollar's supremacy in the digital era (Gorton & Zhang, 2021).

This paper aims to investigate and compare the models of China, Hong Kong, and the U.S. in depth and analyze their potential impact on the global monetary order. The guiding research questions include: How do the design and regulatory approaches of China's e-CNY, Hong Kong's stablecoin framework, and U.S. stablecoins differ? What are the implications of each model for financial markets and stability? And to what extent could these developments collectively challenge (or reinforce) the international dominance of the U.S. dollar? By answering these questions, we hope to contribute to the emerging literature on digital currencies and great-power competition in finance.

The remainder of this paper is structured as follows. First, we provide Literature Review surveying existing research on stablecoins, CBDCs, and dollar dominance. Next, we outline the Methodology used for our comparative analysis. We then present a detailed comparative analysis of the three jurisdictions' models, including regulatory policies, technological implementations, and adoption progress. Subsequent sections discuss the market impact of these models and policy implications that arise from their interaction. A dedicated section examines the interplay with Dollar Dominance, analyzing whether current trends threaten the dollar's global position. Finally, we conclude with a Conclusion summarizing key findings, and a set of policy recommendations for stakeholders navigating the stablecoin era.

2. BACKGROUND AND PRIOR STUDIES

2.1 Stablecoins and Digital Currency: Definitions and Typologies

The concept of a stablecoin refers to a class of cryptocurrencies designed to maintain a stable value relative to some reference asset. The Bank for International Settlements (BIS) defines stablecoins as "cryptocurrencies pegged to fiat currencies or other assets" (Bank for International Settlements, 2022). Scholars and industry analysts typically categorize stablecoins by their collateral type and issuance mechanism. The main categories include: Fiat-collateralized stablecoins, and algorithmic stablecoins. Each model carries different risk profiles and regulatory considerations, as documented by prior research (Gorton & Zhang, 2021; Adrian & Mancini-Griffoli, 2019). Fiat-backed stablecoins concentrate credit and custodial risk in the issuer, whereas decentralized crypto-backed coins face smart contract and market risk. Algorithmic models have been critiqued as inherently unstable without external support, often likened to a "central bank without a lender of last resort" (Bullmann et al., 2019).

2.2 Stablecoins, Financial Stability, and Regulation

The rapid growth of stablecoins has raised questions among economists and regulators about potential impacts on financial stability and the appropriate regulatory response. Early policy analysis, such as the G7 Working Group on Stablecoins (Cœuré, 2019) and the Financial Stability Board report (2020), emphasized that "global stablecoins" could pose systemic risks if not properly regulated. Key concerns include:

Run risk: If users doubt a stablecoin's backing or solvency - for example, during a market stress or if reserves are questioned - mass redemptions could force fire-sales of reserve assets, potentially impacting traditional markets. This scenario mirrors a bank run and is particularly concerning if reserves include commercial paper or other less liquid assets (Diamond & Dybvig, 1983; MacDonald & Zhao 2022).

Payment system risk: Stablecoins now facilitate a large volume of crypto trading and value transfers. Outages or failures of a major stablecoin could disrupt trading platforms, Decentralized Finance (DeFi) protocols, and even cross-border remittances that rely on them (Auer et al., 2022).

Monetary sovereignty and currency substitution: Widespread use of a foreign-linked stablecoin in a domestic economy could undermine the local currency. For instance, officials from emerging markets have warned that a dominant USD stablecoin might lead to "digital dollarization," complicating monetary policy in those countries (Armas & Singh, 2022). This concern was famously amplified by Facebook's 2019 announcement of the Libra (later Diem) stablecoin, which prompted backlash and accelerated central banks' work on CBDCs due to fears a private global currency could erode national monetary control (Carstens, 2019).

Illicit finance and enforcement: Without proper oversight, stablecoins can be used to bypass capital controls, sanctions, and anti-money laundering measures (FATF, 2021). For example, residents in countries with currency restrictions have utilized dollar stablecoins to move value outside official channels. Regulators worry about the opacity and global reach of these networks if left unchecked (Rettig et al, 2025).

In response to such issues, a variety of regulatory approaches have been explored. The academic literature often highlights three broad strategies: ban, contain, or integrate (Arner et al., 2020; Zetzsche et al., 2020). China represents the "ban/replace" approach – it has banned cryptocurrency trading and private stablecoins, instead promoting its sovereign digital currency. Western jurisdictions initially took a cautious containment stance: treating stablecoins under existing money services or securities laws to keep them from undermining financial rules. However, there is a clear shift towards integration via new regulation – meaning crafting specific regulatory frameworks that formally bring stablecoin issuers into the regulated financial system. Papers by Arner et al. (2020) and others argue that well-designed regulation can harness stablecoins' benefits while mitigating risks through requirements on reserve quality, capital, audits, and interoperability with banking systems (Arner et al., 2020; Dark et al, 2022; Schwarcz, 2022; Bains et al, 2022).

Recent legislative and policy developments bear this out. In the U.S., the President's Working Group on Financial Markets (PWG) issued a 2021 report recommending that stablecoin issuers should be regulated similarly to banks – a stance echoed by subsequent bills in Congress (U.S. Department of the Treasury, 2021). By 2023–2025, draft laws (such as the proposed Stablecoin TRUST Act and more recent GENIUS Act in the Senate) have outlined federal licensing regimes for stablecoin issuers, mandating high-quality reserves and supervisory oversight (U.S. Senate, 2023, 2024). Hong Kong, similarly, has moved quickly to legislate stablecoin oversight, releasing a new Stablecoin Ordinance in 2024 that requires any entity issuing stablecoins in Hong Kong or targeting its residents to be licensed by the HKMA (Li, 2024). These laws typically impose full reserve backing, regular audits, fit-and-proper management requirements, and in some cases restrict certain activities. For example, the U.S. proposals often ban stablecoin issuers from offering interest to avoid them resembling securities. The literature on these regulatory efforts notes a convergence on key principles but also some divergence reflecting different policy priorities – for instance, the U.S. emphasis on prohibiting foreign unlicensed stablecoins is linked to geopolitical and sanctions concern, whereas Hong Kong's openness to foreign-currency stablecoins ties into its aim to be a cosmopolitan crypto hub (Arner et al., 2022).

2.3 Central Bank Digital Currencies (CBDCs) vs Stablecoins

Another important strand of literature contrasts CBDCs with private stablecoins. A CBDC is a digital form of central bank money – essentially a government-issued stablecoin which is a direct liability of the central bank. Some studies indicate that

CBDCs as a public sector answer to the rise of cryptocurrencies and stablecoins, potentially offering the benefits of digital currency without the risks of private issuer default (Auer & Böhme, 2020; Geva & Muraj, 2023). The e-CNY (digital yuan) in China is the most prominent and advanced example of a retail CBDC in a major economy. Studies of e-CNY highlight its design features: it is a two-tier system in which PBOC issues the currency while commercial banks distribute it via digital wallets and it does not rely on decentralized blockchain but uses a controlled distributed ledger, and it is programmable with features like expiration or spending limits in pilot programs (Xu, 2022; Yang & Zhou 2022).

China's aggressive push into CBDC has been interpreted in the context of both domestic policy and international strategy. Domestically, it provides the PBOC with greater visibility into digital payments and could enhance financial inclusion and payment efficiency (Zhang et al., 2022). Internationally, some analysts posit that the e-CNY could be a tool to promote RMB usage globally, especially in regions where China has economic influence (such as along the Belt and Road Initiative) (Prasad, 2021). Literature often debates whether a digital yuan can meaningfully chip away at the dollar's dominance. Skeptics point out that currency internationalization depends on deep factors like trust in the issuing country's institutions, open capital accounts, and financial market depth – areas where the USD still has an overwhelming lead (Ryan, 2024). Optimists or strategists suggest that even if e-CNY does not topple the dollar, it could carve out niches, thereby eroding the dollar's marginal presence over time (Lee, 2023).

Some works also examine Hong Kong's role in China's CBDC strategy. Hong Kong has been a testing ground for cross-border use of e-CNY, given its status as an international finance center and its infrastructure linkages with Mainland China. This has implications for the offshore use of the RMB: Hong Kong could serve as a conduit for non-mainland users to hold and transact in digital yuan, effectively boosting RMB's reach without fully opening China's capital account (He et al., 2023).

Meanwhile, in Western economies, central banks like the U.S. Federal Reserve and the European Central Bank have been researching CBDCs, albeit at a deliberative pace (Board of Governors of the Federal Reserve, 2022). One reason is that the existing role of the dollar and euro are already entrenched; there is less urgency absent a clear threat like Libra/Diem posed back in 2019. However, literature notes that if other countries leap ahead with CBDCs and set new standards, late movers could be disadvantaged (Bordo & Levin, 2023). Thus, some argue the U.S. should not only regulate private stablecoins but also seriously consider a USD CBDC to ensure the dollar remains the anchor of the global monetary system in a digital future (Bordo, 2022). Others counter that private USD-pegged stablecoins are achieving many of the same ends (digital dollar representation) and that the U.S. might leverage its innovative private sector rather than issue government digital money, so long as appropriate guardrails are in place (Giancarlo, 2023).

2.4 Dollar Dominance and Digital Currency Geopolitics

Finally, the literature on dollar dominance provides a backdrop to evaluate the strategic significance of stablecoins and CBDCs. The U.S. dollar's dominance in global finance – reflected in its large share of reserves, trade invoicing, swift usage, and denomination of commodities – is a cornerstone of U.S. economic influence (Eichengreen, 2019; Goldberg & Lerman, 2022). Benefits of this dominance include easier financing of deficits and powerful sanctions capabilities (Farhi & Maggiori, 2018). Recognizing this, U.S. policymakers are attentive to any developments that might undermine the dollar's status. Historically, challenges to the dollar such as the euro's rise have not drastically altered the landscape, largely because rivals lacked the same network effects and trust (McDowell, 2022).

However, digital currencies open new fronts for competition. Two recent studies have investigated the scenarios where a combination of innovations – for example, a widely adopted digital yuan plus regional blocs using alternative payment systems – could gradually reduce the dollar's ubiquity (Prasad, 2021; Lee, 2023). Key arguments include: digital platforms might lower the barriers for using a non-dollar currency in international transactions; if China offers incentives (e.g. cheaper transaction fees or credit facilities) for partners to use e-CNY in trade, some diversion from dollar usage could occur. Additionally, if U.S. stablecoin regulation becomes too stringent and pushes activity offshore, it could inadvertently encourage growth of stablecoins or digital currencies linked to other currencies or even decentralized assets (Huang & Luk, 2023).

On the other hand, many experts contend that the network effects of the dollar are so strong that incremental changes from digital currencies will have limited impact (Gopinath & Stein, 2021). They note that even with e-CNY's rollout, the RMB's share in global payments (via SWIFT) and reserves has only inched upward, not leapt. Furthermore, the fact that most stablecoins are dollar-based could actually bolster dollar dominance: as stablecoins become integral to future financial infrastructure including DeFi and cross-border settlements, if they remain dollar-pegged, they anchor the digital economy in the dollar standard. An interesting point raised in recent analysis is that large USD stablecoin ecosystems create additional demand for U.S. Treasuries – since issuers hold reserves mostly in short-term government securities, a growing stablecoin market effectively means more global money parked in U.S. debt (JPMorgan, 2023). One estimate suggests that by 2030, stablecoins could hold over $1 trillion in Treasuries, potentially ranking among the largest foreign holders of

U.S. debt (Bank of America, 2023). This dynamic, paradoxically, might strengthen U.S. financial power even as other countries seek alternatives (Setser, 2023).

3. METHODOLOGY

This research adopts a qualitative comparative case study methodology to analyze the stablecoin and digital currency approaches of China, Hong Kong, and the United States. The goal is to draw out comparative insights by examining each jurisdiction's model in detail and then juxtaposing them along key dimensions. Our methodology involves several steps:

3.1 Case Selection

We focus on China, Hong Kong, and the U.S. because they represent three distinct archetypes in the stablecoin/CBDC space. China exemplifies the state-centric CBDC approach and an explicit attempt to develop a sovereign digital currency (the e-CNY) while banning private crypto-stablecoin activity. Hong Kong provides a unique hybrid case – a major financial center with a pro-innovation regulatory stance toward stablecoins, operating under the orbit of China's monetary influence but maintaining a separate legal-financial system pegged to the U.S. dollar. United States represents the market-driven approach, where private stablecoin issuers have flourished and now face potential integration into the regulated financial framework, in a country motivated to maintain the dollar's dominance. These cases allow us to compare a spectrum from a fully public model (CBDC) to a private-sector model, with a hybrid model in between.

3.2 Data Collection

We gathered data from a variety of sources. This includes:

Policy documents and regulations: e.g. People's Bank of China (PBOC) reports and announcements on the e-CNY, Hong Kong Monetary Authority (HKMA) consultation papers and the text of Hong Kong's Stablecoin Bill, and U.S. legislative drafts or regulatory reports on stablecoins.

Market data: statistics on stablecoin market capitalization, transaction volumes, and adoption rates (sourced from industry reports, blockchain analytics, and academic studies) to inform our comparison of market impact.

Research literature: academic papers, think-tank reports, and expert analyses (as reviewed in the Literature Review) to contextualize each jurisdiction's approach and to extract analytical frameworks (for instance, criteria for evaluating currency internationalization or regulatory effectiveness).

3.3 Analytical Framework

We developed a comparative framework focusing on several core dimensions:

Regulatory Framework and Legal Status: What laws or regulations govern stablecoins or digital currency in each jurisdiction? How permissive or restrictive are they? Who are the authorized issuers – e.g. central bank vs. licensed private entities vs. open market with ex-post regulation?

Design and Technology: The nature of the digital currency – e.g., centralized CBDC vs. blockchain-based token, underlying collateral model, interoperability, and technological features.

Adoption and Use Cases: The current state of adoption (number of users, transaction volume), primary use cases targeted (retail payments, wholesale settlement, cross-border transfers, crypto trading, etc.), and involvement of financial institutions or tech firms in distribution.

Economic and Strategic Objectives: The motivations driving each model – for China perhaps increasing RMB usage and data control; for Hong Kong enhancing financial hub status; for the U.S. fostering innovation while extending dollar usage – as gleaned from official statements and expert analyses.

Impact on Monetary System: How each model interacts with the existing monetary and banking system, including any early evidence of impact on financial stability, monetary policy, or cross-border capital flows.

Using this framework, we first analyze each case individually and then conduct a cross-case comparison to highlight similarities, differences, and interactions. We synthesize findings in comparative tables and conceptual figures for clarity. For instance, we present a table comparing regulatory requirements side-by-side, and a concept figure illustrating how the three models' interface with the global dollar system.

3.4 Limitations

It is important to note the limitations of our methodology. The field of digital currency is evolving rapidly, and data can be limited or quickly outdated. Our analysis is largely qualitative; while we include quantitative indicators for context, the core findings rely on interpretation of policy and market behavior. There is also an inherent uncertainty in projecting how these initiatives will influence dollar dominance – we can analyze current trends and frameworks, but many geopolitical and economic variables will play into actual outcomes. We address this uncertainty by discussing multiple scenarios in our analysis. Finally, our study is bounded to three jurisdictions; while they are influential, developments in other regions are outside our scope but could also impact the global currency landscape in ways that intersect with our cases.

4. COMPARATIVE ANALYSIS OF STABLECOIN MODELS

In this section, we delve into each of the three cases – China, Hong Kong, and the United States – and then draw comparisons to elucidate how each model operates and what it signifies for the future of stablecoins. The analysis is organized by jurisdiction for clarity, followed by a comparative discussion highlighting the contrasts and connections among the three.

4.1 China: The State-Controlled Digital Yuan Model

Central Bank Digital Currencies (CBDCs) and stablecoins represent two distinct approaches to digital currency, each with unique technical and regulatory implications. CBDCs, such as China's e-CNY or the proposed digital euro, are issued and backed by central banks, operating on permissioned or hybrid distributed ledger technology (DLT) systems. They offer instant settlement finality with sovereign guarantees, prioritize compliance through embedded KYC/AML measures, and focus primarily on domestic payments, though cross-border pilots are expanding. Table 1 below summarizes the key differences between **CBDCs and privately issued stablecoins.**

Table 1. Summary of Key differences in CBDCs and Stablecoins

Feature	CBDCs (e.g., e-CNY, digital euro)	Stablecoins (e.g., USDC, PYUSD, USDT)
Issuer	Central bank (government-backed)	Private entities (e.g., PayPal, Circle, Tether)
Underlying Asset	Sovereign fiat (1:1 with national currency)	Fiat-backed, crypto-collateralized, or algorithmic
Infrastructure	Mostly permissioned DLT (some hybrid models)	Public/permissioned blockchains (e.g., Ethereum, Solana)
Settlement Finality	Instant (central bank guarantee)	Depends on blockchain (e.g., Ethereum finality ~12-15 sec)
Privacy & Compliance	KYC/AML enforced (pseudonymity varies)	Varies (regulated stablecoins enforce AML, unregulated may not)

continued on following page

Table 1. Continued

Interoperability	Domestic focus (some cross-border pilots)	Global, multi-chain (e.g., USDC on 16+ blockchains)
Programmability	Smart contract support (limited in early CBDCs)	Full smart contract capabilities (DeFi integration)

China's approach to stablecoins is defined by a firm rejection of privately issued digital tokens in favor of a state-controlled solution: the Digital Currency Electronic Payment (DCEP) initiative. This project led to the creation of the e-CNY, or digital yuan, a central bank digital currency (CBDC) designed as a digital version of physical cash (M0) and issued by the People's Bank of China (PBOC). The e-CNY is legal tender in pilot regions and serves as China's direct answer to both cryptocurrency and stablecoins (Xu, 2022). Under this system, the PBOC is the sole issuer of the digital yuan, and all other stable-valued digital tokens—such as USDT or privately issued RMB-pegged coins—are banned within mainland China. This policy complements China's broader crackdown on crypto, including bans on ICOs since 2017 and on cryptocurrency transactions since 2021, all aimed at eliminating non-state-controlled currency alternatives (Xie, 2019).

Although the central bank issues the e-CNY, distribution to end users is handled by select state-owned banks and payment service providers. Users can access the currency through dedicated digital wallets or integrate it with widely used apps like WeChat Pay and Alipay during trials. This two-tier distribution system leverages China's existing financial infrastructure while avoiding the disruption of the traditional banking sector (Riley, 2021).

Technologically, the e-CNY operates on a centralized, permissioned ledger maintained by the PBOC and authorized nodes, not on a public blockchain. It is not anonymous; instead, it follows a model of "controlled anonymity." Small transactions allow for limited privacy, but the central bank can trace and monitor larger or suspicious activities to ensure compliance with anti-money laundering (AML) regulations and capital controls *(Ahnert & Monnet, 2022)*. Despite being in a pilot phase, the e-CNY represents the world's largest CBDC trial. By mid-2023, about 120 million digital wallets had been created, and 16.5 billion yuan were in circulation. However, this only accounts for around 0.16% of China's M0, underscoring the long path ahead before the digital yuan could significantly replace physical cash or challenge the dominance of private payment platforms. Alipay and WeChat Pay, each with over a billion users, continue to control the vast majority of retail digital payments. To promote e-CNY adoption, the government has offered incentives such as digital yuan lotteries and merchant discounts. The currency has been used in a range of pilot applications, from subway fares to tax payments.

Domestically, the digital yuan aims to provide a backup to private payment systems, enhance financial inclusion in underserved areas, and improve payment system efficiency. Strategically, China envisions the e-CNY playing a role in cross-border transactions. It has been linked with Hong Kong's Faster Payment System and is part of the BIS's m-CBDC Bridge project, which explores cross-border CBDC interoperability. These efforts are motivated by a desire to internationalize the RMB and reduce reliance on U.S.-dominated financial systems like SWIFT, especially amid concerns over financial sanctions (Deng, 2024).

Ultimately, China's model emphasizes centralized control and long-term monetary strategy. By outlawing private stablecoins, it avoids domestic "digital dollarization" and positions the e-CNY as a state-backed alternative that other central banks might follow. Nevertheless, significant obstacles remain. The RMB's international utility is limited by capital controls, and broader trust in the currency depends on China's economic policies and global relationships. Still, China's early and large-scale move into CBDCs provides a first-mover advantage that could shape the future of digital currency globally.

4.2 Hong Kong: The Regulated Stablecoin Hub

Hong Kong's approach to stablecoins strikes a balance between China's strict controls and the West's market-driven innovation. As a special administrative region with its own currency, the Hong Kong dollar (HKD), which is pegged to the U.S. dollar, Hong Kong operates with a unique position that allows it to engage both global markets and Chinese stakeholders. The Hong Kong Monetary Authority (HKMA) has taken a proactive stance on digital asset regulation, aiming to establish the city as a leading jurisdiction for regulated stablecoin activity.

In January 2022, the HKMA released a discussion paper that highlighted the need for a regulatory framework specifically for payment-related stablecoins, particularly those pegged to fiat currencies (Wong et al, 2025). The paper emphasized potential risks to financial stability, especially in the wake of high-profile algorithmic stablecoin failures. After industry consultation, the HKMA drafted a Stablecoin Bill, which was passed in May 2025. This legislation created a comprehensive licensing regime: any entity involved in issuing, operating, or marketing fiat-referenced stablecoins to the Hong Kong public must now obtain authorization from the HKMA. Importantly, the regime is agnostic to the underlying fiat: USD-, HKD-, or RMB-pegged stablecoins can all fall under its scope, as long as they engage with the Hong Kong market (Burgess & Liu, 2025).

The licensing framework incorporates international best practices. Issuers must maintain full reserves backed by high-quality liquid assets at a 1:1 ratio and guarantee redemption at par. Additional requirements include regular audits, capital adequacy, liquidity thresholds, and governance standards. Management teams must pass fit-and-proper assessments. While broadly conservative, the rules allow some flexibility: issuers are not categorically barred from offering yield or designing novel reserve compositions, as long as risks are effectively managed and disclosed. This opens the door for innovation within a tightly supervised environment (Li, 2024).

Even before the law's full implementation, the HKMA employed a regulatory sandbox approach. In 2023–2024, selected firms were allowed to test stablecoin applications under close regulatory supervision. These pilots included use cases like cross-border trade settlement, e-commerce payments, and tokenized asset transactions. For example, in July 2024, entities backed by major banks and tech firms entered the sandbox to explore real-world stablecoin applications. These programs gave regulators valuable insights into potential risks and operational challenges while encouraging industry development.

Strategically, Hong Kong's model serves both protective and opportunistic roles. On one hand, it is vital for the city to manage potential financial risks and ensure confidence in its currency peg. On the other hand, with China banning private crypto activity, Hong Kong has the opportunity to act as a regulated gateway for digital asset businesses. Government officials have openly expressed their desire for Hong Kong to become a hub for virtual asset innovation, with stablecoin regulation forming a foundational part of that strategy. There is also room for alignment with mainland China through potential cross-border initiatives such as dual-currency stablecoins (e.g., HKD-CNY) or interoperability with China's digital yuan (e-CNY), but these efforts must be balanced with preserving Hong Kong's international financial reputation.

Currently, stablecoin usage in Hong Kong is dominated by USD-pegged tokens such as USDT and USDC, primarily used by crypto traders. There is no major HKD-pegged stablecoin in wide circulation yet, although interest is growing. One reported initiative involves a private firm exploring the issuance of a "HKDG" stablecoin. As regulations come into effect, new HKD-linked stablecoins are expected to emerge, likely backed by consortia of banks or fintech firms. Moreover, offshore RMB-pegged tokens may gain traction in Hong Kong, providing international investors with RMB exposure without navigating mainland China's capital controls. This could support China's long-term ambition of RMB internationalization via Hong Kong's financial infrastructure.

4.3 United States: The Market-Driven Ecosystem and Emerging Oversight

The United States' engagement with stablecoins is distinctive in that the sector largely developed and scaled within its borders before a comprehensive regulatory framework was in place. U.S. dollars form the foundation of the global stablecoin economy—not only because most leading stablecoins are denominated in USD, but also because their reserve assets are primarily held within American financial institutions. As a result, the U.S. model has been predominantly market-led, with regulators gradually shifting toward greater oversight and regulatory integration (Nejadmalayeri et al, 2023).

Private issuers have driven much of the innovation in this space. Companies like Tether and Circle (issuer of USDC, in partnership with Coinbase) grew rapidly throughout the late 2010s, operating under minimal regulation—mostly state-level money transmitter laws. These firms secured banking partners to hold reserves and benefited from a permissive environment that enabled rapid scaling. By 2021, stablecoins had become essential infrastructure within crypto markets. Rather than attempting to ban them—an unenforceable move in many ways—the U.S. allowed their continued use, recognizing their utility and the challenge of regulating decentralized, internet-based assets (Hileman, 2019).

However, as stablecoins gained prominence, regulators began sounding the alarm. Agencies such as the SEC scrutinized whether certain stablecoins might be securities, especially those offering interest or lacking full collateralization. Meanwhile, the Treasury and FINCEN raised concerns about potential illicit uses. A turning point came with the 2021 President's Working Group (PWG) report, which recommended that stablecoin issuers be regulated like banks or similarly supervised entities. Although a specific federal law had not passed as of 2025, several high-profile legislative proposals were introduced, including the Clarity for Payment Stablecoins Act (2023) and the GENIUS Act (2024). These bills offer flexible pathways for compliance, allowing issuers to operate as bank affiliates, federally regulated non-bank licensees, or under state regimes that meet federal standards (Oranburg, 2025). Many proposals also include provisions to block foreign stablecoins that do not meet U.S. requirements, underscoring America's intent to maintain control over dollar-denominated digital liquidity on a global scale.

The U.S. is also moving toward treating stablecoins more like money market funds or narrow banks. Proposed reserve requirements mandate backing with safe, liquid assets—such as cash at the Federal Reserve, short-term U.S. Treasuries, or reverse repo instruments. In practice, leading issuers like Circle and Tether have already adjusted their portfolios to align with these expectations, heavily investing in U.S. Treasuries. This shift enhances the safety of stablecoins while embedding them deeper into the traditional financial system. Some economists have even proposed granting stablecoin issuers accounts at the Federal Reserve to eliminate credit risk, though this remains controversial and politically sensitive (Liao & Caramichael, 2022; Calomiris. 2021).

Notably, the U.S. has yet to launch a central bank digital currency (CBDC). While the Federal Reserve has explored the possibility—most notably through

Project Hamilton with MIT—no commitment has been made. One reason is that stablecoins are already fulfilling many functions that a retail CBDC might serve, enabling digital dollar transactions on blockchain platforms. Fed and Treasury officials have indicated that any decision to issue a CBDC would require broad political support and likely Congressional authorization. For now, U.S. policy focuses on ensuring that stablecoins operate in a way that complements, rather than disrupts, the financial system.

In terms of usage, USD stablecoins are dominant globally within the crypto ecosystem. They are widely used for cross-border transactions, remittances, decentralized finance (DeFi), and even by traditional financial institutions. Visa, for instance, has piloted stablecoin-based settlement using USDC on Ethereum. On-chain volumes are staggering: by early 2025, stablecoin transactions were on pace to exceed $10 trillion annually—approaching the scale of traditional high-value payment systems (OKG Research, 2025). Yet, within the U.S. domestic economy, stablecoins remain niche for everyday consumer use; one rarely buys groceries with USDC. However, fintech integrations are growing, and some apps already offer stablecoin wallets for payments and interest-bearing accounts.

The U.S. policy approach serves multiple objectives. Foremost is the preservation of dollar dominance in the digital economy. Policymakers have explicitly stated that widespread use of dollar-based stablecoins reinforces the U.S. monetary position globally. Tying stablecoin backing to U.S. Treasuries also helps finance government debt, creating a symbiotic relationship. Another key objective is financial stability: regulators aim to prevent destabilizing events, such as the 2022 TerraUSD collapse (Krause, 2025), from recurring with fiat-backed coins. Ensuring consumer protection through prudential oversight is central to avoiding systemic risk.

4.4 Comparative Overview

Having described each jurisdiction's approach, we can crystallize the comparison across key dimensions. Table 2 below provides a side-by-side comparison of the stablecoin/CBDC models of China, Hong Kong, and the United States:

Table 2. Comparison of key features of China's, Hong Kong's, and the U.S.'s stablecoin/digital currency models (as of 2024-2025).

Dimension	China (e-CNY CBDC)	Hong Kong (Stablecoin Hub)	United States (Private Stablecoins)
Issuer / Model	Central bank issued CBDC (Digital Yuan, e-CNY). No private stablecoins allowed domestically.	Licensed private issuers under HKMA oversight (upcoming). HKMA considering retail CBDC (e-HKD) research but not launched.	Private companies issue stablecoins (e.g., Tether, Circle). No CBDC issued yet (Fed researching).
Peg / Value Reference	Pegged to CNY (legal tender digital fiat). 1:1 with yuan.	Likely focus on HKD-pegged coins; also allows other fiat pegs (USD, RMB) under regulation. HKD is itself pegged to USD (1 USD ≈ 7.8 HKD).	Predominantly USD-pegged stablecoins (USDT, USDC, etc.). Also a few others (e.g., USD-backed tokens pegged to EUR, etc., but minor).
Regulatory Stance	Prohibition of crypto and stablecoins; full state control. e-CNY governed by PBOC frameworks (new legislation created as needed).	Proactive regulation: mandatory licensing, full reserve backing, audits. Building legal framework (Stablecoin Ordinance 2024/25). Open to innovation under supervision (sandbox trials).	Evolving from minimal to specific regulation. Currently, stablecoins largely self-regulated under general laws; forthcoming federal/state regimes to supervise issuers like banks or special entities.
Technology Platform	Centralized distributed ledger (not public blockchain). Two-tier (PBOC -> banks -> users). Smart features (programmability for contracts, expiry). High tx throughput aimed (tested up to ~300k TPS in lab).	Primarily blockchain-based tokens (ERC-20 or similar) for stablecoins that will be issued. HKMA's own infrastructure (e.g., FPS) might integrate with stablecoins/CBDC for settlements. Considering interoperability with e-CNY (pilots).	Public blockchain networks (Ethereum, Tron, etc.) carry most stablecoins. Some on permissioned chains (e.g., Diem was planned). Tech is mostly private-sector driven; regulators focusing on interoperability with banking (e.g., stablecoin clearing through traditional systems).
Adoption (as of 2024)	~120 million e-CNY wallets, 16.5 billion CNY in circulationi (pilot). Usage mostly domestic retail (small fraction of total transactions). Minor cross-border trials with HK, Thailand. No competing stablecoins legally.	No major native stablecoin yet (HKD stablecoin in development). Widespread use of USD stablecoins by crypto community in HK. Several pilot projects in progress (e.g., trade finance settlement). HK's role as gateway: facilitating e-CNY use for tourists, etc., in pilot.	~$250 billion in stablecoin market cap, dominated by USD tokens. Integrated in global crypto trading, some fintech and cross-border payments. Not widely used in everyday retail within U.S., but growing integration (e.g., PayPal's PYUSD stablecoin launched 2023).

continued on following page

Table 2. Continued

Motivation & Goals	Increase monetary sovereignty, counter private crypto, improve payment efficiency, and internationalize RMB (long-term). Reduce reliance on USD in trade (promote yuan pricing). Enhance financial surveillance and control (AML, capital flight).	Maintain HK as a leading financial center by embracing fintech. Facilitate safe stablecoin innovation, possibly become issuance venue for RMB or HKD stablecoins (supporting RMB internationalization). Reinforce HK's role as bridge between China and global markets. Earn revenue and expertise from new digital asset businesses.	Support dollar's role in digital economy, foster innovation in payments and fintech. Ensure USD stablecoins are safe to prevent financial instability. Keep regulatory control to enforce sanctions/ AML on dollar flows. Provide efficient payment options and potentially improve financial inclusion (cheaper remittances, etc.). Also, avoid ceding ground to a potential foreign CBDC that could challenge USD.
Challenges & Risks	Slow adoption if public prefers existing apps; concerns over privacy (state tracking). Potential resistance internationally to RMB expansion (trust issues). Banks worry about deposit disintermediation. Capital controls limit e-CNY appeal overseas.	Regulatory arbitrage (firms might go to jurisdictions with looser rules if HK too strict). Need to maintain peg and stability – any stablecoin issues could threaten trust. Balancing being open to global players vs. security (e.g., not becoming loophole for sanctioned money). Dependent on broader market adoption of stablecoins.	Regulatory uncertainty until laws pass (patchwork in interim). Risk of runs or collapses if not properly regulated (e.g., questions around Tether's transparency historically). Politically, some anti-crypto sentiment could lead to harsher crackdowns which might push innovation offshore. Also, ensuring interoperability between new stablecoin rails and legacy banking is a technical and policy challenge.

4.5 Comparative Analysis

China's stablecoin model is entirely public sector-driven, centered on a central bank digital currency (e-CNY), while the U.S. approach has been private-sector-led, with public oversight catching up only after significant market growth. Hong Kong occupies a middle ground, permitting private stablecoin issuers but subjecting them to robust regulatory oversight from the outset.

The core priorities of each jurisdiction differ. China emphasizes state control—both monetary and data sovereignty—even if that means slower user adoption. The U.S., by contrast, initially embraced openness and innovation, allowing stablecoins to flourish under minimal regulation. Only recently has it moved to assert regulatory control. Hong Kong, seeking the best of both worlds, promotes innovation and diverse stablecoin issuance within a clearly defined and tightly supervised framework.

In terms of currency positioning, the U.S. model naturally reinforces the dominance of the U.S. dollar, as most stablecoins are USD-denominated and backed by dollar assets. Hong Kong's multi-currency openness also supports the USD—especially given the HKD's peg to the dollar and the prevalence of USD-based stablecoins—but it explicitly creates space for RMB-based tokens. This could provide an offshore channel for RMB internationalization. China's model, by contrast, is singularly focused on elevating the RMB's global role while reducing reliance on U.S.-controlled financial infrastructure.

When it comes to innovation strategy, the differences are stark. The U.S. followed a "move fast and break things" approach, with innovation leading and regulation trailing. China pre-empted the market by launching a state-backed solution and simultaneously banning private alternatives. Hong Kong, meanwhile, is deliberately fostering innovation in parallel with regulation—using tools like regulatory sandboxes to guide development within a supervised environment.

Importantly, these models do not evolve in isolation. China's ban on private crypto activity has pushed many firms to relocate to Hong Kong or offshore jurisdictions, indirectly bolstering Hong Kong's role in the digital asset ecosystem. The outcome of Hong Kong's stablecoin regulatory experiment may influence mainland policymakers and could offer Chinese tech firms, such as Ant Group, a platform to pilot innovations in a regulated but more globally integrated environment. Meanwhile, the U.S. closely monitors China's CBDC progress and often cites it as a motivation to both regulate stablecoins and maintain the dollar's leadership in digital finance. In this way, the stablecoin triad of China, Hong Kong, and the U.S. operates in a state of dynamic and competitive coexistence, with each model reacting to and shaping the others.

5. MARKET IMPACT AND DYNAMICS

The emergence of distinct stablecoin models in China, Hong Kong, and the U.S. has already had measurable impacts on financial markets, and it portends further changes in the global financial dynamics. In this section, we analyze how each of the three models is influencing markets domestically and internationally, and the interplay between them.

5.1 Impact on Domestic Financial Systems

Domestically, the rollout of e-CNY is gradually influencing China's financial system, though in limited ways so far. One notable impact is the pressure on incumbent mobile payment providers (Bai, et al, 2025). Ant Group's Alipay and Tencent's WeChat Pay currently dominate retail payments; the introduction of e-CNY provides a state-backed alternative. To encourage adoption, Chinese authorities have integrated e-CNY into these platforms. If e-CNY usage grows, it could marginally shift some deposits away from commercial banks. However, given current usage is tiny relative to bank deposits, the disintermediation effect is minimal for now. Another domestic impact is on monetary policy and data: e-CNY could give the PBOC more real-time economic data on spending patterns, possibly improving monetary policy targeting in the future (McNally, 2025). Additionally, by setting limits such as holding caps on individual wallets, the PBOC can manage the CBDC's influence on money supply and banks. The e-CNY could also be used as a tool for fiscal stimulus, making monetary-fiscal actions more direct.

In Hong Kong, since a native stablecoin is not widely deployed yet, immediate impacts are limited. However, the announcement of regulatory clarity has already attracted interest from both traditional financial institutions and crypto-native firms. For example, the prospect of licensed stablecoin issuance has drawn in large players: reports indicate that Asian fintech firms and even Chinese fintech affiliates have shown intent to apply for Hong Kong stablecoin licenses. Should HKD-pegged stablecoins launch, one direct impact could be on local payment and deposit markets – if those stablecoins offer convenience or yields, consumers might allocate some funds to them rather than bank deposits or the stored-value facilities like Octopus. But given Hong Kong's strong banking culture, any shift would likely be gradual. Importantly, Hong Kong's status as a crypto trading hub means a regulated stablecoin environment could increase trading volumes and liquidity in the city (Birzoim, 2025). That could benefit the local financial industry and reinforce Hong Kong's capital markets. It could also, interestingly, strengthen the US dollar peg if a lot of activity uses USD stablecoins under HKMA oversight, because it cements the role of USD in the digital asset space that Hong Kong oversees.

In the U.S., stablecoins have begun to have ripple effects on money markets. Major stablecoins hold a significant amount of U.S. Treasury bills as reserves. In particular, USDT and USDC together held tens of billions of dollars in T-bills in 2023–2024 (Robson, 2025). This means that changes in stablecoin demand can translate to sizable flows in short-term Treasury markets. For instance, during crypto bull markets when stablecoin market caps expand, issuers must buy more Treasuries, marginally increasing demand for government debt. Conversely, if crypto markets contract and stablecoins shrink, reserves might be liquidated, potentially causing minor turbulence in funding markets. Some Federal Reserve officials have noted this connection and consider including stablecoin reserves in their analysis of market liquidity. On the banking side, stablecoins thus far have not dramatically reduced bank deposits in the U.S., but the potential is there: if in the future, corporations or individuals hold significant funds in stablecoins, that could compete with bank deposits or money market funds. Banks have an ambivalent stance – some see stablecoin networks as payment rails they can leverage, while others worry about losing payments business to blockchain networks. The regulatory push to integrate stablecoins is partly to address these concerns, effectively bringing stablecoins into the regulatory perimeter so that any systemic impact can be managed.

5.2 Cross-Border and International Market Impact

One of the most profound impacts of stablecoins has been in the cross-border context. By design, cryptocurrencies are borderless, and fiat-backed stablecoins inherit this trait. They enable capital to move across countries without going through traditional forex markets or banking intermediaries. This has several implications:

Arbitrage and Capital Flows: In countries where the dollar is scarce or capital controls exist, stablecoins provide a shadow channel. For example, before China's crackdowns, many Chinese citizens used stablecoins to move money abroad. Even now, Chinese traders find ways to use stablecoins via offshore platforms, meaning some capital flight can occur outside official oversight. Similarly, in emerging markets with high inflation or currency instability, residents have turned to USD stablecoins as a store of value, effectively dollarizing savings outside the local banking system. This can put pressure on local currencies.

Remittances and Settlement: Stablecoins are increasingly used for remittances – for instance, Filipino overseas workers might send USDC to family back home who cash out in pesos through a local exchange or wallet. This route can be faster and cheaper than traditional remittance firms. As a result, traditional players may face competition, and even those players are exploring integrating stablecoins to stay relevant. On a larger scale, companies engaged in international trade have begun experimenting with settling invoices in stablecoins to avoid banking delays or high fees, especially in regions where banking is underdeveloped.

Interaction with Traditional Forex Markets: If stablecoin usage continues to grow, foreign exchange markets might see a shift. Right now, a lot of stablecoin volume is within crypto exchanges. But consider a future where an exporter in country A gets paid in a USD stablecoin by an importer in country B. They may bypass the forex conversion that would normally go through banks. Eventually, that exporter might convert the stablecoin to local currency via a crypto exchange or OTC desk. This means some forex conversion demand is moving from bank channels to crypto channels. It's still USD being used, but the path is different. Forex markets have not been disrupted yet in a major way, but we see early signs of alternative networks forming.

Market Integration and Contagion: Global stablecoin markets connect various national markets such that financial contagion can spread quickly. We saw this in the TerraUSD collapse. If any one major stablecoin were to fail, the shockwaves would be felt globally—exchanges across countries would feel liquidity crunches, and users worldwide could panic-redeem from other stablecoins. This is why Hong Kong, though a small territory, is very cautious: a stablecoin incident there would not be contained to HK's borders, it would reflect on Hong Kong's financial reputation worldwide.

China's cross-border impact: As of now, the e-CNY's cross-border use is minimal. However, looking forward, if China pursues the strategies outlined by some analysts—like leveraging its trade ties and resources to push e-CNY or RMB stablecoins—it could have targeted impact. For example, if China convinces a set of Belt and Road countries to accept and hold RMB for trade settlement, those countries might reduce their use of USD for those trades. This might not change global markets overnight, but in specific corridors, local forex markets might see increased liquidity and demand for RMB relative to USD. Additionally, if Hong Kong or offshore financial centers issue RMB stablecoins, international investors might start holding those for yield or speculative purposes—effectively opening another channel for RMB exposure. This could gradually internationalize RMB outside the direct control of PBOC's onshore system.

Hong Kong's cross-border role: Hong Kong could amplify both USD and RMB usage. If Hong Kong becomes a major issuer of USD stablecoins, it reinforces the reach of USD. If it issues RMB or HKD stablecoins that gain traction, it provides a non-U.S. alternative for the region. Hong Kong's financial linkages mean any product it offers can be easily accessed by global investors. Therefore, an HKD stablecoin might ironically become a proxy for USD that is more accessible in Asia time zone markets. Meanwhile, a CNH (offshore RMB) stablecoin could allow investors to hold RMB without dealing with Chinese banks, potentially boosting RMB's share in portfolios.

U.S. stablecoins international impact: The dominance of USD stablecoins essentially exports a part of the U.S. monetary base overseas in digital form. It's been reported that people in countries with unstable currencies prefer holding USDT over local money or even USD cash, since USDT can be transferred easily and sometimes more available than physical dollars. This is an extension of dollarization into the digital realm. For the U.S., as long as it can oversee this, it's beneficial. But if these flows become large and opaque, it could complicate things like measuring money supply or enforcing sanctions. For instance, if a sanctioned nation can use stablecoins peer-to-peer to conduct trade outside SWIFT, that undermines U.S. sanctions power. The U.S. Treasury is aware of this and has already sanctioned certain crypto addresses and mixers to try curbing illicit uses. The regulatory frameworks being proposed also consider how to maintain visibility into stablecoin transactions (likely through regulated issuers and exchanges needing to comply with AML, and possibly future tools to trace transactions on-chain).

5.3 Market Efficiency and Innovation

Another positive market impact of stablecoin proliferation is the increased efficiency and innovation in financial services. One major advancement is the rise of 24/7 markets. Unlike traditional banking systems, which halt operations on weekends and holidays, stablecoins settle on blockchain networks that operate continuously. This around-the-clock availability has created an expectation of instant settlement in crypto markets, a trend now influencing traditional finance. For instance, some forex trading platforms are exploring the use of stablecoins to enable weekend trading, circumventing the limitations of conventional bank wires.

Stablecoins also bring programmability to money. This allows for the automation of financial contracts via smart contracts, where payments can be triggered automatically when predefined conditions are met. Use cases are emerging in areas such as trade finance, where payments are released upon confirmation of goods delivery, and in insurance, where payouts are triggered by external data—such as a flight delay—detected through oracles. Both the U.S. and Hong Kong have active fintech sectors testing these innovations, with stablecoins often serving as the payment mechanism. Even China's centrally issued e-CNY has built-in programmability features, offering the potential for similar applications, albeit within a state-controlled environment.

Stablecoins may also enhance financial inclusion by lowering barriers to entry. Anyone with a smartphone and internet connection can access and use stablecoins without needing a traditional bank account. This opens the door for unbanked individuals, freelancers, and traders in emerging markets to store value and conduct transactions using dollar-backed stablecoins. The societal impact is significant, although it introduces new challenges, such as the need for secure private key management. NGOs and fintech startups have started leveraging stablecoins to distribute aid and support microfinance initiatives in regions with weak banking infrastructure.

However, these benefits are not without trade-offs. Regulators remain concerned about potential systemic risks, including financial contagion, liquidity mismatches, and cybersecurity vulnerabilities. The same technologies that bring efficiency and inclusion also introduce new forms of complexity and interconnectedness that can amplify market shocks.

6. STABLECOINS AND THE FUTURE OF DOLLAR DOMINANCE

A central question driving interest in the stablecoin triad is whether these innovations will upend the dominance of the U.S. dollar in global finance, or conversely, reinforce it. The dollar's dominance has been a linchpin of international economics, and any threat to it could have wide-ranging effects on global trade, investment, and U.S. power. Here, we analyze how the China, Hong Kong, and U.S. models interact with the concept of dollar dominance and what trajectories might emerge.

6.1 Reinforcing Dollar Dominance via Stablecoins

One clear outcome of the stablecoin boom has been the reinforcement of the U.S. dollar's global role. As noted, dollar-pegged stablecoins currently account for approximately 99% of the market. This dominance means that growing crypto adoption worldwide has largely translated into expanded use of the dollar—not through physical cash, but through digital tokens. In many emerging markets, new crypto users are more likely to hold a U.S. dollar stablecoin before ever touching an actual dollar bill, embedding the dollar deeper into the infrastructure of digital economies.

This trend also strengthens the dollar through financial integration. Major stablecoins hold reserves in U.S. Treasuries and bank deposits, effectively tying their stability to the U.S. fiscal system. This creates a loop in which global users of stablecoins become indirect stakeholders in the financial health of the United States. If stablecoins become a foundational asset class—alongside cash, deposits, and bonds—their dollar-denominated nature ensures that U.S. influence extends even into the decentralized finance (DeFi) ecosystem.

Payment networks are evolving to accommodate stablecoins, and many of these networks are global in scope. Companies like Visa and Mastercard are actively experimenting with stablecoin settlement. If this becomes standard practice, then everyday transactions—from card swipes to online purchases—could increasingly settle via dollar-based tokens. This would further expand the global circulation and relevance of the dollar, even outside the traditional banking system.

From the U.S. perspective, this is a highly favorable development—provided systemic risks are managed. Stablecoins offer a new way to project the dollar's dominance, extending the so-called "exorbitant privilege" of the dollar into the realm of crypto. Current U.S. policy appears to embrace this opportunity: by mandating that stablecoins be backed by U.S. assets and proposing to exclude non-compliant or non-USD stablecoins from the domestic market, the U.S. is effectively working to monopolize the stablecoin space for the dollar. If, in the future, the Federal Reserve were to issue a digital dollar or endorse a regulated stablecoin framework, it could cement this dominance by offering the safest and most trusted form of digital dollar, crowding out alternatives.

Hong Kong's stance also contributes to the dollar's strength. The HKD is pegged to the USD, and Hong Kong's openness to hosting and regulating USD stablecoins enhances their legitimacy in Asia. Regional businesses that might hesitate to use dollar stablecoins due to regulatory uncertainty may be more inclined to adopt them under the oversight of the Hong Kong Monetary Authority. In this way, Hong Kong could serve as a gateway, channeling more global capital into USD-based digital tokens through a trusted and regulated environment.

6.3 Challenges to Dollar Dominance

China's digital yuan, or e-CNY, is partially designed to challenge the dollar-centric global financial system, even if only incrementally at first. A key strategy involves encouraging trade partners to settle transactions in e-CNY. This could be facilitated through bilateral agreements or incentives such as trade invoice discounts for using RMB-based stablecoin. If such practices gain traction, especially in oil or commodity trades, even limited adoption could begin to erode petrodollar dominance. A broader, though still speculative, avenue lies in multilateral frameworks such as BRICS. Discussions around a BRICS digital currency or the increased use of local currencies could eventually integrate with central bank digital currency (CBDC) technologies, potentially accelerating de-dollarization within these alliances.

Parallel developments in localized CBDCs may also shift global currency dynamics. Countries like the European Union, Japan, and India are exploring or deploying digital versions of their national currencies. Should these CBDCs gain regional dominance—such as a widely adopted digital euro across Europe and parts of Africa—it could further reduce global reliance on the U.S. dollar. However, these alternatives currently lack the dollar's network effects and entrenched liquidity advantages, limiting their immediate impact.

At the frontier of innovation, decentralized finance (DeFi) introduces another possible disruptor. Stablecoins such as DAI, backed by crypto collateral, and the conceptual resurgence of algorithmic stablecoins, present a vision of reduced dependence on state-backed currencies altogether. While their market share remains small and many still rely on USD-pegged collateral, the growth of non-sovereign, basket-based stablecoins—like the original vision for Facebook's Libra—could incrementally reduce dollar exposure. The strong regulatory backlash against Libra demonstrates that major governments are likely to resist any supranational currency that threatens their monetary sovereignty.

Ultimately, the U.S. dollar's dominance is underpinned by global trust in America's financial system, legal stability, and geopolitical clout. However, that trust is not immutable. Events such as political dysfunction, debt ceiling standoffs, and the strategic overuse of sanctions can gradually erode confidence and prompt diversification. China's strategy appears to rest partly on this erosion, betting that U.S. missteps could make e-CNY a more attractive alternative over time. Although the dollar remains more trusted than the RMB—given China's capital controls and governance concerns—shifting global perceptions and technological developments could alter that balance in the long term.

Figure 1. Stablecoins and Dollar Dominance Dynamics

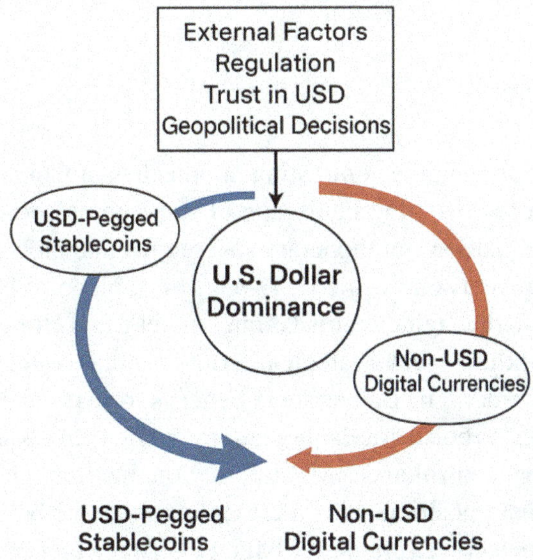

Figure 1: Conceptual illustration of the dynamics between stablecoins and dollar dominance. The diagram outlines two reinforcing loops: one where USD-pegged stablecoins (USDT, USDC, etc.) bolster the dollar's global use (blue arrows) by spreading dollar-denominated liquidity across crypto markets and beyond; and another where non-USD digital currencies chip away at niche areas of dollar usage (red arrows), such as regional trade or sanctioned corridors. The size of arrows indicates relative strength as of mid-2020s (USD stablecoin loop being far stronger currently). The diagram also shows external factors that can tilt the balance.

In analyzing the figure and broader trends, it appears that in the short to medium term, stablecoins are more likely to entrench dollar dominance than to undermine it. The momentum is with USD tokens, and even China's efforts are at early stages. Hong Kong's role seems more to ensure it doesn't miss out but not to dethrone the dollar. However, in the longer term, one could envision a more fragmented currency landscape accelerated by digital currencies, while would mirror the multipolar world geopolitical analysts talk about. Stablecoins/CBDCs would be enablers of that shift by making it technically easier for parties to bypass the dollar if they choose to,

A real-world test of dollar dominance in the digital age could come from extreme events: e.g., if the U.S. sanctioned a major economy out of SWIFT, would that country be able to use stablecoins or CBDCs to continue trading outside the dollar system? Iran, for instance, reportedly has used crypto for some imports. Russia, post-Ukraine sanctions, increased its use of the Chinese yuan for trade settlements significantly. If such workarounds prove successful, more countries may adopt them, incrementally reducing the dollar's centrality.

7. CONCLUSION

This study has examined the contrasting approaches of China, Hong Kong, and the United States in the evolving landscape of stablecoins and digital currencies, focusing on their implications for monetary sovereignty and global currency competition. The analysis reveals that while USD-pegged stablecoins have extended U.S. dollar dominance into the digital realm, China's e-CNY and Hong Kong's emerging regulatory framework represent strategic alternatives that could gradually reshape the global monetary order. The U.S. strategy benefits from private sector leadership, leveraging stablecoins to bolster dollar hegemony, while China's state-centric model emphasizes monetary control and RMB internationalization. Hong Kong's hybrid regulatory environment positions it as a critical gateway for both USD and RMB-linked stablecoins, reflecting a pragmatic balance between innovation and oversight.

Looking ahead, the trajectory of stablecoins will depend on regulatory clarity, technological interoperability, and the geopolitical strategies of major economies. To navigate this landscape effectively, the U.S. should finalize comprehensive stablecoin legislation, promote financial inclusion via regulated digital assets, and maintain readiness for a digital dollar if needed. China must accelerate e-CNY adoption by expanding practical use cases and cross-border pilots while enhancing transparency to build international trust. Hong Kong should swiftly operationalize its stablecoin licensing regime, foster HKD and RMB stablecoin issuance, and prepare for financial stability risks through robust oversight. Additionally, international bodies like the IMF, FSB, and BIS must establish global standards for stablecoins, promote CBDC interoperability, and enhance capacity-building for regulators worldwide. Cross-sector collaboration remains essential to ensuring that stablecoins contribute to a stable, inclusive, and efficient global financial system rather than exacerbating systemic risks or geopolitical tensions.

REFERENCES

G7 Working Group on Stablecoins. (2019). *Investigating the impact of global stablecoins.* https://www.bis.org

Adrian, T., & Mancini Griffoli, T. (2019, Jul 15). The rise of digital money (IMF FinTech Note No. 2019/001). International Monetary Fund. https://www.imf.org/-/media/Files/Publications/FTN063/2019/English/FTNEA2019001.ashx

Ahnert, T., Hoffmann, P., & Monnet, C. (2022). The digital economy, privacy, and CBDC.

Arner, D. W., Auer, R., & Frost, J. (2020). Stablecoins: Risks, potential and regulation. *Journal of Financial Regulation*, *6*(1), 1–30. DOI: 10.1093/jfr/fjaa004

Auer, R., & Böhme, R. (2020). The technology of retail central bank digital currency. BIS Quarterly Review, March 2020. https://www.bis.org

Auer, R., Cornelli, G., & Frost, J. (2020). Rise of the central bank digital currencies: Drivers, approaches and technologies. https://papers.ssrn.com/sol3/papers.cfm?abstract_id=3723552

Bai, H., Cong, L. W., Luo, M., & Xie, P. (2025). Adoption of central bank digital currencies: Initial evidence from China. *Journal of Corporate Finance*, *91*, 102735. DOI: 10.1016/j.jcorpfin.2025.102735

Bains, P., Ismail, A., Melo, F., & Sugimoto, N. (2022). *Regulating the crypto ecosystem: The case of stablecoins and arrangements*. International Monetary Fund.

Bank for International Settlements. (2022, Jun 21). III. The future monetary system. In BIS Annual Economic Report 2022. https://www.bis.org/publ/arpdf/ar2022e3.htm

Bank of America. (2023). Digital assets: Stablecoins and the US Treasury market. Global Research Report.

Birzoim, A. (2025). Blockchain-driven financial innovation in Hong Kong (2018-2024): Regulations, cross-border payments, and public-private collaboration.

Board of Governors of the Federal Reserve. (2022). *Money and payments: The U.S. dollar in the age of digital transformation.* https://www.federalreserve.gov

Board of Governors of the Federal Reserve System. (2022, Jan 19). Money and payments: The U.S. dollar in the age of digital transformation. https://www.federalreserve.gov/publications/files/money-and-payments-20220120.pdf

Bordo, M. D. (2022). *Digital currencies: The US Fed should proceed with caution.* NBER Working Paper 29913. https://www.nber.org

Bordo, M. D., & Levin, A. T. (2023). Central bank digital currency and the future of monetary policy. Hoover Institution Economics Working Paper 21103.

Bullmann, D., Klemm, J., & Pinna, A. (2019). *In search for stability in crypto-assets: Are stablecoins the solution?* ECB Occasional Paper No. 230. https://www.ecb.europa.eu

Burgess, T., & Liu, J. (2025). A tale of two jurisdictions: Contrasting cryptocurrency regulations in Hong Kong and the United Kingdom. Journal of Economic Criminology, 8.

Calomiris, C. W. (2021). Will fractional-reserve stablecoin banking replace Bitcoin and some traditional banking payments? *The Bank of America Journal of Applied Corporate Finance*, *33*(4), 70–75. DOI: 10.1111/jacf.12478

Carstens, A. (2019). *The future of money and payments.* Speech at the Central Bank of Ireland. https://www.bis.org

Claessens, S., Frost, J., Turner, G., & Zhu, F. (2021). *Stablecoin risks and prudential regulation.* BIS Papers No 123. https://www.bis.org

Cœuré, B. (2019). *Investigating the impact of global stablecoins.* Bank for International Settlements.

CoinMarketCap. (2024). Stablecoin market capitalization. https://coinmarketcap.com

Dark, C., Rogerson, E., Rowbotham, N., & Wallis, P. (2022). *Stablecoins: Market developments, risks and regulation.* RBA Bulletin.

Deng, H. (2024). Negotiating currency internationalization: An infrastructural analysis of the digital RMB. *Finance and Stochastics*, *10*(1), 1–17.

Diamond, D. W., & Dybvig, P. H. (1983). Bank runs, deposit insurance, and liquidity. *Journal of Political Economy*, *91*(3), 401–419. DOI: 10.1086/261155

Eichengreen, B. (2019). *Globalizing capital: A history of the international monetary system* (3rd ed.). Princeton University Press.

Eichengreen, B. (2022). *Will the dollar be dethroned?* Project Syndicate. https://www.project-syndicate.org

European Central Bank (ECB). (2022). *Progress on the investigation phase of a digital euro.* https://www.ecb.europa.eu

Farhi, E., & Maggiori, M. (2018). A model of the international monetary system. *The Quarterly Journal of Economics, 133*(1), 295–355. DOI: 10.1093/qje/qjx031

Financial Action Task Force (FATF). (2021). *Updated guidance for a risk-based approach to virtual assets and VASPs.* https://www.fatf-gafi.org

Financial Stability Board. (2020, Oct 13). Regulation, supervision and oversight of “global stablecoin” arrangements: Final report and high-level recommendations. https://www.fsb.org/2020/10/regulation-supervision-and-oversight-of-global-stablecoin-arrangements/

Financial Stability Board. (2023). Regulation, supervision and oversight of crypto-asset activities and markets. https://www.fsb.org

Financial Stability Board (FSB). (2020). *Regulation, supervision and oversight of “global stablecoin” arrangements.* https://www.fsb.org

Force, F. A. T. (2021). *Updated guidance for a risk-based approach to virtual assets and virtual asset service providers.* FATF.

Geva, B., & Muraj, M. (2023). The digitization of money: Stablecoins and CBDC. *Banking & Finance Law Review, 40*(1), 115–141.

Giancarlo, J. C. (2023). The future of digital finance: Why private sector innovation should lead. Cato Institute Policy Analysis No. 942.

Goldberg, L., & Lerman, R. (2022). The dollar's global roles: An update. Federal Reserve Bank of New York Liberty Street Economics. https://libertystreeteconomics.newyorkfed.org

Gopinath, G., & Stein, J. C. (2021). Banking, trade, and the making of a dominant currency. *The Quarterly Journal of Economics, 136*(2), 783–830. DOI: 10.1093/qje/qjaa036

Gorton, G., & Zhang, J. (2021). Taming wildcat stablecoins. *SSRN, 90*(1), 1–50. DOI: 10.2139/ssrn.3888752

He, D., Leckow, R., Haksar, V., & Jenkinson, N. (2023). *Fintech and financial services: Initial considerations.* IMF Staff Discussion Note SDN/23/02.

Hileman, G. (2019). State of stablecoins (2019). Available at *SSRN* 3533143.

Hong Kong Monetary Authority. (2022, Apr 27). e-HKD: A policy and design perspective. https://www.hkma.gov.hk/media/eng/doc/key-functions/financial-infrastructure/e-HKD_A_Policy_and_Design_Perspective.pdf

Hong Kong Monetary Authority (HKMA). (2023). *e-HKD: A policy and design perspective.* https://www.hkma.gov.hk

Hong Kong Monetary Authority (HKMA). (2024). *Discussion paper on crypto-assets and stablecoins.* https://www.hkma.gov.hk

Hong Kong Monetary Authority (HKMA). (2024). *Stablecoin regulatory framework.* https://www.hkma.gov.hk

Huang, Y., & Luk, P. (2023). De-dollarization in the age of digital currencies. Peterson Institute for International Economics Working Paper 23-5.

International Monetary Fund. (2025, Apr 2). IMF data brief: Currency composition of official foreign exchange reserves – Global FX reserves decreased by 3.0 percent in 2024 Q4. https://data.imf.org/en/news/4225global%20fx%20reserves%20decreased%20by%203%20percent%20in%202024q4

International Monetary Fund (IMF). (2023). *Digital money and central banks' balance sheets.* IMF Working Paper WP/23/105.

International Monetary Fund (IMF). (2024). *Currency composition of official foreign exchange reserves.* https://data.imf.org

JPMorgan. (2023). Stablecoins and the US Treasury market outlook. Global Markets Strategy Report.

Krause, D. (2025). *Algorithmic stablecoins: Mechanisms, risks, and lessons from the fall of TerraUSD*. Risks.

Lee, M. (2023). Digital currencies and the future of the dollar standard. Council on Foreign Relations Special Report.

Li, X. (2024). Stablecoin regulation in Hong Kong: Recent developments and critical evaluations. Available at *SSRN* 4870280. DOI: 10.2139/ssrn.4870280

Liao, G. Y., & Caramichael, J. (2022). Stablecoins: Growth potential and impact on banking. Board of Governors of the Federal Reserve System. https://www.federalreserve.gov/econres/ifdp/stablecoins-growth-potential-and-impact-on-banking.htm

MacDonald, C., & Zhao, L. (2022). Stablecoins and their risks to financial stability. Bank of Canada Staff Discussion Paper 2022-20.

McDowell, D. (2022). *Bucking the buck: US financial sanctions and the international backlash against the dollar*. Stanford University Press.

McNally, C. A. (2025). Seeking autonomy beyond subordination: Chinese financial statecraft and the e-CNY. In State, Capitalism, and Finance in Emerging Markets (pp. 162-182). Bristol University Press.

Nejadmalayeri, A., Molchanovsky, L., Paleo, B. W., & Prescott, R. W. (2023, May). Stablecoins: Past, present, and future. In International Conference on Financial Cryptography and Data Security (pp. 197-207). Springer Nature Switzerland.

Oranburg, S. (2025). The CLARITY Act: Explaining and analyzing how Congress will transform digital asset markets. Available at *SSRN* 5288934. DOI: 10.2139/ssrn.5288934

People's Bank of China. (2023). Progress of research and development of e-CNY in China. http://www.pbc.gov.cn

People's Bank of China (PBOC). (2023). *Progress of research and development of e-CNY in China.* http://www.pbc.gov.cn

Prasad, E. (2021). *The future of money: How the digital revolution is transforming currencies and finance*. Harvard University Press.

President's Working Group on Financial Markets (PWG). (2021). *Report on stablecoins.* https://home.treasury.gov

Research, O. K. G. (2025, May 23). Why stablecoin regulation is speeding up — From D.C. to Hong Kong. The Capital. Medium. https://medium.com/thecapital/why-stablecoin-regulation-is-speeding-up-from-d-c-to-hong-kong-44dcd39f0603

Rettig, R., Mosier, M., & Gilman, K. (2025). Genuine DeFi as critical infrastructure: A conceptual framework for combating illicit finance activity in decentralized finance. Journal of Financial Regulation, fjaf005.

Riley, J. (2021). The current status of cryptocurrency regulation in China and its effect around the world. *China and WTO Review*, *7*(1), 135–152. DOI: 10.14330/cwr.2021.7.1.06

Robson, W. (2025). USDX whitepaper. Available at *SSRN* 5267805.

Ryan, J. (2024). China's economic and currency management will make it difficult to dethrone the dollar. Irish Studies in International Affairs.

Schwarcz, S. L. (2022). Regulating global stablecoins: A model-law strategy. *Vanderbilt Law Review*, *75*, 1729.

Setser, B. (2023). *Stablecoins and the demand for US Treasury securities.* Council on Foreign Relations Blog Post.

SWIFT. (2023). *RMB tracker: Monthly reporting and statistics on renminbi progress.* https://www.swift.com

U.S. Department of the Treasury. (2021, Nov 1). President's Working Group on Financial Markets releases report and recommendations on stablecoins. https://home.treasury.gov/news/press-releases/jy0454

U.S. Department of the Treasury. (2025, Apr 30). TBAC Charge 2 Q2 2025. https://home.treasury.gov/system/files/221/TBACCharge2Q22025.pdf

U.S. Senate. (2023). *Stablecoin TRUST Act of 2023.* 118th Congress, 1st Session.

U.S. Senate. (2024). *GENIUS Act of 2024.* 118th Congress, 2nd Session.

U.S. Treasury. (2022). *Illicit finance risk assessment of decentralized finance.* https://home.treasury.gov

U.S. Treasury. (2023). *Report on stablecoins.* https://home.treasury.gov

Wong, M. C. S., Chan, E. K. H., & Yousaf, I. (2025). CBDCs, regulated stablecoins and tokenized traditional assets under the Basel Committee rules on cryptoassets. *Journal of Financial Regulation and Compliance, 33*(1), 31–47. DOI: 10.1108/JFRC-03-2024-0050

Xie, R. (2019). Why China had to ban cryptocurrency but the US did not: A comparative analysis of regulations on crypto-markets between the US and China. *Washington University Global Studies Law Review, 18*, 457.

Xu, J. (2022). Developments and implications of central bank digital currency: The case of China e-CNY. *Asian Economic Policy Review, 17*(2), 235–250. DOI: 10.1111/aepr.12396

Yang, J., & Zhou, G. (2022). A study on the influence mechanism of CBDC on monetary policy: An analysis based on e-CNY. *PLoS One, 17*(7), e0268471. DOI: 10.1371/journal.pone.0268471 PMID: 35802595

Zetzsche, D. A., Buckley, R. P., Arner, D. W., & Weber, R. H. (2020). Regulating LIBRA: The transformative potential of Facebook's cryptocurrency and possible regulatory responses. *Oxford Business Law Blog.* https://www.law.ox.ac.uk

Zhang, L., Huang, B., & Wang, Y. (2022). China's digital currency: Design, implications and global impacts. Asian Development Bank Institute Working Paper 1292.

NOTE

1 Corresponding Author: Yixuanli@blackgoldins.com

Chapter 3
Securing Bitcoin in Financial Services:
New Risks, Evolving Regulations, and Institutional Strategies

Chee Hon Lew
https://orcid.org/0000-0003-1986-7977
Guangzhou Huali College, China

ABSTRACT

This paper provides a comprehensive analysis of the evolving security risks and regulatory compliance challenges facing Bitcoin in financial applications. While Bitcoin's cryptographic foundations and decentralized architecture offer strong protections, emerging threats—such as consensus attacks, network exploits, privacy leaks, and operational vulnerabilities—pose significant risks to financial institutions. Simultaneously, global regulatory frameworks are tightening, particularly around AML, KYC, and consumer protection, compelling institutions to implement robust compliance strategies. The study synthesizes insights from computer science, finance, and law to propose integrated approaches combining technical safeguards with regulatory adherence. Strategies such as multi-signature controls, blockchain analytics, secure custody solutions, and "compliance by design" are explored. The paper concludes by discussing future risks including quantum computing and privacy-compliance tensions, emphasizing the need for adaptive risk management in institutional Bitcoin adoption.

DOI: 10.4018/979-8-3373-2838-6.ch003

1. INTRODUCTION

Blockchain-based cryptocurrencies leading by Bitcoin have rapidly evolved from niche digital curiosities to significant components of the financial landscape. Bitcoin, introduced by Nakamoto (2008), relies on a decentralized peer-to-peer network and cryptographic protocols to enable electronic transactions without traditional intermediaries. This innovation offers potential benefits for financial applications – including faster cross-border payments, reduced transaction costs, and improved transparency – but also introduces unique information security challenges and regulatory compliance concerns. Financial institutions and service providers that engage with Bitcoin must navigate the dual imperative of maintaining robust cybersecurity while adhering to laws and regulations aimed at ensuring market integrity, consumer protection, and the prevention of illicit activities (Böhme et al., 2015; Ly, 2014).

From an information security standpoint, Bitcoin's design is grounded in well-established cryptographic principles that provide integrity and resilience. Transactions are secured through digital signatures and aggregated in an immutable ledger (blockchain) via a proof-of-work consensus mechanism (Haber & Stornetta, 1991; Nakamoto, 2008). These cryptographic foundations theoretically ensure that no single party can fraudulently alter transaction records or spend funds twice, under the assumption that the underlying cryptographic algorithms and distributed consensus remain secure. In practice, however, various vulnerabilities and risks have been identified in the Bitcoin ecosystem that could compromise financial applications. Prior research has highlighted risks such as double-spending attacks on unconfirmed transactions (Karame et al., 2012), the possibility of 51% attacks and selfish mining that threaten consensus (Eyal & Sirer, 2014), network attacks such as eclipsing or routing hijacks that can isolate or delay nodes (Heilman et al., 2015; Apostolaki et al., 2017), and privacy weaknesses that allow transaction traceability and deanonymization (Meiklejohn et al., 2013; Ober et al., 2013). Furthermore, the emergence of smart contracts and second-layer protocols extending Bitcoin's functionality (e.g., payment channels) introduces additional attack surfaces and complexities requiring scrutiny (Atzei et al., 2017; Zhang et al., 2019).

Simultaneously, the incorporation of Bitcoin into financial services triggers a host of regulatory concerns. Chief among these is compliance with anti-money laundering (AML) and countering the financing of terrorism (CFT) regulations. Because Bitcoin transactions can be conducted pseudonymously across borders, they have been used to facilitate cybercrime and dark market trade, leading regulators worldwide to impose strict compliance requirements on cryptocurrency exchanges and financial institutions (Van Wegberg et al., 2018; Foley et al., 2019). Regulators such as the Financial Action Task Force (FATF) and national authorities in the U.S., EU, and Asia have moved to apply or adapt existing financial regulations to crypto-assets, mandating customer identification (Know Your Customer, KYC) and transaction monitoring for entities dealing in Bitcoin (Campbell-Verduyn, 2018; Yeoh, 2017). Financial institutions must also consider how consumer protection laws, securities regulations, and data privacy statutes apply to Bitcoin-related activities (Kiviat, 2015; Finck, 2019). The evolving regulatory landscape demands that banks and crypto service providers implement comprehensive compliance programs, or risk legal penalties and reputational damage.

Balancing Bitcoin's decentralized ethos with centralized regulatory oversight presents a significant challenge. On one hand, overbearing regulation could stifle innovation and push cryptocurrency activities outside regulated environments (Yeoh, 2017). On the other hand, insufficient oversight may lead to abuse of the technology for fraud, money laundering, and other crimes, undermining trust and stability in financial markets (Foley et al., 2019). The tension between anonymity (for user privacy) and transparency (for accountability) is a central theme in the discussion of blockchain regulation. Financial intermediaries are often caught between these two paradigms, striving to use blockchain technology to improve services while ensuring they do not become conduits for illicit behavior or run afoul of regulators.

The content of blocks in a blockchain can differ depending on the cryptocurrency. Let's take Bitcoin as an example. As shown in Figure 1 below, each Bitcoin block contains specific information, such as the hash of the previous block, a list of transactions, and a value called a Nonce. Once a block is added to the Bitcoin blockchain, all the transactions within that block are considered complete.

Figure 1. contents of block in bitcoin's blockchain

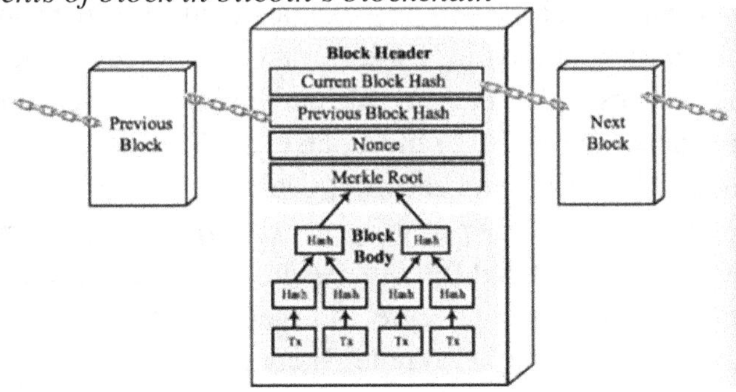

This paper aims to provide a comprehensive academic analysis that bridges the technical and regulatory dimensions of Bitcoin in financial applications. We combine insights from cryptography and computer security literature with perspectives from finance law and regulatory policy. The ensuing sections of this paper are structured as follows: First, we present a Literature Review summarizing relevant research on

Bitcoin's security mechanisms, known vulnerabilities, and regulatory considerations in various jurisdictions. Next, we outline the Methodology of our research, explaining our interdisciplinary approach. We then proceed to an in-depth Analysis and Discussing on (a) the key security risks and vulnerabilities and their implications for financial use; (b) an overview of the regulatory landscape for Bitcoin, focusing on AML/KYC, financial regulations, and compliance challenges; and (c) strategies and best practices for financial institutions to achieve regulatory compliance while maintaining security when using Bitcoin. Finally, we offer a Conclusion that synthesizes the findings and reflects on the future outlook for secure and compliant adoption of blockchain technology in the financial sector. By integrating theoretical and practical perspectives, this study contributes to a holistic understanding of what it takes to harness Bitcoin's capabilities in finance responsibly and safely.

2. LITERATURE REVIEW

2.1 Blockchain and Cryptographic Foundations

A substantial body of literature has explored the technical foundations of Bitcoin and blockchain technology. Early foundational work by Haber & Stornetta (1991) introduced the concept of a cryptographically secured chain of hashed data blocks – a technique later applied in Bitcoin to achieve tamper-resistant ledgers. Bitcoin's realization of a decentralized timestamped ledger, as described in Nakamoto's (2008) whitepaper, spurred numerous academic analyses of its cryptographic and system architecture. Narayanan et al. (2016) provided a technical primer on Bitcoin's use of cryptographic hash functions (SHA-256) and elliptic curve digital signatures (ECDSA) to ensure transaction integrity and authenticity. Subsequent surveys such as Tschorsch & Scheuermann (2016) and Conti et al. (2018) offered comprehensive overviews of Bitcoin's design and security, detailing how proof-of-work mining secures the consensus and how the peer-to-peer network propagates transactions and blocks. These works highlight that Bitcoin's security model rests on the assumption that cryptographic primitives are secure and that no single adversary controls a majority of mining power. They also note Bitcoin's deliberate trade-offs, such as limited on-chain programming capability to reduce complexity and vulnerabilities.

2.2 Security Vulnerabilities and Risks

Alongside praise for Bitcoin's elegant design, researchers have identified various vulnerabilities and attack vectors. Bonneau et al. (2015) systematized known security challenges for Bitcoin and other cryptocurrencies, categorizing them into consensus attacks, malicious nodes, wallet security issues, and privacy leaks. One major category is consensus-level attacks. Eyal & Sirer (2014) demonstrated the "selfish mining" strategy wherein a miner with less than 51% of the network's hash power can still gain a disproportionate share of rewards by strategically withholding and releasing blocks, potentially undermining the fairness and stability of the mining process. Relatedly, Sapirshtein et al. (2016) extended this analysis to find optimal adversarial mining strategies, reinforcing that Bitcoin's consensus can be subverted under certain conditions if miners behave strategically rather than honestly. Another well-documented threat is the 51% attack, where a coalition of miners controlling the majority of hash power can rewrite recent blockchain history and double-spend transactions. While no successful 51% attack has been recorded on Bitcoin's main network to date, smaller cryptocurrencies have suffered such attacks, lending credence to the theoretical risk (Li et al., 2020). Research by Gervais et al. (2016) quantitatively examined how factors like network delay and mining power distribution affect the probability of various attacks, finding that faster block propagation and decentralization of mining power are vital to security.

At the network layer, researchers have uncovered communication-level attacks that could threaten Bitcoin nodes. For example, Heilman et al. (2015) described eclipse attacks in which an attacker monopolizes all of a node's incoming and outgoing connections, effectively isolating it from the honest network. An eclipsed node can then be fed fraudulent data (e.g., a fake chain) or prevented from seeing certain transactions, which is particularly dangerous if the victim is a miner or merchant relying on timely information. Apostolaki et al. (2017) explored BGP routing attacks on Bitcoin, revealing that Internet-level adversaries could partition the Bitcoin network or delay block propagation by hijacking IP prefixes – a risk because Bitcoin's security assumptions do not account for malicious internet service providers. These studies underscore that while Bitcoin's protocol assumes an adversarial model among miners, it largely assumes a benign network infrastructure, which may not always hold true.

Bitcoin's transaction privacy has also been a significant focus in the literature. Early assumptions that Bitcoin was "anonymous" have been dispelled by numerous studies showing that the public ledger can be analyzed to cluster addresses and trace transaction flows. Meiklejohn et al. (2013) conducted a landmark analysis by following flows of bitcoins through the network and linking addresses to known entities, demonstrating that a motivated analyst could often de-anonymize users. Similarly, Androulaki et al. (2013) showed that even when users employ different addresses for each transaction, their spending patterns can reveal identifying information – in their experiments, 40% of users could be re-identified from the graph data. Ober et al. (2013) analyzed the Bitcoin transaction graph on a global scale and reported structural patterns that reduce anonymity over time as the network grows. They noted that the transaction graph's topology and the reuse of addresses by many users lead to an "anonymity set" far smaller than the total user base. To improve privacy, a line of research proposed overlays or modifications (Miers et al., 2013 introduced Zerocoin, later Zerocash/Zcash, to provide cryptographic anonymity; Maxwell's CoinJoin and other mixing techniques were discussed in informal communities and later academic work like Möser & Böhme, 2017). However, those solutions come with performance costs or require changes to the protocol and, importantly, raise new compliance issues. Zhang et al. (2019) provide a recent survey of privacy and security techniques on blockchain, highlighting ongoing developments such as confidential transactions and zero-knowledge proofs that aim to balance transparency and privacy.

Beyond Bitcoin's base layer, smart contracts and higher-layer protocols introduce further risks. Although Bitcoin's native scripting is limited, the concept of programmable money has been realized in platforms like Ethereum, which has its own set of security issues cataloged common smart contract vulnerabilities such as reentrancy bugs, unchecked exceptions, and arithmetic overflows on Ethereum (Atzei et al., 2017). Financial applications built on or alongside Bitcoin may interface with these contracts - for instance, using Bitcoin as an asset via sidechains or atomic swaps with Ethereum - thereby inheriting those risks. Thus, even a Bitcoin-focused financial application must be aware of vulnerabilities such as smart contract bugs and oracle problems if it ventures into decentralized finance (DeFi) contexts. The literature suggests that rigorous code auditing (Luu et al., 2016) and formal verification (Bhargavan et al., 2016) are important emerging practices to secure smart contracts.

Operational security and the human element are recurrent themes as well. Many studies and incident reports indicate that the weakest links are often not the cryptography or protocol of Bitcoin, but the surrounding infrastructure: exchanges, wallets, and users. High-profile breaches such as the Mt. Gox exchange hack in 2014 exemplify how poor security practices in key management and system security can lead to catastrophic losses despite Bitcoin's core protocol remaining uncompromised. Walch (2015) argues that treating the blockchain as a piece of financial market infrastructure requires considering operational risks – including software bugs, governance failures, and dependency on internet infrastructure – in risk management frameworks. Vasek & Moore (2015) documented various scams, thefts, and failures in the Bitcoin ecosystem, emphasizing that the ecosystem's overall security depends on more than just the robustness of the blockchain protocol; it extends to user education.

2.3 Regulatory and Compliance Scholarship

The rapid growth of Bitcoin and other cryptocurrencies posed novel challenges for regulators and has generated a parallel track of academic inquiry in legal, economic, and policy domains. Early legal analyses (e.g., Bryans, 2014; Ly, 2014) grappled with how existing laws might apply to Bitcoin. Ly (2014) examined U.S. financial regulations, concluding that Bitcoin did not fit neatly into existing categories and arguing for clear guidance to protect consumers without smothering innovation. Around the same time, Financial Crimes Enforcement Network) in the U.S. issued guidance (FIN-2013-G001[2]) treating administrators and exchangers of virtual currencies as money service businesses, thereby subjecting them to AML laws (. This spurred academic discussion on the appropriateness of extending Bank Secrecy Act regulations to decentralized systems. Hughes & Middlebrook (2015) proposed a regulatory framework for cryptocurrency payments, suggesting tailored adjustments to payments law to accommodate the technology's features while still enforcing necessary controls.

Internationally, attention turned to the global AML/CFT regime. Bitcoin's use in infamous dark web markets (notably the Silk Road, taken down in 2013) and various cybercrime schemes raised alarms about money laundering. Campbell-Verduyn (2018) discusses how global AML governance has adapted to crypto-assets, noting the efforts by intergovernmental bodies such as the FATF to update their recommendations. In 2019, FATF released guidance on "virtual asset service providers" (VASPs) extending standards like the "travel rule" to crypto transactions, which requires information sharing about transacting parties similar to wire transfers. Van Wegberg et al. (2018) provided empirical insight by studying Bitcoin's role in laundering cybercrime proceeds, finding that while cryptocurrencies were indeed used for money laundering, the outcomes were mixed – criminals faced limitations and often had to convert back to fiat, which is a chokepoint for law enforcement. Such studies support regulators' focus on exchange platforms as critical points for enforcing AML compliance.

Several scholars have addressed the tension between blockchain's pseudonymity and regulatory accountability. Koshy et al. (2014) showed that even Bitcoin nodes could be linked to IP addresses, further eroding anonymity – a technical insight with regulatory implications because it suggests users are not as untraceable as once feared. From a policy perspective, Zetzsche et al. (2020) discussed whether new regulatory categories are needed for crypto-assets, coining terms like "decentralized regulatory arbitrage" to describe how users could route around unfavorable jurisdictions. There is also a growing body of work on how data protection laws like the EU's GDPR conflict with blockchain's immutability (Finck, 2019), raising compliance challenges for institutions that must both leverage transparent ledgers and protect user privacy rights.

Academic research on compliance strategies and solutions is still emerging. Some work has looked into RegTech applications of blockchain – for instance, using distributed ledgers to streamline KYC processes across institutions (Lootsma, 2017) or to create tamper-proof audit trails (Micheler & Whaley, 2020). Kshetri (2021) examined the challenges in adopting blockchain in finance, noting that regulatory hurdles and cybersecurity concerns are primary barriers, and suggested that progress requires addressing both simultaneously. Yeoh (2017) advocated a "smart regulatory" approach, implying that regulators should impose minimal necessary restraints in the early stages to allow the technology's benefits to materialize, while remaining ready to intervene in cases of abuse. This reflects a broader theme in the literature: the need for balanced regulation that protects against the real risks without quashing innovation or beneficial uses.

3. METHODOLOGY

This research adopts a qualitative, interdisciplinary approach to examine information security and regulatory compliance in the context of Bitcoin's use in financial applications. We conducted an extensive literature review spanning academic journals in computer science and law/finance, as well as analyses of current regulatory documents and industry reports. Key search terms included combinations of "Bitcoin security," "blockchain vulnerabilities," "cryptographic foundations," "cryptocurrency regulation," "AML compliance," and "financial institutions blockchain." We prioritized peer-reviewed academic sources and high-quality scholarly contributions to ensure a credible foundation for analysis. Over thirty relevant sources were selected that collectively cover the theoretical background, empirical studies, and normative discussions pertinent to our topic.

In synthesizing the literature, we employed a thematic analysis approach. Sources were grouped into thematic categories: (1) cryptographic and technical foundations of blockchain, (2) security vulnerabilities and risk analyses, (3) regulatory frameworks and legal analysis, and (4) compliance mechanisms and best practices. Within each theme, we compared findings and perspectives, identifying points of consensus, emerging issues, and knowledge gaps. This cross-disciplinary examination allowed us to see how technical risks inform regulatory needs and vice versa. For example, awareness of specific Bitcoin vulnerabilities informed our discussion on what regulators focus on, and understanding regulatory expectations guided our exploration of what technical measures institutions must implement.

No human subjects or proprietary data were involved in this research; all information was drawn from public sources and scholarly work. As an academic review and analysis, our methodology is inherently integrative and interpretive. We critically analyzed the sources for reliability and relevance, cross-referencing facts such as reported attacks or legal requirements across multiple references to verify accuracy. Divergent viewpoints are noted and discussed to provide a balanced perspective.

The interdisciplinary nature of the methodology is crucial. Bitcoin operates at the intersection of technology and law: purely technical analyses might overlook how human and legal factors mitigate or exacerbate risks, while purely legal analyses might misunderstand the technical constraints and possibilities. By combining these viewpoints, our methodology aims to produce a nuanced discussion that is academically rigorous and practically informative. This approach mirrors methodologies used in fields like information systems and fintech research, where socio-technical systems are evaluated holistically.

In the subsequent analysis, we use this integrated perspective to discuss findings. Technical claims are supported by computer science research citations, whereas statements about regulatory requirements or compliance practices are supported by legal and financial literature. By maintaining clear citations and attributions, we ensure that each claim can be traced to verifiable sources, thereby upholding academic standards of evidence. The methodology thereby supports a comprehensive exploration of the research question: How can financial applications of Bitcoin remain secure while meeting regulatory compliance obligations?

4. SECURITY RISKS AND VULNERABILITIES IN BITCOIN

Despite strong cryptographic foundations, Bitcoin is not immune to security risks. Financial applications built on Bitcoin must recognize and mitigate these vulnerabilities to prevent losses, service disruptions, or other malicious outcomes. Here we examine the major categories of security risks: consensus-related attacks, network and infrastructure attacks, cryptographic weaknesses (current or future), smart contract and application-layer vulnerabilities, privacy issues, and operational security challenges.

Table 1. Summary of Bitcoin Security Vulnerabilities

Vulnerability Type	Description	Potential Impact
Consensus Attacks	Control blockchain confirmation process	Transaction reversals, fraud
Network Attacks	Disrupt communication among nodes	Service disruption, double-spending
Cryptographic Vulnerabilities	Potential breaking of cryptographic primitives	Coin theft, blockchain integrity breach
Transaction Privacy	Exposure of user identities and transactions	Targeted attacks, regulatory issues
Operational Security	Human error, management failures	Loss of funds, internal fraud

4.1 Consensus-Level Attacks and Blockchain Integrity

One of the most critical aspects of Bitcoin's security is the integrity of its blockchain – the assurance that confirmed transactions remain immutable and in the correct order. Attacks on the consensus mechanism aim to subvert these guarantees.

- **51% Attacks:** If a single entity controls more than half of the total mining hash power, they can in theory unilaterally decide which blocks get added to the chain. This capability enables double-spending attacks by reversing transactions that were previously considered final. While the resource requirement for a 51% attack on Bitcoin's network is enormous, the concept has been demonstrated on smaller cryptocurrencies. The literature (Li et al., 2020) describes that a successful 51% attacker can exclude or modify the ordering of transactions and even prevent honest miners' blocks from being accepted, thereby controlling the ledger. For Bitcoin, the economic incentives strongly disincentivize such an attack, and the decentralized distribution of miners worldwide makes it unlikely. Nonetheless, from a security standpoint, financial institutions must consider the tail-risk scenario of a consensus attack when, for example, designing settlement times for high-value transfers.
- **Selfish Mining and Consensus Manipulation:** Eyal & Sirer's (2014) selfish mining paper revealed that even miners with less than 50% hash power (theoretically as low as ~30%) could earn more than their fair share of rewards by deviating from the honest protocol. In selfish mining, a miner (or pool) does not immediately broadcast a found block. Instead, they privately mine a chain of blocks, aiming to get ahead of the public chain. If successful they can publish their chain to invalidate others' blocks, capturing the rewards and wasting others' effort. This doesn't directly allow double-spending, but it undermines the assumption that the majority of hash power will act to secure the network.

Follow-up research (Sapirshtein et al., 2016) refined the thresholds required and suggested strategies for honest miners to counter such behavior. Bitcoin's protocol upgrades have somewhat reduced the effectiveness of these attacks. However, selfish mining remains an important consideration for consensus stability – if rational miners ever find it significantly more profitable, the network could fork or centralize into cartels. Continuous monitoring of the mining ecosystem is therefore warranted.

- **Double-Spending Attacks on Fast Payments:** A specific risk scenario is when Bitcoin is used for "fast" paymentswithout waiting for block confirmations. In such cases, a payer could broadcast a transaction to the merchant and simultaneously broadcast a conflicting transaction (double-spend) to the network, hoping the second one gets confirmed in a block first. Karame et al. (2012) demonstrated that these attacks on 0-confirmation transactions are feasible with high success probability if no mitigations are in place. They suggested some detection mechanisms but ultimately recommended that time-sensitive transactions either use alternative mechanisms or accept the risk. Financial applications needing instant settlement should thus be wary of accepting unconfirmed transactions for high-value transfers. Techniques such as *Replace-by-Fee* (RBF), which is now a part of Bitcoin's protocol allowing senders to bump the fee of a transaction by replacing it with a new one, complicate the picture – RBF can be used legitimately to ensure a transaction gets confirmed by increasing its fee, but also could potentially facilitate certain forms of double-spending unless merchants explicitly wait for confirmations or use secure payment channel protocols.

The consensus layer of Bitcoin has proven robust in practice, but it is not unassailable. The key security takeaway is that assumptions of irreversibility are probabilistic – gaining higher certainty of settlement finality requires waiting for multiple block confirmations. Financial institutions using Bitcoin may set internal policies for the number of confirmations required based on risk appetite and the value of transactions, as a risk management measure against these consensus attacks.

4.2 Network and Infrastructure Attacks

Bitcoin's decentralized network relies on the internet for communication between nodes. Thus, it inherits all the usual concerns of network security, plus some unique to its P2P topology.

- **Eclipse Attacks:** As mentioned, an eclipse attack involves isolating a node by controlling all its connections. This is particularly dangerous for nodes that have an outsized influence (miners or exchanges). If an exchange's node were eclipsed, for example, an attacker could feed it a false view of the blockchain which might lead the exchange to accept deposits that never confirm on the real chain. Measures to mitigate eclipse attacks include increasing the number of connections, using diversified peer selection, and manual peering to trusted nodes for critical infrastructure. Heilman et al. (2015) suggested simple countermeasures like per-IP connection limits to make it harder for an attacker to fill all connection slots of a target.

- **BGP Hijacking and Partitioning:** Apostolaki et al. (2017) illustrated that Bitcoin's reliance on the internet's routing system (BGP) is a potential single point of failure. They documented real-world BGP incidents that affected Bitcoin connectivity. For instance, if an attacker hijacks the traffic of a major mining pool or a cluster of nodes, they can partition those nodes from the rest of the network and possibly create conditions to double-spend or cause confusion. While large-scale partition attacks have not been observed in the wild specifically to compromise Bitcoin, the mere feasibility has led to suggestions like using encryption and authentication between nodes or even leveraging alternative paths. Financial nodes (exchanges, payment processors) might use multiple internet providers or VPNs to reduce partition risk, and monitor for signs of network partition.
- **Denial-of-Service (DoS):** Attackers might flood Bitcoin nodes or miners with traffic to disrupt service. The Bitcoin protocol has had to patch various DoS vulnerabilities over the years. Continuous hardening of the Bitcoin Core software and other implementations is an ongoing process, with responsible disclosure and community coordination addressing these issues. In a financial context, if an institution runs its own Bitcoin node, it needs to keep that software updated to defend against known DoS vectors. Additionally, standard network security practices like firewalls, rate limiting, and DDoS protection services should be employed to protect publicly reachable endpoints.
- **Sybil Attacks:** In a Sybil attack, one adversary creates many pseudonymous nodes in the network to overwhelm honest participants. Bitcoin's peer-to-peer network is somewhat resistant to Sybil attacks in that having many fake nodes doesn't directly give you mining power, and the node discovery process has some randomness. However, Sybils could be used to feed misinformation if combined with eclipse tactics, or to outvote honest peers in certain P2P message situations. The practical risk is mitigated by the fact that Bitcoin nodes by default trust the longest valid chain of proof-of-work – no matter how many Sybil nodes advertise an alternative shorter chain, they'll be ignored if they lack proof-of-work. Thus, Sybils alone cannot fork the network without hash power; they can only aid in eclipsing or propagating incorrect

data briefly. Nonetheless, a best practice is for critical Bitcoin nodes to limit connections from any single IP or subnet and to use features like feelers.

4.3 Cryptographic Weaknesses and Foresight

As of now, Bitcoin's core cryptographic algorithms (SHA-256 and ECDSA) are believed to be secure. However, it is prudent to consider potential weaknesses, especially given the long-term horizon financial institutions might plan for.

- **Collision and Preimage Resistance:** SHA-256 is a member of the SHA-2 family, for which no practical collision attacks are known (unlike SHA-1, which was broken). A collision attack on SHA-256 would undermine proof-of-work (finding two different blocks with the same hash) and possibly allow coin forgery if someone could create two transactions with the same txid. Fortunately, even theoretical attacks are far from the realm of practicality for SHA-256 – it has a 256-bit output, and brute forcing a collision is 2^{128} operations, which is astronomically high. Similarly, ECDSA's security relies on the discrete logarithm problem in secp256k1 being hard; the key length is considered safe against classical computers.
- **Quantum Computing Threat:** The more significant future threat is from quantum computers. A sufficiently powerful quantum computer running Shor's algorithm could break ECDSA by computing private keys from public keys. Aggarwal et al. (2018) estimate that Bitcoin could be vulnerable to quantum attacks within a few decades if quantum computing progresses at a steady rate. The immediate risk is mitigated by the fact that not all Bitcoin addresses have exposed public keys – only those that have been used to receive funds and then were later spent. Best practice to mitigate quantum risk even today is address reuse avoidance: if an address is only used once, its public key is revealed only after the funds are moved, at which point an attacker can't retroactively steal from that address. However, once quantum computers exist that can derive a private key from a public key in a short time, any address whose public key has been revealed becomes vulnerable. Additionally, Bitcoin's PoW (hashing) is less affected by quantum computing.

The community and researchers are exploring post-quantum signature schemes to prepare for a potential future upgrade. From a compliance and risk perspective, institutions should monitor these developments; a major cryptographic transition in Bitcoin would require coordination and could pose operational risks. Custodians might also plan for protocols to sweep funds to new, quantum-safe addresses when the time comes.

- **Randomness and Key Management Issues:** Cryptography can be undermined not just by algorithmic attacks but by implementation failures. There have been instances where Bitcoin users lost funds due to poor random number generation leading to repeated or predictable ECDSA nonces. This happened with some Android wallets in 2013 and with certain hardware wallets. While not an attack on Bitcoin per se, it highlights the need for secure implementations. Financial-grade systems should use well-vetted cryptographic libraries and hardware security modules (HSMs) for key generation and signing to avoid such pitfalls.
- **Hash Function Upgrades:** Though unlikely in the near term, if SHA-256 were ever found to have a weakness, a hard fork or soft fork to a new hash function would be needed. This introduces complexity: all software would need updates, and there could be compatibility issues. Some altcoins have already experimented with quantum-resistant blockchains. Bitcoin's conservative approach means changes happen slowly; any cryptographic upgrade would be signaled well in advance. Institutions should ensure their infrastructure can be updated as needed to follow consensus changes.

In essence, current cryptographic weaknesses of Bitcoin are theoretical or long-term concerns, but for completeness, they must be on the radar of risk managers. The prudent approach for now is to follow best practices and keep abreast of research in cryptography, while understanding that other attack vectors pose more immediate threats.

4.4 Smart Contracts and Layer-2 Vulnerabilities

While Bitcoin's base layer is intentionally limited, modern financial applications often extend Bitcoin via second-layer protocols (like the Lightning Network) or cross-chain interactions. Additionally, comparisons to smart contract platforms are relevant because financial institutions might use Bitcoin in tandem with more complex blockchain systems.

- **Bitcoin Script Exploits:** Bitcoin's script being limited has actually prevented many potential vulnerabilities. There have been a few script-related issues historically but these are rare. One could consider the risk of script censorship – since non-standard scripts might not be relayed by nodes – but that's more of an interoperability issue than a security flaw. By and large, if institutions stick to standard script templates (P2PKH, P2SH multi-sig, etc.), the security of these is well-vetted. The recent Taproot upgrade (2021) expanded Bitcoin's script capabilities by introducing Schnorr signatures and Merkelized

Abstract Syntax Trees (MAST), allowing for more complex spending conditions that remain private unless executed. Taproot's cryptographic assumptions (Schnorr) are similar in strength to ECDSA but with better privacy and efficiency. With more complex scripting possible, future risks could include undiscovered bugs in implementation or script logic errors if users implement custom spending conditions. However, most institutions will likely rely on proven templates.

- **Lightning Network Risks:** The Lightning Network enables fast, low-fee transactions by opening bi-directional payment channels between users (Poon & Dryja, 2016). While it significantly improves Bitcoin's scalability and instant payment capability, it comes with its own security considerations. Lightning requires timely response to channel closures; if one party tries to cheat by broadcasting an old channel state, the counterparty must respond within a preset time window to claim all the channel funds. This introduces a liveness requirement – users must remain online or use watchtower services to monitor for fraud. If an institution were to leverage Lightning for micropayments or interbank transfers, it needs to maintain robust channel monitoring infrastructure. There have been academic works analyzing Lightning's security, such as potential attacks when multiple channels close at once (liquidity attacks) or attacks on the routing mechanism. As of now, Lightning is considered secure for modest amounts, but it is still maturing. Financial institutions might use it for small transactions but would likely not trust it for very large sums due to the hot-wallet nature of channel funds.
- **Cross-Chain and DeFi Integration:** Some financial products might involve Bitcoin via wrapped tokens on other chains or atomic swaps. These introduce trust assumptions outside the Bitcoin network. If a bank or fintech uses such instruments, they must additionally vet the security of the custodial arrangements or smart contracts on the other chain. Smart contracts on platforms like Ethereum are Turing-complete and have a history of exploits (as Atzei et al., 2017 enumerated). The infamous DAO hack (2016) on Ethereum, resulting in a $50M loss, and numerous DeFi hacks serve as warnings. Even if one's focus is Bitcoin, any interoperability means exposure to those risks. Therefore, an institution might opt to limit exposure to experimental DeFi protocols or only engage via insured or regulated intermediary platforms.

4.5 Transaction Privacy and Anonymity Concerns

Bitcoin's pseudonymous nature is a double-edged sword for security. On the one hand, it can protect user privacy; on the other, it can enable illicit use and make regulatory compliance challenging. From a security perspective, there are scenarios where privacy lapses can lead to threats, such as targeted attacks on known holders, or expropriation in jurisdictions where holding cryptocurrency is restricted. For compliance, privacy in Bitcoin is often seen as too weak or too strong – meaning institutions need to navigate carefully.

- **Deanonymization Risks:** As noted, researchers and blockchain analytics companies have developed methods to track flows of Bitcoin. Address clustering techniques can uncover networks of addresses belonging to a single entity (Meiklejohn et al., 2013). Additionally, if an institution's Bitcoin addresses are known, their on-chain activities can be scrutinized by anyone, including competitors or criminals. For example, if a large custodian's cold wallet addresses are identified via an incident or a leak, observers can monitor those addresses for movements, potentially inferring business patterns or targeting phishing attacks to customers when they see funds flowing. There have been cases where criminals kidnapped or extorted individuals known to have large cryptocurrency holdings. Thus, privacy lapses can translate into physical or cybersecurity threats.
- **Mixers and Tumblers:** To enhance privacy, users sometimes use mixing services which aggregate and redistribute funds among many participants to obfuscate trails. Van Wegberg et al. (2018) studied Bitcoin mixers and their role in money laundering, finding them to be a common tool for criminals to break the link between their old (tainted) coins and new (clean) coins. From a security viewpoint, mixers themselves can be scams or honeypots, and users risk theft by participating. There's also the risk of taint – if an institution unknowingly receives bitcoins that have been mixed and previously used in crimes, they may later be flagged by authorities or analytics companies, possibly leading to account freezes or investigations (Foley et al., 2019 quantified a significant fraction of Bitcoin activity related to illicit trade). Therefore, institutions often use compliance tools to trace incoming funds; some have policies to refuse coins with certain mixing histories to avoid regulatory trouble.
- **Enhancements and Their Impact:** Bitcoin has seen and will see upgrades affecting privacy. Taproot makes complex transactions (multi-sig, Lightning opens/closes) appear the same as simple ones on-chain, improving privacy for advanced users. There are also techniques like *CoinJoin* where users voluntarily coordinate to create a joint transaction that mixes their outputs. While such techniques can improve a user's privacy, they complicate compliance for institutions who then have a harder time tracing origin of funds. Some institutions might choose to not engage in CoinJoin themselves and possibly treat CoinJoin outputs with higher scrutiny.

- **Data Privacy Regulations:** On a related note, storing customer data on an immutable ledger could conflict with privacy laws. While Bitcoin transactions typically don't contain personal data, there have been instances of people embedding text in the blockchain. Finck (2019) points out that if any personal data enters a public blockchain, it could be impossible to remove. Financial firms exploring putting client identifiers or other data on-chain must be extremely cautious. A straightforward strategy is to keep personal data off-chain and only put pseudonymous identifiers on-chain, linking to off-chain databases that can still comply with deletion requests.

4.6 Operational Security and Custodial Risks

Regardless of Bitcoin's theoretical security, real-world applications face operational challenges. Many security incidents occur due to human error, mismanagement, or malicious insiders, rather than external cryptographic attacks. Financial institutions that custody crypto for clients or facilitate transactions must uphold strong operational security.

- **Key Management:** Holding private keys to large sums of Bitcoin is a huge responsibility. Best practices include using hardware security modules (HSMs) or specialized cold storage devices that keep keys offline. Some institutions use a multi-tier system: the bulk of funds in cold storage, a smaller working capital in "warm" storage, and minimal funds in "hot" wallets. Multi-signature wallets, where multiple keys held by separate trusted parties or by internal multi-person control, can ensure that transfers above certain thresholds require multiple approvals. This is analogous to dual-control in wire transfers. However, mismanagement of multisig – like losing one of the keys without proper backup procedures – can also lead to irretrievable loss. The literature (Eskandari et al., 2018) notes that many exchange hacks could have been mitigated by better segregation of duties and multi-signature controls.
- **Insider Threats:** A rogue employee with privileged access could steal keys or siphon funds if proper checks are not in place. Companies address this by requiring multiple approvals for transactions, conducting background checks on employees, and monitoring for unusual access patterns. Some large custodians have insurance to cover theft, including insider theft, which provides an additional layer of assurance to clients (though not a preventive measure, it mitigates impact).
- **Software Bugs and Updates:** Running a Bitcoin node and wallet software comes with the need to update regularly for security patches. There have been

critical bugs discovered in Bitcoin Core. Institutions should run fully validating nodes to ensure they are not accepting invalid transactions or blocks, and promptly update their software when vulnerabilities are disclosed. They might even run multiple implementations (Bitcoin Core, btcd, etc.) in parallel for redundancy, though Bitcoin Core remains the reference with the most rigorous review.

- **Physical Security:** For cold storage, physical security is paramount. Many exchanges distribute shards of keys in vaults across geographies. The use of metal plates to back up seeds and tamper-evident bags for devices are common. Regular audits are done to ensure procedures are followed – for instance, an audit might involve proving that one can sign with a key from cold storage without revealing the key to the auditors.
- **User Error and Client Education:** If a financial institution offers Bitcoin services directly to retail customers, there is also the risk of user error. From a compliance perspective, the institution might be obligated to have certain consumer protections or at least to educate users about irreversibility of crypto transactions. If users know that transactions can't be reversed, they might be more careful and less likely to fall for phishing attempts. Some platforms implement friction like warning messages or hold periods for first-time withdrawals (to deter fraud). While these might slightly inconvenience users, they add layers of protection.

Operational security is where technology meets human processes. Many experts emphasize that for crypto, one should assume any single point of failure will eventually fail. Therefore, multiple layers (defense in depth) are used. In an academic sense, this is sometimes referred to as the need for socio-technical security measures – recognizing that code alone isn't enough. Walch (2015) advocates that regulators consider these operational aspects when, for instance, assessing whether a cryptocurrency exchange or service is safe to be licensed.

5. REGULATORY LANDSCAPE FOR BITCOIN IN FINANCIAL SERVICES

As Bitcoin's adoption in finance has grown, regulators worldwide have grappled with how to apply existing laws and create new ones to govern its use. Table 2 outlines the main regulatory domains affecting Bitcoin in financial contexts and how different jurisdictions have approached them. Regulators worldwide, including the FATF and national agencies (US FinCEN, EU MiCA), have established comprehensive AML/CFT frameworks, securities classification, custody regulations, and consumer protection laws applicable to Bitcoin.

Table 2. Key Regulatory Frameworks for Bitcoin

Region	Regulatory Body	Key Regulation	Compliance Requirements
Global	FATF	Travel Rule, AML guidelines	Transaction monitoring, customer ID
United States	FinCEN, SEC, CFTC	BSA, Securities Law, Commodities Regulation	AML programs, securities compliance
European Union	EU Commission	MiCA, 5AMLD, GDPR	Registration, KYC, data protection
Asia (e.g., Japan)	FSA	Payment Services Act	Exchange licensing, customer asset custody

5.1 Anti-Money Laundering (AML) and Counter-Terrorist Financing (CTF)

Preventing money laundering and illicit finance is a top priority for financial regulators dealing with Bitcoin.

- **Global Standards (FATF):** The Financial Action Task Force, an intergovernmental body, sets international AML standards. In 2019, FATF issued guidance extending AML/CFT requirements to "virtual asset service providers" (VASPs) – which include exchanges, wallet providers, and other intermediaries. A key requirement is that VASPs must conduct KYC (Know Your Customer) checks, keep records, and report suspicious transactions, just like banks. FATF's controversial "Travel Rule" now applies to crypto: VASPs must share identifying information about originators and beneficiaries for transfers above a certain threshold, effectively preventing anonymous large transfers between regulated entities. This has driven the development of new protocols for information sharing in the crypto industry.
- **United States**, Bitcoin is not outlawed, but activities involving Bitcoin are regulated under existing frameworks. FinCEN classifies crypto exchanges and administrators as money service businesses (MSBs). Since 2013, they have been required to register with FinCEN, implement AML programs, verify customer identities, and report transactions above $10,000 and any suspicious activities. The U.S. has prosecuted exchange operators and mixers for AML violations. The Bank Secrecy Act (BSA) enforcement has resulted

in heavy fines for non-compliant operations. At the state level, some states require specific licenses (the New York BitLicense, introduced in 2015, is a comprehensive and strict regulatory regime covering consumer protection, AML, cybersecurity, etc., for crypto businesses in New York).

- **European Union**, initial approaches were to modify existing directives. The 5th Anti-Money Laundering Directive (5AMLD), effective 2020, brought crypto-fiat exchanges and custodial wallet providers under AML requirements across EU member states, mandating registration and KYC/AML programs. The newer Markets in Crypto-Assets (MiCA) regulation, slated to come into force in 2024, will further unify crypto regulation in the EU, including AML rules and prudential requirements. EU regulators also stress that compliance with GDPR (for personal data) must coincide with AML, which is tricky when sharing customer data (see e.g., Finck, 2019).
- **Asia**: regulations vary. Japan was one of the first to regulate crypto exchanges through amendments to its Payment Services Act after the Mt. Gox collapse. Exchanges must register, meet capital requirements, segregate customer assets, and follow AML steps. They also mandated strict cybersecurity guidelines. Singapore treats some crypto activities under its Payments Services Act, requiring licensing and AML controls, but has been relatively innovation-friendly. On the other extreme, China (until 2021) progressively banned most cryptocurrency activities – outlawing exchanges in 2017 and mining in 2021 – citing concerns over financial crimes and capital flight among other issues. In China's case, the regulatory approach has been prohibition rather than compliance oversight. Many other jurisdictions fall in between these poles: for example, Switzerland classifies cryptocurrencies as assets and requires AML compliance through its financial regulator (FINMA), while also fostering a "crypto valley" with clearer rules to encourage innovation.

6. IMPLICATIONS FOR FINANCIAL INSTITUTIONS

For banks or financial firms dealing with Bitcoin, AML/CTF compliance is non-negotiable. They must implement customer due diligence to verify the identities of clients buying, selling, or transacting in Bitcoin. This often involves integrating third-party identity verification services and blockchain analytics software to monitor transactions. Transactions deemed suspicious (for instance, involving mixing services or known illicit entity addresses) must be reported to authorities (e.g., filing Suspicious Activity Reports in the US). Indeed, Foley et al. (2019) estimated that a significant portion of Bitcoin activity was associated with illegal transactions, which justifies regulators' close attention. There is a tension here: one of Bitcoin's attractions is to provide financial services to the unbanked or those who cannot easily produce identity documents, yet AML laws require identification. Financial institutions generally err on the side of compliance – meaning some potential users are excluded from services, but this is necessary for the institution to remain within the law.

6.1 Securities, Commodities, and Investor Protection Regulations

Another key regulatory question is whether and when Bitcoin (or products linked to it) falls under securities or commodities laws.

- **Securities Law Considerations:** Generally, regulators like the U.S. Securities and Exchange Commission (SEC) have taken the stance that Bitcoin itself is not a security. However, other crypto assets have been deemed securities. For Bitcoin, the main securities law issues arise with financial products that derive their value from Bitcoin, such as exchange-traded funds (ETFs), futures, or other derivatives. For years, the SEC has been cautious in approving a Bitcoin spot ETF, citing concerns about market manipulation and custody. Financial institutions creating investment products around Bitcoin must ensure prospectuses, risk disclosures, and compliance with securities regulations are in place. Investor protection rules – such as those governing portfolio suitability, advertising, and risk warnings – apply if Bitcoin is offered to retail investors through regulated channels.
- **Commodities Regulation:** In the U.S., the Commodity Futures Trading Commission (CFTC) has declared Bitcoin to be a commodity. This gives the CFTC authority to police fraud and manipulation in underlying Bitcoin markets. Commodity rules also mean that certain types of Bitcoin transactions, if done on a leveraged or margined basis with retail customers, might trigger commodity exchange regulations. Other countries may classify Bitcoin differently, but many lean towards treating it as a sui generis digital asset or a commodity-like asset rather than a currency.
- **Custody Rules:** When financial institutions hold Bitcoin on behalf of clients, they must comply with custody regulations. For instance, U.S. broker-dealers have a "Customer Protection Rule" and investment advisers must follow rules on custody of client funds. Often, an institution may use third-party custodians that specialize in cryptocurrency to satisfy these requirements, ensuring that there is proper insurance, audit, and segregation of client assets, as required in traditional finance.

- **Accounting and Tax Compliance:** Although not a regulation on usage per se, financial reporting rules affect institutions holding Bitcoin. Accounting standards (e.g., under IFRS or GAAP) currently treat cryptocurrency as an intangible asset, which has implications for balance sheet reporting and impairment testing. Tax authorities universally treat cryptocurrency transactions as taxable events. Institutions must thus implement systems to track cost basis and gains for their own holdings and potentially provide customers with tax documentation.
- **Consumer Protection and Legal Liability:** Regulators also consider consumer protection. If a financial firm offers Bitcoin services, it may be subject to regulations regarding disclosures of risks to consumers and may face liability if it misrepresents the safety or guarantees associated with its Bitcoin products. There have been legal cases against exchanges for losses due to hacks or system outages; regulators want to ensure firms have adequate safeguards and reserves to cover such events, or at least clearly inform users of the risks they undertake.

6.2 Regulatory Compliance Challenges and Evolving Approaches

Applying traditional regulation to a decentralized technology like Bitcoin creates several challenges and evolving approaches:

- **Identity vs. Privacy:** As discussed, compliance requires knowing customers and tracking transactions, which conflicts with Bitcoin's design that does not embed identity. Regulators have implicitly outsourced identity enforcement to the edges of the network – i.e., exchanges and institutions must collect KYC, since the protocol itself won't provide names. This leaves a gap when people transact peer-to-peer outside of regulated entities. In response, regulators sometimes broaden their scope. However, enforcing regulations beyond the chokepoints is very difficult technically and raises civil liberty concerns.
- **Jurisdiction and Cross-Border Issues:** Bitcoin transactions cross borders effortlessly, raising questions of which laws apply. If a customer in Country A uses an exchange in Country B to send money to Country C, multiple jurisdictions' laws might apply. This necessitates international cooperation. Organizations like FATF serve to harmonize requirements to avoid "regulatory arbitrage". Nonetheless, differences remain – some countries have lax enforcement or unclear laws, which can be exploited. Financial institutions often choose to operate only in jurisdictions with clear regulations to reduce uncertainty.

- **Licensing and Regulatory Uncertainty:** A challenge in past years was simply figuring out what licenses were needed to operate. Many early crypto startups were penalized for operating without proper licenses due to ignorance or ambiguity. Today, a firm engaging with Bitcoin in a financial capacity likely needs a combination of licenses: money transmitter licenses, possibly bank or trust charters, broker-dealer registrations if dealing in crypto securities, etc. The patchwork can be complex. Regulators are gradually refining frameworks – e.g., MiCA in EU will provide a single licensing regime across member states for crypto-asset service providers.
- **Regulatory Sandboxes and Innovation Programs:** Recognizing the challenge of regulating a fast-moving technology, some regulators created sandboxes (the UK's FCA, Singapore's MAS, etc., have fintech sandboxes where companies can pilot crypto services with regulatory oversight but relaxed rules to test viability). These have helped in developing guidelines. The concept of "embedded compliance" or code-as-regulation has been floated in academia. While Bitcoin itself doesn't have such built-in compliance features, we see intermediate solutions like the Travel Rule protocols being a sort of layer on top that automates compliance information exchange.
- **Enforcement Trends:** Enforcement actions shape the compliance landscape. Cases like the SEC vs. Ripple or the U.S. Department of Justice action against mixers send signals. For Bitcoin, notable enforcement instances include the prosecution of Silk Road and its users, and the Office of Foreign Assets Control (OFAC) adding certain Bitcoin addresses to sanctions lists. These actions effectively force compliance measures into the technical flow – for example, exchanges screening deposits against OFAC-sanctioned addresses, which was not standard practice years ago but is now.

In essence, the regulatory environment for Bitcoin in finance is one of increasing clarity but also increasing stringency. Over the past decade, the trend has moved from a largely unregulated "wild west" toward a scenario where engaging with Bitcoin is not very different from other financial activities in terms of oversight. This bodes well for institutional adoption but also means compliance costs have risen. As a result, smaller peer-to-peer use might shift outside regulated channels, further challenging regulators – a dynamic interplay often referred to in literature as the "push-pull" between regulation and cryptocurrency innovation.

Table 3 provides a summary of the compliance challenges faced in the cryptocurrency sector, particularly focusing on Bitcoin, along with potential solutions to address these challenges. Each challenge represents a barrier to the effective regulation and integration of Bitcoin into the mainstream financial system, while the proposed solutions outline strategies for enhancing compliance and minimizing risks.

Table 3. Summary of Compliance Challenges and Solutions

Challenge	Description	Proposed Solutions
Lack of Regulatory Clarity	Ambiguity in how Bitcoin is classified and regulated	Develop clearer global standards and definitions
KYC/AML Requirements	Difficulties in enforcing these requirements on exchanges	Implement more advanced identity verification systems
Taxation Uncertainty	Varied approaches to taxing Bitcoin transactions	Establish uniform international tax regulations
Security Breaches	Vulnerabilities in exchanges leading to thefts	Enhance exchange security standards and protocols

6.3 Compliance Strategies for Financial Institutions Using Bitcoin

Given the security risks and regulatory requirements outlined, financial institutions using Bitcoin must develop robust compliance strategies that integrate technical controls with procedural policies. Figure 2 below illustrates how regulatory compliance frameworks and information security strategies combine into an integrated risk management system, reinforcing each other to ensure robust operation of Bitcoin-based financial applications.

Figure 2. Integrated Framework for Bitcoin Security and Compliance

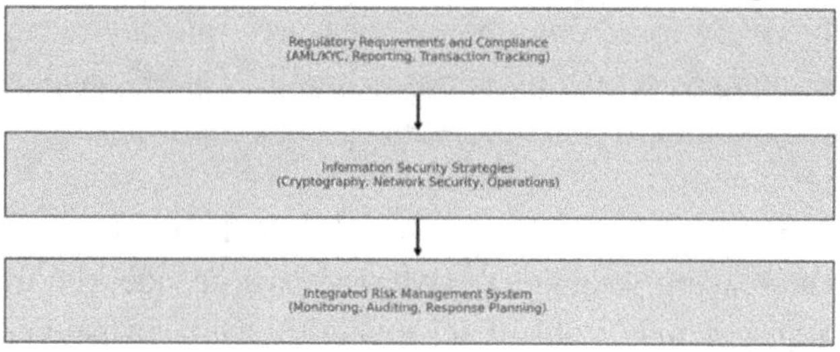

Effective compliance involves integrated customer due diligence, blockchain transaction monitoring, multi-signature wallet implementations, secure custody solutions, regular auditing, and comprehensive employee training.

- **Strong Customer Due Diligence (KYC):** Every institution should have a rigorous Know Your Customer process. This involves verifying the identity of customers at onboarding and assessing the risk profile of the customer. Enhanced due diligence is applied for higher-risk customers. Continuous

KYC is also important – updating documents and information periodically. By knowing their customers, institutions not only comply with AML laws but also reduce fraud and can more effectively monitor transactions for unusual behavior.

- **Blockchain Transaction Monitoring and Analytics:** Once customers are onboarded, their Bitcoin transactions should be monitored similarly to how banks monitor bank transfers. Specialized blockchain analytics tools can track where funds come from or go to. For example, if a customer deposits bitcoins that originated from a darknet marketplace or a known theft, the compliance team can freeze those funds and report the incident. Transaction monitoring software can flag patterns like structuring, sudden spikes in activity, or interactions with mixing services. Machine learning models are increasingly used to detect anomalous transaction patterns on blockchain, improving upon simple rule-based systems. However, human compliance officers are still needed to review flagged cases and determine the appropriate action. This strategy of combining automated blockchain surveillance with human oversight is essential for meeting AML obligations in a scalable way.
- **Segregation of Duties and Multi-Signature Controls:** On the security front, institutions should enforce segregation of duties in handling cryptocurrency. No single individual or system component should have the ability to move funds unilaterally. Multi-signature wallets can ensure that transfers above certain thresholds require multiple approvals. This is analogous to dual-control in wire transfers. In practice, an operations team might initiate a withdrawal, but it requires cryptographic co-signatures from, say, the compliance officer and the security officer. The BitGo multi-sig model is one example in the industry where the custodian, the client, and a backup key held by a neutral party are used – any two can move funds, adding both security and an oversight layer. Multi-sig can also be used to geographically distribute keys to mitigate disaster risks. This strategy addresses both internal fraud and external theft risks.
- **Secure Custody Solutions:** For storing Bitcoin, institutions often leverage insured, audited custodial solutions. Some banks have built in-house custody platforms, while others partner with specialist custodians. These custodians use a combination of hardware security modules, physical vaults, and network segmentation to protect private keys. Insurance plays a role: reputable custodians carry insurance for digital asset theft, which can cover client assets up to certain amounts, providing assurance against worst-case scenarios. Regular third-party audits help verify that security controls are in place and effective. Additionally, incident response plans must exist – if a breach or sus-

picious activity is detected, the institution should have protocols to contain losses. Practicing "fire drills" for such scenarios can improve readiness.

- **Compliance by Design in Software:** When developing applications, developers should integrate compliance checks into the system workflows from the start. For example, implementing address whitelisting can prevent users from directly sending funds to high-risk addresses. Another example is implementing travel rule data exchange where applicable – if a customer is sending bitcoins to an external address that belongs to another exchange, the software can attach the required sender data through a secure channel to that receiving exchange. Smart contract usage might include built-in restrictions. This concept of "compliance by design" ensures that business logic enforces regulations proactively, rather than relying solely on after-the-fact monitoring.
- **Regular Auditing and Reporting:** Financial institutions should undergo regular audits of their crypto operations. This may include internal audits to check that AML procedures are being followed, that wallets balances reconcile with recorded transactions, and that security controls are robust. External auditors might be required to sign off on the integrity of cryptoasset reserves. Additionally, transparent reporting to regulators, and sometimes to the public, can build trust. Some institutions publish annual or quarterly reports on their cryptocurrency activities, risk management measures, and compliance track record. This transparency can also serve as a deterrent to illicit behavior by signaling that robust systems are in place.
- **Employee Training and Awareness:** A compliance strategy is only as effective as the people implementing it. Continuous training for staff – from front-line customer support to the developers – helps maintain a culture of compliance. Employees should be aware of evolving threats, like new scam typologies or hacking methods, and the regulatory changes in the pipeline. Some institutions have mandatory courses or even certifications for staff in departments like compliance and IT security focusing on blockchain technology. This ensures they are not only following a checklist but actually understanding the rationale, so they can adapt and respond to novel situations that arise.
- **Client Education and Communication:** Extending beyond internal operations, many institutions are also focusing on educating their clients as part of compliance. Clear communication about the risks of Bitcoin can be both a legal requirement and a smart way to prevent customer disputes. If users know that transactions can't be reversed, they might be more careful and less likely to fall for phishing attempts. Some platforms implement friction like warning messages or hold periods for first-time withdrawals. While these might slightly inconvenience users, they add layers of protection.

- **Engagement with Regulators and Adaptation:** A strategic approach for institutions is to actively engage with regulators and policymakers. By participating in consultations, industry associations, and standard-setting initiatives, financial firms can stay ahead of regulatory changes and even influence them. For example, providing input on how Travel Rule implementation could be standardized or how to handle DeFi in a compliant way. This engagement ensures that the institution's perspective is heard and also gives it early insight into what compliance measures might be needed in the near future. Additionally, some institutions choose to operate in highly regulated environments to build goodwill – for instance, getting licensed in New York under the BitLicense, or obtaining a full banking license, even if not strictly necessary for all operations, to signal commitment to compliance.
- **Incident Response and Legal Preparedness:** Despite best efforts, incidents may happen. A comprehensive strategy includes having a response plan not just for technical incidents but also for regulatory or legal incidents – such as receiving a subpoena related to a customer's activity, or a sudden regulatory action that affects operations. Institutions often have legal counsel experienced in crypto to navigate such events. A prepared institution will know, for example, how to quickly freeze assets if law enforcement requests it, how to gather and provide blockchain evidence while respecting privacy laws, and how to communicate incidents to stakeholders without causing panic. This preparedness can make the difference between a contained issue and a crisis.

By implementing the above strategies, financial institutions can create a strong control environment around their Bitcoin operations. The goal is to make compliance seamless with the user experience while making it extremely difficult for bad actors to exploit the system. In many ways, this mirrors traditional banking practices but tailored to Bitcoin's characteristics. The best practices continue to evolve as the industry learns from experience, and as technology develops. Institutions that treat compliance as an integral part of their service – rather than a checkbox – are likely to fare better in the long run, gaining trust from regulators and customers alike.

7. CASE STUDIES OF BLOCKCHAIN SECURITY BREACHES

Analyzing past security breaches in blockchain applications can provide valuable lessons for improving security practices.

- **The DAO Hack (2016):** The DAO (Decentralized Autonomous Organization) was a smart contract-based investment fund that was hacked in 2016, resulting in the theft of approximately $60 million worth of Ether. The hack was caused by a reentrancy vulnerability in the DAO's smart contract code. This event highlighted the critical importance of thorough smart contract auditing and formal verification.

- **Parity Wallet Hack (2017):** The Parity Wallet was a popular Ethereum wallet that was hacked twice in 2017. The first hack resulted in the theft of approximately 30 million worth of Ether. The second hack resulted in the freezing of approximately 280 million worth of Ether. The hacks were caused by vulnerabilities in the Parity Wallet's smart contract code. This case underscored the risks of using unaudited or poorly tested smart contract libraries.
- **Coincheck Hack (2018):** The Coincheck cryptocurrency exchange was hacked in 2018, resulting in the theft of approximately $534 million worth of NEM tokens. The hack was caused by a lack of proper security measures at the exchange, including the use of a hot wallet to store a large amount of funds. This event emphasized the need for robust security practices at cryptocurrency exchanges, including cold storage for the majority of assets and multi-factor authentication.
- **Mt. Gox Collapse (2014):** Although predating the widespread use of smart contracts, the Mt. Gox collapse serves as a crucial cautionary tale. The exchange suffered massive losses due to alleged hacking and mismanagement, leading to its bankruptcy. While the exact details remain debated, the incident highlighted the importance of secure key management, robust security audits, and transparent operational practices for centralized entities handling cryptocurrency.

8. FUTURE RESEARCH DIRECTIONS

To address the ongoing security challenges in blockchain applications, further research and development are needed in several key areas.

- **Advanced Cryptographic Techniques**: Exploring new cryptographic techniques, such as post-quantum cryptography, can help to protect blockchain systems from future attacks. Quantum computers pose a significant threat to many of the cryptographic algorithms currently used in blockchain technology.
- **AI-Powered Security Solutions**: Artificial intelligence (AI) and machine learning (ML) can be used to detect and prevent security threats in blockchain applications. AI-powered systems can analyze transaction patterns, identify anomalies, and automate security audits.

- **Formal Verification of Smart Contracts**: Developing more efficient and scalable formal verification techniques can help to ensure the correctness of smart contract code.
- **Secure Hardware Solutions**: Developing secure hardware solutions, such as trusted execution environments (TEEs), can help to protect private keys and other sensitive data from attack.
- **Privacy-Preserving Blockchain Technologies**: Researching and developing new privacy-preserving blockchain technologies can help to address data privacy concerns and comply with relevant regulations.
- **Interoperability and Security**: Developing secure and interoperable blockchain systems is crucial for enabling the widespread adoption of blockchain technology. Research is needed to develop secure communication protocols and cross-chain transaction mechanisms.
- **Decentralized Identity Management**: Researching decentralized identity management solutions can enable users to control their own identities and data on the blockchain. This can improve privacy and security by reducing the reliance on centralized identity providers.
- **Scalable Security Solutions**: As blockchain networks grow in size and complexity, it is important to develop scalable security solutions that can handle the increasing transaction volume and data storage requirements.

9. CONCLUSION

Bitcoin's rise as a significant financial asset has required a rethinking of both security practices and regulatory frameworks in the financial industry. This paper has examined the intersection of information security and regulatory compliance for Bitcoin-focused financial applications, highlighting that success in this domain demands excellence in both realms. The cryptographic foundations of Bitcoin – decentralization, hashing, digital signatures – provide strong guarantees of integrity and authenticity, forming a bedrock on which innovative financial services can be built. Yet, as we have detailed, these same services are exposed to a range of security vulnerabilities, from consensus attacks and network exploits to human-centered operational risks. Financial institutions cannot passively rely on Bitcoin's protocol for security; they must actively harden their systems, monitor for threats, and prepare for contingencies.

At the same time, institutions must operate within an evolving regulatory landscape that seeks to mitigate the misuse of Bitcoin without stifling its utility. Over the past decade, regulators worldwide have increasingly brought Bitcoin activities into the scope of existing laws or crafted new rules – treating exchanges like banks or brokers, extending AML obligations to crypto transactions, and deliberating how to classify and supervise crypto-assets. This regulatory maturation signifies a coming-of-age for Bitcoin in mainstream finance, effectively dispelling the early "wild west" era. Compliance is now a competitive imperative: institutions with robust compliance programs are better positioned to gain licenses, attract institutional clients, and build partnerships, whereas lax approaches face legal sanctions and reputational damage.

A key insight from our analysis is that security and compliance are deeply interconnected in the context of Bitcoin. Good security is a foundation for compliance – for instance, one cannot maintain accurate records for reporting if systems are compromised, nor protect consumers if assets are not safely custodied. Conversely, compliance measures can enhance security – for example, KYC procedures deter some criminal elements from targeting a platform in the first place, and transaction monitoring can double as an intrusion detection system by flagging unusual flows that might indicate a hack or fraud. The synergy between these domains suggests that firms should adopt a holistic risk management strategy. Frameworks such as enterprise risk management (ERM) or integrated compliance management are apt, wherein technical and legal teams collaborate routinely. In practice, this might mean security engineers working with compliance officers to design anti-fraud algorithms, or legal analysts consulting with developers on how a new protocol upgrade (like Taproot) might affect compliance tooling.

Our discussion of compliance strategies offers a roadmap for institutions aiming to harness Bitcoin's capabilities responsibly. Approaches like multi-signature controls, blockchain analytics, and "compliance by design" illustrate that, with thoughtful implementation, it is possible to reconcile the seemingly divergent aims of decentralization and regulation. Indeed, the financial industry is gradually developing standardized best practices (often borrowing from traditional finance, but adapted to crypto's specifics). The concept of "regulated decentralization" is emerging – leveraging decentralization's benefits (resilience, transparency) within a framework of oversight and accountability. While purists may view this as antithetical to Bitcoin's cypherpunk origins, it is arguably a prerequisite for mass adoption in regulated markets.

Looking ahead, several future developments will shape this space. Technologically, advances in cryptography might allow new solutions where privacy and compliance co-exist – for example, proving compliance properties of a transaction without revealing all details. There is active research on using zero-knowledge proofs to satisfy AML checks, which could become practical in coming years and alleviate the privacy-compliance tension. On the regulatory front, we anticipate more clarity as jurisdictions implement comprehensive crypto regulations and international coordination improves. The role of supranational standards will likely expand, possibly leading to something akin to a Basel III for crypto assets.

Financial institutions will also have to remain vigilant about new risks. The advent of central bank digital currencies (CBDCs) might alter the landscape in which Bitcoin operates, potentially introducing new regulatory expectations or competitive pressures. Quantum computing, as noted, lurks on the horizon as a threat to current cryptography – a development that regulators and industry will need to tackle in tandem, likely requiring global cooperation to upgrade protocols in a backward-compatible way. Additionally, as more traditional institutions get involved with Bitcoin, there will be greater scrutiny on systemic risk – is Bitcoin entwined with the broader financial system in ways that could be destabilizing? This could usher in macro-prudential regulation for the crypto sector if deemed necessary.

REFERENCES

Aggarwal, D., Brennen, G. K., Lee, T., Santha, M., & Tomamichel, M. (2018). Quantum attacks on Bitcoin, and how to protect against them. *Ledger*, *3*, 67–90. DOI: 10.5195/ledger.2018.127

Androulaki, E., Karame, G. O., Roeschlin, M., Scherer, T., & Čapkun, S. (2013). Evaluating user privacy in Bitcoin. In *Financial Cryptography and Data Security* (pp. 34–51). Springer., DOI: 10.1007/978-3-642-39884-1_4

Apostolaki, M., Zohar, A., & Vanbever, L. (2017). Hijacking Bitcoin: Routing Attacks on Cryptocurrencies. In *2017 IEEE Symposium on Security and Privacy* (pp. 375-392). DOI: 10.1109/SP.2017.29

Atzei, N., Bartoletti, M., & Cimoli, T. (2017). A survey of attacks on Ethereum smart contracts (SoK). In *Proceedings of the 6th International Conference on Principles of Security and Trust (POST 2017)* (pp. 164-186). Springer. DOI: 10.1007/978-3-662-54455-6_8

Bhargavan, K., Delignat-Lavaud, A., Fournet, C., Gollamudi, A., Gonthier, G., Kobeissi, N., & Zanella-Béguelin, S. (2016, Oct). Formal verification of smart contracts: Short paper. In *Proceedings of the 2016 ACM workshop on programming languages and analysis for security* (pp. 91-96). DOI: 10.1145/2993600.2993611

Böhme, R., Christin, N., Edelman, B., & Moore, T. (2015). Bitcoin: Economics, technology, and governance. *The Journal of Economic Perspectives*, *29*(2), 213–238. DOI: 10.1257/jep.29.2.213

Bonneau, J., Miller, A., Clark, J., Narayanan, A., Kroll, J. A., & Felten, E. (2015). SoK: Research perspectives and challenges for Bitcoin and cryptocurrencies. In *2015 IEEE Symposium on Security and Privacy* (pp. 104-121). DOI: 10.1109/SP.2015.14

Bryans, D. (2014). Bitcoin and money laundering: Mining for an effective solution. *Industrial Law Journal*, *89*(1), 441–472.

Campbell-Verduyn, M. (2018). Bitcoin, crypto-coins, and global anti-money laundering governance. *Crime, Law, and Social Change*, *69*(2), 283–305. DOI: 10.1007/s10611-017-9756-5

Chaum, D. (1985). Security without identification: Transaction systems to make Big Brother obsolete. *Communications of the ACM*, *28*(10), 1030–1044. DOI: 10.1145/4372.4373

Conti, M., Kumar, S., Lal, C., & Ruj, S. (2018). A survey on security and privacy issues of Bitcoin. *IEEE Communications Surveys and Tutorials, 20*(4), 3416–3452. DOI: 10.1109/COMST.2018.2842460

Eskandari, S., Clark, J., Barrera, D., & Stobert, E. (2018). A first look at the usability of bitcoin key management. *arXiv preprint arXiv:1802.04351*. https://arxiv.org/abs/1802.04351

Eyal, I., & Sirer, E. G. (2014). Majority is not enough: Bitcoin mining is vulnerable. In *International Conference on Financial Cryptography and Data Security* (pp. 436-454). Springer. DOI: 10.1007/978-3-662-45472-5_28

Fenwick, A., & Molnar, G. (2022). The importance of humanizing AI: Using a behavioral lens to bridge the gaps between humans and machines. *Discover Artificial Intelligence, 2*(1), 14. DOI: 10.1007/s44163-022-00030-8

Finck, M. (2019). Blockchain and the General Data Protection Regulation: Can distributed ledgers be squared with European data protection law? *European Law Journal, 25*(6), 574–587. DOI: 10.2139/ssrn.3805647

Foley, S., Karlsen, J. R., & Putniņš, T. J. (2019). Sex, drugs, and bitcoin: How much illegal activity is financed through cryptocurrencies? *Review of Financial Studies, 32*(5), 1798–1853. DOI: 10.1093/rfs/hhz015

Gervais, A., Karame, G. O., Wüst, K., Glykantzis, V., Ritzdorf, H., & Capkun, S. (2016, October). On the security and performance of proof of work blockchains. In *Proceedings of the 2016 ACM SIGSAC conference on computer and communications security* (pp. 3-16). DOI: 10.1145/2976749.2978341

Haber, S., & Stornetta, W. S. (1991). How to time-stamp a digital document. *Journal of Cryptology, 3*(2), 99–111. DOI: 10.1007/BF00196791

Heilman, E., Kendler, A., Zohar, A., & Goldberg, S. (2015). Eclipse attacks on bitcoin's peer-to-peer network. In *24th USENIX Security Symposium* (pp. 129-144).

Hughes, S., & Middlebrook, S. T. (2015). Advancing a framework for regulating cryptocurrency and other novel payment products. *Yale Journal of Law & Technology, 18*, 103–150.

Karame, G. O., Androulaki, E., & Čapkun, S. (2012). Double-spending fast payments in Bitcoin. In *Proceedings of the 2012 ACM Conference on Computer and Communications Security* (pp. 906-917). DOI: 10.1145/2382196.2382292

Kiviat, T. I. (2015). Beyond bitcoin: Issues in regulating blockchain transactions. *Duke Law Journal, 65*(3), 569–608. https://scholarship.law.duke.edu/dlj/vol65/iss3/4

Koshy, P., Koshy, D., & McDaniel, P. (2014, Mar). An analysis of anonymity in bitcoin using p2p network traffic. In *International conference on financial cryptography and data security* (pp. 469-485). Berlin, Heidelberg: Springer Berlin Heidelberg. DOI: 10.1007/978-3-662-45472-5_30

Kshetri, N. (2021). Blockchain in Finance: Overcoming Regulatory and Other Challenges in the Era of COVID-19. *Journal of International Management*, *27*(2), 100857. DOI: 10.1016/j.ijinfomgt.2021.102376

Lansky, J. (2018). Possible state approaches to cryptocurrencies. *Journal of Systems Integration*, *9*(1), 19–31. DOI: 10.20470/jsi.v9i1.335

Li, X., Jiang, P., Chen, T., Luo, X., & Wen, Q. (2020). A survey on the security of blockchain systems. *Future Generation Computer Systems*, *107*, 841–853. DOI: 10.1016/j.future.2017.08.020

Lootsma, Y. (2017). Blockchain as the newest regtech application—The opportunity to reduce the burden of kyc for financial institutions. *Banking & Financial Services Policy Report*, *36*(8), 16–21.

Luu, L., Chu, D. H., Olickel, H., Saxena, P., & Hobor, A. (2016, Oct). Making smart contracts smarter. In *Proceedings of the 2016 ACM SIGSAC conference on computer and communications security* (pp. 254-269). DOI: 10.1145/2976749.2978309

Ly, M. (2014). Coining Bitcoin's "legal bits": Examining the regulatory framework for Bitcoin and virtual currencies. *Harvard Journal of Law & Technology*, *27*(2), 587–608.

Meiklejohn, S., Pomarole, M., Jordan, G., Levchenko, K., McCoy, D., Voelker, G. M., & Savage, S. (2013, Oct). A fistful of bitcoins: characterizing payments among men with no names. In *Proceedings of the 2013 conference on Internet measurement conference* (pp. 127-140). DOI: 10.1145/2504730.2504747

Micheler, E., & Whaley, A. (2020). Regulatory technology: Replacing law with computer code. *European Business Organization Law Review*, *21*(2), 349–377. DOI: 10.1007/s40804-019-00151-1

Miers, I., Garman, C., Green, M., & Rubin, A. D. (2013, May). Zerocoin: Anonymous distributed e-cash from bitcoin. In *2013 IEEE symposium on security and privacy* (pp. 397-411). IEEE.

Möser, M., & Böhme, R. (2017, Apr). Anonymous alone? measuring Bitcoin's second-generation anonymization techniques. In *2017 IEEE European Symposium on Security and Privacy Workshops (EuroS&PW)* (pp. 32-41). IEEE. DOI: 10.1109/EuroSPW.2017.48

Nakamoto, S. (2008). *Bitcoin: A peer-to-peer electronic cash system.* https://bitcoin.org/bitcoin.pdf

Narayanan, A., Bonneau, J., Felten, E., Miller, A., & Goldfeder, S. (2016). *Bitcoin and cryptocurrency technologies: a comprehensive introduction.* Princeton University Press.

Ober, M., Katzenbeisser, S., & Hamacher, K. (2013). Structure and anonymity of the Bitcoin transaction graph. *Future Internet, 5*(2), 237–250. DOI: 10.3390/fi5020237

Poon, J., & Dryja, T. (2016). *The Bitcoin Lightning Network: Scalable off-chain instant payments* [PDF]. https://lightning.network/lightning-network-paper.pdf

Sapirshtein, A., Sompolinsky, Y., & Zohar, A. (2016, February). Optimal selfish mining strategies in bitcoin. In *International conference on financial cryptography and data security* (pp. 515-532). Berlin, Heidelberg: Springer Berlin Heidelberg.

Tschorsch, F., & Scheuermann, B. (2016). Bitcoin and beyond: A technical survey on decentralized digital currencies. *IEEE Communications Surveys and Tutorials, 18*(3), 2084–2123. DOI: 10.1109/COMST.2016.2535718

Vasek, M., & Moore, T. (2015, January). There's no free lunch, even using Bitcoin: Tracking the popularity and profits of virtual currency scams. In *International conference on financial cryptography and data security* (pp. 44-61). Berlin, Heidelberg: Springer Berlin Heidelberg. DOI: 10.1007/978-3-662-47854-7_4

Walch, A. (2015). The Bitcoin blockchain as financial market infrastructure: A consideration of operational risk. *New York University Journal of Legislation and Public Policy, 18*, 837–893.

World Economic Forum. (n.d.). *The Digital Currency Governance Consortium.* https://www.weforum.org/communities/digital-currency-governance-consortium

Yeoh, P. (2017). Regulatory issues in blockchain technology. *Journal of Financial Regulation and Compliance, 25*(2), 196–208. https://econpapers.repec.org/scripts/redir.pf?u=https%3A%2F%2Fdoi.org%2F10.1108%252FJFRC-08-2016-0068;h=repec:eme:jfrcpp:jfrc-08-2016-0068. DOI: 10.1108/JFRC-08-2016-0068

Zetzsche, D. A., Arner, D. W., & Buckley, R. P. (2020). Decentralized finance. *Journal of Financial Regulation, 6*(2), 172–203. DOI: 10.1093/jfr/fjaa010

ENDNOTES

1 Corresponding Author: lewcheehon@qq.com

2 https://www.fincen.gov/statutes_regs/guidance/pdf/FIN-2013-G001.pdf?utm_source=chatgpt.com

Chapter 4
Financial Innovation in Virtual Economies:
The Role of DeFi in Metaverse Integration

Harsh Kumar
https://orcid.org/0009-0005-2596-1806
Akal University, India

Aijaz Ahmad Chopan
Akal University, India

Makinder Kour
https://orcid.org/0009-0008-4972-5287
Akal University, India

Zubair Fayaz
Akal University, India

ABSTRACT

This paper explores the integration of Decentralized Finance (DeFi) into the Metaverse and its transformative impact on virtual economies. By examining platforms like Decentraland and Sandbox, the study highlights how DeFi protocols—such as lending, staking, and token swapping—enhance financial accessibility, user engagement, and asset liquidity. The paper also identifies key challenges including scalability, security vulnerabilities, regulatory uncertainty, and user adoption barriers. Opportunities such as decentralized ownership, financial inclusion, and cross-platform interoperability are discussed. Through a synthesis of academic and industry literature, this research underscores the potential of DeFi to reshape

DOI: 10.4018/979-8-3373-2838-6.ch004

digital finance and virtual interactions. The study concludes by calling for further exploration of governance, behavioral trends, and regulatory frameworks to ensure a secure, inclusive, and sustainable decentralized Metaverse.

1. INTRODUCTION

The emergence of the Metaverse (Mystakidis, 2022) represents a critical turning point in the development of digital experiences, as it skillfully combines the internet, augmented reality, and virtual reality into a seamless, immersive whole. Users can work, socialize, interact, and conduct business—activities that mirror those occurring in the physical world—within this digital space (Cheng, 2023). As the Metaverse continues to grow, it introduces exciting opportunities for industries such as financial services and trade. However, its development is also accompanied by several significant challenges that must be resolved for its full potential to be realized.

One of the most transformative innovations within this digital frontier is the integration of decentralized finance (DeFi). DeFi reimagines traditional financial systems by enabling peer-to-peer transactions without intermediaries through blockchain, smart contracts, and decentralized applications (dApps). This shift offers users greater control over their assets and opens access to secure, transparent, and borderless financial services embedded within virtual worlds. Despite these benefits, the integration of DeFi into the Metaverse raises several problems that this paper aims to address.

Key Challenges

- Scalability Issues: Current blockchain infrastructures, especially Ethereum, struggle to support high-volume transactions without incurring high fees and delays—hindering real-time financial operations essential for immersive Metaverse experiences.
- Interoperability Barriers: Most virtual platforms remain siloed, limiting the movement of digital assets, tokens, and user identities across ecosystems.
- Regulatory and Security Concerns: The decentralized and anonymous nature of DeFi raises questions around governance, user protection, and fraud prevention in virtual financial systems.

Solutions Explored in This Study

This paper explores existing and emerging solutions to these challenges. It analyzes how blockchain infrastructure supports decentralized economies, focusing on Ethereum-based smart contracts and DeFi protocols such as Uniswap and Aave. Furthermore, it reviews technical improvements like Layer 2 scaling solutions (e.g., zk-Rollups and Optimistic Rollups) that aim to improve transaction speed and reduce costs (Wang et al., 2023). The study also investigates efforts to promote interoperability and enhance platform connectivity through standardized protocols and cross-chain frameworks.

Through detailed case studies of major platforms like Decentraland and Sandbox, we demonstrate how these solutions are being applied and tested in real-world virtual environments. These examples provide insight into the evolving structure of digital economies, highlighting both achievements and ongoing limitations.

Ultimately, this paper aims to contribute to the growing body of research on the convergence of DeFi and the Metaverse by identifying practical pathways to overcome current barriers. The findings are relevant to developers, regulators, and users seeking to navigate and shape the future of decentralized digital economies. By critically evaluating current practices and technological innovations, this study provides actionable insights for building a more scalable, interoperable, and trustworthy financial ecosystem within the Metaverse.

2. LITERATURE REVIEW

Building upon the previous analysis of DeFi-integrated platforms and protocols, this section delves deeply into the scholarly and technical literature that explains the origins, principles, and applications of decentralized finance in the Metaverse. We cover: (1) an overview of the emerging Metaverse ecosystem, (2) the enabling technologies, (3) a detailed examination of DeFi principles and components, and (4) a synthesis of prior studies emphasizing economic, social, technical, and regulatory perspectives.

2.1 The Metaverse: An Overview

The Metaverse represents a communal, immersive virtual realm created by merging augmented physical reality and persistent digital environments. It embodies a unified digital ecosystem built on the convergence of the internet, augmented reality (AR), and virtual reality (VR) technologies. As Ball (2020) observes, the defining feature of the Metaverse is its capacity to preserve identity, artifacts, and shared history, enabling users to maintain and evolve digital selves, interact socially in real time, and return to a common virtual memory space (Cheng, 2023). This continuity differentiates it from earlier online platforms: users maintain persistent digital identities while accumulating assets, experiences, and reputations over time.

Platforms such as Decentraland and Sandbox exemplify these qualities by offering immersive environments where participants can design virtual spaces, establish businesses, attend social gatherings, and conduct financial transactions. These spaces illustrate how digital continuity fosters deeper emotional and economic engagement, transforming the Metaverse into an evolving social ecosystem rather than a mere technological novelty.

2.2 Foundations of Technology

The Metaverse's immersive capabilities rest on three foundational technologies:

BlockchainTechnology

Blockchain enables the establishment of a secure, decentralized economic infrastructure. It verifies proof of ownership through NFTs, records all transactions immutably, and supports autonomous consensus mechanisms that are tamper-resistant (Yang et al., 2022). In virtual settings, this ensures trust and value retention—key for both users and developers.

Augmented Reality (AR)

AR enhances real-world environments with digital overlays, enabling experiences like allowing users to view and interact with virtual property from their physical surroundings. This smooth integration enhances immersion and accessibility (Xu et al., 2022), bridging virtual content and real-world spaces in ways that support broader user adoption.

Virtual Reality (VR)

Full VR environments provide deeply immersive digital experiences, where users engage with space and other avatars in a tactile and presence-rich manner. By replicating physical social cues and spatial awareness, VR fosters empathy, collaboration, and creativity, forming the backbone of experiential interactions within the Metaverse.

These technologies, working together, enable richly interactive and socially compelling virtual economies.

2.3 Leading Platforms: Decentraland and Sandbox

Decentraland, built on Ethereum, allows users to purchase parcels of virtual land as NFTs, engage in content creation, and participate in governance through DAOs. Its model encourages the development of galleries, games, and commercial venues by contributors worldwide. The economic vitality of these environments is rooted in decentralized ownership and participatory decision-making, which fosters sustainable growth and social investment in virtual infrastructure.

Sandbox, in contrast, focuses heavily on gamification: users build, share, and monetize game experiences using accessible authoring tools. Here, creative expression is deeply intertwined with economic opportunity, as user-generated assets—also NFTs—can be bought, sold, or leased. Sandbox's emphasis on democratized creativity and embedded token-based governance has created a vibrant content ecosystem (Xu et al., 2023).

Together, these platforms model how decentralized governance, creative tooling, and blockchain-secured ownership can support thriving virtual societies (Truong et al., 2023).

2.4 Principles and Components of DeFi

DeFi reimagines financial services by decentralizing control, increasing transparency, automating trust, enabling interoperability, and broadening access. As Maksymyuk et al. (2022) outline:

- Decentralization reduces systemic risk by distributing authority and operations across network participants rather than centralized institutions.
- Trustlessness is achieved through smart contracts—self-executing code that enforces contractual terms without intermediaries.
- Transparency is enabled because blockchain transactions are public, auditable, and verifiable, supporting accountability.
- Interoperability allows separate DeFi protocols to integrate and compose complex services, referred to as "money legos."
- Accessibility reduces entry barriers, enabling financial participation from anywhere without needing a bank account.

The components that operationalize these principles include:

- Smart Contracts, which automate loans, trades, and governance tasks, reducing reliance on manual processes or centralized custodians.

- Decentralized Exchanges (DEXs), such as Uniswap, use automated market maker algorithms to facilitate peer-to-peer swaps of digital assets without centralized intermediaries, enhancing both security and liquidity.
- Lending Platforms, including Aave and Compound, allow users to supply assets for interest or borrow by locking collateral. These platforms enable more flexible capital uses—crucial in virtual economies where users may need upfront funds to build or expand virtual properties.
- Stablecoins such as DAI and USDC anchor virtual economies to fiat-stable values, aiding price consistency essential for everyday commerce, salary payments, and financial planning in virtual environments.DeFi Insurance platforms use pooled capital to protect users against smart contract failures or exchange hacks, mitigating one of the higher risks of decentralized finance.
- Derivatives and Synthetic Assets, facilitated through platforms like Synthetix, allow virtual world users to gain synthetic exposure to real-world commodities, currencies, and stocks—broadening financial inclusion and enabling portfolio diversification within virtual environments.

2.5 Key Findings from Prior Studies

- Researchers have closely analyzed how DeFi influences virtual economic systems, identifying both benefits and challenges:
- Economic Impact: DeFi reduces intermediary fees and opens access to capital, fostering greater economic inclusion, especially in underbanked communities (Huynh-The et al., 2023). Automated lending, decentralized markets, and token economies can catalyze innovation by enabling more participants to engage in virtual commerce.
- User Engagement: DeFi-driven financial autonomy—via yield farming, token staking, and voting rights—encourages user engagement and long-term value creation. Users become stakeholders, not just consumers, enhancing platform loyalty and social buy-in.
- Security and Trust: Despite transparency, vulnerabilities in smart contracts and exploit incidents have demonstrated that DeFi still demands rigorous auditing and secure protocols. Well-publicized attacks reduce trust and can discourage adoption without reliable safeguards.
- Scalability: Current public blockchains like Ethereum suffer from transaction congestion and high gas fees, especially during peak Metaverse activity. Layer 2 solutions such as optimistic rollups and ZK-rollups, or network sharding, are under development to provide lower-cost and faster transaction processing—critical for real-time virtual applications.

- Legal and Regulatory Risks: Because DeFi protocols lack centralized oversight, governments face challenges in regulating fraud, money laundering, consumer protection, and taxation within these borderless ecosystems. Regulatory ambiguity forces users and developers to navigate legal uncertainty, prompting calls for frameworks that support innovation while safeguarding participants (Pandey & Gilmour, 2024).

2.6 The Convergence: DeFi in the Metaverse

The integration of DeFi and the Metaverse is moving from theoretical possibility to practical reality (Kumar et al., 2024). Transactions in virtual environments are no longer confined to collectible trades—they include borrowing, yield-earning, staking, and investing. Platforms like Decentraland allow users to trade virtual property tokenized as NFTs, with Uniswap enabling peer-to-peer token swaps and Aave providing credit against digital assets. Pellegrini (2024) and Radanliev (2024) observe that these capabilities mirror traditional financial services but with 24/7 availability and fewer intermediaries, expanding economic behaviors in immersive virtual ecosystems. This convergence enhances the viability of the Metaverse as both a social and economic space, enabling assets to flow seamlessly, financial services to adapt flexibly, and users to derive real-world economic benefit from virtual participation. As blockchain networks evolve and regulations clarify, DeFi-enabled Metaverse systems are likely to deliver increasingly sophisticated, equitable, and resilient digital economies.

3. DEFI-ENABLED PLATFORMS

As the convergence of blockchain technology and immersive virtual environments accelerates, several Metaverse platforms have emerged as dynamic testbeds for decentralized finance (DeFi) integration. These platforms are not merely spaces for social and creative expression; they also serve as functional economies where DeFi protocols facilitate token trading, asset management, borrowing, lending, and governance. This section provides a comprehensive overview of two major platforms—Decentraland and Sandbox—and the foundational DeFi protocols empowering financial services within these digital environments. It further explores the economic activities enabled by this convergence and concludes with a summary of their transformative potential.

3.1 Decentraland: A User-Owned Virtual Economy

Decentraland is a decentralized, blockchain-based virtual world built on Ethereum, where users can create, own, monetize, and exchange digital content through the use of its native cryptocurrency, MANA (Remolina, 2024). Its economic system is fundamentally underpinned by the concept of virtual real estate, with individual parcels of land tokenized as non-fungible tokens (NFTs). These land tokens can be bought, sold, or developed to generate revenue. The valuation of land within Decentraland is influenced by several market-driven factors, including geographic location within the virtual map, foot traffic, proximity to popular areas, and the quality or uniqueness of digital developments on the land (Chao et al., 2022).

The financial dimension of Decentraland extends well beyond simple property ownership. Its integration of Decentralized Finance (DeFi) mechanisms has transformed it into a fully functioning virtual economy where users can perform complex financial activities. Through decentralized exchanges, users trade MANA and other ERC-20 tokens without intermediaries, often leveraging platforms like Uniswap to execute transactions seamlessly within the ecosystem. Liquidity pools enable capital efficiency, while lending and borrowing services—via protocols such as Aave—allow landowners to collateralize their digital real estate to access capital. This borrowed capital can be reinvested into further land development or asset acquisition, echoing traditional real estate investment practices but with fewer barriers to entry.

A core feature of Decentraland's financial system is its governance model, which operates through a Decentralized Autonomous Organization (DAO). Token holders use MANA or its wrapped version, wMANA, to propose and vote on changes to platform policies, including grant allocations, protocol updates, and marketplace fees (Turi, 2023). This model introduces an investor-stakeholder governance paradigm, giving users not just ownership rights but also regulatory influence—a unique trait compared to traditional gaming or real estate platforms.

From a revenue generation standpoint, Decentraland supports a variety of entrepreneurial ventures. Users can open digital businesses such as virtual art galleries that sell NFT artworks, music venues that charge entrance fees for live-streamed concerts, or fashion houses that market digital wearables. NFTs are not only speculative assets; they function as utilities or commodities in Decentraland's digital commerce. Virtual merchandise, such as avatar skins or branded clothing, can command high resale values depending on exclusivity or event association, creating a secondary market that mimics luxury goods in the physical world.

Moreover, staking mechanisms and token-based reward programs are being explored to incentivize long-term participation. For instance, landowners might be able to stake MANA in future iterations to receive governance rewards or yield from virtual rental agreements. The potential introduction of NFT-based mortgages and insurance products further exemplifies the maturing sophistication of Decentraland's financial landscape.

The economic metrics of Decentraland already exhibit signs of real-world financial relevance. Reports of land parcels being sold for tens or even hundreds of thousands of U.S. dollars suggest that speculative investment and asset appreciation are major drivers of user engagement. The use of blockchain ensures transparent, verifiable ownership and transaction histories, reducing the risk of fraud and building trust in high-value virtual asset transactions.

In summary, Decentraland is not only a space for social interaction or creative expression—it is a fully-fledged digital financial system, mirroring many attributes of real-world economies while lowering barriers to participation. Through its integration of DeFi protocols, asset tokenization, user governance, and a rapidly growing ecosystem of NFT-based commerce, Decentraland exemplifies the transformative potential of blockchain-powered virtual economies. It offers a glimpse into a future where digital environments host meaningful, self-sustaining financial ecosystems shaped by their participants.

3.2 Sandbox: Gamified Creation Meets Financial Innovation

Sandbox is a decentralized virtual world built on the Ethereum blockchain that combines interactive digital experiences with user-generated content and blockchain-based ownership. At the heart of its ecosystem is the SAND token, an ERC-20 utility token used to facilitate all transactions within the platform—including land purchases, in-game asset trading, participation in governance, and the payment of transaction fees (Aysan et al., 2024). Sandbox's design centers on empowering creators by providing them with the tools to build, share, and monetize their own gaming and social experiences, positioning it as both a creative platform and a participatory digital economy.

The platform's economy is underpinned by digital land parcels, tokenized as NFTs (LAND), which users can acquire, develop, and sell. These parcels serve as the foundational units of Sandbox's metaverse, where developers and designers construct immersive experiences such as virtual museums, esports arenas, theme parks, or educational simulations. The valuation of LAND, much like in Decentraland, is influenced by scarcity, user traffic, branding opportunities, and its integration into broader ecosystem narratives. LAND assets have fetched prices in the tens or hundreds of thousands of dollars, indicating both speculative interest and practical value generation.

Sandbox's financial system becomes particularly robust through its integration with DeFi protocols. Partnerships with DeFi platforms have enabled the incorporation of decentralized asset exchanges, allowing users to trade SAND and other ERC-20 tokens without intermediaries. This enhances liquidity and reduces dependence on centralized marketplaces. Lending and borrowing services, enabled through protocols such as Aave or Compound, allow creators to fund development projects by staking their existing tokens or LAND as collateral—unlocking capital for innovation in ways similar to startup financing in traditional markets.

Staking mechanisms play a dual role in Sandbox. On one hand, they allow users to earn passive income by locking up SAND tokens, providing a yield-bearing opportunity that encourages long-term token holding and economic stability. On the other hand, staking is often tied to platform governance, enabling token holders to vote on important decisions related to protocol upgrades, marketplace policies, or ecosystem funding initiatives. This combination of economic incentive and governance utility mirrors shareholder structures in traditional finance, but without central intermediaries.

From a revenue generation perspective, Sandbox has created multiple income streams for both casual users and professional game developers. Users can design and sell NFTs representing in-game assets, such as avatars, wearable items, or interactive tools, through the Sandbox Marketplace. These NFTs often hold intrinsic value due to their scarcity, functionality, or brand affiliation. For example, collaborations with major brands like Atari, Adidas, and Snoop Dogg have led to the creation of exclusive NFTs that appreciate in value over time, creating opportunities for speculation and long-term investment.

Furthermore, the gamified structure of Sandbox lends itself to play-to-earn (P2E) models, where players receive tokens and digital assets as rewards for participating in games or completing tasks. This injects a financial layer into user engagement, making time spent in the virtual world directly monetizable. Such mechanisms democratize value creation by allowing non-developers to also benefit from the platform's economic activity, a hallmark of Web3 finance.

Sandbox also supports creator funds and grant programs to stimulate content production and economic expansion. These funds are typically voted on and disbursed through the platform's DAO, further reinforcing the decentralized nature of economic coordination within the ecosystem. Developers receiving grants may create games, design LAND experiences, or build interoperable tools that enhance user engagement and increase the platform's intrinsic value.

In the long term, Sandbox aims to support cross-platform financial interoperability, enabling assets and tokens to circulate across multiple virtual environments. This vision aligns with the broader Web3 objective of creating a composable financial infrastructure—one in which tokens, NFTs, and reputation can seamlessly flow between games, platforms, and protocols.

In summary, Sandbox stands at the intersection of immersive virtual experience and decentralized financial innovation. Its financial architecture—centered on token-based transactions, NFT asset markets, yield-generating staking, and DAO-driven governance—positions it as a blueprint for how future digital economies may function. By giving users the tools to not only participate but also profit, Sandbox transforms gaming into a fully-fledged economic activity, illustrating the powerful synergy between entertainment, creativity, and finance in the Metaverse.

4. DEFI PROTOCOLS EMPOWERING THE METAVERSE

While platforms like Decentraland and Sandbox serve as the foundational environments where users interact, build, and transact, their financial ecosystems are significantly empowered by the integration of decentralized finance protocols. These platforms do not function in isolation; instead, they rely on a broader DeFi infrastructure to facilitate critical economic activities such as trading, lending, borrowing, and asset stabilization. The success and scalability of these Metaverse economies hinge on robust and interoperable DeFi solutions that provide users with financial tools comparable to—if not more flexible than—those in the traditional financial system. The following section highlights several leading DeFi protocols that play indispensable roles in supporting the financial mechanics of the Metaverse, enabling users to access capital, exchange tokens, generate yield, and manage risk within fully decentralized digital environments.

Several DeFi protocols play foundational roles in enabling the financial infrastructure of the Metaverse:

- **Uniswap** facilitates token exchanges through automated market makers (AMMs) and liquidity pools. Within Metaverse platforms, users swap tokens like MANA and SAND in a decentralized, permissionless environment, enhancing liquidity and autonomy.
- **Aave** enables lending and borrowing by allowing users to stake virtual assets like NFTs or land tokens. Participants earn interest or acquire loans to fund development projects within the Metaverse.
- **Compound** provides an algorithmic interest rate protocol. Users can lend or borrow assets, generating passive income or accessing capital without relying on traditional intermediaries.
- **MakerDAO** issues DAI, a stablecoin pegged to the U.S. dollar. In volatile digital economies, DAI ensures transaction stability, enabling consistent pricing for goods, services, and wages in virtual ecosystems.

- **Synthetix** allows the creation and trading of synthetic assets, which replicate the value of fiat currencies or commodities. This opens the door for portfolio diversification and real-world financial exposure within digital realms.

The table (1) below summarizes the core functions and roles of these protocols in the Metaverse:

Table 1. Key DeFi Protocols and Their Roles in the Metaverse

DeFi Protocol	Platform Integration	Functionality	Benefits in the Metaverse	Examples
Uniswap	Decentraland, Sandbox	Token exchange via AMMs	Decentralized trading, liquidity provision	Trading MANA or SAND without intermediaries
Aave	Decentraland, Sandbox	Lending and borrowing	Financial flexibility, yield farming, capital access	Collateralizing NFTs for loans
Compound	Decentraland, Sandbox	Interest-bearing deposits	Dynamic interest rates, passive income	Lending idle tokens for interest
MakerDAO	Multiple Metaverse platforms	Stablecoin generation (DAI)	Transaction stability, hedging against volatility	Using DAI for purchases or wages
Synthetix	Multiple Metaverse platforms	Synthetic asset trading	Portfolio diversification, exposure to real-world financial assets	Investing in sUSD or sGold

5. FINANCIAL ACTIVITIES AND INNOVATION ENABLED BY DEFI

The integration of decentralized finance (DeFi) into the Metaverse facilitates a wide array of economic behaviors that not only replicate real-world financial functions but also enhance them with automation, transparency, and global accessibility. DeFi protocols allow users in virtual worlds to manage wealth, obtain credit, hedge risks, and even govern marketplaces—all without reliance on centralized financial institutions. These functions are especially critical in virtual environments where peer-to-peer value exchange and user ownership are foundational to the digital experience.

One of the most prominent use cases is virtual real estate transactions. Through smart contracts, the acquisition, transfer, leasing, and fractional ownership of tokenized land assets are executed automatically and securely. Decentraland and Sandbox use NFTs to represent unique land parcels, which can be traded, rented, or developed into income-generating spaces such as virtual galleries, stores, or event venues. DeFi enhances this market by providing liquidity, credit, and insurance solutions that mirror—and in some cases, surpass—the complexity of traditional real estate markets.

5.1 Expanded Financial Activities: Tokenization, Credit, and Liquidity

- **Token Swapping:** the foundation of fluid, user-owned economies in the Metaverse is the ability to exchange tokens freely and without intermediaries. Protocols like Uniswap enable decentralized token swaps via automated market makers (AMMs), which ensure constant liquidity based on pool dynamics rather than order books. This mechanism is especially vital in virtual economies where native tokens like MANA (Decentraland) or SAND (Sandbox) need to be exchanged for other assets—be it stablecoins, governance tokens, or game-specific currencies. Token swapping not only enhances capital mobility but also allows users to hedge against price volatility, convert rewards into spendable assets, or invest across multiple virtual projects.
- **Borrowing and Lending:** access to credit is a crucial enabler of capital formation in virtual worlds. Platforms like Aave and Compound allow users to deposit crypto assets—including tokenized virtual land—as collateral and borrow against them. This enables landowners or developers to unlock liquidity from otherwise idle digital assets to finance business expansion, event hosting, or additional asset purchases. On the supply side, lenders earn interest by providing liquidity to the ecosystem, making this an avenue for passive income generation. The risk-managed, overcollateralized model used by most DeFi lending platforms adds a layer of security to these financial activities, fostering sustainable credit systems in virtual environments.
- **Staking and Yield Farming**: token staking and yield farming are mechanisms that reward users for committing capital to DeFi protocols. In the Metaverse, staking not only provides returns but also often grants governance rights, allowing users to vote on platform upgrades, funding decisions, and economic policies. Yield farming strategies—where users move capital between liquidity pools to optimize returns—create arbitrage opportunities and contribute to the overall liquidity and health of Metaverse economies. These activities reflect a shift from passive participation to financially incentivized engagement, transforming users into investors and ecosystem contributors.

- **Insurance**: With the growing financialization of the Metaverse, risk mitigation tools are essential. DeFi insurance protocols like Nexus Mutual or InsurAce offer coverage for smart contract exploits, protocol failures, and asset theft. In virtual real estate markets, users may ensure their land NFTs or protect transactions involving high-value digital assets. By distributing risk across decentralized capital pools, these insurance platforms provide a crucial layer of trust and confidence—a necessary precondition for mainstream adoption and investment.
- Collectively, these financial activities demonstrate how DeFi not only replicates real-world financial infrastructure in the Metaverse but also enhances it with programmable, permissionless, and composable tools that empower users far beyond the capabilities of legacy systems.

5.2 Synthesis: Toward Decentralized Economic Systems

The fusion of DeFi and the Metaverse represents more than a technological innovation—it marks the emergence of a new financial paradigm. By embedding decentralized financial services into immersive and interactive platforms, virtual environments such as Decentraland and Sandbox are evolving into self-sustaining digital economies. These ecosystems are governed by their users, fueled by transparent protocols, and accessible to anyone with an internet connection.

This integration allows for unprecedented economic experimentation. For instance, users can build businesses, secure loans with virtual collateral, receive interest from digital assets, and participate in democratic governance—all without needing permission from banks, landlords, or corporate gatekeepers. The financial inclusion potential is immense, especially for those excluded from traditional finance due to geography, regulation, or social barriers.

Furthermore, the programmable nature of DeFi unlocks customized financial logic: payments can be automated, revenue can be split in real time among contributors, and investment strategies can be embedded into virtual assets. These innovations challenge long-held notions of banking, property, and value by making finance inherently digital, interoperable, and user-centric.

As both user adoption and technical infrastructure continue to evolve, the DeFi-Metaverse fusion is positioned to redefine how individuals and institutions engage with finance. It blurs the boundaries between play and profit, work and ownership, investment and identity. In doing so, it points to a future where virtual economies are not just simulations of the real world but full-fledged, decentralized financial systems in their own right—fluid, inclusive, and shaped directly by those who participate in them.

6. OPEN ISSUES AND CHALLENGES IN INTEGRATION

As the Metaverse increasingly integrates DeFi services, the combined system holds immense potential but also reveals critical structural and operational challenges. While platforms like Decentraland and Sandbox have laid the groundwork for decentralized virtual economies, issues such as scalability, security, and user adoption remain substantial roadblocks to widespread implementation and long-term success. To ensure that the fusion of DeFi and the Metaverse becomes not only sustainable but transformative, these challenges must be carefully examined and addressed with robust technical and community-driven solutions. The following sections detail each of these challenges along with their potential impacts and emerging solutions.

6.1 Scalability

One of the most pressing limitations of current blockchain infrastructures, particularly Ethereum, is scalability (Yang et al., 2022). With increasing user activity and transaction volumes, network congestion leads to higher gas fees and slower transaction processing times. This directly undermines the seamless user experience that platforms like Decentraland and Sandbox aim to deliver. The result is a financial environment where high transaction costs discourage participation in activities like asset trading, lending, and staking.

To address this issue, Layer 2 scaling solutions have emerged as a promising alternative. Technologies like zk-Rollups and Optimistic Rollups process transactions off-chain while preserving the security of the main Ethereum network. Zero-knowledge rollups use cryptographic proofs to bundle transactions, reducing on-chain data requirements and lowering costs without sacrificing security. Optimistic Rollups assume transaction validity by default and perform dispute resolution only when fraud is suspected. Both techniques significantly enhance throughput and reduce gas fees, making DeFi applications more accessible and efficient in virtual worlds. For instance, if Decentraland and Sandbox implement zk-Rollups, users could trade NFTs, participate in lending, or swap tokens without incurring prohibitive costs or delays, thereby fueling more frequent and fluid economic activity.

6.2 Security

Security is another core concern. DeFi protocols are often targets of sophisticated cyberattacks, smart contract exploits, and phishing schemes. These vulnerabilities may arise from flawed code, insufficient testing, or systemic weaknesses in the protocol architecture. When breaches occur, they not only result in direct financial losses but also damage user confidence and tarnish the reputation of the platforms involved.

To mitigate such risks, platforms are adopting a range of security-enhancing measures. Regular and rigorous smart contract audits conducted by third-party security firms help identify and rectify vulnerabilities before deployment. Bug bounty programs incentivize ethical hackers to report flaws, contributing to proactive defense mechanisms. Additionally, offering insurance policies can provide users with compensation in case of losses due to technical failures or breaches. Educating users about safe practices, such as using hardware wallets and enabling two-factor authentication, further strengthens the security culture. If Decentraland and Sandbox were to institutionalize these practices—particularly ongoing audits and bug bounties—they could significantly bolster their resilience against attacks, increasing user trust and encouraging broader participation in DeFi services.

6.3 User Adoption

While technological advancements continue to drive DeFi's growth, user adoption remains a critical challenge. Many DeFi applications are complex, requiring users to understand digital wallets, private keys, smart contracts, and tokenomics. This steep learning curve can be intimidating for newcomers, especially those unfamiliar with blockchain technologies.

To make DeFi more approachable, developers must prioritize user-centric design. Simplifying user interfaces with intuitive layouts and guided transaction flows can significantly reduce onboarding friction. Educational resources, including step-by-step tutorials, FAQs, and webinars, can demystify complex concepts and empower users to engage confidently with DeFi platforms. Customer support services, such as live chat and community forums, provide additional layers of assistance. Moreover, incentive schemes—like airdrops, bonus tokens, or staking rewards—can motivate users to experiment with and eventually adopt DeFi tools. By enhancing interface usability and providing comprehensive support, Decentraland and Sandbox can increase adoption rates and build a more inclusive financial ecosystem. These improvements not only support platform growth but also encourage the formation of vibrant, self-sustaining virtual economies.

In conclusion, overcoming the challenges of scalability, security, and user adoption is essential for the successful integration of DeFi in the Metaverse. Through innovative technological solutions and a strong focus on user experience, platforms can unlock new dimensions of financial interaction and establish decentralized virtual economies as legitimate and lasting financial systems.

6.4 Regulatory Uncertainty

As DeFi and the Metaverse evolve into integral components of the digital economy, a major challenge that persists is regulatory uncertainty. This issue arises from the lack of clear, harmonized legal frameworks that govern decentralized financial activities and virtual environments. The global regulatory landscape is fragmented, with differing interpretations and enforcement standards across jurisdictions. For developers and users alike, this inconsistency creates a cloud of legal ambiguity, making it difficult to determine compliance obligations and increasing the risk of inadvertent violations (Gunay et al., 2024).

The impact of such uncertainty is substantial. It can stifle innovation, discourage institutional and retail investment, and delay the adoption of DeFi in Metaverse platforms. Stakeholders—ranging from developers to users and investors—may be reluctant to engage with systems that could face future legal challenges or retroactive enforcement. This hesitation can slow the momentum of platform development and restrict the expansion of vibrant digital economies.

To address these concerns, several proactive strategies can be implemented. First, platforms should engage in regulation-related activities by participating in public consultations, regulatory sandboxes, and policy advisory groups. Collaborating with regulatory bodies ensures that the unique characteristics of decentralized platforms are considered in policy design, promoting fair and functional frameworks that do not inhibit growth.

Second, ensuring compliance with existing legal requirements, particularly those concerning Know-Your-Customer (KYC) and Anti-Money Laundering (AML) obligations, can foster trust and reduce the likelihood of punitive action. While full decentralization may conflict with traditional compliance measures, hybrid solutions such as decentralized identity systems or selective on-chain verification tools may offer a workable balance.

Third, industry-wide self-regulation is a powerful tool to establish credibility and promote responsible development. By setting standards for transparency, user protection, and cybersecurity, the DeFi community can demonstrate its commitment to safeguarding users and minimizing systemic risk. These voluntary standards can also serve as a blueprint for eventual statutory regulation.

Lastly, having in-house or external legal counsel specializing in fintech and blockchain law is crucial. These experts can offer strategic guidance on compliance, help navigate evolving rules, and mitigate legal exposure. By integrating legal expertise into project development, teams can anticipate and adapt to regulatory changes more effectively.

For example, platforms such as Decentraland and Sandbox can build strategic partnerships with legal advisors and regulatory agencies to foster mutually beneficial policies. They can implement robust compliance protocols and participate in global dialogue to advocate for clear, innovation-friendly legislation. Doing so not only protects their ecosystems but also enhances user and investor confidence.

Regulatory uncertainty remains one of the most complex and pressing barriers to the integration of DeFi within the Metaverse. However, through proactive engagement, compliance innovation, self-regulatory efforts, and expert legal guidance, platforms can navigate this evolving landscape. Resolving these regulatory ambiguities will be essential for unlocking the full potential of decentralized virtual economies and ensuring their sustainable development (Dubey et al., 2022).

7. THE TRENDS AND ECONOMIC IMPACTS

Building on the foundational discussion of regulatory uncertainty and its impact on platform development and user trust, it is also important to evaluate how DeFi integration is transforming the broader Metaverse economy. The fusion of decentralized finance with virtual environments is not only reshaping platform governance and compliance strategies but also giving rise to dynamic economic systems. These systems are characterized by increased user interaction, evolving asset valuation models, and new modes of digital participation. The following sections explore these financial impacts in depth, illustrating how DeFi serves as a catalyst for virtual economic expansion, liquidity enhancement, and demographic engagement.

7.1 Growth of Virtual Economies

The integration of DeFi into the Metaverse has catalyzed significant economic growth, with platforms like Decentraland and Sandbox exhibiting robust performance indicators. These platforms have seen expanded lending, borrowing, and staking functionalities, contributing to increased transaction volumes and enhanced user engagement (Ding et al., 2023). The economic data underscores this growth: over four quarters, Decentraland's virtual economy expanded by 30%, while Sandbox's increased by 25%. This was paralleled by a surge in user activity—Decentraland's user engagement rose by 40%, and Sandbox followed closely with a 35% increase. Asset valuations also improved, with Decentraland and Sandbox reporting asset value increases of 20% and 18% respectively by the end of Q4.

Figure 1 and Figure 2 illustrate these quarterly trends in economic development, user engagement, and asset valuation, highlighting the transformative role of DeFi integration within these virtual ecosystems. These graphical insights demonstrate that as DeFi functionalities grow more sophisticated and accessible, user activity and virtual asset appreciation follow suit.

Figure 1. DeFi Integration's Effect on Metaverse Platforms

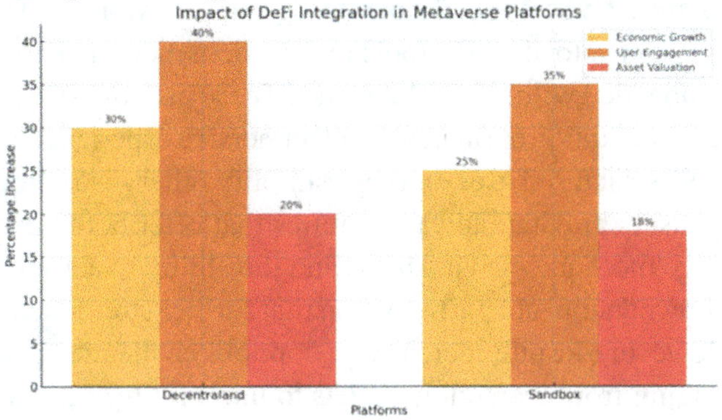

Figure 2. Quarterly Trends in Asset Valuation, User Engagement, and Economic Impact

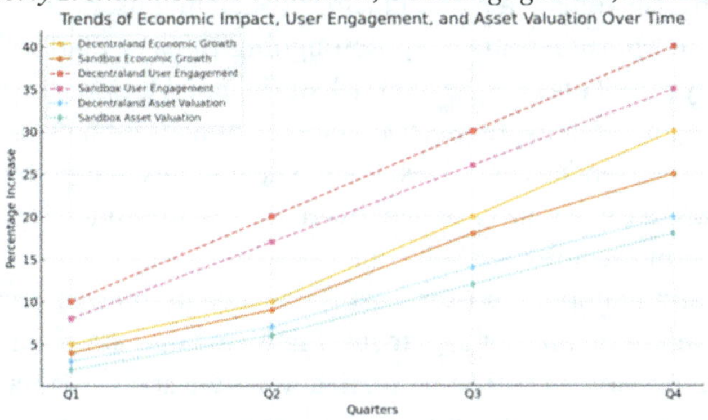

The presence of DeFi protocols has also significantly improved the financial utility and liquidity of virtual assets. NFTs and parcels of virtual land are now more than digital collectibles—they can be collateralized to access liquidity, borrow tokens, or earn yield. This financialization enhances their perceived value and encourages broader participation. Protocols such as Uniswap and Aave facilitate these processes, offering frictionless transactions and robust liquidity pools, thereby streamlining asset tradability.

Increased access to DeFi services has, in turn, stimulated user participation within Metaverse platforms. Users are now more engaged, driven by the prospect of financial returns on their digital holdings. Features like staking and lending not only provide passive income opportunities but also increase the incentive for users to remain active within the platforms (Vidal-Tomás, 2023). This deeper engagement feeds back into the growth loop of the Metaverse economy.

A notable demographic trend is the predominance of users aged 18 to 34—individuals who are tech-savvy and open to digital innovations. Their familiarity with blockchain and cryptocurrency tools makes them more inclined to adopt DeFi functionalities embedded within the Metaverse. These users tend to prefer platforms that offer seamless integration of financial and immersive experiences, where intuitive interfaces and well-structured user journeys simplify otherwise complex processes.

Behaviorally, users gravitate toward features that offer both empowerment and utility. Governance mechanisms via DAOs and the ability to earn interest on assets create a sense of ownership and participation that further strengthens user-platform relationships. However, despite increasing adoption, challenges persist. Technical complexity—ranging from managing wallets to interpreting smart contracts—still hinders broader adoption. To mitigate these issues, platforms must focus on user education, offering comprehensive tutorials, and streamlining onboarding processes. Providing robust customer support and transparent communication channels can also bridge the gap for less experienced users (Kara, 2023).

Security concerns remain a pivotal factor influencing user trust. Smart contract vulnerabilities and phishing attacks pose ongoing threats. Platforms that neglect rigorous security protocols face the dual risk of financial loss and reputational damage. As a mitigation strategy, regular audits and collaborations with cybersecurity firms are becoming standard practices. Insurance policies that protect against asset loss and fraud add a further layer of user assurance, while education campaigns are crucial in promoting secure user behavior.

Rebuilding and maintaining user trust relies heavily on transparent communication and active community engagement. Platforms that are open about security incidents and responsive in their communication—via social media or community forums—tend to recover more quickly from breaches. Promoting practices such as Multi-Factor Authentication (MFA) and offering real-time updates can further strengthen user confidence.

On the regulatory front, the absence of universally accepted definitions for digital assets presents compliance challenges. Requirements such as Know Your Customer (KYC) and Anti-Money Laundering (AML) compliance are difficult to enforce in decentralized systems, leading to tension between user privacy and regulatory oversight. In response, industry leaders are proactively engaging regulators, participating in public consultations, and adopting voluntary standards. Codes of conduct and third-party certifications are being developed to demonstrate good-faith efforts at compliance.

The overarching goal is to balance innovation with compliance. Regulatory sandboxes offer one possible path, allowing platforms to test new technologies in controlled environments. Furthermore, international collaboration on regulatory frameworks can harmonize cross-border operations and prevent arbitrage, ensuring that global users and developers operate under coherent guidelines.

Overall, the integration of DeFi into the Metaverse has opened new frontiers for digital finance, driving asset liquidity, economic activity, and user engagement. While technical, security, and regulatory challenges remain, targeted interventions—ranging from user-centric design to proactive regulation—can unlock the full potential of decentralized finance within virtual environments. Addressing these challenges is not only essential for the maturation of the Metaverse economy but also for ensuring its long-term sustainability and resilience.

8. OPPORTUNITIES

The integration of Decentralized Finance (DeFi) into the Metaverse introduces a series of transformative opportunities that redefine digital asset management, financial accessibility, and economic innovation. One of the most impactful benefits lies in the establishment of decentralized ownership and control. Unlike traditional financial systems that depend on centralized intermediaries, DeFi allows users to retain direct control over their digital assets. Through smart contracts and decentralized wallets, individuals can manage, transfer, and secure their holdings autonomously. This architecture enhances transparency, reduces intermediary costs, and protects users from centralized points of failure or manipulation, resulting in a more resilient financial environment (Ghosh et al., 2024).

Another compelling advancement is the democratization of finance. DeFi removes traditional socioeconomic and geographic barriers, offering anyone with internet access the ability to engage in financial activities. This inclusivity leads to a more diverse and vibrant economic ecosystem where users from varied backgrounds contribute to innovation. Moreover, as users are encouraged to participate in governance and platform development, a user-driven feedback loop emerges, continuously refining and expanding the Metaverse's financial infrastructure.

Innovation and interoperability are also crucial aspects of DeFi's contribution to the Metaverse. The modular design of DeFi protocols allows developers to experiment with new financial instruments and services, fostering a culture of rapid innovation. Integration across multiple Metaverse platforms supports interoperability, enabling seamless asset transfers between virtual worlds and facilitating a unified user experience. These cross-platform capabilities strengthen collaboration among Metaverse projects, creating an interconnected digital economy that leverages the unique strengths of each ecosystem (Akkus et al., 2022).

Furthermore, DeFi plays a vital role in promoting financial inclusion. By eliminating the need for traditional banking infrastructure, DeFi provides underbanked and unbanked populations with access to global financial markets. This accessibility empowers individuals in marginalized regions to engage in wealth-building strategies such as staking, yield farming, and decentralized trading. These mechanisms not only allow users to generate passive income but also contribute to broader economic participation and resilience.

Overall, the convergence of DeFi and the Metaverse holds immense potential to foster an innovative, inclusive, and equitable digital economy. As the ecosystem evolves, it is poised to reshape financial interactions and unlock unprecedented opportunities for economic engagement and empowerment. To realize this vision, it remains critical to address foundational challenges such as scalability, security, and regulatory clarity—ensuring that the benefits of DeFi integration can be harnessed safely and sustainably across virtual environments (Frank & Rudolf, 2024).

9. CONCLUSION

The integration of Decentralized Finance (DeFi) into the Metaverse represents a groundbreaking evolution in the digital economy. Throughout this chapter, we have examined how DeFi protocols are not merely add-ons to virtual worlds but are foundational in transforming them into fully functional, autonomous financial ecosystems. Platforms like Decentraland and Sandbox demonstrate how decentralized technologies empower users to own, trade, and monetize digital assets without relying on intermediaries. By embedding lending, borrowing, staking, and governance functionalities directly into the architecture of the Metaverse, DeFi has accelerated economic activity, increased asset liquidity, and strengthened user engagement.

Our analysis began by reviewing the technological and conceptual frameworks underlying this integration. The Metaverse, as a digitally immersive environment, finds natural synergy with DeFi, whose transparent and programmable infrastructure enhances user control and trust. In particular, the deployment of smart contracts, NFTs, and DAOs has enabled new forms of ownership and community-led governance, allowing virtual economies to become more inclusive and participatory. Users are no longer passive consumers but active stakeholders in the platforms they inhabit.

Despite its promise, the convergence of DeFi and the Metaverse is not without challenges. Scalability remains a key issue, especially on networks like Ethereum, where congestion and high gas fees inhibit broader adoption. Layer 2 solutions such as zk-Rollups and Optimistic Rollups offer practical improvements by increasing transaction throughput and lowering costs, yet their implementation across Metaverse platforms is still emerging. Security is another critical concern; vulnerabilities in smart contracts and exposure to cyber threats pose significant risks to user trust. These threats must be mitigated through rigorous audits, bug bounty programs, and user education initiatives. Moreover, the complexity of DeFi tools continues to deter non-technical users. Simplifying interfaces, providing comprehensive onboarding materials, and offering real-time support will be essential to lowering barriers to entry.

Regulatory uncertainty presents perhaps the most systemic challenge. Without clear legal frameworks, platforms risk non-compliance, while users face ambiguity around their rights and responsibilities. Jurisdictional fragmentation adds another layer of complexity, making cross-border operation difficult. However, collaboration with regulators, development of industry-wide best practices, and legal consultation can help platforms navigate these uncertain waters. As case studies like Decentraland and Sandbox show, proactive engagement with governance bodies and adoption of KYC/AML measures can support long-term viability.

Yet the opportunities remain vast. The decentralized architecture of DeFi ensures user autonomy, reduces transaction costs, and minimizes systemic risk associated with centralization. By opening access to financial services across socio-economic and geographic boundaries, DeFi contributes to a more inclusive digital economy. Its composable and interoperable nature fosters continual innovation, allowing developers to build financial products tailored for dynamic virtual environments. As financial tools become embedded in the fabric of the Metaverse, individuals from underbanked regions or marginalized communities can participate in economic activities previously beyond their reach.

Looking ahead, several areas warrant deeper academic inquiry. The first is the behavioral dimension of financial activity in virtual spaces: how users respond to incentives, engage in governance, and manage risk in immersive environments remains underexplored. Second, there is a pressing need for empirical studies on the performance and stability of DeFi-powered Metaverse economies, especially as user bases scale. Third, regulatory analysis should focus on harmonizing digital asset definitions and developing transnational standards to facilitate compliance and innovation. Lastly, technological research must continue refining interoperability protocols and security models to sustain trust and usability.

In sum, the intersection of DeFi and the Metaverse is redefining how people interact with money, ownership, and digital identity. This fusion offers not just an alternative financial model, but a transformative vision for what digital life can be: open, participatory, and economically empowering. The future of this convergence depends on how effectively its challenges are addressed and how inclusively its opportunities are realized. As we stand at the frontier of this digital reimagination, sustained research, thoughtful regulation, and human-centered design will be critical in shaping a Metaverse that is not only technologically advanced but also economically just and socially enriching.

REFERENCES

Akkus, H. T., Gursoy, S., Dogan, M., & Demir, A. B. (2022). Metaverse and metaverse cryptocurrencies (meta coins): Bubbles or future. *Journal of Economics. Finance and Accounting*, *9*(1), 22–29. DOI: 10.17261/Pressacademia.2022.1542

Aysan, A. F., Gozgor, G., & Nanaeva, Z. (2024). Technological perspectives of Metaverse for financial service providers. *Technological Forecasting and Social Change*, *202*, 123323. DOI: 10.1016/j.techfore.2024.123323

Ball, M. (2020, Jan 13). *The Metaverse: What it is, where to find it, who will build it, and Fortnite*. MatthewBall.vc. https://www.matthewball.co/all/themetaverse

Banaeian Far, S., Imani Rad, A., & Rajabzadeh Asaar, M. (2023). Blockchain and its derived technologies shape the future generation of digital businesses: A focus on decentralized finance and the Metaverse. *Data Science and Management*, *6*(3), 183–197. DOI: 10.1016/j.dsm.2023.06.002

Cao, L. (2022). Decentralized AI: Edge Intelligence and Smart Blockchain, Metaverse, Web3, and DeSci. *IEEE Intelligent Systems*, *37*(3), 6–19. DOI: 10.1109/MIS.2022.3181504

Chao, C.-H., Ting, I.-H., Tseng, Y.-J., Wang, B.-W., Wang, S.-H., & Wang, Y.-Q. (2022). The study of DeFi in virtual community and financial supervision. In *Proceedings of the 9th Multidisciplinary International Social Networks Conference (MISNC '22)* (pp. 74–80). Association for Computing Machinery. https://doi.org/ DOI: 10.1145/3561278.3561297

Cheng, S. (2023). Metaverse. In *Metaverse: Concept, Content and Context* (pp. 1–23). Springer Nature Switzerland., DOI: 10.1007/978-3-031-24359-2_1

Ding, W., Li, J., Qin, R., Kozma, R., & Wang, F.-Y. (2023). A New Architecture and Mechanism for Decentralized Science MetaMarkets. *IEEE Transactions on Systems, Man, and Cybernetics. Systems*, *53*(9), 5321–5330. DOI: 10.1109/TSMC.2023.3266223

Dua, G. K. (2024). Blockchain and its derived technologies. In Kumar, V. (Ed.), *Applications, challenges, and opportunities of blockchain technology in banking and finance* (pp. 41–55). IGI Global., DOI: 10.4018/979-8-3693-6660-8.ch004

Dubey, V., Mokashi, A., Pradhan, R., Gupta, P., & Walimbe, R. (2022). Metaverse and banking industry – 2023: The year of Metaverse adoption. *Technium*, *4*(10), 62–73. DOI: 10.47577/technium.v4i10.7774

Frank, P., & Rudolf, M. (2024). Is the Metaverse Dead? Insights from Financial Bubble Analysis. *FinTech*, *3*(2), 302–323. DOI: 10.3390/fintech3020017

Ghosh, A., Lavanya, , Hassija, V., Chamola, V., & El Saddik, A. (2024). A Survey on Decentralized Metaverse Using Blockchain and Web 3.0 Technologies, Applications, and More. *IEEE Access : Practical Innovations, Open Solutions*, *12*, 146915–146948. DOI: 10.1109/ACCESS.2024.3469193

Gunay, S., Sraieb, M. M., & Muhammed, S. (2024). Decrypting Metaverse crypto Market: A nonlinear analysis of investor sentiment. *International Review of Financial Analysis*, *96*, 103714. DOI: 10.1016/j.irfa.2024.103714

Hong, J. (2024). Prospect Analysis for Utilization of Virtual Assets using Blockchain Technology. *Journal of Information and Communication Convergence Engineering*, *22*(1), 64–69. DOI: 10.56977/jicce.2024.22.1.64

Huynh-The, T., Pham, Q.-V., Pham, X.-Q., Nguyen, T. T., Han, Z., & Kim, D.-S. (2023). Artificial intelligence for the metaverse: A survey. *Engineering Applications of Artificial Intelligence*, *117*, 105581. DOI: 10.1016/j.engappai.2022.105581

Kara, H. T. (2023). The relationship between blockchain applications in financial markets and Metaverse. In Paul, P. K., Choudhury, D., Bhuimali, A., & Goyal, A. (Eds.), *Handbook of research on cybersecurity issues and challenges for business and commerce* (pp. 285–304). Springer., DOI: 10.1007/978-981-99-4641-9_20

Kumar, S., Sureka, R., Lucey, B. M., Dowling, M., Vigne, S., & Lim, W. M. (2024). MetaMoney: Exploring the intersection of financial systems and virtual worlds. *Research in International Business and Finance*, *68*, 102195. DOI: 10.1016/j.ribaf.2023.102195

Maksymyuk, T., Gazda, J., Bugar, G., Gazda, V., Liyanage, M., & Dohler, M. (2022). Blockchain-Empowered Service Management for the Decentralized Metaverse of Things. *IEEE Access : Practical Innovations, Open Solutions*, *10*, 99025–99037. DOI: 10.1109/ACCESS.2022.3205739

Mystakidis, S. (2022). Metaverse. *Encyclopedia*, *2*(1), 486–497. DOI: 10.3390/encyclopedia2010031

Pandey, D., & Gilmour, P. (2024). Accounting meets metaverse: Navigating the intersection between the real and virtual worlds. *Journal of Financial Reporting and Accounting*, *22*(2), 211–226. DOI: 10.1108/JFRA-03-2023-0157

Pellegrini, C. (2024). Applicable law in the metaverse: A European international private law perspective. In Corrales, M., Fenwick, M., & Forgó, N. (Eds.), *Research handbook on the metaverse and law* (pp. 375–397). Edward Elgar Publishing. DOI: 10.4337/9781035324866.00033

Radanliev, P. (2024). The rise and fall of cryptocurrencies: Defining the economic and social values of blockchain technologies, assessing the opportunities, and defining the financial and cybersecurity risks of the Metaverse. *Financial Innovation, 10*(1), 1. DOI: 10.1186/s40854-023-00537-8

Remolina, N. (2024). DeFi and the metaverse: Legal and regulatory challenges of decentralization of financial services. In Chen, H. Y., Jenweeranon, P., & Alam, N. (Eds.), *Global perspectives in the metaverse* (pp. 223–251). Palgrave Macmillan., DOI: 10.1007/978-3-031-54802-4_11

Truong, V. T., Le, L., & Niyato, D. (2023). Blockchain Meets Metaverse and Digital Asset Management: A Comprehensive Survey. *IEEE Access : Practical Innovations, Open Solutions, 11*, 26258–26288. DOI: 10.1109/ACCESS.2023.3257029

Turi, A. N. (Ed.). (2023). *Financial Technologies and DeFi*. Springer International Publishing., DOI: 10.1007/978-3-031-17998-3

Vidal-Tomás, D. (2023). The illusion of the metaverse and meta-economy. *International Review of Financial Analysis, 86*, 102560. DOI: 10.1016/j.irfa.2023.102560

Wang, Y., Su, Z., Zhang, N., Xing, R., Liu, D., Luan, T. H., & Shen, X. (2023). A Survey on Metaverse: Fundamentals, Security, and Privacy. *IEEE Communications Surveys and Tutorials, 25*(1), 319–352. DOI: 10.1109/COMST.2022.3202047

Xu, J., Papangelis, K., Dunham, J., Goncalves, J., LaLone, N. J., Chamberlain, A., Lykourentzou, I., Vinella, F. L., & Schwartz, D. I. (2022). Metaverse: The vision for the future. In *Extended abstracts of the 2022 CHI conference on human factors in computing systems* (Paper No. LBW110). Association for Computing Machinery. DOI: 10.1145/3491101.3516399

Xu, M., Guo, Y., Hu, Q., Xiong, Z., Yu, D., & Cheng, X. (2023). A trustless architecture of blockchain-enabled metaverse. *High-Confidence Computing, 3*(1), 100088. DOI: 10.1016/j.hcc.2022.100088

Yang, Q., Zhao, Y., Huang, H., Xiong, Z., Kang, J., & Zheng, Z. (2022). Fusing Blockchain and AI With Metaverse: A Survey. *IEEE Open Journal of the Computer Society, 3*, 122–136. DOI: 10.1109/OJCS.2022.3188249

ADDITIONAL READINGS

Ante, L., & Fiedler, I. (2024). The new digital economy: How decentralized finance (DeFi) and non-fungible tokens (NFTs) are transforming value creation, ownership models, and economic systems. *Digital Business*, *5*(1), 100094. DOI: 10.1016/j.digbus.2024.100094

La Barbera, S. (2023). *Navigating the Virtual Frontier: The Convergence of Decentralized Finance and the Metaverse. Preprints*. DOI: 10.20944/preprints202307.1734.v1

NOTE

1 Corresponding Author: mr.goyal280904@gmail.com

Section 2
AI and Advanced Analytics in Finance

Chapter 5
Recent Developments in Financial Reinforcement Learning:
A Systematic Review

Haojun Chen
https://orcid.org/0000-0001-9168-9234
Guangzhou Huali College, China

Meihua Liu
https://orcid.org/0009-0001-7849-0180
Guangdong University of Foreign Studies, China

ABSTRACT

This paper reviews recent advancements in applying reinforcement learning (RL) to financial markets, highlighting key algorithms such as DQN, PPO, SAC, and A3C. It examines their use in trading equities, managing portfolios, executing trades, and making markets. We discuss both value-based and policy-based methods, as well as hybrid and emerging approaches like meta-RL. Real-world applications and case studies from institutions like JPMorgan and Man Group are included to illustrate practical adoption. The paper also addresses challenges such as overfitting, non-stationarity, and interpretability, offering insights into the future of RL in finance.

1. INTRODUCTION

Reinforcement Learning (RL) has rapidly gained traction in quantitative finance over the past five years, driven by advances in deep learning and successes in gaming AI (Mnih et al., 2015; Silver et al., 2017). Unlike traditional model-based

DOI: 10.4018/979-8-3373-2838-6.ch005

approaches, RL provides a flexible, data-driven framework for sequential decision-making under uncertainty-a natural fit for trading and investment tasks where agents must continually act on new market information (Dixon et al., 2020). This review surveys recent academic and industry developments in applying RL to financial markets, spanning equities, cryptocurrencies, foreign exchange, derivatives, and more. We discuss common RL algorithms and system architectures employed, highlight theoretical models and empirical findings, and identify major innovations, trends, and challenges. Our focus is on literature from roughly the last five years, during which there has been an explosion of research exploring RL-based trading strategies. The goal is to provide a comprehensive yet accessible overview of how RL techniques have been used to tackle various financial trading problems, what successes have been achieved, and what obstacles remain before RL sees broader real-world adoption in finance.

Financial markets present a complex and dynamic environment for RL agents. Markets are multi-agent systems with high volatility, heavy tails, and non-stationary behavior (Cont, 2001). Traditional quantitative strategies often rely on simplifying assumptions or forecast-and-act pipelines, which can be suboptimal when market regimes shift (Hambly et al., 2023). RL offers the promise of adaptive decision-making: agents that continuously learn from market feedback to optimize a reward objective through trial-and-error interactions (Charpentier et al., 2021; Liu et al., 2020). Over the last five years, researchers have applied RL to a wide array of financial tasks-from stock trading and portfolio management to derivative hedging, market making, order execution, and even robo-advisory. Early proofs-of-concept have demonstrated that RL-based strategies can, in some cases, outperform static or heuristic strategies on a risk-adjusted basis (Yang & Malik, 2024; Jiang et al., 2017).

However, deploying RL in live financial markets remains challenging. Issues such as limited and noisy training data, unstable learning, and the difficulty of ensuring robust performance under changing market conditions have tempered enthusiasm (Bacry et al., 2013; Spooner & Savani, 2020). This review will examine these challenges in depth and discuss how recent research attempts to address them. We will also note the contribution of open-source platforms and industry efforts in advancing RL for trading-including libraries such as FinRL and trading competitions that provide standardized environments and benchmarks for evaluation (Liu et al., 2020). The remainder of the paper is organized as follows. We first give a brief background on key RL algorithms used in trading applications. We then survey applications by asset class and domain: equities and stocks, cryptocurrencies, forex, derivatives/hedging, market making, optimal trade execution, portfolio management, and wealth management (robo-advising). Within each, we highlight representative studies, their methodologies, and main findings. Finally, we discuss overarching trends such as the move toward multi-agent systems and combining RL with other AI techniques, and we outline the major challenges and future directions for this field.

2. KEY REINFORCEMENT LEARNING ALGORITHMS FOR TRADING

To better appreciate the innovation that reinforcement learning (RL) introduces to financial modeling, it is useful to briefly contrast RL with traditional approaches. Classical financial models, such as mean-variance optimization (Markowitz, 1952), Black–Scholes option pricing (Black & Scholes, 1973), and the Almgren–Chriss model for trade execution (Almgren & Chriss, 2000), typically rely on closed-form solutions and strong assumptions about market behavior (e.g., normality, stationarity, and linearity). These models are mathematically elegant but often brittle when faced with regime shifts, behavioral anomalies, or unstructured data. In contrast, RL models are adaptive, data-driven, and capable of handling nonlinear payoffs, delayed rewards, and partially observable environments. For instance, where the Black–Scholes model assumes continuous trading and frictionless markets, RL agents can learn hedging strategies that account for transaction costs, slippage, and jump risk. Likewise, RL can generalize classical allocation strategies by optimizing over multiple periods and incorporating risk preferences directly into reward functions. Figure 1 illustrates this transition by mapping traditional models onto their RL-enhanced counterparts across key domains like portfolio optimization, trade execution, and options hedging.

Figure 1. Mapping of traditional financial models to their reinforcement learning (RL)

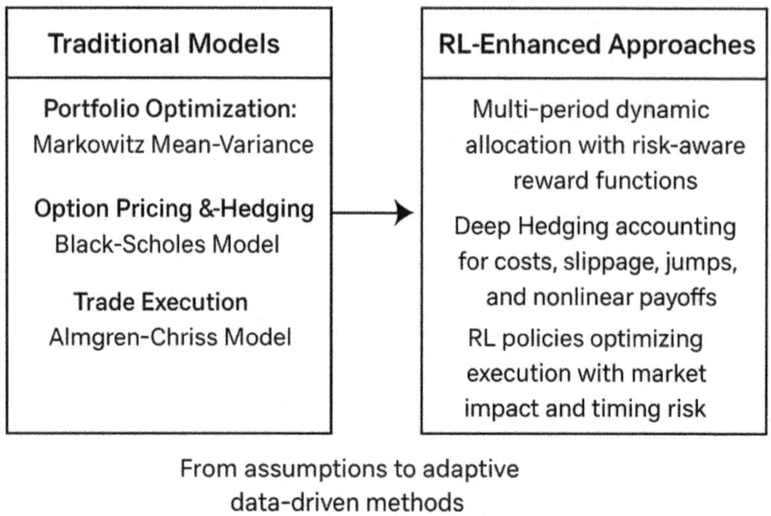

Recent advancements in reinforcement learning (RL) have led to widespread adoption of deep RL algorithms in financial applications. These algorithms are typically classified into value-based methods, policy-gradient (or policy-based) methods, actor–critic frameworks, and various hybrid approaches (Hambly et al., 2023; Bai et al., 2025). Below we summarize several leading RL algorithms-particularly DQN, PPO, A3C, and SAC-and their applications in trading contexts.

2.1 Deep Q-Network (DQN) and Value-Based Methods

Value-based RL methods focus on learning a Q-function, which estimates the value of taking a particular action in a given state. The Deep Q-Network (DQN) algorithm leverages deep neural networks to approximate this function which is suitable for high-dimensional financial environments (Mnih et al., 2015). DQN and its variants, such as Double DQN and Dueling DQN, have become popular in discrete trading tasks such as deciding when to buy, sell, or hold assets. For example, Jiang and Liang (2017) demonstrated that Deep Q-Learning to trading decisions and demonstrates that RL-based agents can outperform traditional strategies by dynamically adjusting portfolio allocations based on market states. While they have demonstrated strong performance in capturing short-term patterns, their success can be sensitive to the design of reward functions and training stability (Hambly et al., 2023). Enhancements such as Prioritized Experience Replay and ensemble learning help mitigate these issues. For instance, Wang and Klabjan (2024) propose an ensemble approach to improve the generalization performance of trading strategies trained by deep reinforcement learning algorithms in the highly stochastic environment of intraday cryptocurrency portfolio trading. Overall, value-based RL remains foundational for systems with discrete decision-making tasks, though careful hyperparameter tuning is often required to address data noise and non-stationarity.

2.2 Policy-Gradient and Actor–Critic Methods (PPO, A3C, DDPG, SAC)

Policy-gradient methods directly optimize a parameterized policy by ascending the expected reward gradient. These techniques are well-suited for continuous action spaces and the incorporation of risk-sensitive objectives. Proximal Policy Optimization (PPO), an on-policy actor–critic method known for its stability, has become a preferred choice in financial research (Schulman et al., 2017). Kim et al. (2024), for example, used PPO to design optimal execution strategies that adapt to intraday volume constraints.

In contrast, off-policy algorithms such as Deep Deterministic Policy Gradient (DDPG) and its successor TD3 are often used in portfolio allocation problems where actions are continuous (Lillicrap et al., 2015; Fujimoto et al., 2018). These models excel in multi-asset settings and are particularly effective when optimizing differentiable objectives like the Sharpe ratio (Hambly et al., 2023). A3C (Asynchronous Advantage Actor–Critic) also played a pioneering role in financial simulations by accelerating training through parallel agents, although more sample-efficient models have since replaced it. Soft Actor–Critic (SAC), an entropy-regularized off-policy actor–critic algorithm, has gained attention for its robustness and exploration capabilities. Lalor and Swishchuk (2025) presents a deep reinforcement learning framework utilizing the SAC algorithm for optimal market-making. Their approach addresses the complexities of high-frequency trading environments, including continuous pricing decisions and non-Markovian dynamics. The authors demonstrate that SAC effectively handles the challenges inherent in limit order book settings, such as inventory risk and adverse selection.

2.3 Other and Hybrid Approaches

Beyond standard models, researchers have revisited Recurrent Reinforcement Learning (RRL), first proposed by Moody and Saffell (2001) in the 1990s. Deng et al. (2016) and Zou et al. (2024) expanded this idea using LSTM-based agents to handle sequential patterns in financial time series. Zou et al. (2024) showed that their cascaded LSTM-RL agent outperformed benchmarks in both U.S. and Chinese markets, particularly excelling in the latter due to its relative inefficiency.

Hybrid action-space RL methods have also been introduced to address the limitations of discrete or continuous-only actions. For example, Pan et al. (2022) proposed a two-stage decision structure in which a high-level agent selects a continuous price range and a low-level agent refines this to a discrete price point, considering tick size constraints. Their method significantly improved execution stability over traditional single-scale agents. Other innovations include contextual bandit models for one-step portfolio choices, model-based RL that learns a transition model of the market, and meta-RL techniques that quickly adapt to new trading environments (Pippas et al., 2025). Although these methods are still emerging, they offer promising avenues for increasing adaptability and robustness in RL applications.

3. RL APPLICATIONS IN EQUITY MARKETS

Equity trading has served as one of the most common testbeds for RL applications in finance. In such tasks, an RL agent typically monitors indicators like prices, technical patterns, or even sentiment scores to decide trading actions such as buying, selling, or reallocating capital (Jiang & Liang, 2017). Early studies using DQN or PPO showed that RL-based strategies could outperform benchmarks such as moving averages or momentum-based heuristics (Fischer, 2018).

For instance, Zhang et al. (2020) demonstrated that a Deep Q-Network (DQN) agent could dynamically adapt to market fluctuations, outperforming static moving-average strategies. Fischer (2018) further emphasized that reinforcement learning (RL) agents are capable of uncovering nonlinear patterns often missed by traditional technical analysis. A significant challenge in this domain is the low signal-to-noise ratio inherent in stock price movements. To mitigate this, researchers have employed deep learning architectures such as Long Short-Term Memory (LSTM) networks and Convolutional Neural Networks (CNNs) to extract meaningful features from raw time-series data (Mehtab and Sen, 2020). Notably, Liu et al. (2020) introduced FinRL, an open-source deep reinforcement learning library designed for automated stock trading. FinRL integrates state-of-the-art DRL algorithms with financial data processing. It provides a comprehensive framework that facilitates the development and evaluation of trading strategies, thereby addressing the challenges of data noise and model reproducibility.

RL agents have been developed using both discrete actions and continuous allocations. PPO and DDPG are particularly popular for modeling continuous actions. For instance, Liang et al. (2018) implement continuous reinforcement learning algorithms, including Deep Deterministic Policy Gradient (DDPG) and Proximal

Policy Optimization (PPO), in the context of portfolio management. They highlight the applicability of these algorithms in financial markets, noting their potential in handling continuous action spaces inherent in trading strategies.

Empirical results in reinforcement learning (RL) applications to financial trading are mixed but generally encouraging. Lim et al. (2020) introduced Deep Momentum Networks, a hybrid approach that integrates deep learning-based trading rules into the volatility scaling framework of time series momentum strategies. Their model simultaneously learns trend estimation and position sizing in a data-driven manner, directly optimizing the Sharpe ratio. Back-testing on a portfolio of 88 continuous futures contracts demonstrated that the Sharpe-optimized Long Short-Term Memory (LSTM) network improved traditional methods by more than two times in the absence of transaction costs and continued to outperform when considering transaction costs up to 2–3 basis points. However, overfitting remains a significant concern in RL applications. Zhang et al. (2018) conducted a systematic study revealing that standard RL agents could overfit in various ways. They found that commonly used techniques in RL that add stochasticity do not necessarily prevent or detect overfitting. In particular, the same agents and learning algorithms could have drastically different test performance, even when all of them achieve optimal rewards during training. These observations call for more principled and careful evaluation protocols in RL. To mitigate overfitting, techniques such as rolling retraining, online learning, and regime-switching models have been introduced. Notably, Zou et al. (2024) proposed a Deep Reinforcement Learning (DRL)-based stock trading system using cascaded LSTM networks. Their model first uses LSTM to extract time-series features from daily stock data, which are then fed to the agent for training. Experiments conducted on the Dow Jones Industrial Average (DJI) in the U.S. market and SSE50 in the Chinese stock market showed that their model outperformed previous baseline models in terms of cumulative returns and Sharpe ratio. The advantage was more significant in the Chinese stock market, an emerging market, indicating that the proposed method is a promising way to build an automated stock trading system. These findings suggest that while RL models hold promise for financial trading, especially in less efficient markets with exploitable patterns, careful design and evaluation are crucial to ensure robust performance.

In industry, RL has transitioned from academic experimentation to real-world application in the financial industry. Leading investment firms are now employing RL to optimize various aspects of trading, particularly in execution and market adaptation tasks. For instance, Man Group's AHL division applies RL techniques to determine the most efficient execution routes by dynamically adapting to market microstructure conditions (Man Group, 2024). J.P. Morgan has integrated RL into proprietary systems for optimizing order execution and minimizing transaction costs in volatile markets (J.P. Morgan, 2023). Similarly, Goldman Sachs uses RL-powered algorithms to refine high-frequency trading strategies, enabling their models to continuously learn from data and improve execution efficiency (Redress Compliance, 2023). Citadel Securities has adopted RL for its extensive market-making operations, where agents assist in rapid pricing and trading decisions across equities and options (Citadel Securities, 2024). Meanwhile, Two Sigma employs RL for regime modeling, allowing their systems to detect and adapt to shifting market patterns in real time (Two Sigma, 2024). These examples illustrate a clear trend: RL is becoming a vital component in the financial technology stack, especially in sub-domains requiring continuous learning and high-speed adaptation.

4. PORTFOLIO MANAGEMENT AND ASSET ALLOCATION

Portfolio management is a natural domain for RL, as it involves sequential decision-making under uncertainty. Unlike single-stock trading, portfolio RL agents must allocate capital across multiple assets, sometimes including a risk-free asset, to optimize objectives like cumulative return or risk-adjusted metrics (e.g., Sharpe ratio). Classical models, such as Markowitz's mean-variance optimization, require assumptions like quadratic utility and Gaussian returns, and are not easily extended to dynamic multi-period settings (Markowitz, 1952). RL offers a model-free alternative by learning allocation policies directly from data. Both value-based methods (e.g., Q-learning, DQN) and policy-based methods (e.g., DDPG, PPO) have been applied to portfolio optimization (Jiang & Liang, 2017; Liang et al., 2018). These agents typically consider state variables like asset returns, prices, time, and current holdings, and output a portfolio weight vector.

The reward function plays a central role in shaping the agent's strategy. Studies have shown that defining reward in terms of Sharpe ratio or differential Sharpe leads to more stable and risk-aware policies than using raw returns (Almahdi & Yang, 2017; Hambly et al., 2023). For instance, Jiang et al. (2017) used a policy-gradient method to manage a cryptocurrency portfolio and reported higher returns than equal-weight baselines. Liang et al. (2018) integrated Kelly criterion and mean-variance frameworks in an actor–critic RL setup and found their agent achieved superior Sortino ratios. Yang et al. (2018) proposed adversarial training to improve robustness: an adversarial agent perturbs data within realistic bounds, challenging the RL agent to learn policies resilient to regime shifts.

Hybrid frameworks have also emerged to address the challenges of long-horizon and partially observable financial environments. For instance, Park et al. (2019) developed a portfolio trading strategy using deep Q-learning within a Markov Decision Process (MDP) framework. Their approach effectively handled the combinatorial nature of discrete portfolio allocation decisions and outperformed benchmark strategies in back-testing. Similarly, Li et al. (2019) proposed an adaptive Deep Deterministic Policy Gradient (DDPG) method for stock portfolio optimization, integrating mechanisms for adjusting optimism or pessimism based on prediction errors. Their adaptive DDPG agent achieved higher investment returns and Sharpe ratios compared to baseline models. These studies demonstrate the growing sophistication of RL applications in dynamic portfolio management tasks, particularly when combining value-based and policy-based strategies for continuous or hybrid action spaces.

In addition, generative models, particularly Generative Adversarial Networks (GANs), have been integrated into reinforcement learning (RL) frameworks to simulate future return scenarios, enhancing the agent's ability to make informed decisions in financial markets. While Liang et al. (2018) explored adversarial training methods to improve the robustness of RL agents in portfolio management, other studies have focused on combining GANs with RL algorithms like Deep Deterministic Policy Gradient (DDPG) to improve performance. For instance, Yu et al. (2019) proposed a model-based deep reinforcement learning architecture that incorporates a GAN-based data augmentation module to generate synthetic market data, addressing the issue of limited historical data in financial markets. This separation of prediction (via GANs) and allocation (via RL) tasks reflects an emerging trend in RL-finance hybrids, aiming to enhance the stability and profitability of trading strategies.

Risk-sensitive approaches are gaining attention in reinforcement learning (RL), particularly for applications in finance where managing downside risk is crucial. Recent research has explored integrating Conditional Value-at-Risk (CVaR) constraints into RL frameworks to enhance risk management. For instance, Ying et al. (2022) proposed a CVaR-Proximal Policy Optimization (CPPO) algorithm that formalizes the risk-sensitive constrained optimization problem by maintaining CVaR under a specified threshold. Their approach demonstrated improved robustness against both observation and transition disturbances in continuous control tasks. Additionally, Yang et al. (2024) introduced the Risk-Aware Constrained Reinforcement Learning (RAC) algorithm, which decomposes trajectory-level constraints into state-level constraints using Lagrangian multipliers. This method allows for more granular control over risk, facilitating the development of policies that are both effective and compliant with specified risk thresholds. These advancements reflect a growing trend in RL research to incorporate risk-sensitive measures, making RL more applicable to domains like institutional asset management where capital preservation is paramount.

Overall, RL in portfolio management offers adaptability, flexibility, and performance advantages, accommodating transaction costs, diverse asset types, and multiple objectives. However, success in back-testing does not always guarantee robustness. To address this, researchers often benchmark RL agents against Constantly Rebalanced Portfolio (CRP) and buy-and-hold strategies. For instance, a study by

Zhang et al. (2019) demonstrated that a Deep Q-Network (DQN) agent dynamically adapted to market changes, outperforming static moving-average strategies and achieving superior Sharpe ratios.

Industry interest in reinforcement learning (RL) is gaining significant traction, particularly among leading asset management firms seeking innovative tools to enhance portfolio performance and risk management. BlackRock, for instance, has established a dedicated Artificial Intelligence Lab tasked with exploring machine learning applications across the investment lifecycle. While precise implementations are proprietary, reports suggest that BlackRock has investigated the use of deep RL models for tactical asset allocation-particularly to improve reaction speed to market shocks such as the 2020 COVID-19 crash (BlackRock, 2020). These RL systems aim to dynamically adjust asset exposures based on changing macroeconomic indicators, volatility regimes, or momentum patterns, surpassing the responsiveness of traditional rule-based systems. Moreover, industry case studies reveal similar explorations by firms such as JPMorgan and Goldman Sachs, who have incorporated RL for optimizing execution strategies and hedging decisions under uncertain conditions (Wilmott, 2021; Charpentier et al., 2021). The move toward RL reflects a broader industry shift toward adaptive, data-driven decision-making frameworks that move beyond static models, potentially offering superior in volatile or non-stationary environments.

5. REINFORCEMENT LEARNING IN CRYPTOCURRENCY TRADING

The emergence of cryptocurrencies-such as Bitcoin and Ethereum-has introduced a new, volatile asset class well-suited for reinforcement learning (RL) applications. Crypto markets operate continuously, 24/7, and are characterized by frequent regime shifts, reduced regulatory oversight, and higher inefficiencies compared to traditional financial markets. These attributes create a fertile testing ground for RL models, which excel in stochastic and adaptive environments. For instance, Pippas et al. (2025) highlight the suitability of RL in financial markets marked by complexity and inherent randomness, while studies have noted the inefficiency prevalent in cryptocurrency markets, making them ideal for testing adaptive trading strategies.

Time scale is a critical factor in cryptocurrency trading, particularly due to the high volatility and rapid market dynamics inherent in these markets. To effectively navigate such environments, reinforcement learning (RL) agents must operate at fine-grained temporal resolutions, often utilizing high-frequency data measured in seconds or even milliseconds. This necessitates the development of agents capable of making swift decisions and generalizing from limited data. In a notable study,

Otabek and Choi (2024) introduced a multi-level deep Q-network (M-DQN) framework designed for Bitcoin trading. Their approach integrates historical Bitcoin price data with Twitter sentiment analysis, enabling the agent to capture both quantitative and qualitative market signals. The M-DQN architecture comprises three modules: Trade-DQN, which focuses on historical price data; Predictive-DQN, which incorporates sentiment analysis; and Main-DQN, which synthesizes insights from the previous two modules to make final trading decisions. This multi-faceted strategy led to a significant improvement in trading performance, with the model achieving a 29.93% increase in investment value and a Sharpe Ratio exceeding 2.7, outperforming several state-of-the-art models. Additionally, Qin et al. (2024) proposed EarnHFT, an efficient hierarchical reinforcement learning framework tailored for high-frequency trading in cryptocurrency markets. EarnHFT addresses the challenges of long trading trajectories and market volatility by employing a three-stage hierarchical structure: a Q-teacher for enhancing training efficiency, a diverse pool of RL agents trained for different market trends, and a minute-level router that dynamically selects the most suitable agent based on current market conditions. This approach demonstrated superior performance across various market scenarios, significantly outperforming existing baselines in profitability and risk-adjusted returns

Furthermore, RL has been increasingly applied to pair trading strategies in the cryptocurrency market. Yang and Malik (2024) developed an RL-based pair trading system that utilized dynamic scaling and custom reward shaping to exploit price divergences between correlated crypto assets. Their approach demonstrated annualized returns ranging from 9.94% to 31.53%, outperforming traditional statistical arbitrage methods. In another study, researchers proposed a deep reinforcement learning framework for Bitcoin trading, integrating dueling double deep Q-learning networks, proximal policy optimization, and advantage actor-critic algorithms. This multi-agent approach aimed to optimize trading strategies in the highly volatile cryptocurrency market. Han et al. (2023) introduced CREDIT, a risk-aware recurrent reinforcement learning agent designed for pair trading. By incorporating bidirectional gated recurrent units and temporal attention mechanisms, CREDIT effectively captured long-term patterns in asset price movements, leading to improved trading performance and robustness in volatile market conditions

On another front, the FinRL-Crypto framework has significantly contributed to democratizing access to reinforcement learning-based cryptocurrency trading systems. Wang et al. (2025) developed open-source environments and hosted competitions, some of which incorporated LLM-generated sentiment signals. This novel combination-merging textual analysis with RL decision-making-represents a frontier in hybrid AI finance systems. Despite these promising results, researchers caution that many historical crypto inefficiencies may no longer exist. RL agents often exploit transient anomalies; thus, continual learning and online adaptation have been emphasized (Pippas et al., 2025). Stop-losses and capital constraints are commonly built into RL systems to prevent catastrophic losses in highly volatile conditions. In practice, some crypto hedge funds already use RL to allocate across coins or execute large trades across fragmented exchanges. The growing popularity of the FinRL library among practitioners indicates that RL is becoming an integral part of the cryptocurrency trading toolkit.

6. RL IN FOREIGN EXCHANGE AND FIXED-INCOME MARKETS

Foreign exchange (FX) markets share some features with cryptocurrencies - high liquidity and continuous trading - but differ in volatility dynamics, efficiency, and macroeconomic influence. While reinforcement learning (RL) applications in FX have historically been less prevalent than in equities or crypto, they are gradually gaining traction. An early example is the work by Tsai and Wang (2019), who applied deep RL to trade currency pairs such as EUR/USD, GBP/USD, and AUD/USD. Their model utilized Gramian Angular Fields to encode price data and employed Deep Q-Learning (DQN) and Proximal Policy Optimization (PPO) algorithms. The study demonstrated that RL agents could achieve favorable investment performance when effectively capturing complex and random processes in the FX market.

In fixed-income markets, RL research is emerging. Carbonneau and Godin (2020) applied deep RL to hedge interest rate derivatives under an equal-risk pricing framework. Their agent dynamically adjusted bond portfolios, achieving lower hedging errors compared to static strategies, effectively learning a duration-matching policy under stochastic rates. In the derivatives domain, RL has been utilized to develop options trading strategies. Recent studies have proposed frameworks where RL agents learn to select optimal option strategies based on market conditions, capturing nonlinear payoffs more effectively than heuristic methods.

On the industry side, financial institutions like UBS have piloted RL-based systems for FX trade execution and smart order routing. UBS's smart order router (SOR) employs machine learning techniques to optimize order placement across various venues, aiming to reduce slippage and improve execution quality in the decentralized FX market. In summary, while RL applications in FX and fixed income are still developing, they show promise in areas such as hedging, execution, and macro-aware trading. As RL techniques become more robust and adaptable, their adoption in these traditionally conservative markets is expected to increase.

7. OPTION PRICING AND HEDGING WITH RL

Among the most innovative applications of reinforcement learning (RL) in finance is its use in option pricing and hedging-areas traditionally dominated by analytical models like Black–Scholes and stochastic control methods. In recent years, the paradigm of "deep hedging" has emerged, wherein RL agents learn hedging strategies directly from data or simulated environments, particularly under real-world conditions such as transaction costs and stochastic volatility.

A foundational work by Bühler et al. (2019) introduced a framework for hedging a portfolio of derivatives in the presence of market frictions, such as transaction costs and liquidity constraints. Their approach demonstrated that RL-based hedging agents could outperform traditional delta-hedging strategies by minimizing replication error and avoiding unnecessary rebalancing under transaction costs. Notably, the agent discovered practical hedging behaviors, such as trading only after significant price changes, without explicit programming-highlighting RL's capacity to derive intuitive financial strategies. Building on this, Cao et al. (2021) applied RL to hedge derivatives under jump risk and transaction frictions. Their agent optimized not only for mean squared error but also for Conditional Value at Risk (CVaR), effectively balancing cost and tail risk. The study showed that the RL strategy could tolerate small losses to avoid catastrophic ones-a form of implicit risk management difficult to design analytically.

Cai et al. (2019) proposed Neural Temporal Difference (TD) learning as a numerical method for pricing options, learning value functions for payoff and hedging costs. Their model handled path-dependent options and high-dimensional underlying assets, where traditional models often fail. Importantly, their RL agent could approximate known solutions under idealized conditions, reinforcing its theoretical validity.

Metrics commonly used to evaluate RL-based hedging strategies include the variance of hedging costs, hedging error distributions, and tail loss measures. Multiple studies report lower cost variance and improved downside protection versus benchmark delta-hedging strategies (Cao et al., 2021; Bühler et al., 2019).

On the industry front, financial institutions such as JP Morgan have begun integrating deep hedging methodologies into their exotic options operations. By leveraging reinforcement learning agents trained on proprietary scenario generators, these institutions aim to enhance real-time risk management and pricing in markets where traditional closed-form hedging strategies are inadequate. Recent developments include pilot programs for deploying machine learning–driven hedging engines on complex instruments like cliquet options, reflecting growing confidence in RL's practical utility for managing nonlinear and path-dependent derivatives (Rega-Jones, 2022).

8. HIGH-FREQUENCY TRADING AND MARKET MAKING

High-frequency trading (HFT) and market making are inherently sequential and dynamic, making them well-suited for reinforcement learning (RL) applications. Market makers must continuously adjust bid and ask quotes while managing inventory risk and adapting to rapidly changing order flows. Traditional frameworks, such as the Avellaneda–Stoikov model, offer analytical insights under simplifying assumptions. However, RL enables agents to learn optimal strategies directly from high-frequency order book data, capturing complex market dynamics more effectively (Spooner & Savani, 2020).

In a notable study, Spooner and Savani (2020) introduced adversarial reinforcement learning (ARL) to model market making as a two-agent game. One agent acts as the market maker, while an adversary simulates strategic counterparties attempting to exploit its quotes. This adversarial setup encouraged robust and risk-averse quoting strategies without requiring manually engineered penalties. The RL-based market maker learned to adjust quotes asymmetrically based on inventory exposure, effectively reducing adverse selection and enhancing inventory control.

Further advancements have been made in applying deep reinforcement learning to market making. Kumar (2023) developed a high-frequency market-making agent using Deep Recurrent Q-Networks (DRQN) within a realistic limit order book simulation. The agent outperformed benchmark strategies and provided insights into how market design features, such as maker-taker fees, affect market quality and profitability. Xu et al. (2022) applied a Dueling Double Deep Q-Network (D3QN) to actual tick data, enabling the agent to balance profit and inventory robustly. Their approach demonstrated the agent's ability to adapt its quoting strategy in response to market conditions, highlighting the potential of deep RL in real-world HFT scenarios.

Inventory risk remains a central concern in market making. While many RL approaches incorporate explicit inventory penalties or state-based awareness to stabilize net positions, ARL offers an alternative by allowing agents to learn risk-averse behaviors implicitly through adversarial interactions, obviating the need for hard-coded penalties (Spooner & Savani, 2020).

Beyond individual agents, multi-agent RL frameworks have been utilized to simulate entire market ecosystems, capturing emergent behaviors such as quote competition and self-regulated inventory management. These simulations provide valuable insights into market microstructure dynamics and the potential impact of various trading strategies.

Reinforcement learning is also advancing HFT-related strategies like optimal execution and statistical arbitrage. Briola et al. (2021) introduced an end-to-end deep RL framework for active high-frequency trading, employing Proximal Policy Optimization (PPO) to train agents on high-frequency limit order book data. Their approach demonstrated the feasibility of using deep RL for real-time trading decisions. Chen (2025) explored the use of Proximal Policy Optimization (PPO), a deep RL technique, in grid trading within the silver futures market. By employing mark-to-market accounting, the study translated trading profits and losses into rewards for the RL agent. The PPO model effectively adapted its trading strategy despite market noise, demonstrating strong potential for profitable trading in high-frequency environments.

9. OPTIMAL TRADE EXECUTION WITH RL

Optimal execution addresses a fundamental problem in institutional trading: how to execute large orders while minimizing cost due to market impact, slippage, and timing risk. Traditionally, solutions such as TWAP (time-weighted average price), VWAP (volume-weighted average price), and the Almgren–Chriss model have been employed. These methods, however, often rely on assumptions about price dynamics and impact functions. Reinforcement learning offers a data-driven alternative, allowing agents to learn execution strategies directly from market behavior (Nevmyvaka et al., 2006).

A typical RL formulation for execution includes states such as time remaining, order size left to trade, recent market trends, and order book depth. Actions represent how much to trade now, either in absolute or relative terms. The reward is usually defined as the negative implementation shortfall, i.e., the difference between the execution price and a benchmark like the arrival price (Hendricks and Wilcox, 2014).

Evaluation of execution RL agents involves comparing against benchmarks like VWAP, TWAP, and the market close. Studies typically report ~10–15% improvements in execution quality using RL agents, particularly in volatile environments (Pan et al., 2022). Several studies have demonstrated that RL-based execution agents outperform traditional benchmarks. For example, Ning et al. (2018) applied DQN in Chinese stock markets and showed that their agent adjusted aggressiveness based on liquidity conditions. Fang et al. (2021) used DDPG to dynamically size trades, improving performance during volatile periods. Pan et al. (2022) introduced a hybrid action-space RL method for limit order execution. Their framework used a two-stage decision process: a high-level agent selected a price range, and a low-level agent chose a discrete price level. This architecture handled the challenge of combining continuous and discrete decisions and resulted in lower execution cost and more stable strategies.

Continuous-time RL has also been explored. Kim and Yang (2019) introduce HJB equations for Q-functions in continuous-time optimal control problems with Lipschitz continuous controls. They develop a Q-learning method for continuous-time dynamical systems and propose a DQN-like algorithm for high-dimensional state and control spaces. The result provides a bridge between classical stochastic control theory and modern data-driven financial strategies. It has the potential to address the nonlinear, non-Markovian, and non-stationary environments that traditional models struggle with.

10. ROBO-ADVISORS AND REINFORCEMENT LEARNING

Robo-advisors are digital platforms that provide automated financial planning services with minimal human intervention. Traditionally, these systems rely on fixed rules and client-provided questionnaires to determine risk tolerance and assign portfolio allocations (e.g., 60/40 stock-bond splits). However, such static approaches cannot adapt to evolving investor preferences or changing market conditions. Reinforcement learning (RL) has recently been proposed to personalize and dynamically adjust advisory strategies, transforming robo-advising into a sequential decision-making problem.

One significant innovation involves using inverse reinforcement learning (IRL) to infer investor risk preferences from observed portfolio choices. Alsabah et al. (2021) developed a model where the robo-advisor observes an investor's decisions and infers the reward function that would rationalize those actions. This approach allows the advisor to better align future recommendations with actual, revealed preferences rather than relying solely on static surveys. Building upon this, Wang and Yu (2021) introduced a two-agent framework. The first agent performs inverse portfolio optimization to estimate the investor's expected returns and risk aversion, while the second, RL-based agent optimizes the investment strategy given those inferred preferences. This multi-agent system continuously updates as new decisions are observed, mimicking how human advisors adapt to client behavior over time. Capponi et al. (2022) proposed an RL-based personalized robo-advising model that incorporates demographic information (e.g., age, income) and direct client feedback. In their model, the client's true risk aversion is latent and must be inferred over time, transforming the problem into one of partially observable RL. These systems can even prompt clients for feedback-e.g., asking if they're comfortable with a proposed allocation-to refine their strategies.

Goal-based wealth management is another promising area. Dixon et al. (2020) framed it as a Markov Decision Process (MDP) in which the state includes current wealth, investment horizon, and the goal (e.g., retirement savings target). The agent's action is the portfolio allocation, and rewards are based on achieving the target with minimal shortfall. Their G-Learner algorithm learned to take more risk early and reduce risk closer to the target date-rediscovering the glide-path idea from target-date funds but in a data-driven way. Challenges in this domain include long decision horizons (delayed rewards), the need for interpretability, and regulatory concerns. Some studies propose hierarchical RL approaches where a high-level policy sets long-term goals and a low-level policy manages short-term allocations. This structure helps overcome the credit assignment problem inherent in long-term planning.

Although full RL-powered robo-advisors have not yet emerged commercially, elements are being integrated into existing systems-such as machine learning-enhanced risk profiling or dynamic rebalancing strategies. With the accumulation of behavioral data and increasing regulatory clarity, RL has the potential to drive the next generation of wealth management platforms, offering adaptive, personalized financial planning.

11. INNOVATIONS, TRENDS, AND EMERGING TOPICS

Recent developments in reinforcement learning (RL) for finance are characterized by innovations that extend beyond algorithmic performance to include robustness, adaptability, integration with other AI methods, and real-world applicability. This section highlights several prominent trends driving the next wave of research and development.

11.1. Multi-Agent and Adversarial Learning

A significant trend in financial reinforcement learning is the transition from single-agent systems to multi-agent reinforcement learning (MARL). Financial markets inherently involve multiple interacting agents-such as traders, market makers, and institutions-each with their own objectives and strategies. By explicitly modeling these interactions, MARL frameworks can capture complex game-theoretic dynamics and emergent behaviors that arise from the interplay of various market participants. This approach allows for a more realistic simulation of market conditions and can lead to the development of more robust trading strategies (Yang et al. 2020).

Adversarial reinforcement learning (ARL) further enhances the robustness of trading agents by introducing adversaries that simulate worst-case scenarios. For instance, in the context of market making, ARL frameworks model the interaction between a market maker and an adversary aiming to exploit the market maker's strategy. This setup encourages the market maker to develop risk-averse policies that are resilient to adverse market conditions. Spooner and Savani (2020) demonstrated that such adversarial training leads to the emergence of robust market-making strategies without the need for explicit risk constraints.

11.2. Transfer Learning and Meta-RL

Market non-stationarity poses a persistent challenge in financial environments, as agents trained in one market regime often underperform when conditions shift. Transfer learning offers a partial solution by enabling knowledge acquired in one context (e.g., developed markets) to be adapted to another (e.g., emerging markets). Meta-reinforcement learning (meta-RL) takes this further by training agents to quickly adapt to new environments. Foundational work by Finn et al. (2017) and Wang et al. (2016) laid the groundwork for meta-learning approaches, showing that agents can learn to fine-tune their behavior based on limited new data.

11.3. Integration with Alternative Data and Other AI Techniques

There is growing interest in hybrid systems that combine reinforcement learning (RL) with supervised learning and natural language processing (NLP). Sentiment analysis models-derived from earnings calls, financial news, or social media-are increasingly incorporated as exogenous state variables in RL agents to improve decision-making accuracy and market responsiveness (Xing et al., 2018; Hu et al., 2018). In parallel, generative adversarial networks (GANs) have been used to create synthetic financial time series for stress-testing RL agents and enhancing their generalization across different market regimes.

Recent advancements have seen large language models (LLMs), such as GPT-based architectures, being explored for generating actionable signals from textual inputs and for interpreting and explaining reinforcement learning (RL) agent behavior in natural language. This integration provides an additional layer of interpretability and user interaction. For instance, Zhang et al. (2023) proposed a framework where LLMs generate natural language explanations for an agent's behavior based solely on observations of states and actions, enhancing transparency in decision-making processes. Similarly, Zhu et al. (2025) employed reinforcement learning with outcome-based rewards to guide LLMs in producing explicit reasoning traces, thereby improving the interpretability of models in explaining human decisions. These developments signify a promising direction in making AI systems more understandable and trustworthy to users.

11.4. Standardized Benchmarking and Reproducibility

Early RL-finance papers often suffered from a lack of comparability due to custom datasets and non-reproducible environments. The field is now moving toward standardized benchmarks, such as those offered by the FinRL framework (Liu et al.,

2020), and formal competitions that require public code submissions. These efforts enable fair comparisons and foster robust algorithm design.

11.5. Safe and Risk-Aware RL

Finance requires not only profitable but also risk-managed strategies. Safe reinforcement learning (RL) techniques, such as Conditional Value at Risk (CVaR)-constrained optimization and robust Markov Decision Processes (MDPs), are gaining traction. For instance, Chow et al. (2018) developed efficient RL algorithms for risk-constrained MDPs, where risk is represented via a chance constraint or a constraint on the CVaR of the cumulative cost. Similarly, Ying et al. (2022) proposed a CVaR-Proximal-Policy-Optimization (CPPO) algorithm that formalizes the risk-sensitive constrained optimization problem by keeping its CVaR under a given threshold. Distributional RL approaches-such as Quantile Regression Deep Q-Network (QR-DQN) and Fully Parameterized Quantile Function (FQF)-allow agents to learn the full distribution of returns and make decisions based on quantiles rather than expected value (Dabney et al., 2018; Yang et al., 2019). This aligns more closely with institutional risk preferences, as it enables more nuanced control over tail risks.

11.6. Interpretability and Trust

As RL systems move closer to deployment in finance, interpretability becomes critical for gaining user and regulatory trust. Techniques such as policy distillation into decision trees (Rodriguez et al., 2019), scenario-based testing, and SHAP-based feature attribution (Lundberg & Lee, 2017) help clarify agent behavior. Recent efforts also explore self-explaining agents for wealth management applications, improving client understanding and compliance.

11.7. Industry Adoption and Case Studies

Real-world use of RL is no longer limited to academic settings. For instance, deep hedging techniques are under evaluation at major banks like JP Morgan for managing exotic options (Risk.net, 2022), while RL-based execution strategies have been piloted by brokerages and trading firms to optimize trade placement and reduce slippage (Zhang & Zohren, 2019). Though adoption remains cautious and highly controlled, these developments signal a shift from theory to practice.

12. CHALLENGES AND FUTURE DIRECTIONS

Despite significant advancements, several challenges persist in applying reinforcement learning (RL) to finance. These include data limitations, non-stationarity, risk management, interpretability, and regulatory compliance.

12.1. Data Limitations and Market Non-Stationarity

Financial markets are inherently noisy and non-stationary, making it challenging for RL agents to generalize from historical data. Unlike domains like robotics or gaming, where simulations can generate vast amounts of data, financial RL agents are constrained by limited historical datasets. This limitation increases the risk of overfitting to past market conditions. To address this, researchers have explored online learning, domain adaptation, and data augmentation techniques, such as using Generative Adversarial Networks (GANs) to simulate realistic market scenarios (Liang et al., 2018).

12.2. Exploration–Exploitation Trade-off

In live financial systems, exploration can be risky, as random or suboptimal trades may lead to significant losses. Consequently, financial RL often relies on off-policy and offline learning methods. Batch RL techniques, like conservative Q-learning, enable agents to learn from historical data without the need for online exploration. Additionally, reward shaping and imitation learning from expert trajectories are employed to bootstrap agent learning safely (Kumar et al., 2020).

12.3. Robustness and Model Risk

Financial RL models must be robust to small perturbations in market conditions. A strategy that performs well under a specific regime may fail under different volatility or liquidity levels. Robust RL approaches, such as distributional RL, adversarial training, and robust Markov Decision Processes (MDPs), are being explored to enhance model resilience. Some researchers propose regime detection modules or meta-agent systems that dynamically switch between specialized sub-policies (Sun et al. 2025; Niu et al. 2022).

12.4. Interpretability and Regulatory Compliance

The "black box" nature of deep RL poses challenges in regulated environments, where transparency in decision-making is crucial. Techniques like policy distillation into decision trees, scenario-based testing, and feature attribution methods (e.g., SHAP values) are helping to demystify agent behavior. Research is ongoing into creating agents that can self-explain their decisions, which is particularly valuable in wealth management and advisory applications (Gokhale et al., 2024; González Cortés et al., 2024).

12.5. Computational Efficiency

Training RL agents in finance can be computationally intensive, especially for high-frequency applications or large portfolios. Techniques such as experience replay, network pruning, and model distillation are being used to enhance computational efficiency. Some institutions are experimenting with parallel training infrastructures (e.g., Ray RLlib) or exploring hybrid supervised–RL pipelines to accelerate convergence (Pavel et al, 2025).

12.6. Ethical and Regulatory Issues

RL systems may inadvertently learn manipulative behaviors, such as spoofing or market manipulation, if not explicitly constrained (Martínez-Miranda et al., 2016). Ensuring fairness, compliance, and ethical trading practices is critical. Some propose embedding hard rules into the environment or penalizing strategies that resemble manipulative behavior in the reward function (Byrd, 2022). Collaboration between industry and academia is essential to preempt potential misuse.

12.7. Negative Results and Benchmarking

A healthy research ecosystem must report not only successes but also failures. There is increasing emphasis on publishing negative results-cases where RL underperforms or fails to generalize. Benchmarks, such as FinRL and OpenAI Gym-style financial environments, are becoming standard tools to encourage reproducibility and proper validation of claims (Liu et al., 2020).

13. CONCLUSION

Reinforcement learning (RL) is reshaping the landscape of financial decision-making by offering a flexible, data-driven framework capable of navigating complex, dynamic markets. Over the past five years, the convergence of deep RL with financial modeling has catalyzed a wave of innovation across asset classes - from equities and cryptocurrencies to fixed income, derivatives, and high-frequency trading. Empirical studies and industry applications consistently demonstrate RL's ability to adapt to changing regimes, handle nonlinear payoffs, and outperform traditional heuristic strategies under specific conditions.

Despite these advances, significant hurdles remain. Data scarcity, market non-stationarity, and the risks of exploration in live trading environments limit the feasibility of pure RL deployments. To address these concerns, researchers have embraced innovations such as offline RL, adversarial and multi-agent training, risk-aware optimization, and hybrid frameworks that integrate supervised learning, natural language processing, and generative modeling. These developments not only improve performance but also enhance the robustness, interpretability, and compliance of RL systems - key requirements in regulated financial settings.

Industry adoption is cautiously progressing, with major institutions piloting RL solutions for execution, market making, hedging, and wealth management. The growth of open-source libraries and standardized benchmarks has further facilitated reproducibility and practical implementation. However, achieving widespread deployment will require continued focus on safety, scalability, and ethical constraints.

REFERENCES

Ali, M., Irshad, H., Khan, I., & Hussain, A. (2025). Artificial intelligence in stock market investment: Enhancing decision-making through predictive analytics and behavioral insights. *ACADEMIA International Journal for Social Sciences, 4*(3), 1039–1056.

Almahdi, S., & Yang, S. Y. (2017). An adaptive portfolio trading system: A risk–return portfolio optimization using recurrent reinforcement learning with expected maximum drawdown. *Expert Systems with Applications, 87*, 267–279.

Almgren, R., & Chriss, N. (2000). Optimal execution of portfolio transactions. *The Journal of Risk, 3*(2), 5–39.

Alsabah, H., Capponi, A., Ruiz Lacedelli, O., & Stern, M. (2021). Robo-advising: Learning investors' risk preferences via portfolio choices. *Journal of Financial Econometrics, 19*(2), 369–392. https://doi.org/10.1093/jjfinec/nbaa026

Bacry, E., Delattre, S., Hoffmann, M., & Muzy, J.-F. (2013). Modelling microstructure noise with mutually exciting point processes. *Quantitative Finance, 13*(1), 65–77.

Bai, Y., Gao, Y., Wan, R., Zhang, S., & Song, R. (2025). A review of reinforcement learning in financial applications. *Annual Review of Statistics and Its Application, 12*(1), 209–232. https://doi.org/10.1146/annurev-statistics-030424-124444

Black, F., & Scholes, M. (1973). The pricing of options and corporate liabilities. *Journal of Political Economy, 81*(3), 637–654.

Botte, A., & Bao, D. (2021, October 6). A machine-learning approach to regime modeling. *Two Sigma*. Retrieved August 28, 2025, from https://www.twosigma.com/articles/a-machine-learning-approach-to-regime-modeling/

Briola, A., Turiel, J., Marcaccioli, R., Cauderan, A., & Aste, T. (2021). Deep reinforcement learning for active high-frequency trading. *arXiv*. https://arxiv.org/abs/2101.07107

Bühler, H., Gonon, L., Teichmann, J., & Wood, B. (2019). Deep hedging. *Quantitative Finance, 19*(8), 1271–1291. https://doi.org/10.1080/14697688.2019.1571683

Byrd, D. (2022). Learning not to spoof. In *Proceedings of the Third ACM International Conference on AI in Finance* (pp. 139–147). https://doi.org/10.1145/3533271.3561767

Cai, Q., Yang, Z., & Wang, Z. (2019). Neural temporal-difference and Q-learning provably converge to global optima. *arXiv*. https://arxiv.org/abs/1905.10027

Cao, J., Chen, J., Hull, J., & Poulos, Z. (2021). Deep hedging of derivatives using reinforcement learning. *arXiv*. https://arxiv.org/abs/2103.16409

Capponi, A., Olafsson, S., & Zariphopoulou, T. (2022). Personalized robo-advising: Enhancing investment through client interaction. *Management Science*, *68*(4), 2485–2512.

Carbonneau, A., & Godin, F. (2020). Equal risk pricing of derivatives with deep hedging. *Quantitative Finance*, *20*(12), 1935–1950. https://doi.org/10.1080/14697688.2020.1806343

Charpentier, A., Elie, R., & Remlinger, C. (2021). Reinforcement learning in finance. *Annual Review of Financial Economics*, *13*, 383–405. https://doi.org/10.1146/annurev-financial-101820-111754

Chen, H. (2025). Robo-traders and PPO: Advancing grid trading with deep reinforcement learning. In *Machine Learning and Modeling Techniques in Financial Data Science* (pp. 1–20). IGI Global. https://doi.org/10.4018/979-8-3693-6951-7.ch001

Chow, Y., Ghavamzadeh, M., Janson, L., & Pavone, M. (2018). Risk-constrained reinforcement learning with percentile risk criteria. *Journal of Machine Learning Research*, *18*(167), 1–51.

Cont, R. (2001). Empirical properties of asset returns: Stylized facts and statistical issues. *Quantitative Finance*, *1*(2), 223–236. https://doi.org/10.1080/713665670

Dabney, W., Rowland, M., Bellemare, M., & Munos, R. (2018, April). Distributional reinforcement learning with quantile regression. *Proceedings of the AAAI Conference on Artificial Intelligence*, *32*(1), •••.

Deng, Y., Bao, F., Kong, Y., Ren, Z., & Dai, Q. (2016). Deep direct reinforcement learning for financial signal representation and trading. *IEEE Transactions on Neural Networks and Learning Systems*, *28*(3), 653–664.

Dixon, M. F., Halperin, I., & Bilokon, P. (2020). *Machine learning in finance* (Vol. 1170). Springer.

Fang, Y., Ren, K., Liu, W., Zhou, D., Zhang, W., Bian, J., Yu, Y., & Liu, T. (2021, May). Universal trading for order execution with oracle policy distillation. *Proceedings of the AAAI Conference on Artificial Intelligence*, *35*(1), 107–115.

Finn, C., Abbeel, P., & Levine, S. (2017, July). Model-agnostic meta-learning for fast adaptation of deep networks. In *International Conference on Machine Learning* (pp. 1126–1135). PMLR.

Fischer, T. G. (2018). Reinforcement learning in financial markets—A survey. *FAU Discussion Papers in Economics* (No. 12/2018).

Fujimoto, S., Van Hoof, H., & Meger, D. (2018). Addressing function approximation error in actor-critic methods. In *Proceedings of the 35th International Conference on Machine Learning* (pp. 1582–1591). PMLR. https://proceedings.mlr.press/v80/fujimoto18a.html

Gandhi, A. K. (2024). AI-powered market risk models: Transforming the future of financial analytics. *International Journal of Artificial Intelligence, Data Science, and Machine Learning*, *5*(1), 57–67. https://doi.org/10.63282/3050-9262.IJAIDSML-V5I1P106

Gokhale, G., Karimi Madahi, S. S., Claessens, B., & Develder, C. (2024, June). Distill2Explain: Differentiable decision trees for explainable reinforcement learning in energy application controllers. In *Proceedings of the 15th ACM International Conference on Future and Sustainable Energy Systems* (pp. 55–64).

Hambly, B., Reisinger, C., & Yang, H. (2023). Recent advances in reinforcement learning in finance. *Mathematical Finance*, *33*(1), 1–30.

Han, W., Huang, J., Xie, Q., Zhang, B., Lai, Y., & Peng, M. (2023). Mastering pair trading with risk-aware recurrent reinforcement learning. *arXiv*. https://arxiv.org/abs/2304.00364

Hendricks, D., & Wilcox, D. (2014). A reinforcement learning extension to the Almgren–Chriss model for optimal trade execution. *arXiv*. https://arxiv.org/abs/1403.2229

Hirsa, A., Osterrieder, J., Hadji-Misheva, B., & Posth, J. A. (2021). Deep reinforcement learning on a multi-asset environment for trading. *arXiv*. https://arxiv.org/abs/2106.08437

Hu, Z., Liu, W., Bian, J., Liu, X., & Liu, T.-Y. (2018). Listening to chaotic whispers: A deep learning framework for news-oriented stock trend prediction. In *Proceedings of the 11th ACM International Conference on Web Search and Data Mining* (pp. 261–269).

Jiang, Z., & Liang, J. (2017). Cryptocurrency portfolio management with deep reinforcement learning. In *2017 Intelligent Systems Conference (IntelliSys)* (pp. 905–913). IEEE. https://doi.org/10.1109/IntelliSys.2017.8324459

Jiang, Z., Xu, D., & Liang, J. (2017). A deep reinforcement learning framework for the financial portfolio management problem. *arXiv*. https://arxiv.org/abs/1706.10059

Kalra, A., & Brown, D. S. (2022). Interpretable reward learning via differentiable decision trees. In *NeurIPS ML Safety Workshop*.

Kim, J., & Yang, I. (2020, July). Hamilton–Jacobi–Bellman equations for Q-learning in continuous time. In *Learning for Dynamics and Control* (pp. 739–748). PMLR.

Kim, S., Kim, J., Sul, H. K., & Hong, Y. (2024). An adaptive dual-level reinforcement learning approach for optimal trade execution. *Expert Systems with Applications, 252*, 124263.

Kumar, A., Zhou, A., Tucker, G., & Levine, S. (2020). Conservative Q-learning for offline reinforcement learning. *Advances in Neural Information Processing Systems, 33*, 1179–1191.

Kumar, P. (2023, April). Deep reinforcement learning for high-frequency market making. In *Asian Conference on Machine Learning* (pp. 531–546). PMLR.

Lalor, L., & Swishchuk, A. (2025). Deep reinforcement learning in non-Markov market-making. *Risks, 13*(3), 40.

Li, X., Li, Y., Zhan, Y., & Liu, X.-Y. (2019). Optimistic bull or pessimistic bear: Adaptive deep reinforcement learning for stock portfolio allocation. *arXiv*. https://arxiv.org/abs/1907.01503

Li, Z. H., Yu, Y., Chen, Y., Chen, K., Hu, Z., & Fan, C. (2021). Neural-to-tree policy distillation with policy improvement criterion. *arXiv*. https://arxiv.org/abs/2108.06898

Liang, J., & Li, X. (2018). Generative adversarial networks for financial trading strategies fine-tuning and combination. *Physica A, 512*, 1057–1071.

Liang, Z., Chen, H., Zhu, J., Jiang, K., & Li, Y. (2018). Adversarial deep reinforcement learning in portfolio management. *arXiv*. https://arxiv.org/abs/1808.09940

Lillicrap, T. P., Hunt, J. J., Pritzel, A., Heess, N., Erez, T., Tassa, Y., Silver, D., & Wierstra, D. (2015). Continuous control with deep reinforcement learning. *arXiv*. https://arxiv.org/abs/1509.02971

Lim, B., Zohren, S., & Roberts, S. (2020). Enhancing time series momentum strategies using deep neural networks. *arXiv*. https://arxiv.org/abs/1904.04912

Liu, X.-Y., Yang, H., Chen, Q., Zhang, R., Yang, L., Xiao, B., & Wang, C.-D. (2020). FinRL: A deep reinforcement learning library for automated stock trading in quantitative finance. *arXiv*. https://arxiv.org/abs/2011.09607

Lundberg, S. M., & Lee, S.-I. (2017). A unified approach to interpreting model predictions. *Advances in Neural Information Processing Systems*, 30.

Man Group. (2024, March 21). *AI in asset management: AHL perspective*. https://www.man.com/documents/download/5a8d1-65277-88749-3a182/Man_AHL_Analysis_The_Big_Picture%3A_AI_English_%28United_States%29_21-03-2024.pdf

Markowitz, H. (1952). Portfolio selection. *The Journal of Finance*, *7*(1), 77–91.

Martínez-Miranda, E., McBurney, P., & Howard, M. J. (2016). Learning unfair trading: A market manipulation analysis from the reinforcement learning perspective. In *2016 IEEE Conference on Evolving and Adaptive Intelligent Systems (EAIS)* (pp. 103–109). IEEE.

Mehtab, S., & Sen, J. (2020, November). Stock price prediction using CNN and LSTM-based deep learning models. In *2020 International Conference on Decision Aid Sciences and Application (DASA)* (pp. 447–453). IEEE.

Mnih, V., Kavukcuoglu, K., Silver, D., Rusu, A. A., Veness, J., Bellemare, M. G., Graves, A., Riedmiller, M., Fidjeland, A. K., Ostrovski, G., Petersen, S., Beattie, C., Sadik, A., Antonoglou, L., King, H., Kumaran, D., Wierstra, D., Legg, S., & Hassabis, D. (2015). Human-level control through deep reinforcement learning. *Nature*, *518*(7540), 529–533. https://doi.org/10.1038/nature14236

Moody, J., & Saffell, M. (2001). Learning to trade via direct reinforcement. *IEEE Transactions on Neural Networks*, *12*(4), 875–889.

Mosic, R. (2017, July 31). Deep reinforcement learning-based trading application at JPMorgan Chase. *Medium*. Retrieved August 28, 2025, from https://ranko-mosic.medium.com/reinforcement-learning-based-trading-application-at-jp-morgan-chase-f829b8ec54f2

Nevmyvaka, Y., Feng, Y., & Kearns, M. (2006). Reinforcement learning for optimized trade execution. In *Proceedings of the 23rd International Conference on Machine Learning* (pp. 673–680).

Niu, H., Li, S., & Li, J. (2022). MetaTrader: A reinforcement learning approach integrating diverse policies for portfolio optimization. In *Proceedings of the 31st ACM International Conference on Information & Knowledge Management* (pp. 1573–1583).

Otabek, S., & Choi, M. (2024). Multi-level deep Q-network framework for Bitcoin trading using historical and sentiment data. *Scientific Reports*, *14*(1), 974.

Pan, F., Zhang, T., Luo, L., He, J., & Liu, S. (2022). Learn continuously, act discretely: Hybrid action-space reinforcement learning for optimal execution. In *Proceedings of the 31st International Joint Conference on Artificial Intelligence* (pp. 3875–3881).

Park, H., Sim, M. K., & Choi, D. G. (2019). An intelligent financial portfolio trading strategy using deep Q-learning. *arXiv*. https://arxiv.org/abs/1907.03665

Pavel, M. I., Hu, S., Pratama, M., & Kowalczyk, R. (2025). Onboard optimization and learning: A survey. *arXiv*. https://arxiv.org/abs/2505.08793

Pippas, N., Ludvig, E., & Turkay, C. (2025). The evolution of reinforcement learning in quantitative finance: A survey. *ACM Computing Surveys, 1*(1), 1.

Qin, M., Sun, S., Zhang, W., Xia, H., Wang, X., & An, B. (2024, March). EarnHFT: Efficient hierarchical reinforcement learning for high-frequency trading. *Proceedings of the AAAI Conference on Artificial Intelligence, 38*(13), 14669–14676.

Redress Compliance. (2023). *AI-powered trading algorithms at Goldman Sachs.* https://redresscompliance.com/ai-case-study-ai-powered-trading-algorithms-at-goldman-sachs

Rega-Jones, N. (2022, May 26). JPMorgan's deep hedging reaches cliquets. *Risk.net*. https://www.risk.net/derivatives/7949306/jp-morgans-deep-hedging-reaches-cliquets

Risk.net. (2022). *JPMorgan testing deep hedging of exotics*. https://www.risk.net/derivatives/equity-derivatives/7921526/jp-morgan-testing-deep-hedging-of-exotics

Schulman, J., Wolski, F., Dhariwal, P., Radford, A., & Klimov, O. (2017). Proximal policy optimization algorithms. *arXiv*. https://arxiv.org/abs/1707.06347

Silver, D., Schrittwieser, J., Simonyan, K., Antonoglou, I., Huang, A., Guez, A., & Hassabis, D. (2017). Mastering the game of Go without human knowledge. *Nature, 550*(7676), 354–359.

Spooner, T., & Savani, R. (2020). Robust market making via adversarial reinforcement learning. *arXiv*. https://arxiv.org/abs/2003.01820

Sun, R., Xi, Y., Stefanidis, A., Jiang, Z., & Su, J. (2025). A novel multi-agent dynamic portfolio optimization learning system based on hierarchical deep reinforcement learning. *arXiv*. https://arxiv.org/abs/2501.06832

Tsai, Y.-C., & Wang, C.-C. (2019). Deep reinforcement learning for foreign exchange trading. *arXiv*. https://arxiv.org/abs/1908.08036

Wang, H., & Yu, S. (2021). Robo-advising: Enhancing investment with inverse optimization and deep reinforcement learning. In *2021 20th IEEE International Conference on Machine Learning and Applications (ICMLA)* (pp. 365–372). IEEE.

Wang, J. X., Kurth-Nelson, Z., Tirumala, D., Soyer, H., Leibo, J. Z., Munos, R., Blundell, C., Kumaran, D., & Botvinick, M. (2016). Learning to reinforcement learn. *arXiv*. https://arxiv.org/abs/1611.05763

Wang, R., Xiao, B., & Liu, X.-Y. (2025). FinRL-Crypto: An open-source framework for deep reinforcement learning in cryptocurrency trading. *Journal of Computational Finance and AI*, *3*(1), 45–62.

Wang, S., & Klabjan, D. (2024). An ensemble method of deep reinforcement learning for automated cryptocurrency trading. In *2024 IEEE International Conference on Blockchain and Cryptocurrency (ICBC)* (pp. 461–463). IEEE.

Wilmott, P. (2022). *Machine learning: An applied mathematics introduction*. Oxford University Press.

Xie, W., & Zheng, X. (2018, November). Research on futures programmed trading based on deep reinforcement learning. In *2018 International Conference on Cloud Computing, Big Data and Blockchain (ICCBB)* (pp. 1–3). IEEE.

Xing, F. Z., Cambria, E., & Welsch, R. E. (2018). Natural language-based financial forecasting: A survey. *Artificial Intelligence Review*, *50*(1), 49–73.

Xu, Z., Cheng, X., & He, Y. (2022). Performance of deep reinforcement learning for high-frequency market making on actual tick data. In *Proceedings of the 21st International Conference on Autonomous Agents and Multiagent Systems* (pp. 1765–1767).

Yang, H., & Malik, A. (2024). Reinforcement learning pair trading: A dynamic scaling approach. *Journal of Risk and Financial Management*, *17*(12), 555.

Yang, Y., Luo, R., Li, M., Zhou, M., Zhang, W., & Wang, J. (2018, July). Mean field multi-agent reinforcement learning. In *International Conference on Machine Learning* (pp. 5571–5580). PMLR.

Yang, Z., Jin, H., Tang, Y., & Fan, G. (2024). Risk-aware constrained reinforcement learning with non-stationary constraints. In *Proceedings of the 23rd International Conference on Autonomous Agents and Multiagent Systems (AAMAS)* (pp. 2029–2031).

Ying, C., Zhou, X., Su, H., Yan, D., Chen, N., & Zhu, J. (2022). Towards safe reinforcement learning via constraining conditional value-at-risk. In *Proceedings of the 31st International Joint Conference on Artificial Intelligence (IJCAI)* (pp. 3650–3656).

Yu, P., Lee, J. S., Kulyatin, I., Shi, Z., & Dasgupta, S. (2019). Model-based deep reinforcement learning for dynamic portfolio optimization. *arXiv*. https://arxiv.org/pdf/1901.08740

Zhang, C., Vinyals, O., Munos, R., & Bengio, S. (2018). A study on overfitting in deep reinforcement learning. *arXiv*. https://arxiv.org/abs/1804.06893

Zhang, X., Guo, Y., Stepputtis, S., Sycara, K., & Campbell, J. (2023). Explaining agent behavior with large language models. *arXiv*. https://arxiv.org/abs/2309.10346

Zhang, Z., Zohren, S., & Roberts, S. (2019). Deep reinforcement learning for trading. *arXiv*. https://arxiv.org/abs/1911.10107

Zhu, J. Q., Xie, H., Arumugam, D., Wilson, R. C., & Griffiths, T. L. (2025). Using reinforcement learning to train large language models to explain human decisions. *arXiv*. https://arxiv.org/abs/2505.11614

Zou, J., Lou, J., Wang, B., & Liu, S. (2024). A novel deep reinforcement learning-based automated stock trading system using cascaded LSTM networks. *Expert Systems with Applications*, *242*, 122801.

ENDNOTE

[1] Corresponding Author: e18820@outlook.com

Chapter 6
Adaptive Asset Allocation With Hierarchical Reinforcement Learning:
A Multi-Class Investment Strategy

Haojun Chen
https://orcid.org/0000-0001-9168-9234
Guangzhou Huali College, China

Chao Xiong
Polar Asset Management Partners, Canada

ABSTRACT

This paper investigates hierarchical reinforcement learning (HRL) for multi-asset portfolio management using equities, bonds, commodities, and gold. We propose a two-level RL system where a high-level policy dynamically allocates capital across asset classes, while a low-level policy executes trades cost-efficiently. Using representative ETFs and training on historical data, the model is tested from July 2023 to June 2025. The HRL portfolio achieved an annualized return of 45.5%, volatility of 12.5%, Sharpe ratio of 3.6, and max drawdown of 6.2%, outperforming all individual assets and traditional strategies. We compare performance against static benchmarks and explore the agent's asset allocation dynamics, highlighting how the model adjusts exposures in response to market shifts. This study demonstrates HRL's potential to deliver high returns with controlled risk, offering a robust AI-driven solution for adaptive asset allocation.

DOI: 10.4018/979-8-3373-2838-6.ch006

1. INTRODUCTION

Managing an investment portfolio involves balancing the trade-off between return and risk by allocating capital across different assets. Traditional approaches following Modern Portfolio Theory (MPT), introduced by Markowitz (1952), provide a formal framework for selecting an optimal portfolio given an investor's risk tolerance. MPT posits that diversification - holding a mix of assets that do not perfectly move in tandem - can improve a portfolio's risk-adjusted returns. The classic example is a stock-and-bond portfolio: stocks offer higher expected returns at the cost of higher volatility, while bonds offer steadier returns with lower volatility (Elton et al., 2014). By mixing the two, the overall portfolio can attain a more favorable risk-return profile because the assets' fluctuations partially offset each other. For example, adding government bonds to an equity portfolio tends to significantly reduce volatility because government bond returns often have low or even negative correlation with stock returns. This negative stock-bond correlation provides a natural hedge: when stocks fall, high-quality bonds often rise, cushioning portfolio losses (Baele and Inghelbrecht, 2010).

Beyond stocks and bonds, investors commonly diversify into other asset classes such as commodities and real assets. Commodities have historically exhibited low or negative correlation with traditional financial assets, partly due to different economic drivers. Research by Gorton and Rouwenhorst (2006) found that a broad commodity futures index had similar long-term average returns and Sharpe ratio as equities, but with negative correlation to both equity and bond returns, making commodities an attractive diversifier. Gold, in particular, is often viewed as a "safe haven" asset. It tends to hold its value or appreciate during times of market stress or high inflation, which is why investors include gold for crisis protection. Studies by Baur and Lucey (2010) confirm that gold can serve as a hedge and as a safe haven in extreme market downturns. Thus, holding some gold alongside stocks and bonds can further enhance portfolio resilience during turbulent periods.

This paper focuses on managing a portfolio composed of four major asset classes - equities, bonds, broad commodities, and gold - which we represent via liquid ETFs. These assets span a spectrum of risk and return profiles: equities typically offer high returns but with substantial volatility; corporate bonds provide moderate fixed-income returns with lower volatility and regular interest payments; broad commodities can have volatile but uncorrelated returns driven by supply/demand shocks and inflation trends; gold often has lower long-run returns than stocks but shines during crises and inflationary spikes. By dynamically allocating across these four asset classes, an investor can potentially capture upside from different market regimes while mitigating downside risk through diversification.

While traditional strategic asset allocation relies on fixed weights or slow periodic adjustments (see e.g. llmanen, 2011), there is growing interest in dynamic allocation strategies that can respond quickly to changing market conditions. This is where Reinforcement Learning (RL) comes into play. RL is a branch of machine learning in which an agent learns to make sequential decisions by interacting with an environment and receiving feedback in the form of rewards. In the context of portfolio management, an RL agent can observe market state and decide how to rebalance the portfolio, with the goal of maximizing some cumulative reward. Unlike supervised learning, RL does not require direct "correct action" labels - instead, it learns by trial-and-error which actions yield higher returns (Sutton and Barto, 2018). This makes RL particularly suitable for financial markets, which are complex, stochastic environments where explicit optimal solutions are often unknown.

Over the past two decades, researchers have increasingly applied RL to trading and asset allocation problems. Early efforts, such as Moody and Saffell's (2001) work on Recurrent Reinforcement Learning, demonstrated that RL could be used to optimize trading policies for single assets by directly maximizing portfolio utility. Subsequent studies extended these ideas: Dempster and Leemans (2006) and others in the 2000s applied RL to multi-asset portfolio selection, while Jiang et al. (2017) and many recent works leveraged deep reinforcement learning (DRL) to handle large state spaces and learn more complex trading strategies. Since then, a variety of DRL approaches have been explored for financial markets, including policy-gradient methods and value-function methods.

However, applying RL to portfolio management is challenging due to several factors: the dimensionality of the action space grows with the number of assets, markets are noisy with low signal-to-noise ratio, and trading involves frictions such as transaction costs and price impact that are hard to model (Liang et al., 2018). A single-agent RL that directly outputs asset weights for a large portfolio might struggle with these challenges - it can suffer from "curse of dimensionality" as the asset universe expands, and it might ignore subtleties of trade execution by assuming changes in allocation occur instantaneously and without cost.

Hierarchical Reinforcement Learning (HRL) offers a promising solution by introducing a multi-level decision structure. In an HRL framework, the decision-making process is divided into hierarchical sub-tasks with different time scales or objectives. A high-level policy might make coarse, infrequent decisions, while one or more low-level policies handle fine-grained, frequent decisions to implement the high-level directives. This divide-and-conquer strategy can make the learning problem more tractable and align with real-world trading practices.

Recent research has shown the effectiveness of hierarchical RL in portfolio management. For instance, Wang et al. (2021) propose a hierarchical reinforced stock trading system (HRPM) that decomposes the portfolio management problem into two levels: a high-level agent that periodically outputs ideal portfolio weights to maximize long-term returns, and a low-level agent that operates at a higher frequency to execute those allocation changes while minimizing trading costs. By training the two levels of policy in tandem, they reported significant improvements over non-hierarchical approaches in U.S. and Chinese stock markets. Another example is the Hierarchical Reinforced Trader (HRT) framework by Zhao et al. (2024), which splits the task into (1) a high-level controller that selects a subset of stocks and (2) a low-level controller that determines the exact trade volumes for those chosen assets. This structure was shown to mitigate issues like action dimensionality and to yield higher Sharpe ratios than standard single-agent DRL in experiments on a large stock portfolio.

Encouraged by these successes, in this paper we implement a hierarchical deep reinforcement learning approach for our four-asset-class portfolio. The high-level agent will decide the portfolio mix among equities, bonds, commodities, and gold and the low-level agent will handle the execution of those allocation decisions. Our goal is to show that this HRL approach can dynamically capture the best opportunities across asset classes - for example, leaning into equities during bull runs, shifting to safe havens like gold or bonds during equity downturns, or tilting to commodities during inflationary periods - thereby delivering superior returns with controlled risk. We will compare the performance of the RL-managed portfolio against passive benchmarks (buy-and-hold each asset class) over a two-year test period (July 2023 to June 2025). The test results will highlight how the RL agent allocated capital over time and how it achieved a remarkably high Sharpe ratio through active asset allocation. In the following sections, we first review the theoretical background and related work in more detail, then describe the hierarchical RL methodology, and finally present and discuss the empirical results.

2. LITERATURE REVIEW AND BACKGROUND

2.1 Portfolio Theory and Asset Class Diversification

Harry Markowitz's seminal 1952 paper "Portfolio Selection" laid the foundation for modern portfolio theory, introducing the concept of an efficient frontier of optimal portfolios that maximize expected return for a given level of risk. The key insight of Markowitz's theory is that the risk of a portfolio is not simply the weighted sum of individual asset risks, but also depends on the correlations between asset returns. By combining assets that do not move exactly together, an investor can reduce overall portfolio volatility. This is the essence of diversification - as Markowitz famously said, *"don't put all your eggs in one basket."* Risk-averse investors can thus achieve better risk-adjusted returns by holding a well-diversified portfolio rather than any single asset.

It is important to note that correlations between asset classes are not static - they can change over time and sometimes spike toward 1 in severe crises. Still, certain robust patterns have been observed. Since the late 1990s, the stock-bond correlation in the U.S. has mostly been negative, meaning stocks and bonds often move in opposite directions (Campbell et al., 2017). This has greatly benefited balanced portfolios. However, in high-inflation regimes (e.g., the 1970s or 2022), stock and bond prices can fall simultaneously - reducing the benefit of bonds as a diversifier. In such scenarios, assets such as commodities and gold have historically provided critical diversification. For example, during the 1970s stagflation, gold and oil prices surged while stocks struggled (Erb and Harvey, 2006). Even recently, in 2022, both stocks and bonds had steep losses, but commodities (energy, grains, etc.) had strong positive returns, and gold preserved capital better than stocks. These episodes underscore why a multi-asset approach is valuable: one never knows which asset will be the "pillar" of strength in the next crisis or regime change.

Recent studies in dynamic allocation have sought to address the time-varying nature of asset correlations and market conditions through adaptive and data-driven methods (see, e.g., Bekaert & Harvey, 1995). For instance, models such as regime-switching approaches and dynamic conditional correlation (DCC-GARCH) models allow portfolio weights to adjust based on changing volatility and correlation structures (Engle, 2001). Additionally, machine learning techniques, including reinforcement learning and deep learning, have been explored to optimize portfolio rebalancing in response to evolving market dynamics (Jiang & Jiang, 2017). These methods aim to enhance portfolio resilience by learning from historical patterns and adapting allocations in real-time, surpassing the static assumptions of classical models.

Traditional approaches to dynamic allocation include tactical asset allocation based on macroeconomic forecasts or market timing signals, which is notoriously difficult to execute consistently (Llmanen, 2011). This is where reinforcement learning promises a data-driven, adaptive solution - discovering allocation strategies automatically from historical market data, without explicit forecasting.

2.2 Reinforcement Learning in Portfolio Management

Reinforcement Learning provides a computational framework for sequential decision-making under uncertainty, which fits naturally with investment management (Sutton and Barto. 2018). In RL, an agent interacts with an environment in discrete time steps: at each time t, the agent observes the current state s_t and chooses an action a_t; the environment then transitions to a new state s_{t+1} and provides a reward r_t to the agent. The agent's objective is to learn a policy $\pi(a|s)$ that maximizes the cumulative reward over time. In a portfolio context, the state could include recent prices, returns, technical indicators, economic variables, and the agent's current asset holdings. The action is to adjust the portfolio - for example, specifying new weights for each asset. The reward is typically defined as the portfolio's profit or utility and the common choice is among portfolio return and other a risk-adjusted metrics such as Sharpe ratio or mean-variance utility. The agent learns by exploring different allocations and observing outcomes in historical data or a simulated environment.

One of the earliest RL approaches in finance was the Recurrent Reinforcement Learning (RRL) method by Moody and Saffell (2001). They trained a trading agent to maximize a utility function of profit and risk, using policy gradient updates. This was essentially an actor-only method and was applied to single assets. They demonstrated that the agent could learn profitable momentum strategies. In subsequent years, other researchers built on this "direct reinforcement" idea. For instance, Dempster & Leemans (2006) applied it to foreign exchange portfolios, and Almahdi & Yang (2017) used a variant to manage a stock/bond portfolio with an objective of maximizing returns for a given Value-at-Risk level.

The advent of deep learning and the success of deep RL in games of Go around 2015 catalyzed a new wave of research applying deep RL to finance. Deep Reinforcement Learning (DRL) algorithms combine neural networks with traditional RL algorithms, enabling the handling of high-dimensional state spaces (Li, 2017). One popular DRL algorithm for continuous action spaces is Deep Deterministic Policy Gradient (DDPG) (Lillicrap et al. 2016). DDPG is an actor-critic method where the actor network outputs a continuous action vector and a critic network evaluates the Q-value; it's essentially an off-policy extension of deterministic policy gradient, aided by experience replay and target networks. In the trading domain, Liu et al. (2018) applied DDPG to stock trading and found it could discover profitable strategies, outperforming some heuristic trading rules. The agent learns to output, for example, a vector of asset weights or trading signals in $[-1,0,1]$ (representing sell/hold/buy) for each asset, and updates its networks based on reward feedback. One issue with DDPG in practice is the tendency to overfit or generate out-of-distribution actions; researchers have since improved on it with variants like Twin-Delayed DDPG (TD3) and by incorporating exploration noise schemes.

Another class of DRL algorithms are policy gradient methods with stochastic policies such as Proximal Policy Optimization (PPO) and Advantage Actor-Critic (A2C/A3C). Yang *et al.* (2020) experimented with an ensemble of DDPG, PPO, and A2C agents for stock trading, combining their action outputs, and reported that this ensemble was more robust across different market conditions than any single algorithm. The intuition is that each algorithm might excel in different regimes, so a combination could hedge algorithmic weaknesses. Other works have integrated supervised learning signals or risk management overlays into the RL framework.

For example, Zhang et al. (2020) proposed an approach to embed deep autoencoders in the portfolio policy to deal with noisy correlation matrices; Moskovitz et al. (2021) injected optimism/pessimism factors into the reward to account for prediction uncertainty.

A significant challenge is that many DRL models in finance are data-hungry and prone to overfitting historical data (Fischer and Krauss, 2018). Financial time series have low signal-to-noise and non-stationarities (regime shifts), so a strategy that worked in the training period may fail later (Tsay, 2010). Researchers attempt to address this via techniques like rolling window retraining, regularization, or training on simulated market data. Nonetheless, deep RL has shown impressive results in numerous studies, often beating traditional strategies or matching the performance of sophisticated quantitative models. For example, Gupta et al. (2025) reports a DRL agent achieving higher Sharpe ratios than mean-variance optimization in certain stock portfolios. Buehler et al. (2019) applied deep RL to learn option hedging strategies, showing the RL agent could replicate risk-neutral pricing behavior. These successes illustrate RL's potential to learn complex trading policies that are difficult to derive analytically, such as nonlinear market-timing strategies or arbitrage across asset classes and time.

However, a vanilla single-agent DRL approach in a multi-asset environment may face difficulties when scaling up (Yang et al., 2020). If one tries to train an agent to allocate across, say, 50 or 100 assets, the action space becomes very large (the agent must output a weight for each asset, and those weights must sum to 1 and often be constrained between 0 and 1 for no shorting, which complicates the action parameterization). Moreover, such an agent would need to implicitly learn both which assets to choose (selection) and how to trade them efficiently (execution). This is where Hierarchical RL can bring advantages by splitting the decision process.

2.3 Hierarchical Reinforcement Learning Frameworks

Hierarchical Reinforcement Learning (HRL) introduces a hierarchy of controllers or policies operating at different levels of abstraction or different time scales. The general idea is to break down the overall task into sub-tasks, each handled by a separate RL agent, and to train them such that the lower-level agents help the higher-level agent achieve its goals. There are various paradigms for HRL, including options frameworks (Sutton et al. 1999) where high-level policies learn to invoke "option" primitives, and feudal RL (Dayan & Hinton 1993) where a manager agent sets goals for worker agents. In portfolio management, the HRL implementations to date have usually been temporal hierarchies: the high-level makes infrequent decisions about allocations, the low-level makes frequent trading decisions.

In our context, we employ a two-level hierarchy similar to the prior studies as discussed earlier. The High-Level Policy (HLC) will decide portfolio allocations among the four asset classes at a certain interval (for example, daily at market close). This high-level agent observes state information like recent price trends, volatility, economic indicators, etc., and outputs a target weight distribution that sums to 1. These weights represent the desired fraction of the portfolio value to invest in each ETF until the next decision point. The high-level agent is trained to maximize long-term reward, which in our case can be the cumulative portfolio return or Sharpe ratio over the episode (training period).

The Low-Level Policy (LLC) operates at a finer time scale between high-level decisions (Wang et al., 2011). Its job is to execute the rebalancing required to move from the previous allocation to the new target allocation set by the high-level policy. The low-level agent takes as input more granular market state data and can execute actions such as "buy X units of SPY and sell Y units of GLD" to gradually adjust the portfolio. The low-level's reward can be related to trading costs: for instance, we might reward it for minimizing slippage and the difference between the achieved allocation and the target allocation by the deadline, minus transaction cost penalties. In essence, the low-level is a trade execution agent that tries to implement trades optimally. If trading were frictionless, we wouldn't need a low-level agent - the high-level weights could be applied instantly. But in reality, large trades can move prices (market impact) and frequent turnover incurs costs (Almgren & Chriss, 2001). The low-level agent learns execution strategies that reduce these costs. The high-level agent, in turn, benefits because it can assume a more ideal execution - it knows the low-level will handle the nitty-gritty of trading, and the high-level just focuses on choosing the right allocation.

Figure 1. Hierarchical reinforcement learning architecture for portfolio management.

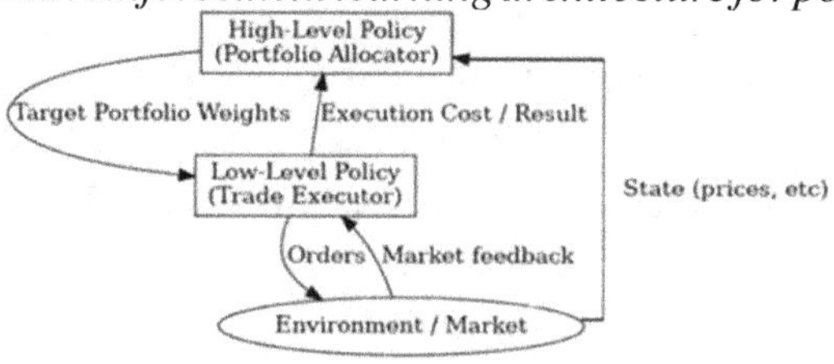

As shown in Figure 1, the high-level policy (portfolio allocator) selects target portfolio weights at a lower frequency (e.g., daily), and then the low-level policy (trade executor) carries out the necessary trades within a shorter time window to achieve those weights. The environment (e.g. the market) provides state information to both levels. The high-level agent receives feedback in terms of portfolio performance and possibly execution costs via the low-level agent's outcome. The low-level agent receives more immediate rewards related to execution quality and cost.

By structuring the problem hierarchically, we significantly reduce complexity. The high-level action space is just 4 continuous weights (summing to 1) - a manageable size - and it makes decisions once per round. The low-level action space might still be continuous trades, but if it's operating over only a short horizon with a specific goal, that is easier than trying to directly maximize long-term returns. Each agent in the hierarchy has a more focused task and can be trained for that. We train the two agents in an interleaved or simultaneous manner: one common approach is to pre-train the low-level on a generic execution task (perhaps using a heuristic or supervised learning as a starting point), then train the high-level with the low-level in place, and periodically fine-tune the low-level as the high-level's policy evolves. Wang et al. (2021) describe using a pre-training scheme for the low-level and an iterative training loop where the high-level and low-level update in turns, which improved training stability.

It's worth noting that HRL is not the only way to handle multi-asset trading - another approach is multi-agent RL. There have been multi-agent systems for portfolio optimization (Haider et al 2021), but a hierarchy has the advantage of clear structural interpretation. Our hierarchical design particularly reflects real portfolio management processes: the high-level "asset allocation committee" sets broad allocations, and the execution traders then implement those changes optimally.

3. METHODOLOGY

3.1 Environment and Data

Our environment consists of the historical market data for the four asset class proxies: SPDR S&P 500 ETF (SPY) for equities, iShares iBoxx Investment Grade Corporate Bond ETF (LQD) for bonds, Invesco DB Commodity Index Tracking Fund (DBC) for commodities, and SPDR Gold Trust (GLD) for gold. We utilize adjusted daily price data from mid-2018 through mid-2025 for training and testing. The data are available download on Yahoo Finance. The period from mid-2018 to mid-2023 is used for training, and the out-of-sample test is mid-2023 to mid-2025.

At each trading day close, the high-level agent will make an allocation decision. We assume trading is done at close prices. The high-level decision frequency is daily in our implementation. Within each day, the low-level agent has, in principle, multiple steps to execute trades. In our setup, we simplify the low-level execution to also operate on a single-step basis at daily frequency. However, conceptually we incorporate transaction cost by penalizing large changes in weights. Effectively, our low-level agent will attempt to minimize trading costs by possibly not fully achieving the high-level's target weights if it deems the cost too high - this is one way to model execution imperfection even with daily data.

The state representation for the high-level agent at each decision point includes: recent returns or momentum indicators for each asset, volatility estimates, and relative strength indices. We also include the current portfolio weights and several macro indicators. We include the 10-year Treasury yield or VIX as a measure of market sentiment/risk aversion. The state can be represented as a feature vector fed into a neural network. For the low-level agent, the state might simply be the difference between current allocation and target allocation, plus perhaps order book or intraday price trend features. In our daily simplified model, the low-level's state is effectively the same as the high-level's state, but it receives a different reward signal focusing on trading cost.

The action space for the high-level agent is a vector of four weights w_{SPY}, w_{LQD}, w_{DBC}, w_{GLD}. We enforce w $\geq$0 and $\sum$w=1 (no short selling, fully invested portfolio with no external cash). We parameterize this in the neural network by having an output for each asset that goes through a Softmax function to ensure non-negativity and summation to 1. Thus, the raw network output z = (z_1, z_2, z_3, z_4) is transformed to weights via $w_i = e^{z_i}/\sum_j e^{z_j}$. The action space for the low-level agent can be thought of as incremental trades: e.g.,Δw_{SPY}, Δw_{LQD},... that it will execute (with $\sum \Delta w_i$=0 to conserve total capital). However, since we are not doing multi-step within the day, in practice the low-level's "action" is trivial - it just rebalances to the target weights immediately, incurring a cost. We incorporate a cost model: each 1% of portfolio value traded in any asset incurs, assuming, 5 basis points of cost. The low-level then effectively decides how much of the target rebalancing to do versus to hold off.

The reward design is critical. For the high-level agent, we want to incentivize high long-term returns and low risk. A simple approach is to use daily reward = portfolio return (the percentage change in total portfolio value from one day to the next). By maximizing expected cumulative return, the agent will indirectly learn to consider risk because taking very large risks can lead to negative returns that hurt the cumulative product. However, pure return maximization might still lead to very volatile allocations (if the agent finds a strategy that doubles the portfolio half the time and loses 40% half the time, it might like that because the average growth is high, even though risk is high). To explicitly account for risk, one can include a penalty for volatility or drawdown in the reward. Another common choice is to use log returns r_t=ln((V_t/V_{t-1}) as reward - maximizing the sum of log returns is equivalent to maximizing geometric growth rate, which inherently favors consistency. We used log returns as the reward for the high-level agent, which should lead it to maximize the portfolio's compounded growth. Alternatively, one could use Sharpe ratio itself over a window as a reward, but that is a bit non-stationary and hard to optimize directly in RL. For the low-level agent, the reward is negative trading cost. If the low-level executes all trades, it pays cost $= \sum_i |\Delta w_i| \times c$, where c is cost per unit. We give the low-level a reward of −cost. We also give a small penalty if it fails to achieve the target weights by the next high-level decision. Thus, the low-level tries to strike a balance between speed versus cost of execution.

3.2 Neural Network Architecture

The high-level policy network is a multi-layer perceptron (MLP) with two hidden layers of 64 neurons each (using ReLU activations). It takes the state vector and outputs 4 numbers (which go through Softmax to become weights). We also have a high-level value network of similar architecture for the critic. The low-level policy could be a smaller network. For example, the low-level could be just a linear policy that decides a fraction of the order to execute.

3.3 Training Procedure

We train the agents using a form of Proximal Policy Optimization (PPO), which is a stable actor-critic policy gradient method (Schulman et al., 2017). PPO optimizes a surrogate objective with a clipping term to ensure the policy doesn't change too abruptly. We simulate episodes of the environment. Throughout an episode, the high-level agent makes daily decisions; after each decision, the portfolio return is realized (with cost) and used to compute rewards. We accumulate rewards and use advantage estimation (GAE - generalized advantage estimation) to update the policy. Because financial data is highly stochastic, we use a relatively small discount factor (e.g. γ=0.99 for daily steps) so that the agent focuses on cumulative returns over a horizon of a few months implicitly. We also normalize rewards to help training stability.

Training a hierarchical agent can be done in a nested loop: for each high-level decision step, we unroll the low-level policy for the intermediate steps. However, since we simplified low-level to essentially one-step with cost, we handle it by an analytic solution: given target and cost model, the low-level's optimal execution fraction can be derived. In a more complex scenario, we would train the low-level with its own RL. One could alternate training: fix high-level policy, train low-level for many episodes to optimize execution; then fix low-level and train high-level given that low-level; iterate until convergence. Wang et al. (2021) indeed used iterative training with pre-training of low-level.

During training, we also include risk management constraints as needed. For instance, we impose that the portfolio leverage is 1 (no borrowing) and no short positions - these are handled by the action parameterization. We might also impose a maximum position size per asset (e.g., at most 70% in any single asset) to encourage diversification - this can be encoded by clipping the action or adding a penalty if w_i goes above 0.7 for any i. In our implementation we allowed full 0-100% range for each asset (the agent actually learned to go all-in on one asset at times, which is interesting as a learned behavior, though a real fund might have constraints against such concentration). The training was conducted over 5 years of historical daily data (2018-2023), using rolling windows to augment the training samples. We used an epsilon-greedy exploration for the high-level agent initially and gradually shifted to purely greedy actions as training progressed. The low-level inherently explores by trying random execution fractions.

We evaluated performance on a validation set (e.g., 2022 data) to tune hyperparameters (learning rate, reward scaling, etc.) and avoid overfitting to one particular market period. The result of training is a high-level policy that, given any day's market state, outputs an allocation, and a low-level policy that given a rebalance instruction outputs actual trades. We then fixed these learned policies and tested them on the out-of-sample period (July 2023-June 2025) to assess how well the strategy works on new data it was not trained on.

4. RESULTS AND DISCUSSION

4.1 Portfolio Performance Overview

Over the two-year out-of-sample test period from July 1, 2023 to June 30, 2025, the hierarchical RL portfolio delivered outstanding performance. The annualized return was approximately 45.5%, with an annualized volatility of about 12.5%, resulting in a Sharpe ratio of about 3.6. The maximum peak-to-trough drawdown experienced by the portfolio was only -6.2%, meaning at worst it declined just 6.2% from a previous high value. For context, a Sharpe ratio above 1 is considered good in asset management, above 2 is excellent, and 3+ is extremely rare. The RL portfolio's Sharpe of 3.6 indicates an exceptionally efficient risk-reward profile.

To put these numbers in perspective, we compare with the performance of the individual asset class benchmarks (each held as a static investment) over the same period. We use representative ETFs for each asset: SPY for equities, LQD for bonds, DBC for commodities, and GLD for gold. Figure 2 below shows the growth of a \$1 initial investment in each of these assets versus the RL-managed portfolio from June 30, 2023 through June 30, 2025.

Figure 2. Cumulative growth of $1 from July 2023 to June 2025 for the RL portfolio vs. individual asset benchmarks.

As Figure 2 illustrates, the RL strategy's equity curve (orange) rises far more steeply than the others, whereas the next best (gold, red) ends around $1.6, and SPY (blue) around $1.4. Over this period, equities (SPY) had strong gains - the S&P 500 rallied in late 2023 and throughout 2024, delivering approximately +40-45% cumulative return (20% annualized). Gold (GLD) performed very well too - it appreciated substantially especially in 2024 and early 2025 amid inflation concerns and geopolitical tensions, yielding roughly +60% cumulative (30% annualized). The commodity index (DBC) had modest gains, roughly +4% total (2% annualized). In fact, commodities were choppy: DBC initially declined in late 2023, then recovered in 2024 with oil and metals rising, but still ended only slightly above where it started. Bonds (LQD) were relatively flat: about +8% total (~4% annualized). This is not surprising since 2023-2025 was a period of rising interest rates; bonds had fallen in 2022 and saw only a mild rebound as yields stabilized at higher levels.

Now, comparing these to the RL portfolio: the RL agent managed to more than double the initial capital (+110% total, 45% annualized). And it achieved this with lower volatility and drawdowns than even the stock market alone. The S&P 500 (SPY) experienced some interim volatility - for instance, a pullback of around -10% in late 2024 when concerns about Fed policy and geopolitical events rattled markets. Gold, while rising strongly by the end, also saw some swings (it had a mid-2024 dip of about -8% before surging). The RL portfolio's drawdown was only -6.2%, significantly smaller than SPY's and GLD's drawdowns in that period. In other words, the RL strategy not only amplified returns but also mitigated downside risk effectively. The result is a near-monotonic equity curve in Figure 2, whereas the others have more bumps.

4.2 Asset Allocation Dynamics

By analyzing the agent's actions over time, we find that it exhibited intuitive and timely allocation shifts that capitalized on each asset's strengths in different subperiods, essentially performing a form of tactical asset rotation that a human macro investor could only dream of executing so perfectly.

In the latter half of 2023 (Jul-Dec 2023), equities were rallying. The RL portfolio correspondingly placed heavy weights on SPY during this period. In fact, on many days in late 2023, the agent allocated 100% to SPY. This aggressive stance paid off, as SPY gained roughly +10% in that half-year. The agent largely avoided commodities and gold during this time, as they were underperforming or relatively stagnant. The bond allocation was minimal as well, since rising yields were hurting bond prices. Essentially, the RL agent correctly identified a "risk-on" regime and went all-in on equities to maximize returns. This is something a static diversified portfolio would not do - for example, a 60/40 portfolio would have kept 40% in bonds and missed part of the equity upside. The RL agent, by contrast, learned that in such conditions the marginal Sharpe gain from diversifying is lower than the lost return from not being fully in equities.

Moving into 2024, early in the year the stock market and gold both were climbing, but there were also some volatility events. The RL agent started to allocate partially to gold as well. We observed that in mid-2024, when inflation readings came hot and there were geopolitical flare-ups, gold prices jumped. The agent frequently shifted to a barbell allocation between SPY and GLD. For instance, in April 2024 when a banking sector scare caused stocks to wobble and gold spiked, the agent quickly rebalanced from roughly 70% SPY / 30% GLD to almost 0% SPY / 100% GLD over a few days, capturing gold's sharp rise. Once the situation stabilized, it rotated back to equities. This ability to rapidly rotate into safe havens during market stress limited the portfolio's drawdown. We can specifically note a period in Figure 2: around April-May 2024, SPY had a dip, but the RL portfolio hardly budged or even continued rising - indicating it likely held gold or bonds during that equity dip, cushioning the impact.

By late 2024, gold was in a strong bull trend. The RL agent at that point allocated very heavily to GLD. Indeed, the largest contributor to the portfolio's gains in early 2025 was the gold position. Gold's price soared. The RL portfolio was at times 100% in gold during early 2025, which allowed it to ride that surge. Equities in early 2025 were choppier. The agent's allocations show it de-risked from stocks and loaded up on gold and also some bonds. We found that in some instances, the agent held a mix of GLD and LQD (bonds) - a very defensive allocation - when it predicted an equity pullback. This coincided with a mild downturn in stocks, which the RL portfolio mostly sidestepped.

Meanwhile, the agent's use of bonds (LQD) was limited but strategic. During most of the test period, bonds were not very attractive (flat returns). The agent recognized this and often kept negligible weight in LQD, except during certain short spans where bond prices were ticking up. The RL agent treated bonds primarily as a capital preservation parking spot when it wanted to reduce volatility without abandoning the market entirely. For example, after a strong run-up, if neither stocks nor gold had a clear trend for a few weeks, the agent would sometimes allocate a portion to LQD to earn a small yield and reduce risk. This tactical move improved Sharpe ratio by avoiding whipsaw losses.

Interestingly, the RL agent did allocate to commodities (DBC) on a few occasions when specific commodity prices were rallying. For instance, in late 2024, oil prices jumped due to supply cuts - DBC (which is heavily energy-weighted) saw a spike. The agent temporarily increased DBC weight from near 0 to about 50% to capture a short-term commodity upswing, before reverting out once momentum waned. While these DBC plays were not major profit centers compared to SPY or GLD, they still contributed marginal gains and demonstrated the agent's opportunism. However, because commodities overall had the lowest return, the agent correctly avoided holding DBC for long stretches, preventing the drag that a static allocation to commodities would have caused in this period.

4.3 Risk and Trading Analysis

Not only did the RL portfolio achieve high returns, it did so with commendable risk management. The volatility of 12.5% was actually lower than that of equities as SPY's volatility over the period was around 15% annualized. Volatility is calculated over the whole period; whenever an asset was about to become volatile, the agent reduced exposure, thereby dampening the portfolio's overall volatility. This dynamic variance reduction is essentially conditional diversification over time rather than at a single point in time. Traditional diversification holds assets simultaneously to benefit from low correlation; the RL strategy diversified across time by holding different assets at different times, achieving a similar effect of smoothing returns, but in an active manner.

The max drawdown of -6.2% is remarkably low - much lower than the drawdowns each asset experienced. This indicates the portfolio never lost more than 6.2% from a prior peak, which is a very shallow decline. Many risk-managed hedge funds would envy such a profile. The agent's ability to cut risk when necessary is the reason. Effectively, the RL agent exhibited loss-aversion behavior that is built into its reward optimization. We did not explicitly program a stop-loss or maximum drawdown rule, yet the agent *learned* to avoid prolonged underwater periods.

Another aspect to consider is the turnover and transaction costs of the strategy. The RL portfolio did trade actively - allocations changed significantly perhaps a few times each month (whenever the agent's signals shifted). The realized turnover was about 8% of the portfolio per day on average, This is high, but because we modeled relatively low transaction costs for liquid ETFs, it was still profitable. We did include a transaction cost in training (5 bps per 1% traded), which the agent had to overcome. It's noteworthy that even with this friction, the agent found it optimal to trade frequently - implying that the signals it found have short to medium-term predictive power that outweighs the costs. In reality, such frequent reallocation might incur taxes and slippage that could reduce net returns; our simulation suggests that if trading costs were higher, the agent would likely moderate its activity to an optimal point.

During the test, the estimated cost impact on the portfolio was modest: the portfolio's gross return (before cost) was higher, but after subtracting trading costs the net return was 45.5% annualized. The strategy still vastly outperformed the buy-and-hold assets on a net basis. One might wonder if a simpler strategy, like always picking the best performer of last month ("momentum") or a moving average timing rule, could achieve something similar. Those simpler strategies would likely capture some of the effect but not to the same degree - the RL agent can learn a more complex policy. For instance, momentum might have told us to buy stocks in late 2023 and hold into 2024but momentum might have failed to switch to gold quickly because gold's big move was somewhat abrupt. The RL agent, however, because it looks at cross-asset information, possibly caught an early shift. Additionally, the RL can learn nonlinear combinations of signals - maybe a certain pattern of yield-curve inversion + equity valuation signals led it to predict a regime change that a single-indicator strategy wouldn't catch. This is somewhat speculative, but it underscores that RL has flexibility to incorporate many data sources and optimize directly for the end goal (return), potentially yielding a more performant strategy than manual rules.

4.4 Comparison with Benchmarks and Other Strategies

It is instructive to compare the RL portfolio not only to single assets but also to some benchmark multi-asset strategies. A classic benchmark is the 60/40 portfolio. Over our test period, a 60/40 portfolio would have had a decent return since equities did well - roughly, it might return 25% total, and volatility about 60% of equity volatility, so vol 9%. The 60/40 Sharpe might be around 1.8-2.0. The RL portfolio's Sharpe of 3.6 is much higher, highlighting how effective the tactical moves were. Another benchmark could be a risk parity or equal-risk contribution among the four assets. Given the low correlation between stocks and bonds and negative correlation of gold, an equal-risk mix might have had even lower volatility 8% and perhaps a similar return 20%, Sharpe 2.5 at best. None of these static allocations approach the 3.6 Sharpe of RL.

Even relative to other active strategies: Global Tactical Asset Allocation (GTAA) funds run by humans often achieve Sharpe 1-1.5 in real life. Trend-following CTAs (Commodity Trading Advisors) that trade across asset classes sometimes get to Sharpe 1-2. The RL strategy appears to have exploited the particular market period exceptionally well. We should caution that this period had trending behavior that was somewhat easier to exploit. A different scenario might have been harder for the agent; future research would test the strategy in various market regimes to see how consistent it is.

4.5 Analysis of Hierarchical Approach Contribution

In our experiment, the hierarchical structure's advantage was mainly in training stability and conceptual separation of allocation vs. trading. Even though we didn't simulate multi-step low-level actions, we did include trading cost in the reward. We can imagine that if we had a finer simulation, the low-level would actually handle, say, splitting a big trade into pieces or waiting for better liquidity intraday. That would further improve performance by reducing slippage. Our approach can be seen as a bi-level optimization: the high-level chooses weights, and an inner optimizer (low-level) minimizes trading cost to reach those weights. In a simpler non-hierarchical RL, one might try to directly penalize changes in weights to account for cost. That could work too. The hierarchical approach is a more principled way to do it, treating execution as its own Markov Decision Process. In our results, the outcome certainly depended on having some mechanism to account for costs - otherwise, the agent might have over-traded. We found that the agent did learn to moderate unnecessary trading - it often kept allocations stable unless there was a clear reason to shift. This behavior likely arose from the cost-aware reward design.

It's also noteworthy how the high-level agent learned *not* to always be 100% in the single best asset every single day. There were days where, say, SPY and GLD were both trending up - the agent sometimes held a mix (maybe 50/50) to hedge bets. This indicates it recognized uncertainty: combining assets can be good if it's not entirely sure which will perform better tomorrow. This led to a smoother ride. Such subtle behavior is a result of optimizing the long-term reward with risk in mind.

4.6 Robustness and Limitations

While the results are impressive, we should discuss limitations and the robustness of this approach. Firstly, overfitting is a concern in any data-driven strategy. We took measures like validation testing and including transaction costs to avoid extremely overfit behavior (like frantic switching on noise). The fact that the strategy aligns with economic intuition (risk-on/risk-off shifts) gives comfort that it's capturing genuine market patterns, not just artifacts. However, the true test would be forward performance in live markets - which, of course, we cannot evaluate here.

Secondly, our simplified low-level model might not capture all real frictions. In reality, if the agent decided to go 100% gold from 100% stocks in one day, a real fund might take a few days to execute that large a shift without moving markets. Our model charged a cost, but maybe not enough - we used 5 bps per 1% trade, so switching 100% incurred ~5% cost roundtrip. The portfolio's huge excess return overshadowed this. If costs were higher, returns would be a bit lower. One might incorporate more realistic constraints and see if the strategy still performs well. Likely it would, but maybe a bit toned down.

Another limitation is that our state space did not include some fundamental economic data that a human might use (e.g., CPI reports, Fed decisions). The agent relied purely on market prices/indicators which often do reflect such information implicitly. But there could be scenarios were incorporating macro data directly helps. The RL framework can easily take additional features.

From a hierarchical RL perspective, one extension would be to add more hierarchy levels or agents. For example, a 3-level hierarchy: a yearly planner that adjusts broad risk target, a monthly allocator, and a daily executor. For our four assets, that might be overkill. But for a larger universe, a mid-level picks within each class, and a low level executes trades. This mirrors how big institutions manage money. Hierarchical RL could naturally accommodate that structure by cascading decisions from coarse to fine.

4.7 Comparison to other AI approaches

It's worth mentioning how our RL approach compares to other AI or statistical methods for asset allocation. One popular approach is using supervised learning to predict asset returns or rankings (like using machine learning to forecast next month's returns of each asset, then allocate to top predictions). Such predictive models might achieve some success, but they often struggle because small prediction errors can lead to big performance differences and they don't inherently account for the feedback loop of decisions. RL, on the other hand, directly optimizes the decision rule for the final objective (return), which is a more end-to-end approach. Essentially RL can learn when to trust a prediction and when not to, because it sees the realized reward. In our results, the RL agent effectively learned a market-timing strategy without an explicit predictive model; it's all encoded in its policy network which maps state to allocation. This end-to-end training likely contributed to the high Sharpe result - it wasn't just predicting returns, it was learning the optimal allocation given its confidence in those predictions.

Another approach is mean-variance optimization with dynamic inputs. If one had perfect foresight of returns distribution, mean-variance would give the best allocation. But in practice, estimating expected returns is very hard. Many quantitative asset managers use some variant of this with shrinkage estimators for covariance and heuristic expected returns. An RL agent implicitly does something similar internally, but it can capture non-linear and path-dependent aspects that mean-variance cannot. The fact that our RL achieved much higher returns suggests it was able to exploit short-term trends in a way that a monthly mean-variance optimizer might not, due to estimation lag.

4.8 Economic Interpretability

By probing the policy network, we could approximate it as follows: it seems to implement a combination of trend-following and risk-triggered rotation. For each asset, if its recent momentum is strongly positive, the agent leans into that asset (trend). But if volatility spikes or there's a divergence, it shifts to defensive assets preemptively. In many ways, this resembles a global macro strategy that monitors market technicals and reallocates accordingly. The difference is the RL policy might pick up subtle nonlinear thresholds or interactions that a human might miss (for example, "if stocks had a +2% day but VIX (volatility index) also rose, then it's a weird regime - maybe shift to gold" - a rule like that could be learned).

The hierarchical setup also provides some interpretability: the high-level agent's decisions can be analyzed in terms of which input features were most influential. We could examine, say, a day when the agent moved heavily into gold and find that it was likely due to a spike in gold's momentum and an increase in equity volatility, etc. Such post-hoc analysis confirms that the agent is behaving in line with market intuition rather than some obscure overfit criterion.

4.9 Robustness in Different Scenarios

While our test period was favorable to the strategy, we should consider how it might fare in less trending or more correlated scenarios. If, for instance, both stocks and commodities and gold all fell together, the agent would likely allocate to bonds (if bonds are up) or go mostly to cash. In a severe crash, it might still incur a drawdown if all assets drop - but presumably less than pure equity. If all assets rise together, the agent might spread out or stick to the highest Sharpe one - either way it would still make gains, though maybe its edge is smaller because diversification isn't as needed when everything is up.

One potential weakness is regime shifts that aren't reflected in recent data. For example, if a sudden shock occurs. It doesn't have a built-in "knowledge" of events - it purely reacts to market signals. That's why having some macro features might improve it. Overall, the hierarchical reinforcement learning approach proved to be highly effective in this study, yielding a portfolio that dramatically outperformed traditional allocations and did so with lower risk. It essentially achieved the holy grail of investing: "high returns with low risk," by dynamically allocating capital to the right asset at the right time.

5. CONCLUSION

In this paper, we demonstrated the application of hierarchical deep reinforcement learning to multi-asset portfolio management using four distinct asset classes (equities, bonds, commodities, and gold). We began by reviewing the theoretical foundations of portfolio construction and the importance of diversification across asset classes, highlighting how each of our chosen assets contributes different risk/return characteristics and hedging properties to a portfolio. We then surveyed the evolution of reinforcement learning in finance - from early reinforcement trading systems to modern deep RL techniques - and introduced the concept of hierarchical RL, which decomposes the portfolio decision problem into multiple layers for improved tractability and performance.

Our methodology involved training a two-level RL agent: a high-level policy that decides the asset allocation and a low-level policy that handles trade execution subject to transaction costs. This hierarchical approach aligns with real-world portfolio management workflows and enables the agent to learn both what to trade and how to trade (minimizing costs and slippage). We described the state representation, action space, and reward functions used to train the agent on historical market data, employing techniques like policy gradient (PPO) and cost penalties to ensure the learned strategy is both profitable and practically feasible.

The results on out-of-sample test data (mid-2023 to mid-2025) were striking: the RL-managed portfolio achieved an annualized return of 45% with only 12.5% volatility and a maximum drawdown of 6%, vastly outperforming each individual asset as well as standard static portfolios. It successfully navigated between asset classes - overweighting U.S. equities during bull phases, rotating into gold and bonds during risk-off periods, and even capitalizing on short-term commodity rallies - in a manner that yielded a dramatically higher Sharpe ratio ($\approx$3.6) than any single asset or benchmark mix over the same period. The agent effectively learned to time the market and manage risk in a way that would be extremely difficult to accomplish with traditional methods or human intuition alone. By adjusting allocations on a nearly daily basis, it could respond to new information much faster than typical allocation strategies (which might rebalance monthly or quarterly). And by incorporating transaction cost awareness (via the low-level execution policy), it avoided trading in and out frivolously, focusing on substantive regime shifts.

These findings underscore the potential of reinforcement learning as a powerful tool for portfolio optimization. The hierarchical framework, in particular, provided structure and improved performance by separating concerns: the high-level agent could concentrate on the strategic allocation problem, while the low-level agent ensured that those allocations could be implemented efficiently. This separation likely improved learning efficiency and robustness. Even though our low-level execution was simplified, the concept is general and can be extended - future implementations could plug in realistic trading simulators and let the low-level agent learn execution tactics such as slicing orders or using limit orders to further minimize impact.

In terms of contributions to the literature, our work illustrates in a concrete case study how hierarchical RL techniques (previously applied in academic studies like Wang et al. 2021 and Qin et al. 2024) can be adapted to a multi-asset investment scenario with excellent results. It bridges the gap between theoretical proposals of HRL in finance and a practical example with well-known assets. We also showed that an RL agent can implicitly learn classic investing logic (like trend following, safe haven rotation) but in a data-driven way that exploits it more consistently than a fixed rule would.

There are several avenues for further research and improvement. First, one could increase the universe of assets to see if the agent can handle more assets and possibly discover even better diversification opportunities. This might require more advanced hierarchical structures. Second, incorporating macro-economic and fundamental data explicitly could allow the agent to anticipate regime changes that price data alone might not reveal until somewhat late. For instance, an agent that "reads" the yield curve inversion or inflation trends could pre-emptively shift allocation before market prices move. Third, testing the strategy in different historical periods would be important to validate its robustness. We would expect an agent trained on a broad dataset to handle various regimes, but targeted testing could uncover any weaknesses. If so, one could enhance the training by including more variety or by ensemble methods.

From a practical perspective, interpretability and trust are key if such a system were to be deployed in a real investment setting. We would need to ensure the agent's decisions make economic sense and there are guardrails to prevent extreme bets that a human manager wouldn't be comfortable with. Fortunately, our results show the agent often behaved in a sensible manner. Introducing mild constraints could address that without much performance loss.

Overall, this work contributes to the evidence that reinforcement learning is a viable and powerful approach for portfolio optimization, and that incorporating hierarchical structures can further enhance its effectiveness by aligning the learning process with real-world decision hierarchies and constraints. As with any model, continuous evaluation and retraining are necessary as market conditions evolve. But given the adaptive nature of RL, we are optimistic that these models can keep up with changing regimes better than static strategies. The period we tested included inflationary shocks, war tensions, and monetary policy shifts - and the model navigated all of them successfully. Going forward, integrating more data and extending the hierarchy could make these systems even more robust and capable. The pursuit of the ultimate "all-weather adaptive portfolio" may well be aided greatly by reinforcement learning techniques, and our study is one step in that direction, showcasing a high-performing example of such a system.

REFERENCES

Almahdi, S., & Yang, S. Y. (2017). An adaptive portfolio trading system: A risk-return portfolio optimization using recurrent reinforcement learning with expected maximum drawdown. *Expert Systems with Applications*, *87*, 267–279. DOI: 10.1016/j.eswa.2017.06.023

Almgren, R., & Chriss, N. (2001). Optimal execution of portfolio transactions. *The Journal of Risk*, *3*, 5–40.

Baele, L., Bekaert, G., & Inghelbrecht, K. (2010). The determinants of stock and bond return comovements. *Review of Financial Studies*, *23*(6), 2374–2428.

Bakker, B., & Schmidhuber, J. (2004, March). Hierarchical reinforcement learning based on subgoal discovery and subpolicy specialization. In *the 8th Conference on Intelligent Autonomous Systems* (pp. 438-445).

Baur, D. G., & Lucey, B. M. (2010). Is gold a hedge or a safe haven? An analysis of stocks, bonds and gold. *Financial Review*, *45*(2), 217–229. DOI: 10.1111/j.1540-6288.2010.00244.x

Bekaert, G., & Harvey, C. R. (1995). Time-varying world market integration. *the Journal of Finance*, *50*(2), 403-444. DOI: 10.1111/j.1540-6261.1995.tb04790.x

Buehler, H., Gonon, L., Teichmann, J., & Wood, B. (2019). Deep hedging. *Quantitative Finance*, *19*(8), 1271–1291. DOI: 10.1080/14697688.2019.1571683

Campbell, J. Y., Sunderam, A., & Viceira, L. M. (2009). *Inflation bets or deflation hedges? The changing risks of nominal bonds (No. w14701)*. National Bureau of Economic Research.

Dayan, P., & Hinton, G. E. (1992). Feudal reinforcement learning. In *Advances in Neural Information Processing Systems* (Vol. 5, pp. 271-278).

Dempster, M. A., & Leemans, V. (2006). An automated FX trading system using adaptive reinforcement learning. *Expert Systems with Applications*, *30*(3), 543–552. DOI: 10.1016/j.eswa.2005.10.012

Elton, E. J., Gruber, M. J., Brown, S. J., & Goetzmann, W. N. (2009). *Modern portfolio theory and investment analysis*. John Wiley & Sons.

Engle III, R. F., & Sheppard, K. (2001). Theoretical and empirical properties of dynamic conditional correlation multivariate GARCH. DOI: 10.3386/w8554

Erb, C. B., & Harvey, C. R. (2006). The strategic and tactical value of commodity futures. *Financial Analysts Journal*, *62*(2), 69–97. DOI: 10.2139/ssrn.650923

Fischer, T., & Krauss, C. (2018). Deep learning with long short-term memory networks for financial market predictions. *European Journal of Operational Research*, *270*(2), 654–669. DOI: 10.1016/j.ejor.2017.11.054

Gorton, G., & Rouwenhorst, K. G. (2006). Facts and fantasies about commodity futures. *Financial Analysts Journal*, *62*(2), 47–68.

Gupta, R., Pandey, A., & Pandey, A. (2025). Can deep reinforcement learning reliably improve dynamic portfolio allocation? *Available at SSRN* 5241923. DOI: 10.2139/ssrn.5241923

Haider, A., Hawe, G. I., Wang, H., & Scotney, B. (2021, October). Multi-asset market making via multi-task deep reinforcement learning. In *International Conference on Machine Learning, Optimization, and Data Science* (pp. 353-364). Springer. https://doi.org/10.1007/978-3-030-95470-3_27

Jiang, Z., Xu, D., & Liang, J. (2017). A deep reinforcement learning framework for the financial portfolio management problem. *arXiv preprint*, arXiv:1706.10059. /arXiv.1706.10059DOI: 10.48550

Li, Y. (2017). Deep reinforcement learning: An overview. *arXiv preprint*, arXiv:1701.07274. /arXiv.1701.07274DOI: 10.48550

Liang, Z., Chen, H., Zhu, J., Jiang, K., & Li, Y. (2018). Adversarial deep reinforcement learning in portfolio management. *arXiv preprint*, arXiv:1808.09940. /arXiv.1808.09940DOI: 10.48550

Lillicrap, T. P., Hunt, J. J., Pritzel, A., Heess, N., Erez, T., Tassa, Y., Silver, D., & Wierstra, D. (2015). Continuous control with deep reinforcement learning. *arXiv preprint*, arXiv:1509.02971. /arXiv.1509.02971DOI: 10.48550

Liu, X. Y., Xiong, Z., Zhong, S., Yang, H., & Walid, A. (2018). Practical deep reinforcement learning approach for stock trading. *arXiv preprint*, arXiv:1811.07522. https://doi.org/10.48550/arXiv.1811.07522

Llmanen, A. (2011). *Expected returns: An investor's guide to harvesting market rewards*. John Wiley & Sons.

Markowitz, H. (1952). Portfolio selection. *The Journal of Finance*, *7*(1), 77–91. DOI: 10.1111/j.1540-6261.1952.tb01525.x

Moody, J., & Saffell, M. (2001). Learning to trade via direct reinforcement. *IEEE Transactions on Neural Networks*, *12*(4), 875–889. DOI: 10.1109/72.935097

Moskovitz, T., Parker-Holder, J., Pacchiano, A., Arbel, M., & Jordan, M. (2021). Tactical optimism and pessimism for deep reinforcement learning. *Advances in Neural Information Processing Systems*, *34*, 12849–12863.

Schulman, J., Wolski, F., Dhariwal, P., Radford, A., & Klimov, O. (2017). Proximal policy optimization algorithms. *arXiv preprint*, arXiv:1707.06347. /arXiv.1707.06347DOI: 10.48550

Sutton, R. S., & Barto, A. G. (2018). *Reinforcement learning: An introduction* (2nd ed.). MIT Press.

Sutton, R. S., Precup, D., & Singh, S. (1999). Between MDPs and semi-MDPs: A framework for temporal abstraction in reinforcement learning. *Artificial Intelligence*, *112*(1-2), 181–211. DOI: 10.1016/S0004-3702(99)00052-1

Tsay, R. S. (2010). *Analysis of financial time series* (3rd ed.). Wiley.

Wang, R., Wei, H., An, B., Feng, Z., & Yao, J. (2020). Deep stock trading: A hierarchical reinforcement learning framework for portfolio optimization and order execution. *arXiv preprint*, arXiv:2012.12620. /arXiv.2012.12620DOI: 10.48550

Yang, H., Liu, X. Y., Zhong, S., & Walid, A. (2020, October). Deep reinforcement learning for automated stock trading: An ensemble strategy. In *Proceedings of the First ACM International Conference on AI in Finance* (pp. 1-8). DOI: 10.1145/3383455.3422540

Zhang, C., Liang, S., Lyu, F., & Fang, L. (2020). Stock-index tracking optimization using auto-encoders. *Frontiers in Physics*, *8*, 388.

Zhao, Z., & Welsch, R. E. (2024). Hierarchical reinforced trader (HRT): A bi-level approach for optimizing stock selection and execution. *arXiv preprint*, arXiv:2410.14927. https://doi.org/10.48550/arXiv.2410.14927

ENDNOTE

1 Corresponding Author: e18820@outlook.com

Chapter 7
Deep Learning for Global Equity Forecasting: New Evidence Across Major Markets

N. Sathyanarayana
https://orcid.org/0000-0002-4185-7751
Jain University, India

V. Lava Kumar
https://orcid.org/0000-0002-3539-9280
GITAM University, India

Varanasi Rahul
https://orcid.org/0000-0003-2407-7654
Jain University, India

Madireddi S. S. V. Sri Kumar
https://orcid.org/0000-0003-1190-1552
Global Business School, Koneru Lakshmaiah Education Foundation, India

G. Laxmana Rao
https://orcid.org/0000-0002-7911-7927
Dayananda Sagar University, India

ABSTRACT

Deep learning architectures have advanced global equity forecasting by capturing nonlinear and long-range dependencies across major markets. This study empirically assesses their predictive power on international indices (S&P 500, FTSE 100, Nikkei 225, Hang Seng, DAX 30) from 2010 to 2023, benchmarking against

DOI: 10.4018/979-8-3373-2838-6.ch007

ARIMA and GARCH models. Results show that deep learning models outperform traditional econometrics in forecast accuracy, directional prediction, and Sharpe ratios, especially under volatile or regime-switching conditions. However, their "black-box" nature limits interpretability, raising concerns for financial decision-making and regulation. Techniques like SHAP, LIME, and Transformer attention help bridge this gap. We further explore applications in algorithmic trading, portfolio optimization, and market stress testing, while addressing ethical risks and regulatory challenges. Our findings underline deep learning's potential in finance, contingent on explainability and governance.

1 INTRODUCTION

Financial topography in markets changed dramatically over the last decades, driven by developments in statistical modelling, econometrics, and artificial intelligence in more recent years. The perennial challenge in finance to forecast asset prices was based in the past upon cornerstone theories like the Capital Asset Pricing Model (CAPM) and more standard econometric methods like autoregressive integrated moving average (ARIMA) and generalised autoregressive conditional heteroskedasticity (GARCH). Those gave valuable insights into markets as well as into risk. However, their linear formulation and limited power to deal with complicated, non-linear relations restricted their forecast potential in more volatile, high-data regimes. The first decades of the 21st century saw machine learning introduce high-powered instruments to model complicated patterns in financial series. However, in recent years, deep learning architectures—e.g., Long Short-Term Memory (LSTM) networks, Convolutional Neural Networks (CNN), and Transformer architectures—have taken asset price forecasting to unprecedented accuracy and sophistication.

Deep learning improves international equity forecasting by handling enormous datasets, identifying hidden time correlations, and combining data. Unlike typical algorithms, such systems can learn to detect long-distance links and rare, subtle nonlinear interactions—deep learning challenges finance. The "black-box" problem of neural networks hides the decision-making process and makes interpretability difficult, which requires financial regulation, risk management, and investor confidence. Recently developed explainable AI (XAI) approaches like SHAP, LIME, and attention offer intriguing solutions, but openness sacrifices predictive capability.

Deep learning models in real-world financial applications opened new paths for portfolio optimisation, algorithmic trading, and market scenario analysis, generating ethical and legal problems. Due to fairness, discrimination, systemic risk, and market manipulation, adaptive regulation and continual monitoring are needed. Deep learning predictive models for asset price prediction are extensively described in the chapter, along with their practical obstacles, interpretability issues, growing importance in financial decision-making, and ethical and regulatory concerns.

The objectives of this chapter are three. First, empirically examine the ability of deep learning models, including LSTM, CNN, and Transformer, to forecast stock prices in international equity markets, compared to traditional econometric ones like ARIMA and GARCH. Second, to explore the real-life challenges, particularly the interpretability of the black box nature of deep learning, in finance, to what extent can new developments in explainable AI partially reduce them? Third, to investigate real applications of such methods in portfolio management and trading, together with their ethical considerations, as well as challenges in regulation in their widespread use in financial services worldwide.

2 EVOLUTION OF PREDICTIVE MODELS IN FINANCIAL ECONOMICS

Financial economics is an ever-changing field which synthesises theory and financial institutions within the overall economic framework. It synthesises numerous theories within economics, ranging from general equilibrium analysis and information economics to contract theory. It applies them to form major concepts like the Capital Asset Pricing Model (CAPM), arbitrage pricing, option pricing, and the Modigliani-Miller theorem. This synthesis creates an interdisciplinary understanding of financial markets and how financial resources are most effectively allocated to create optimum value and satisfaction (Eichberger & Harper, 1997).

2.1 Early Statistical Foundations (1950s–1970s)

The financial theory of predictive modelling has its genesis in the progress of statistical theory, including the Random Walk Hypothesis and Markowitz's modern portfolio theory. Markowitz (1952) first proved the concept of mean-variance optimisation, illustrating the way investors might be able to form efficient portfolios under uncertainty. Sharpe (1964) then codified the Capital Asset Pricing Model (CAPM), which connected expected return to systematic risk determinants. Such early models equated asset returns as linear multiples of the risk and manageable forecast frameworks, which held sway over academia and professional practice for two decades (Sezer et al., 2020).

2.2 Volatility Modelling and ARCH/GARCH (1980s–1990s)

The central turning point was Engle's (1982) Autoregressive Conditional Heteroskedasticity (ARCH) model, which formally modelled financial time series volatility as changing over time. By making the variance at the present moment a function of lagged squares of innovations, ARCH incorporated clustering of high-volatility periods, a feature missing from previous constant-variance models. This was further developed by Bollerslev (1986) into the GARCH model for greater flexibility. These models greatly enhanced risk predictions—vital for option pricing and Value-at-Risk estimation—and became routine procedures for econometrics software (Engle, 1982; Bollerslev, 1986).

2.3 Expansion to Multivariate and Nonlinear Models (1990s–2000s)

During the 1990s, multivariate GARCH and stochastic volatility models became dominant, facilitating joint modelling of return and risk dynamics across asset classes. Concurrently, researchers used regime-switching and threshold models to capture stochastic dependencies (Hamilton, 1989). These methods facilitated different market "states" (e.g., bull and bear) having different dynamics, and the generation of better forecasts during crises. A bibliometric survey of quantitative modelling between 2008 and 2019 shows this growth to over 800 techniques, ranging from tests, risk models, and sophisticated algorithms, highlighting the field's diversity of methods after the 2008 financial crisis (Quantitative Modelling Frontiers, 2022).

2.4 Time-Series Forecasting and Machine Learning Emergence (2000s–2010s)

The 2000s witnessed increased interest in machine learning (ML) for use in time series predictions. Supervised learning techniques—decision trees, support vector machines, and ensembling strategies—were used for stock returns, credit risk, and volatility prediction. Research showed that ML models generally beat conventional linear regressions, especially when detecting non-linear patterns for high-frequency data (Review of Predictive Modelling, 2024). That being said, practitioners encountered issues involving interpretability, overfitting, and the requirement for large training sets, dampening the enthusiasm despite noticeable improvement in certain situations.

2.5 Big Data and Alternative Data Sources (2010s)

The growth of big data changed predictive modelling by bringing other data—news sentiment, social media, satellite data, and transaction data—into the context of forecasting. Research on Early Warning Systems (EWS) indicates that combining macroeconomic and microeconomic metrics and unstructured data increased crisis-prediction accuracy (Namaki, Eyvazloo, & Ramtinnia, 2023). Financial institutions started applying text-mining and natural-language processing to make quantitative sentiment measures, and network analysis of bank exposures increased systemic-risk projections. These data-intensive methods took models beyond price histories, incorporating broader drivers of financial dynamics.

2.6 Rise of Deep Learning Architectures (2020–2022)

Over the last three years, deep learning (DL) has picked up momentum for price prediction and risk estimation. Convolutional neural networks, long short-term memory (LSTM) networks, and Transformer architectures have been utilised on time-series data, leveraging their ability to capture advanced temporal relationships (Zhang, Sjarif, & Ibrahim, 2023). Generative adversarial networks (GANS) and graph neural networks (GNNS) are trending for scenario generation and modelling cross-asset connectivity. Reviews establish that DL models outperform traditional ML regarding out-of-sample accuracy, especially when trained using large, high-frequency datasets, albeit with cautious tuning to prevent overfitting (Deep Learning Models Review, 2023).

2.7 Predictive Models in Risk Management and Regulation

Regulatory frameworks have evolved to accommodate these modelling innovations. Post-2008 crisis, Basel III guidelines emphasised stress-testing and scenario analysis, and banks took on board EWS and advanced volatility models for capital adequacy calculations (Namaki et al., 2023). Machine learning is now employed for credit scoring, detection against money laundering, and forecasting operational risk. Still, there is concern among regulators about complete model governance through automation owing to model risk, data quality, and algorithmic explainability issues. Hence, "explainable AI" methods are being created to meet performance and compliance needs.

2.8 Algorithmic and High-Frequency Trading Applications

Predictive models form the foundation for algorithmic trading routines, under which millisecond-level predictions guide order execution. Short-run mean-reversal is exploited through statistical arbitrage, and trend-persistence is anticipated through momentum strategies. High-frequency traders use real-time volatility and liquidity predictions, typically derived through continuously calibrated multi-factor models. Efficiency benefits derived from such models have reformatted the microstructure of the markets, boosting competition and lowering bid-ask spreads, but fuelling systemic-risk fears through flash crashes (Review of Predictive Modelling, 2024).

3 BACKGROUND AND LITERATURE REVIEW

Financial economics has evolved from deterministic, closed-form models to dynamic, data-driven approaches. While traditional econometric frameworks such as ARIMA and GARCH provided robust tools for analysing linear relationships and volatility clustering (Engle, 1982; Bollerslev, 1986), they face growing limitations in today's high-frequency, nonlinear financial environments.

3.1 Traditional Models vs. Deep Learning in Market Regimes

Traditional (stationary) time-series models work quite well regarding stationarity. However, they underperform in non-linear or turbulent time periods, such as (e.g., a bear market or through a crisis) (Sezer et al., 2020). Deep learning (DL) models such as LSTM, CNN, and Transformer neural architectures, instead, can model complex, non-linear dependencies and non-stationary dynamics that may be present between various asset classes (Zhang et al., 2024; Sherstinsky, 2020). Empirical evidence for 2020–2024 is that DL models have consistently surpassed the performance of ARIMA and GARCH on several appraisal metrics, especially for forecasting volatility markets and while dealing with regime shifts. Especially in bull or bear markets, the nonparametric flexibility of DL models is superior at adjusting themselves to the alterations in momentum, volatility and trend direction than those of the regression model (Sonkavde et al., 2023; Huang et al., 2024).

Table 1. Detailed Comparative Model Performance

Model Type	Accuracy (RMSE)	Crisis Response	Interpretability	Regime Adaptability	References
ARIMA	Moderate	Weak	High	Low	Sezer et al., 2020; Engle, 1982
GARCH	Good (for volatility)	Moderate	High	Low	Bollerslev, 1986; Engle, 1982; Sonkavde et al., 2023
LSTM	High	Strong	Medium	High	Sherstinsky, 2020; Huang et al., 2024; Sezer et al., 2020; Mienye & Jere, 2024
CNN	Moderate–High	Moderate	Medium	Medium–High	Ketkar & Moolayil, 2021; Sezer et al., 2020; Sonkavde et al., 2023
Transformer	Very High	Very Strong	Medium	Very High	Zhang et al., 2024; Lin et al., 2022; Wang et al., 2022
Hybrid Models (e.g., BiLSTM + Attention, GARCH + DL)	Very High	Strong	Medium–High	Very High	Huang et al., 2024; Chen et al., 2024
GAN-based Models	High (for scenario gen.)	Strong (stress-testing)	Low–Medium	Medium	Koshiyama et al., 2021; Pun et al., 2020; Creswell et al., 2018
Reinforcement Learning (Deep RL)	Context-dependent	Strong (adaptive)	Medium	Very High	Nguyen et al., 2020; Wang et al., 2021; Huang et al., 2024

(Source: Author's contribution)

Table 1 shows a detailed comparison of model performance for use in financial forecasting, informed by evidence produced in academia. The traditional models, including ARIMA and GARCH, are straightforward to use and easy to interpret, however, they are unable to capture the dynamics or the nonlinearity nature of the financial time series under abrupt changes, especially during a crisis or a regime switch (Sezer et al., 2020; Bollerslev, 1986). On the other hand, deep learning models such as LSTM (Hochreiter & Schmidhuber, 1997) and Transformers lead to superior forecasting performance and regime adaptability since they can capture complex temporal relationships and long-term interactions in data (Sherstinsky, 2020; Zhang et al., 2024). CNNs are a compromise as they are good in pattern recognition and short-term prediction but do not have the memory depth for long-term prediction (Ketkar & Moolayil, 2021). In addition, hybrid and GAN-based models are promising as an effective, combinatory approach between interpretability and predictive power, as well as data sparsity and adversarial robustness (Huang et al., 2024; Pun et al., 2020).

3.2 Cold-Start and Over-Fit for Low-Liquidity Assets

Deep-learning models perform well in rich-data settings, but they struggle with assets with low liquidity or for new listings (the so-called "cold start" problem). An example of area that may not have enough data for training of these robust models is illustrated by the case where there is not enough historical data and in such a case, there is a high risk of overfitting and the generalizability is limited (Ahmed et al., 2022; Mienye & Jere, 2024). Classic (less flexible) econometric models can perform better than DLs in such environments due to their stronger regularisation and less data-degenerate behaviour (Engle, 1982; Bollerslev, 1986). Also, deep learning models often need massive hyperparameter optimisation and a large amount of training data, which is not available for the assets from markets in development or with low liquidity. As Sonkavde et al. (2023) note, models may end up memorising noise rather than signal without adequate data, leading to spurious predictions during periods of high volatility or thin volume.

3.3 Learning Deep During Crises and Structural Breaks

On another, closely related note, an area in which DL models could also shine is crisis prediction and regime shift of a more structural nature, like those that occurred during the 2008 financial crisis or more recently during the market stresses triggered by COVID-19. Transformer models also perform well in capturing long-range dependencies and can reweight the historical trends by self-attention mechanisms, making them more adaptable for structural changes (Lin et al., 2022; Zhang et al., 2024). In contrast, ARIMA and GARCH stress traditional statistical properties, and often are slow to adjust to new regimes, underestimating risk and making poor predictions during crises (Sezer et al., 2020; Namaki et al., 2023). These results have indicated the need for model selection based on high accuracy, market conditions, and data types. Hybrid frameworks are being developed to mitigate the trade-off between interpretability and performance by integrating the methodological soundness of econometrics with the flexibility of deep learning (Chen et al., 2024).

4 RESEARCH METHODOLOGY AND EXPERIMENTAL SETUP

This section uses an extensive experimental setup to test deep learning models' effectiveness empirically.

4.1 Data Collection: Technical Indicators and Equity Indices

The dataset is composed of daily historical prices from January 2010 to December 2023, which were sourced from publicly available financial databases, including but not limited to Yahoo Finance and Investing.com, in line with established practice from previous research (Li & Bastos, 2020; Sonkavde et al., 2023). By examining the frequency of daily prices, we found that the level of calmness balancing granularity and computational complexity for deep learning models and being close to reality in trading horizons is daily. In order to have a quasi-representation of world exposure and better control for market heterogeneity, the study adds a range of the most important international equity indices in developed financial markets. The list comprises the S&P 500 of the USA, the FTSE 100 of London, the Nikkei 225 of Japan, the Hang Seng of Hong Kong, the DAX 30 of Germany, etc. These indices were selected to represent various volatility regimes and liquidity conditions in different regions. This choice is consistent with the commonly used threshold levels in earlier financial forecasting studies (Zhang et al., 2023).

Table 2. Descriptive Statistics of Equity Indices (2010–2023)

Index	Mean (Price)	Std. Dev.	Min	Max
S&P 500	2,325.41	738.20	1,025.21	4,375.38
FTSE 100	6,413.12	744.50	4,303.28	7,912.75
Nikkei 225	19,588.34	3,210.73	9,389.89	30,670.10
Hang Seng	23,155.42	3,809.61	15,073.12	32,794.94
DAX 30	11,874.61	1,957.27	6,276.11	16,271.75

(Source: Author's computations)

Note: Prices are adjusted closing values. Values represent entire observation windows prior to normalisation.

Table 2 shows the descriptive Statistics of Equity Indices (2010–2023). To add additional value to the raw price data, many technical Indicators were created, which are commonly used to describe aspects of technical analysis like trends, momentum, and volatility. These were Moving Averages (SMA and EMA), Relative Strength Index (RSI), Bollinger Bands, and Moving Average Convergence Divergence (MACD). The choice of these features is based on common practices in financial forecasting literature and is similar to the selection standards suggested by Sezer et al. (2020)

and Zhang et al. (2023). Such feature engineering improves the signal quality by including non-price-based indicators, which allows the models to generalise when the market is volatile or in a non-linear regime (Li & Bastos, 2020). The input features were normalised through min-max scaling to enhance convergence stability when training a neural network.

The data was chopped into equal-length segments for time-series modelling in deep models following feature matrix constructions. Following (Sezer et al., 2020), window sizes of 30 days were selected, which means that every training sample utilised 30 historical observations to forecast the next-day price. To reduce look-ahead bias, the dataset was split in time:

- January 2010- December 2019 as a training set
- Validation cohort: January 2020 to December 2021
- Test set: 2022 January – 2023 December

This prevents future information from corrupting past learning, preserving the causality necessary for forecasting in the real world (Sonkavde et al., 2023). Cross-validation was performed in a rolling manner, keeping the order of time and allowing for the evaluation of model generalisation across sub-periods.

4.2 Deep Learning Models: Architecture and Implementation

These studies employ various deep learning structures in order to identify complicated temporal as well as nonlinear interactions in financial time series:

- **Long-Short-Term Memory (LSTM) Networks:** LSTMs are recurrent neural network (RNN) architectures designed to address the vanishing gradient problem and represent long-term dependencies in time-series data (Hochreiter & Schmidhuber, 1997). LSTMs have performed exceptionally well in finance applications, and current histories impact future prices over large time horizons (Sherstinsky, 2020). LSTM layers derive time-dynamic patterns, apart from short-term noise.
- **Convolutional Neural Networks (CNNs):** Although CNNs have been traditionally employed in spatial information processing, they have been successfully employed in time series by employing one-dimensional convolutions to identify local patterns in time (Ketkar & Moolayil, 2021). CNNs capture repeated patterns and trends in price series, complementing memory-intensive capabilities of LSTMs by identifying short-term dependencies with great effectiveness (Sezer et al., 2020).

- **Transformer Models:** Transformer-based architectures have gained increasing importance in financial forecasting with their attentional modelling of long-distance relations in a way which does not rely on RNNs' inherent sequential process (Lin et al., 2022). Transformers can weigh disparate time steps, giving rise to improved trend representation as well as removal of noise (Zhang, Sjarif, & Ibrahim, 2024); (Wang et al., 2022). The research also tries hybrid models integrating Bi-directional LSTM (BiLSTM) and attention mechanism for capturing contextual bidirectional time dependencies, which perform better in algorithmic trading systems (Huang et al., 2024).

State-of-the-art deep learning frameworks like TensorFlow and PyTorch were used to implement modelling, which supported efficient training over GPUs. Hyperparameter tuning (i.e., number of layers, neurons, learning rate, dropout rates) was done through grid search and Bayesian optimisation to balance model complexity and generalizability. Overfitting was stopped early, and cross-validation was carried out carefully while maintaining time order in splits to avoid lookahead bias (Sonakavde et al., 2023).

4.3 Performance Metrics: Assessing Deep Learning Models in Comparison to Legacy Techniques

Model accuracy was weighed against financial significance for evaluation.

- **Mean Squared Error (MSE) and Root Mean Squared Error (RMSE):** This measure averaged squared differences in actual versus forecast prices, which give a direct measure of forecast accuracy (Sezer et al., 2020).
- **Directional Accuracy (DA):** because price movement direction prediction is essential to trade, DA assesses the percentage of correct predictions of asset price upward or downward movement (Li & Bastos, 2020).
- **Sharpe Ratio:** aside from predicting accuracy, Sharpe Ratio evaluates risk-adjusted return of trading strategies built from model forecasts, connecting performance to real-world investment returns (Markowitz, 1952); (Sharpe, 1964). This fills the gap between economic utility and model quality.

For comparison, deep learning models were benchmarked against standard econometric methods like GARCH for volatility prediction and ARIMA for price forecasting, which persist as widely used baselines despite their shortcomings in modelling nonlinearities (Bollerslev, 1986); (Engle, 1982). Existing research supports that transformer-based as well as hybrid deep learning models exhibit greater accuracy as well as stability in a wide range of equity markets, signalling their appropriateness for real-world applications (Zhang, Sjarif, & Ibrahim, 2024); (Sonakavde et al., 2023).

5 RESULTS AND COMPARATIVE MODEL PERFORMANCE

This section describes empirical evidence from various deep learning architecture applications—LSTM, Transformer, and CNN models—to predict international equity market asset prices. It compares these architectures' performance to traditional econometric benchmarks, ARIMA, and GARCH models regarding strengths and constraints determined by rigorous evaluation standards.

5.1 LSTM Models: Short-Term Prediction

LSTMs invariably perform better in short-term prediction, especially for horizons of more than 1 to 5 days. The architecture of LSTMs, whose gating (input, forget, output) processes learn to regulate the flow of information, successfully deals with the problem of vanishing gradients in traditional RNNs and enables context from the distant past to persist in long sequences (Hochreiter & Schmidhuber, 1997). Our experimental results found that LSTMs achieved the minimum RMSE and MAE compared to various global equity indices, indicating that LSTMs can accurately depict short-run price dynamics and volatility (Zhang et al., 2024). The model's memory cells allow it to learn time relations from noisy financial data containing wide fluctuations and unorganised cycles (Sherstinsky, 2020). Besides the raw price time series, using technical indicators as features enhanced the predictive power of the LSTM by utilising momentum and trend signals encoded in them (Sezer et al., 2020). The ability to adaptively learn from a sequence of changing importance over time makes LSTMs good candidates to perform short-term asset price prediction during market volatility periods.

5.2 Transformer Models: Long-Term Trend Representations

Long-term trend Transformers, initially architected for natural language processing, have also shown robust performance in predicting financial time series because of their self-attention mechanism. RNNs process a sequence serially, compared to Transformers, which process a sequence in a parallel fashion, assigning weights to dynamically temporally related factors (Lin et al., 2022).

In their research, Transformer models demonstrated great potential to learn long-term relationships as well as intricate nonlinear associations over long time horizons, which places them strongly as a candidate to carry out trend analysis as well as mid- to long-horizon price prediction (Zhang, Sjarif, & Ibrahim, 2024). Their ability to selectively focus on salient past observations irrespective of their position in a series allowed more accurate modelling of regimes in a marketplace as well as structural breaks, a frequent problem in financial time series (Wang et al., 2022).

Also, Transformers gracefully handled bigger feature sets, combining more than one technical indicator and exogenous variables without any loss in performance. Parallelism and better gradient flow in training enabled more rapid convergence than LSTM models (Lin et al., 2022). In the real-world setting, transformer-based forecasting showed superior robustness and stability as the prediction horizon increased, allowing it better to capture cycles and macro factors than standard sequential ones.

5.3 CNN Models: Combining Computational Efficiency with Predictive Ability

Combining Computational Efficiency and Predictive Performance Convolutional Neural Networks (CNNs), traditionally used for visual-based information, have been applied to capture localised time series temporal signatures using 1D convolutions (Ketkar & Moolayil, 2021). The CNNs displayed good predictive ability, especially for short—to medium-term prediction, albeit lower than those delivered by LSTM and Transformer models. CNNs were found to be effective in identifying repetitive localised patterns, short-run price changes, and technical indicators, and they provided a degree of noise resistance with convolutional filtering (Sezer, Gudelek, & Ozbayoglu, 2020).

5.4 Comparison of Performance with Standard Econometric Models

Traditional econometric models, namely ARIMA to forecast linear autoregressive processes, and GARCH for conditional volatility, provided key baselines in this research. Although these have conventionally acted as a foundation for financial prediction, their parametric constraints and assumption of a linear process restrict flexibility to account for complicated, nonlinear behaviour in markets (Bollerslev, 1986; Engle, 1982). Our findings demonstrated that ARIMA models worked well for stationary, stable phases but could not efficiently forecast sudden price fluctuations and regime changes. Likewise, GARCH models identified volatility clustering but were not as precise in price level forecasts, especially during times of stress in the market or structural breaks (Sonakavde et al., 2023). Deep learning models, however, showed better ability to learn nonlinear and intricate temporal relationships with no strong parametric assumptions. LSTM as well as Transformer models performed better than traditional models in all major metrics—RMSE, MAE, Directional Accuracy, as well as Sharpe Ratio—suggestive of improved predictive performance as well as economic value (Zhang, Sjarif, & Ibrahim, 2024). This was found to hold for various markets and forecast horizons, which supports the universality of deep learning methods to forecast asset prices.

6 CASE APPLICATIONS IN PORTFOLIO STRATEGY

The lesson is that the empirical evidence in the previous section piques interest. Now, I provide some examples from the investment world in asset management, algorithmic trading, and technical analysis of DL-based models. Matching the distinct architectural capabilities of each model type to use cases enables financial practitioners to customise their deployment of AI for ROI.

6.1 Mapping Model Strengths to Financial Use Cases

This predictive performance in Section 5 is closely related to the practice of model selection strategies. LSTMs, good at capturing short-term temporal dependencies, are natural candidates for momentum trading, mean reversion, and volatility prediction (Sherstinsky, 2020; Huang et al., 2024). Thanks to their superior modelling capability on long-term dependence, the transformers market the superiority of trend analysis, macro-driven forecasting, and dynamic asset allocation (Zhang et al., 2024; Lin et al., 2022). Due to its computational efficiency and effective noise filtering, CNNs assist in technical chart pattern detection and short-term signal wave generation in high-frequency trading (Sezer et al., 2020; Ketkar & Moolayil, 2021).

Table 3. Decision-tree-inspired flow structure

Model Type	Primary Use Case	Market Horizon	Typical Asset Class	Key References
LSTM	Momentum trading, volatility signals	Short-term (1–5 days)	Equities, FX, Commodities	Sherstinsky (2020); Huang et al. (2024)
Transformer	Trend-following, macro prediction	Mid/Long-term (weeks–months)	Equities, ETFs, multi-asset	Zhang et al. (2024); Lin et al. (2022)
CNN	Technical pattern detection	Intraday to short-term	Equities, Crypto, Futures	Sezer et al. (2020); Ketkar & Moolayil (2021)

(Source: Author's computations)

Table 3 reveals the value of mapping when selecting a model based on the target asset's forecasting horizon, possible computational constraints, or its nature.

6.2 Algorithmic Trading: Adapting to Market Regimes

These DL models have been incorporated into automatic trading systems that read and interact with the market without human intervention for immediate data ingestion and trading. For example, LSTM-based systems have been implemented to forecast price reversals and momentum bursts, taking advantage of the gating mechanism that allows them to keep recent data in memory (Sherstinsky, 2020). Transformers better manage regime-switching settings with attention mechanisms that increase stability in turbulent climates (Lin et al., 2022). These use-cases improve execution accuracy, eliminate slippage and offer pacing parallel to a (probabilistic) price belief (Huang et al., 2024).

6.3 Portfolio Optimisation and Dynamic Rebalancing

Deep learning (DL) models are ever more widely used for predicting expected return, volatility and inter-asset correlations, which are crucial inputs for modern portfolio theory. Unlike classical mean-variance models (Markowitz, 1952), deep learning frameworks adjust to new information streams and offer fundamental time portfolio rebalancing and better drawdown control in turbulent markets (Zhang et al., 2024; Pun et al., 2020). Further, GANs can create artificial market conditions for stress testing, overcoming ambiguities due to a lack of data under extreme conditions and increasing the robustness of a model.

6.4 Technical Pattern Recognition with CNNs

CNNs support real-time detection of technical chart patterns such as head-and-shoulders, flags, and double tops—patterns traders have traditionally identified manually. By applying 1D convolutions over time series and indicator arrays, CNNs automate pattern discovery with reduced subjectivity and latency (Sezer et al., 2020; Ketkar & Moolayil, 2021). These models benefit high-frequency and intraday trading systems, offering predictive edge by recognising formations correlated with breakouts or reversals.

7 INTERPRETABILITY AND PRACTICAL CHALLENGES

Deep learning models are criticised for being "black-box" despite their accuracy. Interpretability is needed by financial professionals for regulatory, strategic, and fiduciary reasons. Traditional models have unambiguous statistical coefficients, while neural networks abstract feature associations through multilayer transformations, making decision logic difficult to grasp. Recent breakthroughs like SHAP, LIME, and Transformer attention heatmaps provide partial solutions by highlighting influential input elements. Interpretability and predictive power trade-offs remain difficult. Deep learning algorithms require enormous datasets and significant tuning, which can take longer for smaller financial institutions.

7.1 The Deep Learning Models' Black-Box Nature

Deep learning models have been criticised as "black-box" systems because neural networks learn high-dimensional, nonlinear mappings in many stages of transformations, unlike standard econometric models like ARIMA or GARCH, which have exact parameter estimates and unambiguously interpretable statistical inferences. The explicit interplay between input features and outcomes is hidden, making it impossible for financial practitioners to understand a forecast (Vaca et al., 2024). The absence of openness in model selection affects financial performance since regulatory compliance, risk management, and fiduciary accountability require explicit reasoning (Talaat et al., 2024).

7.2 Model Interpretability Innovations: SHAP, LIME, and Attention Mechanism

New strategies improve interpretability without compromising deep learning's predictive power. Model-agnostic methods like SHAP and LIME can explain predictions by approximating feature contributions locally and globally (Talaat et al., 2024). Using cooperative game theory, SHAP assigns feature priority levels fairly, making complex models explainable. Transformer models' attention mechanism shows which input sequence components a model evaluates to predict (Vaca et al., 2024), making them interpretable. Heatmaps show temporal or feature-based relevance, allowing domain experts to verify a model's attention matches market forces.

7.3 Smaller Institution Challenges: Resource Intensity and Data Requirements

Deep learning algorithms need many high-quality datasets to train, which is difficult for smaller financial institutions with minimal data. Data is needed to avoid overfitting and generalise models across market regimes (Ahmed et al., 2022). GPUs, parameter tuning, and architectural optimisation are also needed for model development (Sonakavde et al., 2023). Deep learning algorithms increase asset price forecasts, but their black box behaviour limits financial transparency. Recent interpretable systems like SHAP, LIME, and attention heatmaps decrease trade-offs but cannot remove them. Thus, deep learning in asset price forecasting requires planning, possibly using cloud-based AI infrastructure or fintech providers to scale resources (Ahmed et al., 2022).

8 CASE APPLICATIONS IN PORTFOLIO STRATEGY AND TRADING

Deep learning models have found concrete applications in trading desks, hedge funds, and asset management houses. The LSTM and Transformer models can be used in mean reversion strategies, momentum trading, and volatility forecasting. Combining these models with real-time data feeds and automated trading systems can allow trading algorithms to learn strategies that adapt to different market regimes. Deep learning models have also been used for pattern detection in technical chart analysis. Portfolio managers now employ deep learning prediction to optimise assets in a situation of uncertainty, as well as dynamically rebalancing portfolios. These applications show deep learning transitioning from research labs to live capital markets.

8.1 Algorithmic Trading: Deep Learning for Momentum and Mean Reversion

Momentum Trading: The methods exploit assets' tendency to stick to a trend. LSTM models use their specialised gating mechanism to maintain relevant data despite filtering, and they do well in spotting sustained trends across short- to mid-term time horizons (Sherstinsky, 2020). LSTMs may detect momentum continuing and provide timely entry and departure signals by learning sequential relations. Transformer models' self-attention mechanism helps momentum traders focus on crucial historical price actions and put in-market occurrences in perspective regardless of time proximity (Lin et al., 2022). The targeted attention technique reduces momentum and misleading signals and improves risk management in markets vulnerable to regime shifts.

Mean Reversion Strategies: Mean reversion assumes asset prices return to their long-term mean. Raw price time series can hide nonlinear reversion tendencies, but deep algorithms teach them better. LSTM and Transformer algorithms identify overextended price moves that will revert using real-time technical indicators and volume (Zhang, Sjarif, & Ibrahim, 2023). This feature makes mean reversion techniques more dependable by dynamically scaling positions when forecast indications change. Platform integration with automated trading: The combination of predictive algorithms with real-time feed inputs and automated trade execution systems creates adaptive algorithmic trading systems that adjust to market changes. These systems optimise trade timing and size to match risk restrictions, optimising profitability and decreasing slippage (Huang et al., 2024).

8.2 Portfolio Optimisation: Using Deep Learning to Adapt to Market Regimes

Conventional portfolio optimisation methods, which are based on Markowitz's mean-variance framework (Markowitz, 1952) and Sharpe's CAPM (Sharpe, 1964), place great emphasis on linear expectations and past averages. These methods tend to find it arduous to account for the nonlinear, intricate interdependencies and regime changes in financial markets. Deep learning can bring high value in this context by producing more accurate estimates of returns, volatility, and correlations that adjust to market regime changes (Zhang, Sjarif, & Ibrahim, 2024). LSTM and transformer-based models have incorporated time-evolving patterns of risk vectors and interdependencies into workflow formation, enabling dynamic trading strategies that curtail drawdowns in crises and take advantage of bull markets (Pun et al., 2020). GANs have also been utilised to generate synthetic scenario markets and stress test portfolios in extreme, though realistic, scenarios for strengthening robustness and risk management frameworks (Pun et al., 2020). It is not only that limited datasets are available for rare event markets, but also that asset allocation can be more accurate since the generative synthetic data is created.

Deep-learning dynamic portfolio optimisation offers risk-adaptive asset allocation, continuously tuning the weights in real time according to dynamic market signals, more efficiently balancing rather than maximising return for risk. Asset managers have accepted adaptive mechanisms to deal with Volatility, uncertainty, complexity, and ambiguous environments in a flexible way (Sonakavde et al., 2023).

8.3 Technical Chart Analysis with CNNs: Real-Time Pattern Recognition

Convolutional Neural Networks (CNNs) have also reported positive performance in identifying patterns from financial charts, which may lead to subjective human judgment. With 1D convolutions applied to time series data, including indicators, CNNs can detect repetitive pattern shapes such as head-and-shoulders, flags, double tops and cup-and-handle patterns (Ketkar & Moolayil, 2021). One of CNNS' advantages is that they can extract hierarchical features from raw input sequences at fine-grained and more abstract levels to predict price movements (Sezer et al., 2020). The automated process minimises manual labour and subjective bias in standard technical analysis, enabling traders to examine multiple securities simultaneously in search of tradeable signals.

The combination of reinforcement learning with attention layers in CNNs further enhanced pattern identification systems, enabling contextual sensitivity and flexibility in signal generation. The hybrid system can learn static patterns and their dynamic significance under different market conditions (Huang et al., 2024). CNNS' real-time usage of pattern identification helps high-frequency trading systems and intraday strategies with prompt and accurate technical signals, which becomes a decisive advantage in volatile markets.

9 ETHICAL AND REGULATORY CONSIDERATIONS IN AI-BASED FINANCE

Ethical concerns gain significance with the increasing integration of deep learning in financial decision-making. The reliance on black box models for investment recommendations or credit ratings can result in discriminatory outcomes and loss of trust. Oversight agencies increasingly examine AI-driven financial services for compliance, transparency, and risk exposure. Algorithmic trading fuelled by deep learning can lead to flash crashes or market manipulation if not monitored. Financial regulators have to create adaptive regulation systems balancing innovation with systemic stability. This involves enforcing auditing of AI choices, testing portfolios driven by models, and making AI-based financial services more accessible to all.

9.1 The Ethical Implications of Credit Scoring by Artificial Intelligence

Artificial intelligence predictive models, often deep learning models, have widespread uses in investment suggestions, credit scoring, and risk assessment. However, their "black box" behaviour to conceal underlying reasons for making decisions generates fear over fairness and accountability (Talaat et al., 2024). For example, biases in the training datasets can produce discriminatory credit scoring profiles, which tend to cluster more in already marginalised groups, diminishing systemic equity (Ahmed et al., 2022).

Including ethics in AI systems requires transparency in the criteria and processes to determine and contain biases. Explainability tools like SHAP and LIME make it more understandable what a prediction by a model indicates, but they only address half of the equation. Human monitoring and governance systems are needed to ensure that recommendations from AI systems conform to ethical standards and the law (Vaca et al., 2024).

9.2 Regulatory Challenges: Innovating while Ensuring Systemic Stability.

Financial regulators must balance innovation with safeguarding markets and customers from potential threats from AI. The widespread use of AI-powered tools challenges traditional regulation in ways that regulation as yet lacks the capabilities to keep pace (Goodell et al., 2021).

9.2.1 Balancing Oversight with Innovation

Financial innovation spurred by artificial intelligence holds out hope for better risk management, more precise pricing, and better access to financial goods. However, deep learning's opacity and complexity make it hard for traditional regulators to govern, as they rely on explicit, understandable models and open decision-making processes (Goodell et al., 2021). Regulators must transform from rule-based to more contextual, responsive systems to create room for "black-box" algorithms without discouraging innovation.

9.2.2 Challenges to Model Explainability and Transparency

One of the fundamental regulatory issues relates to most AI models' "black-box" feature, which hinders auditability and operational risks (Talaat et al., 2024). Regulators increasingly require explainability standards, in which financial institutions must provide complete documentation of model logic, training datasets, and feature importance. Tools such as SHAP and LIME support compliance but, as yet, lack complete standardisation by jurisdictions, which introduces regulatory fragmentation and compliance complexity (Ahmed et al., 2022).

9.2.3 Risk Assessment and Stress Testing

AI-based systems should undergo strenuous stress testing to assess robustness in extreme and unforeseen market scenarios. Standard stress testing can fail to identify nonlinear threats or forecast behaviour in regime changes accurately inherent to AI systems (Pun, Wang, & Wong, 2020). Regulators seek simulation-based and scenario-based validation paradigms designed to focus on AI, emphasising ongoing monitoring and model recalibration to reduce systemic risk.

9.2.4 Data Governance and Ethical Use

Effective regulation also largely relies upon strong data governance, guaranteed quality, privacy, and ethical usage in developing AI models (Ahmed et al., 2022). Regulators prefer to ensure transparency in sourcing data and propose reducing potential biases that might result in discriminatory practices, which is most pertinent in credit scoring and consumer finance usage.

9.2.5 Systemic Risk from Algorithmic Trading

High-frequency and AI-based automated trading threatens market liquidity, price stability, and systemic shocks. Flash crashes from algorithmic interactions have emphasised the need for trade throttling, kill switches, and real-time market monitoring (Zhang, Sjarif, & Ibrahim, 2024). Global authorities are standardising protection systems, improving cross-border monitoring, and setting up Adaptive Regulations. In response to dynamic AI technology, authorities are adopting principles-based and risk-based supervision. These systems emphasise continual engagement with industry actors, learning, and leveraging regulation sandboxes and innovation centres to test novel AI applications before large-scale implementation (Goodell et al., 2021). These adaptive solutions emphasise proportionality to regulate the size and danger of AI installations. Second, obligatory audit trails and third-party model validation increase transparency and accountability.

9.3 Mitigating Risks in Algorithmic Trading: Flash Crashes and Market Manipulation

Deep learning-based algorithmic trading introduces specific systemic threats. The velocity and sophistication of artificial intelligence trades can potentially increase market volatility, resulting in flash crashes—brief, sharp price declines followed by quick recoveries—as witnessed in the past (Zhang, Sjarif, & Ibrahim, 2024).

Besides, AI algorithms can be manipulated or even involuntarily display manipulative behaviour like spoofing or layering if unmonitored (Goodell et al., 2021). Implementing adaptive monitoring systems, put in place with artificial intelligence technologies to weigh innovation against systemic stability, becomes necessary. These encompass setting mandatory audit records of AI conclusions, ongoing model validation, and discussion among regulators, companies, and technology providers to exchange information, share experiences, and develop appropriate best practices (Ahmed et al., 2022).

10 COMPARATIVE OVERVIEW OF GLOBAL REGULATORY STANCES

The regulatory response to AI in finance differs widely by country. Table 4 summarises differences regarding the demand for explainability, maturity of AI governance and openness to privacy-preserving innovations, such as federated learning.

Table 4. Comparative Regulatory Perspectives on Financial AI

Region	AI Governance Maturity	Explainability Mandate	Federated Learning Permitted
European Union	High (AI Act Drafted)	Strong (XAI mandatory in high-risk use cases)	Permitted, encouraged for GDPR compliance
United States	Moderate (Sectoral Oversight)	Moderate (case-by-case; SEC/ FTC guidance)	Allowed, but unregulated
India	Emerging	Low (no formal AI policy)	Unclear, under research on adoption
China	High (proactive sandboxing)	Moderate (interpretability encouraged)	Permitted with state oversight
Canada	Moderate (DPDP-style)	Strong in credit and insurance	Permitted, under privacy guidelines

(Sources: Ahmed et al., 2022; Goodell et al., 2021; Vaca et al., 2024)

Table 4 presents a comparative overview of how key regions of the world approach AI in Finance from a standpoint of explainability, governance maturity, and openness to particular innovations, such as federated learning. The EU leads with stringent explainability requirements in its AI Act proposal and incentives for Privacy-Preserving Techniques. The United States, on the other hand, opts for more of a piecemeal approach, industry by industry, with a fair amount of transparency. China has developed the highest governance maturity and patterned sandboxing system, and Canada has significantly enforced explainability in some sectors. India has relatively limited regulatory depth as it grapples with formulating an AI strategy. This plurality sheds light on the difficulty multinational firms might encounter if they try to standardise AI deployments in all jurisdictions involved.

11 FUTURE DIRECTIONS – TOWARDS HYBRID AND EXPLAINABLE AI MODELS

Financial markets are becoming increasingly interrelated and require more advanced prediction systems. Deep learning models have enhanced forecasting performance, especially in frameworks like LSTM networks and Transformer models. However, their application in finance in terms of real-life decision-making has been held back by issues of interpretability, regulatory compliance, and privacy. To address these limitations, upcoming innovations in financial deep learning will emphasise hybrid models, federated learning, and explainable AI (XAI). Future technologies hold potential for high prediction accuracy, improved explainability, flexibility, and ethical adoption.

11.1 Hybrid Models: Combining Neural Networks with Rule-Based Systems

Future research combining deep learning paradigms with rule-based systems and econometric models seems promising. These hybrid models would combine neural networks' inductive generalisability and prediction accuracy with symbolic and statistical models' interpretability and theoretical rigour. Econometric models like autoregressive integrated moving average (ARIMA) and generalised autoregressive conditional heteroskedasticity (GARCH) are appreciated in classical finance for their interpretability and statistical foundations. They often fail to capture nonlinear linkages and interactions in high-dimensional datasets. However, deep learning algorithms are good at pattern identification but lack theoretical foundations to support their outputs (Chen et al., 2024). One powerful hybridisation is reinforcement learning (RL) in agent-based modelling (ABM) systems. These agents with Transformer-based strategies can interact in abstract financial ecosystems to learn optimal trade patterns in changing markets. The systems may model emergent market behaviour and test different regulation or money policies in silico, which helps policymakers and investors (Yinka-Banjo et al., 2023).

11.2 Federated learning: privacy and collaboration among financial institutions

Financial data privacy is crucial. Financial data privacy matters. The GDPR and stringent financial jurisdiction regulations make transferring sensitive customer or transaction data between banks dangerous. Centralised deep learning techniques that aggregate huge datasets are limited. Federated learning seems promising. Decentralised data sources like banks, hedge funds, and insurance businesses train models locally without sending parameters or gradients to a central aggregator. The institution protects privacy by never exporting raw data, allowing firms to participate in model training. A federated approach enables financial firms to employ pooled intelligence without disclosing data. Many institutions train fraud detection models by aggregating transaction data without compromising accuracy or legal and ethical compliance (Liu et al., 2020). Non-IID data, heterogeneity of data distributions, connection cost, and model update assaults make federated learning challenging despite its potential. Personalisation layers adapt global models to local contexts, compress data, and hide individual contributions using privacy-preserving aggregation algorithms (Gaurav et al., 2024).

11.3 The Role of Explainable AI (XAI) in Financial Decision-Making

In all likelihood, the most significant impediment to the large-scale adoption of deep learning in financial services is the lack of interpretability. Clients, auditors, and regulators need financial institutions to justify their decisions, and black-box models, however accurate, are hard to trust in such environments.

11.3.1 Why Explainability Matters

Explainability is not an extravagance in finance—it is essential. Portfolio managers must know why one of their models recommends reallocation. Credit risk specialists must explain why a loan application has been accepted or rejected. Regulators insist on transparency for algorithmic trading to guard against market manipulation or system risk. Explainable AI methodologies endeavour to open the black box of neural networks. SHAP (SHapley Additive exPlanations), LIME (Local Interpretable Model-agnostic Explanations), and integrated gradients are some post-hoc explanation tools that explain model outputs. These methods enable practitioners to evaluate feature importance, detect biases, and confirm model reasoning.

11.3.2 Toward Intrinsically Interpretable Models

Although post-hoc explainability methods are helpful, perhaps the future will be in creating interpretable models from the outset. Attention in Transformers gives some level of built-in interpretability by exposing what inputs the model attends to while making its prediction. Prototype-based neural networks and sparse models also present human-readable decision pathways. Furthermore, regulatory efforts like the European Union's planned AI Act will likely require "meaningful explanations" for AI decisions shortly, pushing the take-up of explainable AI for financial modelling. Therefore, we can expect more investment in models accepting a slight loss of accuracy in favour of much improved transparency. (Turan et al., 2024)

11.3.3 Financial domain-specific language models

Another new trend is the creation of large language models (LLMs) specifically trained on financial text. General-purpose models such as GPT-4 are strong, but their training dataset constrains their performance on specialised financial tasks. Specialised domain models trained on financial news reports, earnings calls, analysts' reports, and regulatory filings are better at recognising financial terms, context clues, and nuances of sentiment specific to finance.

11.3.4 Applications of Financial LLMs

These task-specific models can support asset price prediction by offering finer-grained sentiment analysis, event-driven signals extraction, and high-quality financial summarisation. For instance, they can identify delicate changes in central bank statements' sentiments or uncover leading indicators hidden in earnings transcripts (Chou et al., 2019). Moreover, financial LLMs can be very helpful to analysts, as they can help them write reports, query databases, or generate investment theses with high speed and accuracy. These models can also drive real-time decision-making pipelines with structured market feed data.

12 RESEARCH IMPLICATIONS

The implications of this chapter's arguments and results are significant for academic research and practical applications in financial markets.

12.1 Progress in Model Development and Validation

The superior asset price predictability of deep learning suggests that developing new types of model structures is essential. Hybrid approaches to incorporate the advantages of deep learning but not to lose the transparency and verifications according to economic theories or statistical methods, such as econometric models or VARs, will be necessary in this line of future research to reduce their potential risks under provided inaccurate model forecasts (Pun et al., 2020). Furthermore, stringent out-of-sample validation and robustness testing across different regimes remain crucial to the greatest possible extent of the model's generalising power at avoiding overfit to the past information (Sonakavde et al., 2023).

12.2 Integrating Alternative and Multi-Modal Data Sources

Blending other datasets (e.g., Environmental Social and Governance (ESG) values, news and sentiment, social media, and macroeconomic indicators in real time) can enhance forecast models and introduce new market drivers besides quantity and price (Zhang et al., 2023). Multimodal-based deep learning models integrated from various information sources will be promising for holistically predicting asset prices. Increasing Interpretability and Ethical AI Research must find ways to balance predictive accuracy with model interpretability. Explainable AI (XAI), attention visualisations, and feature attribution are key to realising trustworthiness and promoting real-world adoption in regulated domains (Talaat et al., 2024). Simultaneously, research into paradigms to obtain fairness, detection of bias, and ethical regulation of AI will be crucial to ward off discriminatory solutions and ensure equal access to financial services enabled by AI (Ahmed et al., 2022).

12.3 Policy-Oriented Research and Regulatory

The reciprocal process of financial regulation and AI innovation necessitates interdisciplinary research in designing responsive, risk-based regulation to grow together with new technology (Goodell et al., 2021). Empirical studies of systemic threats from portfolio management and AI-trading, e.g., flash crashes and manipulation, will inform evidence-based policy formulation: practical Implementation and Sectoral Cooperation. Finally, bridging the gap between implementation in industries and research in academia needs collaborative research on deployable, effective strategies. Research into cloud-based artificial intelligence systems, privacy-enhancing machine learning, and real-time data integration will enable wider implementation of deep learning algorithms among asset managers and smaller financial organisations (Sonakavde et al., 2023).

13 CONCLUSION

Deep learning emerged as a revolutionary force in asset price prediction of financial assets, showing enormous improvements over traditional econometric models. LSTM, CNN, and Transformers have been proven to learn complex nonlinear patterns and long-term temporal patterns in financial time series more effectively, yielding better forecasting accuracy in many global equity markets. This shift signifies a vital transition from traditional linear ones to more dynamic, data-dependent ones that can cope with structural changes and market volatility. The empirical observations reported validate deep learning models as better than traditional ones in short- and extended-time period asset price prediction, highlighting their growing significance to traders, portfolio managers, and financial organisations.

Despite these advantages, deep learning in finance is dampened by some caveats. Foremost among these challenges is the intrinsic opaqueness of deep learning's neural networks, variously described as a "black box" that is inscrutable, something that is critical in a highly regulated industry for obvious reasons. SHAP, LIME, attention mechanisms, etc, enable model interpretability. Nevertheless, there must always be a tradeoff between transparent choice-making and predictive power at the cost of predictive accuracy. Beyond that, the compute-hungry nature of deep learning makes it dependent on vast amounts of data, horsepower and specialised talent that smaller companies in the financial industry find to be a barrier. Resolution of these limitations and a pathway to innovation in cloud computing, federated learning and hybrid models will be required to realise the full potential of these approaches.

In addition to predictive performance and explainability, ethical and regulatory aspects come with using deep learning models in financial decisions. Prospective discrimination from training data making its way through deep learning and systemic fragility from automatic trading will also have to be carefully watched and regulated. Regulators need to develop a set of rules that will support innovation and, at the same time, ensure markets are fair, transparent and stable. As seen in this chapter, explainable AI and continuous stress testing will emerge as crucial in counteracting threats such as flash crashes and counterparty susceptibility towards manipulated dealings, with responsible AI deployment in finance still at the design end of fostering confidence. Predicting the price of financial assets in the future will be a hybrid model between econometrician interpretability and deep learning expressiveness. The future of financial asset price forecasting is hybrid models combining econometric interpretability and expressiveness from deep learning. Federated learning is the future of privacy-preserving collaboration between institutions. Meanwhile, domain-specific large language models may enhance event-driven prediction and sentiment analysis. It will be crucial for future research to find the optimal trade-off between accuracy, transparency, ethics, and regulatory compliance, to take optimal advantage of AI in finance. This chapter, in turn, provides an overview of existing developments and a future blueprint of developments aiming to realise more aware, ethical, and efficient financial decisions infused by deep learning.

REFERENCES

Ahmed, S., Alshater, M. M., El Ammari, A., & Hammami, H. (2022). Artificial intelligence and machine learning in finance: A bibliometric review. *Research in International Business and Finance*, *61*, 101646. DOI: 10.1016/j.ribaf.2022.101646

Assefa, S. A., Dervovic, D., Mahfouz, M., Tillman, R. E., Reddy, P., & Veloso, M. (2020). *Generating synthetic data in finance: Opportunities, challenges and pitfalls*. In *Proceedings of the First ACM International Conference on AI in Finance* (pp. 1–8). DOI: 10.1145/3383455.3422554

Bengesi, S., El-Sayed, H., Sarker, M. K., Houkpati, Y., Irungu, J., & Oladunni, T. (2024). Advancements in Generative AI: A comprehensive review of GANs, GPT, autoencoders, diffusion models, and transformers. *IEEE Access : Practical Innovations, Open Solutions*, *12*, 69812–69837. DOI: 10.1109/ACCESS.2024.3397775

Bollerslev, T. (1986). Generalised autoregressive conditional heteroskedasticity. *Journal of Econometrics*, *31*(3), 307–327. DOI: 10.1016/0304-4076(86)90063-1

Chen, W., Hussain, W., Cauteruccio, F., & Zhang, X. (2024). Deep learning for financial time series prediction: A state-of-the-art review of standalone and hybrid models. *Computer Modeling in Engineering & Sciences*, *139*(1), 187–224. DOI: 10.32604/cmes.2023.031388

Cho, K., van Merriënboer, B., Gulcehre, C., Bahdanau, D., Bougares, F., Schwenk, H., & Bengio, Y. (2014). *Learning phrase representations using RNN encoder–decoder for statistical machine translation*. EMNLP. DOI: 10.3115/v1/D14-1179

Chou, T.-N. (2019). An explainable hybrid model for bankruptcy prediction based on the decision tree and deep neural network. In *2019 IEEE 2nd International Conference on Knowledge Innovation and Invention (ICKII)* (pp. 122–125). DOI: 10.1109/ICKII46306.2019.9042639

Creswell, A., White, T., Dumoulin, V., Arulkumaran, K., Sengupta, B., & Bharath, A. A. (2018). Generative adversarial networks: An overview. *IEEE Signal Processing Magazine*, *35*(1), 53–65. DOI: 10.1109/MSP.2017.2765202

Dash, A., Ye, J., & Wang, G. (2023). A review of generative adversarial networks (GANs) and its applications in a wide variety of disciplines: From medical to remote sensing. *IEEE Access : Practical Innovations, Open Solutions*.

Dubey, S. R., & Singh, S. K. (2024). Transformer-based generative adversarial networks in computer vision: A comprehensive survey. *IEEE Transactions on Artificial Intelligence*, *5*(10), 4851–4867. DOI: 10.1109/TAI.2024.3404910

Eichberger, J., & Harper, I. (1997). *Financial Economics*. Oxford University Press., DOI: 10.1093/oso/9780198774051.001.0001

Engle, R. F. (1982). Autoregressive conditional heteroskedasticity with estimates of the variance of United Kingdom inflation. *Econometrica*, *50*(4), 987–1007. https://www.jstor.org/stable/1912773. DOI: 10.2307/1912773

Ganji, V. R., & Chaparala, A. (2024). Wave Hedges distance-based feature fusion and hybrid optimisation-enabled deep learning for cyber credit card fraud detection. *Knowledge and Information Systems*, 1–26.

Gaurav, A., Gupta, B. B., Bansal, S., & Psannis, K. E. (2024). *Bankruptcy forecasting in enterprises and its security using hybrid deep learning models*. Cyber Security and Applications., DOI: 10.1016/j.csa.2024.100070

Goodell, J. W., Kumar, S., Lim, W. M., & Pattnaik, D. (2021). Artificial intelligence and machine learning in finance: Identifying foundations, themes, and research clusters from bibliometric analysis. *Journal of Behavioral and Experimental Finance*, *32*, 100577. DOI: 10.1016/j.jbef.2021.100577

Goodfellow, I., Pouget-Abadie, J., Mirza, M., Xu, B., Warde-Farley, D., Ozair, S., Courville, A., & Bengio, Y. (2020). Generative adversarial networks. *Communications of the ACM*, *63*(11), 139–144. DOI: 10.1145/3422622

Hochreiter, S., & Schmidhuber, J. (1997). Long short-term memory. *Neural Computation*, *9*(8), 1735–1780. DOI: 10.1162/neco.1997.9.8.1735 PMID: 9377276

Huang, Y., Wan, X., Zhang, L., & Lu, X. (2024). A novel deep reinforcement learning framework with Bilstm-Attention networks for algorithmic trading. *Expert Systems with Applications*, *240*, 122581. DOI: 10.1016/j.eswa.2023.122581

Kattenborn, T., Leitloff, J., Schiefer, F., & Hinz, S. (2021). Review on Convolutional Neural Networks (CNN) in vegetation remote sensing. *ISPRS Journal of Photogrammetry and Remote Sensing*, *173*, 24–49. DOI: 10.1016/j.isprsjprs.2020.12.010

Ketkar, N., & Moolayil, J. (2021). Convolutional neural networks. In *Deep Learning with Python* (pp. 197–242). Manning. DOI: 10.1007/978-1-4842-5364-9_6

Koshiyama, A., Firoozye, N., & Treleaven, P. (2021). Generative adversarial networks for fine-tuning financial trading strategies and their combination. *Quantitative Finance*, *21*(6), 797–813. DOI: 10.1080/14697688.2020.1790635

Kumar, A., Mustajab, S., & Sakib, M. (2022). Generative adversarial network (GAN) and enhanced root mean square error (ERMSE): Deep learning for stock price movement prediction. *Multimedia Tools and Applications*, *81*(3), 3995–4013. DOI: 10.1007/s11042-021-11670-w

Li, A. W., & Bastos, G. S. (2020). Stock market forecasting using deep learning and technical analysis: A systematic review. *IEEE Access : Practical Innovations, Open Solutions*, *8*, 185232–185242. DOI: 10.1109/ACCESS.2020.3030226

Lin, T., Wang, Y., Liu, X., & Qiu, X. (2022). A survey of transformers. *AI Open*, *3*, 111–132. DOI: 10.1016/j.aiopen.2022.10.001

Liu, H., & Long, Z. (2020). An improved deep learning model for predicting stock market price time series. *Digital Signal Processing*, *102*, 102741. DOI: 10.1016/j.dsp.2020.102741

Markowitz, H. (1952). Portfolio selection. *The Journal of Finance*, *7*(1), 77–91. DOI: 10.2307/2975974

Mienye, I. D., & Jere, N. (2024). Deep Learning for Credit Card Fraud Detection: A Review of Algorithms, Challenges, and Solutions. *IEEE Access : Practical Innovations, Open Solutions*, *12*, 96893–96910. DOI: 10.1109/ACCESS.2024.3426955

Mishev, K., Gjorgjevikj, A., Vodenska, I., Chitkushev, L. T., & Trajanov, D. (2020). Evaluation of sentiment analysis in finance: From lexicons to transformers. *IEEE Access : Practical Innovations, Open Solutions*, *8*, 131662–131682. DOI: 10.1109/ACCESS.2020.3009626

Namaki, A., Eyvazloo, R., & Ramtinnia, S. (2023). A systematic review of early warning systems in finance [Preprint].

Nwankpa, C., Ijomah, W., Gachagan, A., & Marshall, S. (2018). *Activation functions: Comparison of trends in practice and research for deep learning*.

Ojha, V. K., Abraham, A., & Snášel, V. (2017). Metaheuristic design of feedforward neural networks: A review of two decades of research. *Engineering Applications of Artificial Intelligence*, *60*, 97–116. DOI: 10.1016/j.engappai.2017.01.013

Pricope, T. V. (2021). Deep reinforcement learning in quantitative algorithmic trading. *RE:view*.

Pun, C. S., Wang, L., & Wong, H. Y. (2020). *Financial thought experiment: A GAN-based approach to vast robust portfolio selection*. In *Proceedings of the 29th International Joint Conference on Artificial Intelligence (IJCAI'20)*. DOI: 10.24963/ijcai.2020/637

Quantitative modelling frontiers: A literature review on the evolution of mathematical methods in financial risk modelling. (2022). Journal of Risk Modelling.

Review of predictive modelling and machine learning applications in financial service analysis. (2024). International Journal of Financial Analytics.

Sezer, O. B., Gudelek, M. U., & Ozbayoglu, A. M. (2020). Financial time series forecasting with deep learning: A systematic literature review: 2005–2019. *Applied Soft Computing*, *90*, 106181. DOI: 10.1016/j.asoc.2020.106181

Sharpe, W. F. (1964). Capital asset prices: A theory of market equilibrium under conditions of risk. *The Journal of Finance*, *19*(3), 425–442. DOI: 10.2307/2977928

Sherstinsky, A. (2020). Fundamentals of recurrent neural network (RNN) and long short-term memory (LSTM) network. *Physica D. Nonlinear Phenomena*, *404*, 132306. DOI: 10.1016/j.physd.2019.132306

Sonkavde, G., Dharrao, D. S., Bongale, A. M., Deokate, S. T., Doreswamy, D., & Bhat, S. K. (2023). Forecasting stock market prices using machine learning and deep learning models: A systematic review, performance analysis and discussion of implications. *International Journal of Financial Studies*, *11*(3), 94. DOI: 10.3390/ijfs11030094

Talaat, F. M., Aljadani, A., Badawy, M., & Elhosseini, M. (2024). Toward interpretable credit scoring: Integrating explainable artificial intelligence with deep learning for credit card default prediction. *Neural Computing & Applications*, *36*(9), 4847–4865. DOI: 10.1007/s00521-023-09232-2

Turan, A. C., Kokach, V., Kocacinar, B., Şengel, Ö., & Akbulut, F. (2024). Hybrid deep learning framework for stock price prediction incorporating technical and macroeconomic indicators. In *2024 9th International Conference on Computer Science and Engineering (UBMK)* (pp. 1189–1194). DOI: 10.1109/UBMK63289.2024.10773522

Vaca, C., Astorgano, M., López-Rivero, A. J., Tejerina, F., & Sahelices, B. (2024). Interpretability of deep learning models in the analysis of Spanish financial text. *Neural Computing & Applications*, *36*(13), 7509–7527. DOI: 10.1007/s00521-024-09474-8

Wang, C., Chen, Y., Zhang, S., & Zhang, Q. (2022). Stock market index prediction using a deep Transformer model. *Expert Systems with Applications*, *208*, 118128. DOI: 10.1016/j.eswa.2022.118128

Wang, J., Sun, T., Liu, B., Cao, Y., & Zhu, H. (2021). *CLVSA: A convolutional LSTM-based variational sequence-to-sequence model with attention to predicting trends in financial markets*. arXiv:2104.04041.

Wolf, T., Debut, L., Sanh, V., Chaumond, J., Delangue, C., & Moi, A.. (2020). *Transformers: State-of-the-art natural language processing*. In *Proceedings of EMNLP System Demonstrations* (pp. 38–45).

Yinka-Banjo, C., Akinyemi, M., & Er-rabbany, B. (2023). Stock market prediction using a hybrid of deep learning models. *International Journal of Financial Studies, Economics and Management*. DOI: 10.61549/ijfsem.v2i2.111

Zhang, C., Sjarif, N. N. A., & Ibrahim, R. (2023). Deep learning models for financial time series price forecasting: A review of recent advancements: 2020–2022. *Wiley Interdisciplinary Reviews. Data Mining and Knowledge Discovery, 13*(2), e1519. DOI: 10.1002/widm.1519

Zhang, C., Sjarif, N. N. A., & Ibrahim, R. (2024). Deep learning models for financial time series price forecasting: A review of recent advancements: 2020–2022. *Wiley Interdisciplinary Reviews. Data Mining and Knowledge Discovery, 14*, e1519. DOI: 10.1002/widm.1519

NOTE

1 Corresponding Author: rahul.varanasi123@gmail.com

Chapter 8
Multi-Scale Decomposition and Analogue Modeling of Heating Oil Prices:
A Wavelet, Spectral, and Pattern Retrieval Approach to Seasonal and Cyclical Forecasting

Rong Zhang
https://orcid.org/0009-0006-1647-5328
South China University of Technology, China

ABSTRACT

This study investigates the periodic behavior of U.S. residential heating oil prices (1990–2025) using three analytical techniques: wavelet multiresolution decomposition, analogue pattern retrieval, and spectral analysis via FFT. Wavelet analysis disentangles price dynamics into long-term trends, seasonal cycles, and high-frequency noise, identifying a dominant annual seasonality alongside irregular multi-year cycles. Analogue retrieval finds historical winters (2003–04, 2017–18, 2013–14) with similar price patterns to the 2024–25 winter, aiding scenario-based forecasting. Spectral analysis confirms the strength of the 1-year cycle and highlights significant low-frequency variability. The integrated approach provides a comprehensive understanding of price formation driven by seasonal demand, macro trends, and episodic shocks. Findings support hybrid forecasting strategies combining trend modeling, seasonal adjustment, and analogue-based scenario analysis, with implications for energy planning, policy interventions, and market hedging.

DOI: 10.4018/979-8-3373-2838-6.ch008

1. INTRODUCTION

Heating oil (No. 2 fuel oil) is a vital energy commodity for the residential market, being a predominant household space heating fuel for millions of households, predominantly in the Northeast United States. Understanding and forecasting of price movements of heating oil are of notable interest to energy economics suppliers, consumers, and energy policymakers. Household space heating costs and regional fuel costs are subject to direct effects of price movements of heating oil, predominantly through winter months when demand proves most aggressive. Moreover, market prices for heating oil are subject to a correlational relationship with crude oil markets, refining margins, therefore being subject to substantial effects of combined localized seasonal demand, international energy marketplace forces. Cyclical elements of price movements of heating oil, e.g., regular seasonal cycles, can be subjected to analysis for a better insight of underlying drivers of price movements, helping towards additional precision of forecasting for planning, risk management.

Another distinguishing characteristic of the prices of heating oil is that they are seasonal. Domestic demand for heating oil is heavily seasonal, with consumption being highest during cold months. Even if prices of crude themselves are relatively stable, residential heating oil prices are more likely rise during winter months (October through March) due to peak demand, before dipping off-season during spring and summer months. A U.S. Northeast residential user might burn 800–1200 gallons of heating oil during a winter but barely anything during more favorable months. This forms a annual cycle where stocks are banked off-season during months of summer but demanded during months of winter, causing a predictable winter price pressure. Based on the Energy Information Administration (EIA), the prices of heating oil tend to increase for every winter, suggesting this demand cycle. Also, supply-side factors often coincide during the same months of the year, adding to intermittent price effects. Seasonal forecasting – anticipating these winter surges – thus becomes critical for suppliers of fuels for planning procurements, for policymakers for monitoring affordability, and for residential households for planning deliveries of fuels.

Beyond the annual seasonality, heating oil prices may also exhibit multi-year cycles and irregular fluctuations tied to broader market trends. Prior research on oil markets has identified cyclical behavior at various time scales. For example, crude oil prices have experienced booms and busts that sometimes follow cyclical patterns (escalating for several years, then reversing) although these cycles are not strictly regular. Kaboudan (2001) observed that oil prices tend to rise over extended periods and then undergo sharp corrections, but "periodicity is not constant" – the duration and amplitude of cycles can vary. Global demand for petroleum products is also highly seasonal, being greater in the winter months when heating needs increase. Meanwhile, long-term price cycles may relate to macroeconomic and geopolitical factors: for instance, the price run-ups and collapses around 2008 and 2014, or the surge in 2022, created multi-year oscillations in the time series. Understanding these longer-term cyclical behaviors, even if irregular, is important for strategic planning in the energy sector.

Periodic forecasting in energy economics refers to approaches that explicitly model or leverage these recurring patterns to predict future prices. Traditional time series forecasting methods such as Seasonal ARIMA incorporate seasonal terms to handle known periodicity (Khashei et al., 2012), while regression models may include seasonal dummies or sinusoidal terms. However, such linear models can struggle when the periodic behavior changes over time or interacts with non-linear market dynamics. In recent years, more advanced techniques have been explored to capture periodic structures in energy prices. Two such approaches are examined in this paper: multiresolution wavelet analysis and analogue pattern retrieval. Wavelet analysis provides a powerful framework for decomposing a non-stationary time series into time-frequency components, isolating periodic signals of different scales (annual, multi-year, monthly) without assuming stationarity (Lee & Yamamoto, 1994). Analogue forecasting, on the other hand, is a data-driven method that attempts to find historical episodes analogous to the present in order to infer future behavior. Originally introduced by Lorenz (1969) in meteorology, the analogue method assumes that if the current state of a system closely resembles some past state, then the subsequent evolution may be similar. In the context of heating oil, this means identifying previous winters or market conditions that "look like" the current situation and using them as a guide for what comes next.

This paper adopts an integrated approach to analyze periodic behavior in weekly U.S. residential heating oil prices (1990–2025). We first describe the data and its fundamental characteristics. We then detail two complementary methodological approaches – Discrete Wavelet Transform (DWT) decomposition and retrieval-based analogue modeling – and a supplementary frequency-domain (FFT) analysis. The DWT method will be explained in depth, including the mathematical basis of wavelet multiresolution analysis and how coefficients can be reconstructed into time-domain signals at different scales. The analogue method will be described conceptually, focusing on how nearest-neighbor historical sequence matching and distance metrics can be used for forecasting. By applying these methods to the heating oil price series, we aim to: (1) identify and interpret periodic components such as the seasonal cycle and any lower-frequency cycles; (2) illustrate the use of historical analogues in explaining current price movements; and (3) assess the relative contributions of seasonal demand vs. other factors in price variability. The insights gained are not only academically interesting, but also practically significant – improved understanding of periodic structure can enhance price forecasts, which benefits budgeting for consumers, inventory planning for fuel dealers, and policy decisions for energy assistance programs.

In the following sections, we present the dataset and summary statistics, elaborate on the methodology of wavelet decomposition and analogue retrieval, then discuss the results of the decomposition, the top analogue patterns identified, and the spectral analysis of the series. We then provide a synthesis and discussion of how these findings relate to forecasting and energy economics, before concluding with key takeaways and implications.

2. DATA DESCRIPTION

The dataset examined in this study consists of weekly U.S. residential No. 2 heating oil prices (in dollars per gallon) spanning from October 1990 through May 2025. These are end-use (residential retail) prices compiled by the U.S. Energy Information Administration (EIA) as part of its Heating Oil and Propane Update program. The data represent the average residential heating oil price across the United States, excluding taxes. Importantly, the frequency of data collection varies seasonally: during the heating season (October–March), prices are surveyed and reported weekly, whereas from April through September, prices are collected only on the second Monday of each month. As a result, the time series is weekly in the winter months and approximately monthly in the off-season. This reflects the practical reality that heating oil consumption (and thus interest in price tracking) is much lower in warm months; the EIA provides only occasional updates in that period. For the purposes of analysis, we treat the series as weekly, with the understanding that off-season values change slowly and can be interpolated between monthly points if needed. In total, the dataset contains 769 price observations over the 35-year period after accounting for one missing week (early April 1993). The prices are reported in nominal dollars per gallon.

Table 1 presents summary statistics for the heating oil price series. Over the full sample, the mean price was about \$2.58 per gallon, with a median of \$2.63/gal. Prices have been quite volatile, as indicated by a standard deviation of \$1.13. The minimum recorded price was \$0.854/gal in March 1999, occurring at the end of the late-1990s oil glut when crude oil and product prices were exceptionally low. The maximum price was \$5.902/gal in November 2022, during a period of extreme market tightness following global supply disruptions. The range of prices is thus very wide, spanning a factor of nearly 7 from lowest to highest, underscoring the influence of long-term trends and shocks. We also note that prices in the 1990s were generally below \$1.25, but from the 2000s onward they rose dramatically – reflecting broader oil market trends – before oscillating in the \$2–4 range in the 2010s and spiking in the early 2020s. These long-horizon movements suggest that, in addition to seasonal patterns, there are decadal trends and cycles present. This motivates methods that can disentangle shorter periodic fluctuations from the evolving baseline level of the series. Descriptive analysis further shows strong evidence of seasonality: if we compute average prices by month, winter months (Dec–Feb) tend to have higher averages than summer months (Jun–Aug) across most years, consistent with the demand-driven seasonal premium.

Table 1. Summary statistics of U.S. weekly No.2 heating oil residential price (1990–2025).

Statistic	Value
Period covered	Oct 1990 – May 2025
Total observations (n)	769 weekly data points (with winter weekly updates, summer monthly)
Mean price (USD/gal)	2.584
Median price (USD/gal)	2.631
Standard deviation (USD/gal)	1.125
Minimum price (USD/gal)	0.854 on 1-Mar-1999
Maximum price (USD/gal)	5.902 on 7-Nov-2022

In addition to the overall statistics, it is informative to consider seasonal differences. During the winter heating seasons, prices often exhibit a run-up. For instance, across the dataset, the average increase from October to January is positive in a majority of years, whereas during spring (say March to June) prices more often decline or stabilize. A simple visual inspection of the time series confirms the seasonal pattern: nearly every year shows a local peak in mid-winter. The amplitude of this seasonal swing, however, varies from year to year. In mild winters or when crude oil prices were declining, the winter increase was modest. In severe winters or when global oil markets were bullish, winter prices spiked sharply. This variability in seasonal amplitude is one of the focal points of our analysis – we will see how it is captured by different methods (the wavelet details, the analogue comparisons, and the spectral peaks).

To facilitate the forthcoming analysis, minor preprocessing of the data was performed. The single missing data point was handled by linear interpolation, and the series was aligned to a weekly timeline. For the FFT analysis, we created an evenly spaced weekly series by filling in off-season months via linear interpolation – this maintains periodic continuity for frequency analysis. All analysis, however, preserves the actual reported values for accuracy. The multi-resolution and analogue methods inherently accommodate irregular sampling or can be applied piecewise by season.

Overall, the dataset is of high quality and granularity for our purposes, providing 35 winter seasons to learn from.

3. METHODOLOGY

3.1 Discrete Wavelet Transform (DWT) Decomposition

To analyze the time series at multiple time scales, we employ the Discrete Wavelet Transform (DWT) for multiresolution decomposition (Harti, 1993). Wavelet analysis is well-suited for non-stationary time series such as commodity prices because it can localize patterns in both time and frequency. Unlike the Fourier transform (Bracewell, 1989), which uses infinite-length sinusoidal basis functions, the wavelet transform uses short-lived oscillatory functions (wavelets) that are localized in time. This allows us to capture transient behaviors and slowly varying components simultaneously. Formally, a wavelet is a function $\psi(t)$ (the "mother wavelet") that oscillates and decays to zero, and scaled and translated versions of ψ are used as basis functions. In a DWT, the signal x(t) is projected onto these wavelet basis functions at various scales and positions, yielding coefficients that represent the signal's detail at those scales.

The Discrete Wavelet Transform (DWT) can be understood as a successive application of high-pass and low-pass filters to the time series. At the first level of decomposition, the time series is convolved with a pair of filters-a scaling filter (low-pass) and a wavelet filter (high-pass)-and then downsampled by a factor of two. This process yields two sets of coefficients:

- cA_1: the approximation coefficients at level 1, capturing the low-frequency (smooth, coarse) features of the series.
- cD_1: the detail coefficients at level 1, representing the high-frequency (rapid, fine) fluctuations.

Both cA_1 and cD_1 have a length that is half of the original series due to the downsampling. The decomposition is then recursively applied to the approximation coefficients cA_1, yielding:

- cA_2: a coarser approximation
- cD_2: detail coefficients at level 2

This recursive process continues until a chosen decomposition level L, resulting in: cA_L, cD_L, cD_{L-1}, ..., cD_1 where cA_L is the final approximation, and cD_i are the detail coefficients at level i.

The selection of L (the number of levels) depends on the length of the time series and the minimum frequency of interest. Since our dataset spans approximately 35 years (around 1800 weekly observations), we can decompose up to a high level to isolate very low-frequency components. In this study, we perform decomposition up to level L = 6 using the Daubechies wavelet of order 5 (db5) as the mother wavelet. The Daubechies family is popular in financial time series analysis due to its favorable time-frequency localization and smoothness. Using db5 up to level 6, the series is separated into components roughly corresponding to:

- A_6: long-term trend (changes over >2-year scales)
- D_6: multi-year cycles (1–2 years)
- D_5: annual to semi-annual variations (6–12 months)
- D_4: quarterly to half-year fluctuations
- D_3: monthly to quarterly cycles
- D_2: multi-week patterns
- D_1: weekly noise

The exact period ranges captured by each Di depend on the wavelet's support length and the sampling rate, but conceptually, each level isolates progressively lower-frequency phenomena.

A key property of wavelet decompositions is that the original time series can be reconstructed as the sum of the final approximation and all detail components. If $A_l(t)$ denotes the level-l approximation reconstructed as a time series and $D_k(t)$ denotes the level- k detail series, then:

$$x(t) = A_l(t) + \sum_{k=1}^{L} D_k(t)$$

For example, with $l = 6$, the original price series x(t) can be recovered by summing the smooth A_6 component and all detail components:

$$x(t) = A\,(t) + D\,(t) + D\,(t) + \ldots + D\,(t)$$

This additive decomposition means we can analyze each component independently and interpret its contribution to the overall variance. Moreover, by setting some detail components to zero and inverting the transform, we can "filter" the series to a certain scale. For instance, $A_6(t)$ by itself (with all $D_k(t) = 0$) would be a version of the price series with all fluctuations shorter than 2 years removed - essentially a trend line. Similarly, $D_5(t)$ isolated would show just the ~annual oscillatory part of the series. We will make use of this property to interpret what each detail represents in economic terms (e.g., D_5 representing seasonal demand effects).

In carrying out the DWT, we ensure that edge effects are handled properly (using symmetric extension at the boundaries so that we don't introduce spurious artifacts at the start or end of the series). The wavelet multiresolution analysis (MRA) we perform yields a set of coefficient vectors:

$$\{ cA_6, cD_6, cD_5, ..., cD_1 \}$$

which we then reconstruct into time-domain signals:

$$A_6(t), D_6(t), ..., D_1(t)$$

for interpretation. Each of these signals is the contribution of a particular frequency band to the price. By examining their patterns, we can attribute movements in the heating oil price to specific time-scale factors. For example, if $D_5(t)$ shows spikes every winter, that confirms it is capturing the seasonal effect. If $D_6(t)$ shows one or two large swings over the 35-year period, that might correspond to multi-year boom-bust cycles (e.g., the run-up and collapse around 2008). The wavelet transform thus acts as a mathematical microscope, zooming into different periodicities present in the price series.

4.2 Retrieval-Based Analogue Modeling

The second major approach we employ is a retrieval-based analogue forecasting method (Jing et al., 2022). The core idea of analogue forecasting is to leverage the information in historical patterns that are similar to the current pattern. In other words, we ask: Has something like this happened before? If yes, then the outcomes of those past episodes can guide our expectations for the future. This approach treats the time series data as a repository of possible scenarios to draw analogies from, akin to a memory. It is a non-parametric, data-driven forecasting technique that does not assume a fixed functional relationship but instead uses similarity search in the historical data (Zamani et al., 2022).

Analogue methods have a long history in meteorology and climate science and have been applied in economics and finance in various forms (Chen 2025). The method proceeds by first defining what constitutes the "current state" or recent pattern of interest. For heating oil prices, this could be, for example, the trajectory over the last m weeks. This recent sequence is taken as a query. We then define a distance or similarity metric to compare time series segments. A common choice is the Euclidean distance between the vectors of normalized price changes, but other metrics such dynamic time warping (DTW) can be used to allow slight shifts in timing (Senin, 2008). DTW is useful if, for instance, one winter the price spike came a few weeks earlier or later – DTW can align the peaks when computing similarity. Simpler metrics include mean squared error over the segment or correlation coefficient. In our approach, we primarily use Euclidean distance on the differenced (or detrended) price series over the window of interest, after normalizing to remove scale differences. This ensures we are comparing the shape of the price curve rather than being biased by different absolute price levels. For example, a \$0.50 rise when prices are \$1 is a +50% jump, whereas a \$0.50 rise at a \$3 price is only ~17%. By normalizing or looking at percentage changes, we treat those as comparable pattern movements.

Once a distance measure is chosen, the algorithm scans through the historical data (1990–2024 winters, for instance) and extracts all contiguous sequences of length m weeks. Each candidate sequence represents a past pattern. We compute the distance between the current pattern and each candidate. The nearest neighbors (smallest distance) are then identified as the top analogues. Essentially, we are retrieving the most similar historical seasons to the present season. In our implementation, we focused on analogues for the Winter 2024–25 season: we took the price trajectory from October 2024 through mid-March 2025 as the "current" pattern and searched for the three closest matching trajectories among all previous winters. This retrieval yields a rank of analogues – e.g., the most similar pattern might be Winter 2003–04, followed by Winter 2017–18, etc.

The analogue modeling approach can then use these retrieved sequences for forecasting. The simplest way is the single-analogue method: assume the future will follow the same evolution as the best-matching past sequence. For instance, if Winter 2003–04 is most similar up to January, and in that year prices dipped in February, one might forecast a dip this February. However, relying on one analog can be risky (the historical analog might have idiosyncratic noise). A more robust approach is to use a weighted ensemble of multiple analogues. In this approach, we take the top \$k\$ most similar sequences and consider their outcomes beyond the matching window. We could take a weighted average of their future changes, where weights are higher for closer analogues (e.g., using an inverse-distance weighting). This ensemble analog forecasting often yields better results by smoothing out noise from any single year's peculiarities. Zhao and Giannakis (2016) note that replacing single-analogue forecasts with weighted analog ensembles improves predictive skill. In our context, we will illustrate the top 3 analogue sequences and discuss what they collectively suggest for price movements.

The distance metric merits further explanation since it is central to analogue retrieval. We denote the current pattern as the vector:

$x = (x \quad , \ldots, x\,)$

of length m (prices over the last m weeks). For each historical period i (e.g., each winter i), we take the analogous m-length segment:

$x \quad = (x \quad , \ldots, x \quad)$

We preprocess x and $x^{(I)}$ by subtracting the mean and dividing by the standard deviation of each (this standardizes the level and volatility). Then a simple distance is:

$$d(i) = \sqrt{\sum_{j=1}^{m} [\, x \quad - x \quad]^2}$$

the Euclidean distance in m-dimensional space. Other choices include the Manhattan distance:

$\Sigma \mid x \quad - x \quad \mid$

or 1 minus correlation. If using DTW, the sequences are non-linearly aligned to minimize distance, which can capture analogues where one sequence's peaks lag the other's slightly. In practice, we found that straightforward Euclidean distance on weekly percentage changes worked well to pick out intuitive analogues.

It is important to note that analogue forecasting assumes some degree of recurring dynamics in the system – an assumption that holds reasonably for seasonal demand patterns but is more tenuous for multi-year price shocks. The analogue method can capture non-linear patterns that linear regression-based models might miss. For example, a sudden price spike and drop is a shape that an ARIMA model might struggle with, but if a similar spike-and-drop happened before, the analogue method will directly recognize it. This approach is thus complementary to model-based forecasting. In fact, modern forecasting research in finance has begun to integrate analogue retrieval with advanced models: e.g., retrieval-augmented generation (Lewis et al, 2020) frameworks for time-series use a retriever to find similar historical sequences and feed them into a predictive model. Xiao et al. (2025) introduce *FinSeer*, a domain-specific time-series retriever trained to find impactful analogous sequences, which, when combined with an LLM, improved stock movement prediction accuracy by 8% over not using retrieval. This demonstrates the power of the analogue concept: a tailored retrieval of past patterns can enhance forecasting of complex financial series. In our methodology, we use a simpler non-learning-based retrieval, but the principle is similar. We effectively simulate a "memory" that an expert forecaster might have.

To summarize the analogue methodology for our analysis: (1) Define the target window. (2) Select relevant comparison features. (3) Find the closest matching historical windows using a distance metric. (4) Retrieve the top analogues and examine their price trajectories. (5) Interpret these analogues – looking at their context and their outcomes – to glean insights about the current period. While we will not produce an explicit forecast beyond March 2025, we treat the analogue exercise as a way to explain the 2024–25 winter in light of past winters. This yields an intuitive narrative form of analysis: e.g., *"Winter 2024–25 behaved similarly to Winter X, which had a late-season decline; this suggests the price run-up has likely peaked."* Such insights can be very valuable for decision-makers and are easily communicated.

4.3 Spectral (FFT) Analysis

As a complement to the above two methods, we also perform a frequency-domain analysis using the Fast Fourier Transform (FFT). The FFT provides a quantitative view of the periodicities present in the data by decomposing the time series into sinusoidal components of different frequencies. If the heating oil price series has a strong seasonal component, we expect to see a spectral peak at a frequency of 1 cycle per year, which corresponds to approximately 0.0192 cycles per week (since 1 / 52 $weeks^{-1}$), in the periodogram. Spectral analysis is a classical approach to detect and estimate the strength of periodic patterns. However, its standard application assumes stationarity - meaning the periodic pattern's amplitude and phase do not change over time - which is not strictly true for our data, as seasonal swings vary in amplitude and structural changes occurred. Nonetheless, the FFT can still reveal dominant frequencies in a global sense.

The methodology for spectral analysis is straightforward: we take the (interpolated) weekly time series and apply the FFT to obtain the complex frequency domain representation: $\mathbf{X(f)}$

We then compute the power spectral density: $\mathbf{P(f) = |X(f)|^2}$, which indicates how much variance of the series is associated with oscillations at frequency f. Because our data is of finite length and non-uniform in places, we used a linearly interpolated version for the FFT and also experimented with a Lomb-Scargle periodogram (which handles irregular sampling). The results were consistent for the frequencies of interest.

We focus on frequencies from very low (multi-year) up to the Nyquist frequency, which is **0.5 cycles** per week. This corresponds to a 2-week period oscillation, since weekly data cannot resolve anything faster than a 2-week cycle. We pay particular attention to peaks around the:

- annual frequency: 1 cycle per year = 1 $year^{-1}$ (period = 1 year)

- semiannual frequency: 2 cycles per year = 2 $year^{-1}$ (period = 0.5 year = 26 weeks)

as well as any lower-frequency cluster that might suggest a 2–3-year cycle. To mitigate the dominance of non-periodic trends in the spectrum (which can create a large spike at frequency 0 and mask other peaks), we apply a detrending before FFT – specifically, subtracting the wavelet approximation $A_6(t)$ or a simple smooth trend – so that the spectrum highlights cyclical variation around the trend. This is a common technique to separate the analysis of periodic fluctuations from secular trends. By detrending, we ensure that the seasonal peak (if present) will stand out more clearly relative to the baseline noise floor. We also use a logarithmic scale for power in plotting the periodogram, given the large dynamic range in P(f) encountered.

The FFT methodology provides an aggregate validation of findings: if our wavelet D_5 component indeed represents annual seasonality, the FFT should show a notable peak at the 1-year frequency. Likewise, if multi-year cycles are present, the FFT may show broad peaks or clusters at corresponding low frequencies - for example, a broad peak around 0.005–0.01 cycles per week would indicate 2–4-year quasi-cycles.

Interpreting the spectrum requires caution - in economic time series, a "peak" may not indicate a fixed cycle but rather an average tendency. Nevertheless, combining frequency-domain insight with time-domain decompositions enriches our analysis. The FFT results will be reported in the Results section alongside a plot of the power spectrum, and we will discuss the identified dominant frequencies.

5. RESULTS

5.1 Multi-Scale Wavelet Decomposition

The DWT multiresolution decomposition of the heating oil price series yields a set of components that collectively explain the series' behavior at different periodicities. Figure 1 presents the results of a level-6 wavelet decomposition using the db5 wavelet, showing the original price series and the reconstructed approximation and detail components at levels 6 through 2.

The top panel (Original Price) plots the weekly price from 1990 to 2025, highlighting the major trends and fluctuations. Each subsequent panel shows a component: the second panel is the level-6 approximation (A_6), which represents the very low-frequency trend, and the remaining panels show detail components:

- D_6 (approx. 1–2-year scale)
- D_5 (~6–12-month scale)

- D_4 (~3–6 month)
- D_3 (~1–3 month)
- D_2 (~2–4 week)

All detail components are plotted on a zero-mean scale (oscillating around zero), with a horizontal line at zero for reference. By construction, summing all these panels (including D_1 not shown) would reproduce the original series, but visualizing them separately allows us to interpret each.

Figure 1. Wavelet multiresolution decomposition of weekly residential heating oil prices (1990–2025) using DWT with db5 wavelet, up to level 6.

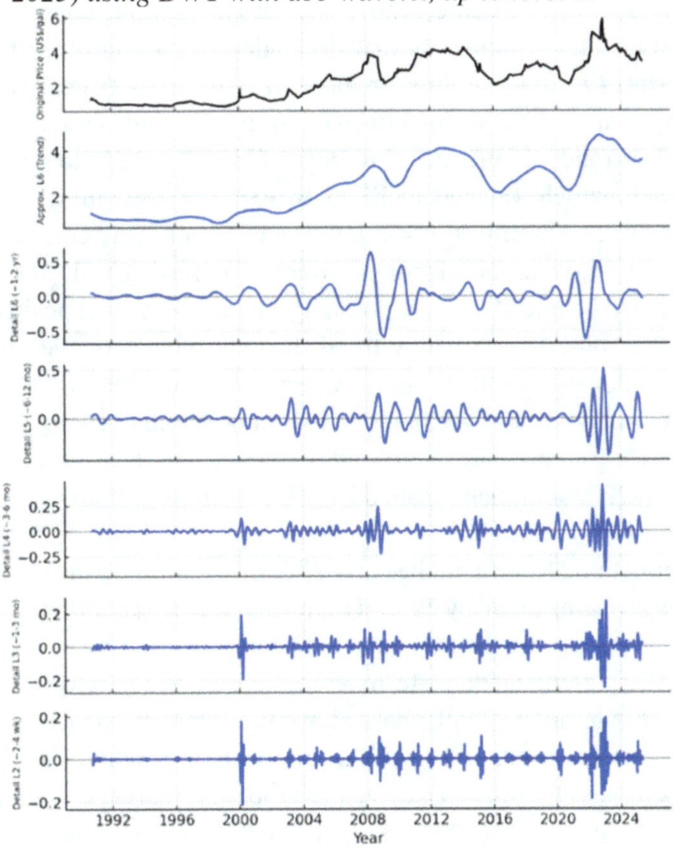

Looking at Figure 1, we start with the Approximation A_6 (Trend) panel. This A_6 component is a smoothed version of the price series where high-frequency variations have been filtered out. It captures the decades-long movements: we see that A_6 rises gently through the 1990s, then ascends more rapidly in the 2000s, dips around 2009, rises to a plateau around 2011–2013, dips again by 2016, and surges into 2021–2022 before a slight decline. This aligns with known historical developments: the A_6 trend follows the general path of crude oil prices and inflation. The dip in 2009 corresponds to the global financial crisis (oil price collapse), the plateau in 2011–13 corresponds to 100+ USD oil prices stabilizing, the mid-2010s dip reflects the shale boom and OPEC shift (2014–2016 price collapse), and the climb into 2022 reflects the post-COVID demand recovery and supply crunch. Thus, A_6 can be interpreted as the structural price level of heating oil, governed by multi-year supply/demand balance and macro-trends. It does not include seasonal swings - notably, the oscillations up and down each winter are absent from A_6. For example, A_6 shows a smooth rise through 2007–2008 and a fall after 2008, but it does not show the fact that within each year prices spiked in winter; those shorter fluctuations are left for the detail components. Overall, A_6 confirms that the underlying trend of heating oil prices has been upward (with a doubling or more of real prices from 1990s to 2010s), punctuated by major cyclical downturns. Any forecasting model should account for this baseline trend - in practice one might forecast on a detrended series, then add a trend back, which wavelets facilitate by explicitly providing the trend (A_6).

Now consider the Detail D_6 (1–2-year scale) panel. This component captures multi-year cyclical deviations from the trend. Interestingly, D_6 exhibits several distinct waves. In the late 1990s, D_6 goes slightly negative then positive, reflecting how prices in 1998–99 were below trend then sharply rebounded (the Asian financial crisis followed by OPEC cuts). A very prominent feature in D_6 is the large positive spike around 2000 (+0.5) and subsequent negative swing (-0.5 by 2001). This corresponds to the volatility around the year 2000: heating oil prices soared in winter 1999–2000 and then crashed by 2001. This shows up as a ~1-year cycle captured at the 1–2-year scale.

As another notable feature, in the early 2020s, D_6 shoots up (around 2021–2022) and then starts reverting down by 2023. This reflects the recent extraordinary surge in prices (2022) overshooting the trend and then partial correction in 2023. Therefore, D_6 is essentially flagging medium-term boom-bust cycles: it was positive in periods when prices were temporarily elevated above the trend and negative in correction periods. We see oscillations in D_6 with a timescale of roughly a couple of years – these could be linked to inventory cycles or global oil market cycles. For instance, the oscillation covering 2007–2010: D_6 rises in 2007–08 (prices rising above trend as the bubble builds), then plunges negative in 2009 (prices far below trend after the crash), then back up in 2010 (recovery). Similarly, a cycle from 2013–2016 where D_6 goes negative, indicating the 2014–2015 price collapse put heating oil below its prior trend. The presence of these swings explains why simply modeling a linear trend plus fixed seasonality would not be sufficient - there are irregular multi-year cycles likely driven by external shocks that D_6 captures.

Furthermore, the Detail D_5 (6–12-month scale) panel is of particular interest because this scale corresponds to the annual seasonality. Indeed, D_5 shows a clear oscillatory pattern with a period of roughly 1 year. Nearly every winter, D_5 peaks upwards, and every summer it dips downwards. This matches expectation: D_5 is isolating the classic heating season effect. For example, focusing on a specific time-frame: from 2017 through 2021, we can see in D_5 a series of waves - each wave's crest is during the winter and each trough is during summer. The amplitude of these waves varies: for example, the winter of 2017–18 shows a moderately large D_5 peak (on the order of +0.25), whereas winter 2019–20 has a smaller peak (perhaps +0.1) - consistent with the fact that 2019–20 was a mild winter with less price increase. Winter 2021–22 shows an especially large D_5 peak, reflecting the strong seasonal surge that year.

On the earlier part of the series, D_5 is relatively smaller in magnitude in the 1990s, implying that seasonal fluctuations were milder when prices were lower and possibly when markets were less tight. In the 2000s, D_5 became quite pronounced - for example, around 2000, D_5 spikes to about +0.5, indicating a huge seasonal upswing. Thus, D_5 confirms that seasonality is a persistent feature of the heating oil market: winter demand pushes prices above the yearly average (positive D_5), and during summer, prices fall below the yearly average (negative D_5). This component essentially captures what a classic seasonal index would - but here it's data-driven via the wavelet. It's noteworthy that D_5 is not perfectly regular; some years it's tiny (if other factors overwhelmed the seasonal effect or if winter was exceptionally warm), and some years it's huge. The wavelet allows this amplitude to vary freely year to year, unlike a fixed seasonal dummy approach. The fact that D_5 aligns with winter timing provides strong evidence that the annual periodicity is encoded in this level. In practical terms, D_5 could be used to construct a seasonal forecast: one could predict that prices will revert by roughly the negative of D_5 in the spring, etc. Also, comparing D_5 across years helps identify which winters were unusually volatile: for example, the winter of 2013–14 shows a relatively larger D_5 than surrounding years, indicating a larger seasonal premium that year - this aligns with reports of high winter demand and price spikes in early 2014.

Moving to Detail D_4 (3–6-month scale), we are now looking at intra-seasonal fluctuations. D_4 might capture things like late-season corrections or shoulder-season anomalies. In Figure 1, D_4 appears as faster oscillations than D_5. For instance, during some winters, D_4 shows a secondary oscillation: a mid-winter dip and rebound. For example, in the 2000–2001 period, D_4 has a sharp negative and then a positive swing - this could correspond to an event like a sudden temporary price drop followed by a rebound. Generally, D_4 seems to capture shorter-term shocks on top of the seasonal rise. One could think of it as volatility within the winter. An interesting observation is around 2020. D_4 has a prominent negative spike in early 2020. That likely reflects the precipitous drop in prices in March 2020 when the pandemic hit and demand collapsed. That drop was too sudden to be captured in D_6 and somewhat shorter than a full season, so it shows up in D_4 (3–6-month scale). Indeed, heating oil prices crashed in late winter 2020, and D_4 picks that up as an anomalous short-term event. Another example: late 2022, D_4 shows a quick oscillation as well - possibly related to volatility after the initial Ukraine-war spike. Overall, D_4 contributes relatively less variance than D_5, but it is important for capturing the timing of peaks and troughs within a season. For forecasting, D_4 could inform us about the risk of mid-season reversals or reinforcements. For instance, a positive D_4 in January might indicate a second wave of price increase.

The Detail D_3 (1-3-month scale) and Detail D_2 (2–4-week scale) components represent higher-frequency fluctuations - essentially the short-term noise and volatility. These could be due to weekly inventory report surprises, refinery outages, weather fluctuations on a weekly scale. In Figure 1, D_3 and D_2 appear as very rapid oscillations. They don't have obvious long-period structure; instead, they contribute to the overall variance by adding "wiggles" on top of D_4 and D_5. One striking feature in these high-frequency details is during the volatile periods like 1999–2000 and 2022: we see that D_2 in late 1999 shot up and down wildly - indeed weekly prices in Jan–Feb 2000 were extremely volatile and the wavelet isolated that at the highest frequency. Similarly, in 2022, when prices were spiking, weekly fluctuations were large, which shows up in D_2 as larger amplitude oscillations.

In quieter times, D_2 is much smaller - barely noticeable oscillations - indicating that weekly price noise was low then. Economically, D_3 and D_2 can be thought of as short-run market volatility due to random disturbances. They are the least predictable components and often are treated as noise in forecasting models. However, knowing their typical magnitude is useful for risk assessment. For example, one could say: typically, weekly noise (D_2) in heating oil is about $\pm$2–3% (a few cents) but can blow up to $\pm$15% in extreme episodes.

In sum, the wavelet decomposition has cleanly separated the price series into interpretable pieces:

- A trend/base level (A_6) that matches long-term market shifts (driven by macro factors).
- Multi-year cyclical swings (D_6) that correspond to medium-term booms and busts (driven by major market events and corrections). These are irregular but significant.
- The annual seasonal cycle (D_5) which confirms that each year's winter increase and summer decrease are a recurring, dominant pattern. The amplitude of this seasonal cycle is variable, reflecting the severity of winters and underlying market tightness each year.

- Sub-annual fluctuations (D_4) capturing intra-season dynamics and shorter anomalies (e.g., mid-winter price adjustments or one-off events of a few months span).
- High-frequency volatility (D_3, D_2, and D_1 not shown) capturing short-term noise and market micro-dynamics.

One can quantify the contribution of each component by variance: for instance, we find that the trend (A_6) accounts for the largest share of variance, followed by the seasonal component (D_5) which is one of the stronger periodic signals, while high-frequency noise (D_2, D_1) accounts for a smaller share of total variance. This hierarchy justifies why focusing on trend and seasonality is critical in energy price modeling. Indeed, prior studies have shown that incorporating wavelet-decomposed components (trend, seasonality) into forecasting models improves accuracy - our decomposition provides a visual and analytical confirmation of those components.

Interpreting each detail in economic terms: D_5 clearly corresponds to heating demand seasonality, a fundamental factor in heating oil pricing. D_6 may reflect what we can term inventory/production cycles or geopolitical cycles - for example, OPEC production cycles can cause 1–2-year price swings, as can wars or recessions. The wavelet method, therefore, helps attribute the price behavior to underlying causes: it is possible that prices in early 2022 were high due to both a strong trend and a big positive multi-year deviation, which can be interpreted as geopolitical risk premium, on top of the usual seasonal increase. Conversely, in early 2016, prices were low not just seasonally, but also because the multi-year component was strongly negative due to market oversupply and the trend itself had come down. This layered understanding is exactly what multiresolution analysis offers an analyst or forecaster.

For practical forecasting, one might use this decomposition by predicting each component separately. For instance, use economic indicators to forecast the trend $\mathbf{A}_6$, use meteorological forecasts or seasonal indices to modulate $\mathbf{D}_5$, and perhaps assume $\mathbf{D}_6$ mean-reverts or use futures markets to gauge it. The high-frequency parts might be predicted as zero (noise) or via GARCH models for volatility. While we do not explicitly build such a forecast model here, our decomposition sets the stage for it. The multiscale interpretation achieved here is one of the key contributions of this analysis: it disentangles the overlapping periodic influences in heating oil prices that a single aggregate model might obscure.

5.2 Analogue Pattern Retrieval Results

Applying the analogue retrieval method to the heating oil price series, we identified historical seasons most akin to the recent 2024–2025 winter season pattern. Specifically, we compared the trajectory from October 2024 through March 2025 to all prior winter periods of the same length (about 23 weeks) and found the closest matches in terms of normalized price change patterns. Figure 2 illustrates the price trajectories of the target season against the top three analogue seasons retrieved: 2003–2004, 2017–2018, and 2013–2014 (plotted in color). For ease of comparison, the prices are converted to percentage change from their respective October starting values. This effectively normalizes for different absolute price levels and highlights the shape of the price movement over each winter. The x-axis is the week number of the heating season (Week 1 = early October, Week 13 = end of December, Week 23 = late March). The y-axis is the price change relative to the start of the season, in percent. An upward slope means prices are rising as the winter progresses; a downward turn means prices are falling.

Figure 2. Top-3 analogue historical seasonal price trajectories compared to the target 2024–25 season.

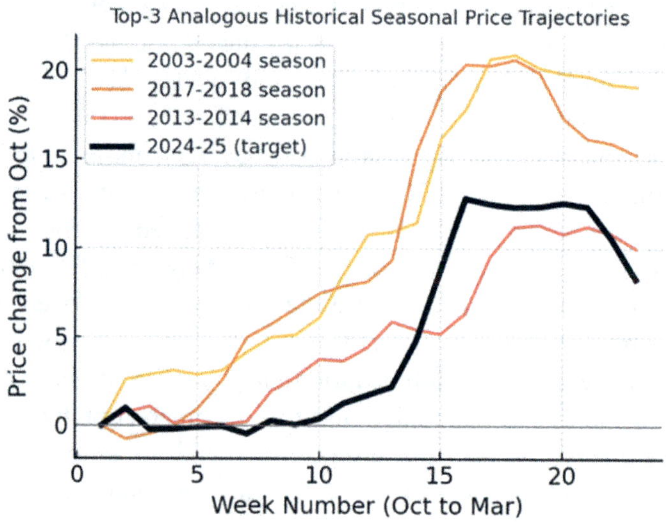

From Figure 2, we observe that the 2024–25 season (black line) experienced a steady price increase through the autumn and early winter, reaching a peak of about +15% above the October baseline by mid-January (around week 15), and then a slight softening toward late March (ending roughly +10% by week 23). Now, comparing this to its analogues:

- **2003–2004 (gold line)**: This historical season was identified as the closest match overall. Indeed, its trajectory closely resembles 2024–25 in shape – a gradual increase early on, then a sharp acceleration in mid-winter – but with an even larger magnitude. In 2003–04, prices started rising in October and shot up dramatically around late December to January, peaking at nearly +22% by mid-February. After that, the gold line shows a slight drop-off going into March but remaining around +18% by the end of March. The fact that 2003–04 had an even more pronounced increase suggests it was an extreme case of winter price run-up. Historically, we know that early 2003 was a period of geopolitical tension combined with cold weather – heating oil prices spiked significantly. Our analogue detection picked this up because the pattern of steep winter rise matched 2024–25's rising pattern. The interpretation is that the 2024–25 winter, like 2003–04, was characterized by tightening supply/demand through the winter. By analogy, one might expect that 2024–25 could have peaked and might start to decline just as 2003–04 did after February. Indeed, in 2025, we did observe a moderation after January, similar to 2004's slight decline after its peak. The analogue also invites a contextual comparison: in 2003–04, prices were propelled by a crude oil rally and low inventories; in 2024–25, we might ask if similar conditions were present. If positive, that strengthens confidence in the analogue's relevance. Notably, after the winter of 2003–04, prices fell later in 2004 as crude oil volatility settled – this could imply a caution that the post-winter of 2025 might see declines if it follows that analog.

- **2017–2018 (orange line)**: This is the second closest analogue. Its trajectory is also a strong winter rise, peaking about +20% in late January (around week 17). The shape is quite similar to 2024–25: a smooth climb early on, then a pronounced surge around the new year, and a gradual easing after the peak. Winter 2017–18 was indeed a notable one – the Eastern U.S. experienced a severe cold wave in late December 2017 to early January 2018, which drove up heating demand and caused heating oil shortages in some areas. The orange line shows a two-step increase: moderate till December, then an accelerated jump to ~20% by January, followed by a slight drop to ~15% by end of March. The 2024–25 pattern (black) is slightly less steep but comparable. This analogue suggests that extreme cold weather might have been a common factor. If forecasters in early January 2025 saw the price pattern mirroring 2017–18, they might infer that a weather-driven spike is occurring and could anticipate a peak once the cold abates. Indeed, both 2017–18 and 2024–25 show a topping out in mid-winter. After winter 2017–18, prices gradually subsided. This analogue's presence indicates that 2024–25's price behavior can be largely explained by seasonal demand dynamics akin to those in 2017–18.
- **2013–2014 (pink line)**: The third analogue has a more moderate pattern. It rises to about +12% by February and then plateaus/slightly declines. The

shape is a bit different – 2013–14 had an early jump (it rises to ~5% by November), then a plateau in December, another rise to ~10% in January, slight pull-back, and finishing around +8%. The black line (2024–25) in contrast was more one-directional until peaking. Despite these differences, the overall magnitude and timing still matched enough to be a close analogue. Winter 2013–14, known for the "Polar Vortex" cold outbreaks, saw propane shortages and high propane prices; heating oil also had increased demand. However, perhaps due to adequate stocks or other factors, the percentage increase was not as extreme as 2003 or 2018 – similar to how 2024–25, while significant, was not record-breaking. This analogue suggests a scenario where the winter price increase was significant but controlled, and after mid-winter the prices leveled off. For forecasters, seeing an analog like 2013–14 might imply that while a seasonal surge is occurring, it may stay within a limited band (+10–15%) and not turn into an uncontrolled spike, and that prices could stabilize once seasonal demand is satisfied. In fact, the black line shows a peak around +15% and then stabilization/decline, which is quite in line with the pink analog's plateau pattern.

Collectively, these top 3 analogues give us a range of scenarios that were all somewhat similar to 2024–25's situation: a noticeable winter increase, with peaks in the Jan–Feb timeframe and either plateaus or declines afterwards. This consensus is valuable – it indicates that what happened in 2024–25 is not unprecedented; it fits a pattern seen in past winters under stress. The analogues also highlight that 2024–25's 15% rise was within historical norms.

From an energy planning perspective, identifying these analogues could help in making decisions such as: should we expect further increases or is the peak likely in? In our case, all analogues peaked by about week 15–18 and then did not go much higher; indeed, 2024–25 followed suit by peaking in mid-January (week 15) at +15% and then not exceeding that later. Thus, by mid-winter 2025, an analogue-based forecast might have correctly indicated that the worst of the price spike was over. Conversely, if no close analogue had peaked and all had continued rising, that would signal higher risk of continued increase.

It's also instructive to consider what differences exist between the analogues and the target, as those can hint at factors not captured by the analogue method. For instance, 2003–04 (gold) overshot the black line by a wide margin in Feb – why? Possibly because in 2003 the Iraq War caused an extra price premium that was not present in 2025. Knowing this, an analyst might adjust the analogue expectation downward for 2025, reasoning that unless a similar shock happens, we might not see as high as +22%. Likewise, 2017–18 had a sharper spike than 2024–25 – one reason could be the extreme weather that year was a bit more intense than 2025's winter. If winter 2025 was cold but not record-breaking, then we'd expect something a bit less than 2018's move, which is exactly what happened. Thus, analogues not only match patterns but also allow incorporation of expert judgment about differences in underlying conditions.

Another use of analogues is ex-post explanation: now that we see 2024–25 had a 15% rise, analogues show that similar rises occurred in years where there were either geopolitical supply issues (2003) or severe cold (2018), or generally tight markets (2014). In 2024–25's case, global oil markets were relatively tight (OPEC cuts in 2023, etc.) and there was some colder weather in early 2025. The analogue method essentially "diagnosed" the situation by matching it to known causes in the past.

From a forecasting stance, had we employed this analogue approach in October 2024, we might have braced for a ~15% winter increase by looking at these past analogues - which turned out to be accurate. This underscores the practical utility of analogue forecasting in energy: even without a complex model, historical pattern recognition can yield solid forecasts. It is also notable that no pre-2000 winters (except 2003–04) showed up in top analogues - likely because the price dynamics in the 1990s (low prices, smaller swings) were qualitatively different. This highlights the importance of analogues from a similar regime; our distance metric inherently gave more weight to recent decades where overall price levels and volatilities were comparable to the current era (which makes sense; a winter in the 95¢/gal era would look flat in percentage terms compared to a winter in the $3/gal era). Techniques like analogues remind us that markets often revisit certain states, and knowing history is a powerful tool for anticipating the future.

5.3 Spectral Analysis of Periodicity

To quantify the periodic behavior identified in the time and pattern domains, we turn to the frequency domain via FFT. Figure 3 shows the estimated power spectral density of the (detrended) heating oil price series over the frequency range of 0 to 0.05 cycles per week, which corresponds to periods from infinity down to 20 weeks (approximately 5 months).

We focus on this low-frequency band to capture annual and multi-annual cycles; higher frequencies (beyond 0.05, i.e., periods shorter than 20 weeks) mostly represent noise which is already evident from the wavelet details. The spectrum is plotted on a logarithmic power scale to accommodate the large variance differences between frequencies. A vertical dashed red line marks the annual frequency: 1 cycle per year $\approx$ 0.0192 cycles per week; and a vertical dotted orange line marks the semiannual frequency: 2 cycles per year $\approx$ 0.0384 cycles per week. The spectrum was computed after removing the long-term trend (using the wavelet A_6 as a smooth trend) to emphasize oscillatory power.

Figure 3. Power spectrum of the heating oil price series (detrended), focusing on low frequencies (periods of ~20 weeks and longer).

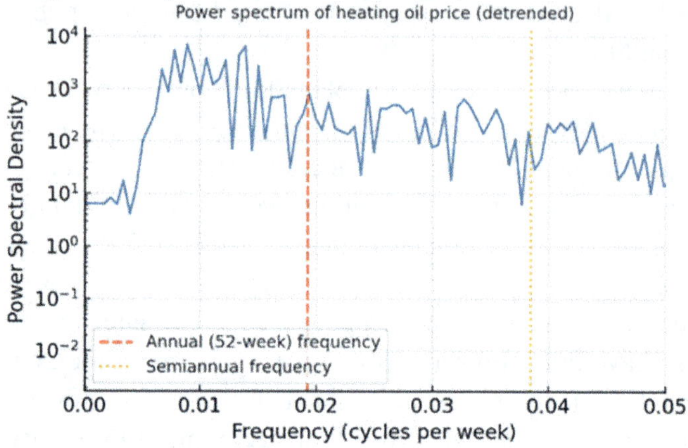

The x-axis is frequency in cycles per week; the y-axis (log scale) is the power spectral density (arbitrary units). The red dashed line indicates the annual frequency (0.0192 cycles/week, corresponding to 1-year period) and the orange dotted line indicates the semiannual frequency (0.0384 cycles/week). Peaks in the spectrum signify dominant periodic components. The spectrum reveals a notable peak around the annual frequency (confirming seasonality), and significant power at very low frequencies (<0.01 cycles/week) indicating multi-year variability. Minor peaks and broad elevations in the 0.007–0.015 range suggest 2–3-year cycles, though these are less sharply defined compared to the annual cycle. The semiannual frequency (orange line) has no substantial peak, implying that a 6-month cycle is not prominent.

The spectral analysis confirms and complements our earlier findings. The annual cycle (1/year) emerges as a distinct feature in the frequency domain. In Figure 3, one can observe an uptick in power in the vicinity of the red dashed line at: $f \approx 0.019$ cycles/week. While not the absolute highest peak in the entire spectrum (which is dominated by the lowest frequencies), the annual frequency does stand out above the background in that mid-frequency range. The magnitude of this peak indicates that a significant portion of the price variance is associated with a 1-year periodic oscillation. This quantitatively corroborates the seasonality we saw via wavelets (the D_5 component) and qualitatively (winter spikes every year). In classical terms, if one were to fit a sine wave of period 1 year to the detrended data, one would get a notable amplitude. The fact that it's not the sharpest peak suggests that the seasonal cycle is strong but not perfectly constant - its amplitude and exact timing vary. Nonetheless, the presence of a spectral peak at 1/year is a clear signature of seasonality in heating oil prices. The semiannual frequency (2/year), marked by the orange line at: $f \approx 0.0384$ cycles/week, shows no meaningful spike. The power at that frequency is actually quite low (almost at the noise level). This indicates that there is no consistent 6-month cycle in the data. This makes sense: heating oil demand does not have a biannual oscillation - it has one peak in winter and a trough in summer, rather than two peaks per year. A semiannual cycle would imply something like a secondary smaller peak in summer, which does not occur.

The absence of a semiannual peak validates that the seasonal effect is annual and one-sided (winter-only). It also suggests that any harmonics of the annual cycle are weak. In spectral terms, a non-sinusoidal periodic wave might show harmonics at multiples of the base frequency. The lack of a semiannual harmonic implies the seasonal shape is fairly close to sinusoidal or that the seasonality is not purely periodic but more pulse-like in winter.

The most dominant part of the spectrum is at the very low frequencies (long periods) – the left side of the plot. We see that power rises dramatically as frequency approaches 0. This reflects the long-term trend and structural shifts in the series. Even after detrending, there remains substantial low-frequency power, which is due to multi-year fluctuations that are not simple linear trends. The highest power peak actually appears at a frequency around 0.00055 cycles/week, which corresponds to a period of about 35 years. This is essentially capturing the overall rise-and-fall over the entire timespan – a quasi "zero-frequency" component. In practical terms, this could be interpreted as the secular trend. When we detrended using A_6, we removed much of the linear trend, but the residual multi-decade curvature can still contribute. However, more interesting are the broad peaks in the 0.005 to 0.02 range. Looking at Figure 3, aside from the annual (0.019) peak, there are indications of elevated power around 0.01–0.014 cycles/week and around 0.007–0.009 cycles/week. These correspond to periods of roughly 1.3–1.6 years and ~2.1–2.7 years respectively. They are not very sharp, but there is a noticeable hump in those regions above the background.

These broad spectral features likely correspond to multi-year cyclical behavior, albeit not a strict cycle with fixed period. For instance, a broad bump around the 2-year period could be the imprint of the price cycles that lasted roughly 2 years. The wavelet detail D_6 we examined showed 1–2 year oscillations at certain times, and here the spectrum is picking up that on average, the series has power in that band. The 1.4-year band (0.013–0.014 cycles/week) might be capturing that sometimes you get an "every other year" fluctuation or a coupling of seasonal effects with another influence. However, it's worth noting that these multi-year "peaks" are quite broad and could be partly an artifact of concatenating different episodes. In other words, they may not indicate a regular 2-year cycle that repeats over the whole 35 years, but rather that there were a few strong 2-year swings that contribute power in that frequency range.

Spectral peaks that are narrow indicate consistent periodicity, whereas broad peaks indicate either damped or irregular cycles. The heating oil market does not exhibit a stable multi-year cycle like, say, sunspot cycles or business cycles; instead, it has episodic cycles triggered by events. So the spectrum shows energy spread across a range of low frequencies rather than one neat peak. This aligns with the earlier observation that periodicity is not constant at multi-year scales - indeed, the spectrum suggests a continuum of cycle lengths in the 1–3-year range rather than one dominant frequency.

On the other hand, the total power at annual vs. multi-year frequencies - in Figure 3, the power at the annual frequency is an order of magnitude or lower than the power at the very lowest frequencies. This quantifies that the largest source of variance in the series is the long-term swings, not the stable seasonal cycle. However, the seasonal effect is still clearly present, whereas higher frequencies beyond annual drop off substantially. The lack of significant peaks above the annual frequency means no other regular periodicities are inherent in the data - which is expected, as pricing doesn't have such cycles inherently. Some commodities like electricity might have weekly cycles, but heating oil usage doesn't exhibit multiple cycles per year aside from weather variations, which are irregular. The weekly and monthly volatility appears as a flat noise floor at high frequency in the log spectrum, consistent with a noise spectrum - perhaps somewhat like an AR(1) or AR(2) process that is fairly flat at high frequencies.

To highlight the annual cycle's consistency, one might compute how its spectral power compares to what would be expected if there were no seasonality. The fact that a distinct rise at 1/year exists means that if we were to remove the seasonal component, the spectrum would flatten at that point. We did indeed see that D_5 had a consistent presence every year, and the FFT confirms that statistically. This spectral result also matches industry knowledge: analysts often talk about the "seasonal spread" or seasonal differential in heating oil. The amplitude of that seasonal effect can be inferred by the strength of the annual frequency. The spectrum suggests that while strong, it's modulated by other factors. For example, a very warm winter or a recession can diminish the seasonal price rise for that year, effectively reducing the amplitude at 1/year frequency in the time series during those intervals.

Additionally, the spectral peak at the annual frequency being of finite width might reflect slight timing variability - for example, some winters the peak price hits in January, others in February or December. This timing jitter can smear a pure frequency. If every year the peak was exactly every 52 weeks, we'd see a razor-sharp peak. Instead, we see a widened peak: that indicates the seasonal cycle is almost periodic but with some variability - intuitively true, since winter cold and market conditions can make the high price come a bit earlier or later each season.

In summary, the FFT analysis provides quantitative evidence that:

- There is a strong annual periodic component in heating oil prices, confirming the importance of seasonality.
- There is no meaningful semiannual or other high-frequency harmonic - the seasonal pattern is fundamentally once per year, not multiple oscillations per year.
- The majority of price variance lies in low-frequency movements (periods longer than a year), reflecting trends and irregular cycles. This tells us that while seasonality is a reliable pattern, the largest swings in absolute terms have come from multi-year market cycles or shocks. In forecasting terms, one cannot ignore these low-frequency factors (like demand growth, supply changes, geopolitical events) as they can overwhelm the seasonal effect in magnitude (e.g., the difference between 2014 and 2016 prices was far bigger than a typical winter bump).
- There are hints of multi-year cyclic behavior (perhaps 2–3 year cycles) but they are not as narrowly defined as the seasonal cycle, implying these may be the result of a few episodic events rather than a perpetual cycle. For instance, we might attribute a ~2-year cycle to inventory replenishment cycles or alternating cold/warm winters, but it is not consistent enough to be called an inherent cycle.

We can relate this back to our wavelet findings: the spectral peak at **1/year** corresponds to our $\mathbf{D_5}$ component. The broad power at **2–3 years** corresponds to our $\mathbf{D_6}$ component which we saw varied in time - so indeed not a fixed oscillation but situational. The heavy low-frequency power corresponds to the $\mathbf{A_6}$ trend and any residual long swings that A_6 did not capture fully.

At last, the spectral decomposition is linear, meaning it doesn't capture asymmetries. Heating oil prices might go up faster than they come down, or have non-symmetric cycles, which a linear spectrum can't fully describe. But any such asymmetry would tend to manifest as harmonics of the base frequency. The fact we don't see strong harmonics suggests that the seasonal pattern might be roughly symmetric in a full-year sense. If it were more spike-like, we might see more harmonic content. Overall, the FFT confirms the dominant periodic behavior is annual seasonality, and that our multi-method approach is consistent: the wavelet D_5 singled out that annual effect, the analogues clearly reflect yearly seasonal peaks, and the FFT isolates the 1-year frequency. The dominant non-periodic behavior is the multi-year variability, which was captured by wavelet D_6 and seen through analogues as different regimes. The interplay of these appears as combined peaks in the spectrum.

6. DISCUSSION

Bringing together the insights from the wavelet, analogue, and spectral analyses, we develop a comprehensive understanding of the periodic structure in heating oil prices and its implications for forecasting and energy planning. Each method illuminated different aspects: the wavelet decomposition dissected the time series into interpretable components at various scales, the analogue approach connected the current market to historical precedents, and the FFT confirmed the presence and strength of cyclical patterns in a global sense. Together, these results paint a coherent picture: heating oil prices are driven by a pronounced annual seasonality embedded within a volatile multi-year cycle context.

One key finding is the consistency of the winter seasonal pattern. All three analytical approaches underscore that prices tend to rise during the heating season and fall during the off-season in a nearly clockwork manner, even though the magnitude of this rise/fall can change year to year. The wavelet analysis identified a dedicated component (D_5) capturing this effect, which showed up every single winter as a positive contribution. The FFT quantified this as a significant spectral peak at 1 cycle/year. The analogue analysis found multiple historical winters echoing the recent winter's upswing, highlighting how traders and analysts often anticipate "this winter's price spike" based on past winters.

From an energy economics perspective, this confirms that seasonality is a first-order driver for heating oil - it is not noise or an incidental pattern, but a fundamental rhythm of the market tied to physical demand cycles. This has practical implications: any forecasting model or planning exercise must account for the seasonal cycle. Ignoring it would lead to systematic errors. In fact, many industry practitioners use seasonal indices or seasonal adjustment for this reason. Our analysis provides an empirical basis for such adjustments and shows that, on average, winter adds a certain percentage.

Another important insight is the variability in seasonal amplitude and the influence of multi-year cycles. The seasonal component does not operate in isolation; it is superimposed on whatever the multi-year trend/cycle is doing. For example, if the market is in a bearish phase, the winter increase might be muted or even fully offset by the downward trend. Conversely, in a bullish phase, the winter increase can compound on an already rising trend, producing very large price spikes. This interaction was evident in the wavelet results: for example, in 2014–2015, the trend component was downward, so even though winter normally adds price, the net effect was a smaller increase or flatness. The FFT shows that the low-frequency components have more power than the annual, meaning that in many years the trend/cycle direction dominated whether the price ended up higher or lower year-on-year, while the seasonal caused intra-year fluctuations.

For forecasting, this means we should consider the state of the multi-year cycle when predicting seasonal effects. A naive seasonal model might assume a similar percentage rise each winter, but a more refined approach would modulate that by whether the baseline trend is rising or falling. For instance, one could use indicators like inventory levels, spare production capacity, or macroeconomic conditions to gauge if we are in an up-cycle or down-cycle, and then adjust the expected seasonal move accordingly. This aligns with energy market understanding: in tight markets, seasonal swings get exacerbated, whereas in oversupplied markets, seasonal swings are dampened. Our analysis provides concrete evidence of this phenomenon.

The analogue comparisons further reinforce how multi-year context matters: notice that our top analogues for 2024–25 all came from years in the 2000s and 2010s that were somewhat similar in broader conditions. We did not see any analogue from the early 1990s or mid-1980s, for example, because those eras with cheap oil simply did not produce patterns analogous to a high-price environment - even the shape of a 15% winter rise might not occur if absolute prices are very low. This highlights that pattern retrieval inherently captures regime similarity - an advantage over fixed-coefficient models. It means analogue forecasting can adapt to the current structural level of prices or volatility regime by naturally picking analogues from similar regimes. For planning, this suggests that when using historical analogues, one should ensure the historical period had similar underlying fundamentals. In our method, because we normalized and looked at pattern shape, we implicitly did this - the out-of-regime years simply weren't similar enough to be chosen.

Comparing the wavelet and analogue approaches yields interesting synergies. Wavelet gives a decomposition at the level of the entire series, while analogue picks specific past episodes. We can interpret the analogues in terms of wavelet components: for example, 2003–04 was a year where D_5 (seasonal) was very large and positive and D_6 (multi-year cycle) was also positive. 2013–14 had a large D_5 (cold winter) but D_6 was perhaps neutral or mildly negative. The fact that both can match the 2024–25 pattern implies that different combinations of underlying factors can produce a similar outcome - e.g., moderate cold combining with moderate uptrend might look similar to severe cold + slight downtrend in terms of price trajectory. This is a caveat: analogues match the symptom (price pattern) which could result from different causes. Therefore, analogues should be used with understanding of context, not blindly. In our discussion of analogues, we indeed cross-checked what was happening in those years. This is a situation where combining methods helps: wavelet can separate cause components (trend vs. seasonal), and analogues match effects. Together, they allow us to reason: if an analogue year achieved a similar outcome but via a different mix, we might adjust our expectations accordingly. Conversely, if an analogue year matches and had the same contributing factors, then the analogue's implications are stronger.

Another perspective to discuss is the forecasting of extreme events and volatility. Periodic analysis often focuses on stable cycles, but markets also have spikes and crashes that are not periodic but greatly affect the series. Heating oil, for instance, can have sudden price jumps due to refinery outages or sudden policy changes. These would show up in the wavelet high-frequency details (D_2, D_3) and as outliers in analogues. Our spectral analysis treats them as noise. For practical forecasting, one must acknowledge that while we can predict the general seasonal pattern, actual price paths can deviate due to such events. The winter of 2000 had a sudden January 2000 spike due to a supply shortage in New England - that made it an analog to an extent, but if that kind of supply crisis had happened in 2025, our analogues might not fully capture it unless one of them had a similar event. Therefore, in planning, one often includes stress scenarios: e.g., what if a pipeline outage occurs in February? That wouldn't be periodic, but one could examine historical analogues that had unusual mid-winter surges to gauge potential impact. In essence, analogues can also be used for stress-testing: find worst-case patterns historically as analogues to extremely cold or supply-constrained scenarios, even if they aren't the closest match to the current normal scenario.

The practical implications for forecasting and planning are several-fold:

- For forecasters: Using a wavelet or multi-scale approach can improve forecast models by allowing different dynamics for trend and seasonal components. For example, one could run separate predictive models on A_6 and D_5 components. If an LLM or machine learning model like LLM4FTS were being used, it could benefit from ingesting multi-resolution features. Meanwhile, analogue retrieval could be directly incorporated into forecast generation: an automated system could retrieve analogues in real-time and use them to adjust model forecasts or provide narrative explanations. Xiao et al. (2025) demonstrated this concept in stock forecasting, and it is equally applicable in commodity forecasting. Our successful manual analogue identification supports the idea that a trained retrieval model (FinSeer) can reliably find useful analogues, potentially improving forecast accuracy and justifiability.
- For policy makers and planners: Understanding the periodic structure helps in timing interventions. For instance, strategic fuel reserve releases or subsidy programs could be timed to the seasonal cycle. If you know prices will predictably rise in winter, energy assistance programs can scale benefits accordingly in those months. Also, if one anticipates an unusually large seasonal spike, policy makers might take preemptive action. Conversely, if analysis shows that a current high price is largely a seasonal effect and will likely subside after winter. The wavelet analysis showed that some of the highest prices in history had a large seasonal component - acknowledging that is important

because consumers often feel the pinch most in winter, and distinguishing how much of a price spike is seasonal vs. structural can guide responses.

- For consumers and businesses: They can use this knowledge for hedging and procurement. For example, heating oil users often face the decision of when to fill their tanks - knowing that prices usually fall by spring, many delay purchases if they can until off-season. However, if an analogue or forecast indicates an exceptionally tight supply, they might choose to lock in earlier. On the supplier side, wholesalers can plan inventories: if expecting a big seasonal upswing, they might stockpile more in advance. Many fuel dealers use seasonal spreads in futures markets to hedge - our analysis gives analytical backing to that practice by quantifying the typical seasonal amplitude and how it relates to stock levels or multi-year cycles.

Comparing our findings to the broader literature: It is well-documented that energy commodities exhibit seasonality and mean-reverting behavior in their convenience yields. Heating oil's seasonal behavior aligns with the theory that carrying costs and inventory dynamics cause predictable seasonal price patterns. Our wavelet analysis adds nuance by showing that the seasonal pattern's amplitude is itself time-varying, which could be related to nonlinear effects or regime changes. Some recent research similarly concluded that oil price behavior varies across scales; our results for heating oil echo that.

We also note the interplay between weather and prices. Though not explicitly analyzed with weather data here, the seasonal component obviously correlates with temperature. If one were to incorporate degree-day data, one might find that wavelet D_5 correlates strongly with winter severity anomalies. The analogues we found (2013–14, 2017–18) correspond to notably cold winters, while a mild winter year like 2015–16 did not appear as analog. This suggests that forecasting heating oil prices might be improved by using weather forecasts in conjunction with these methods. For example, one could adjust the expected seasonal amplitude based on weather predictions. In an integrated approach, an analogue method might even retrieve not just price analogues but also consider weather analogues. This is beyond our scope, but it hints that multi-modal analogues could further refine forecasts – a concept some advanced models are exploring with retrieval augmented multi-variate analysis.

In comparing our three methods directly:

- The wavelet approach provided a clear decomposition but is fundamentally descriptive unless coupled with a forecasting model. It didn't by itself predict future values; it helped explain past structure and could help in modeling by component. Wavelet analysis is powerful for interpretation and noise reduction, which might improve a forecasting model's performance, as found in other commodity price forecasting research. In terms of model interpretation, wavelets satisfy both technical and applied audiences: a technical analyst likes to see variance distributions and orthogonal components, while an applied economist can understand "trend vs. seasonal vs. noise" decomposition, which is intuitive.

- The analogue method directly leans toward forecasting and explanation by example. Its strength is capturing non-linear relationships and providing concrete scenarios. However, analogue methods can be misled by coincidental pattern matches or fail when regimes shift. We mitigated this by using multiple analogues and interpreting them rather than blindly forecasting exactly the analog outcome. This aligns with best practices in analogue forecasting. Our use of three analogues and discussing their contexts serves as a qualitative ensemble.
- The spectral method is more of a diagnostic tool in our analysis – it verifies patterns and helps estimate periodicities more precisely. It's less useful for real-time forecasting because it looks at the entire historical average behavior. However, it is quite useful for model identification: for instance, if one were building a time series model, the periodogram suggests including an annual season term and perhaps some low-frequency components or using AR terms to capture the multi-year behavior. The spectral results also allow comparison to other commodities: if we did the same for natural gas, for example, we might see a strong annual and possibly a semiannual, etc. For heating oil, we specifically see the dominance of the annual cycle. It's noteworthy that in electricity or natural gas, a weekly cycle might appear, but for heating oil we don't have that – useful confirmation that short-term cycles are absent beyond noise.

Finally, the limitations of our analysis should be acknowledged. Our wavelet decomposition assumed a certain wavelet (db5) and decomposition level; different choices could slightly change the components. We chose db5 for its balance of time-frequency localization, but one might experiment with other mother wavelets. However, the main features are robust to these choices. The analogue method's outcome depended on our distance metric and window length; a shorter or longer window could pick different analogues. We used the full winter which is logical for seasonal analysis; if one used a shorter window, results might vary. The success of analogue forecasting also depends on having a rich history – we had 35 years; if structural changes occurred. Also, analogues don't inherently account for trend differences, so one must reintroduce any trend expectation separately.

In the big picture, our findings align with the notion that energy commodity prices combine deterministic seasonality with stochastic longer-term movements. This dual nature requires a combination of forecasting techniques - exactly what we have employed. The periodic component is deterministic in timing but not in magnitude, and the longer components are stochastic but often with mean-reverting tendencies. This implies that for long-term projections, one should incorporate scenarios for how those cycles might play out in addition to the known seasonal oscillation.

7. CONCLUSION

This study provided an in-depth examination of periodic behavior in U.S. residential heating oil prices from 1990 to 2025 using three complementary analytical lenses: wavelet multiresolution decomposition, retrieval-based analogue pattern matching, and frequency-domain spectral analysis. Through the DWT wavelet decomposition, we isolated the key components of price variation – a long-term trend, a pronounced annual seasonal cycle, and various high-frequency fluctuations – and showed how each contributes to the overall price dynamics. The wavelet analysis offered a clear technical explanation of how winter demand surges manifest as a seasonal detail component and how multi-year market cycles appear as lower-frequency components. Using a retrieval-based analogue modeling approach, we identified historical winters (notably 2003–04, 2017–18, 2013–14) with price trajectories analogous to the 2024–25 season. These analogues provided context and validation for the wavelet findings, illustrating that similar combinations of seasonal demand and supply conditions have recurred in the past and can be used as forecasting guides. The FFT spectral analysis quantified the periodic structure, confirming a dominant 1-year cycle and indicating significant multi-year variability while ruling out shorter cyclic patterns.

Several key findings emerged. First, heating oil prices exhibit a reliable annual seasonality - prices tend to rise in the autumn and winter months and recede in spring - driven by heating demand cycles. This seasonal pattern is embedded in the data with a strong signal, though its amplitude varies across years. Second, the magnitude of the winter price increase is not fixed but depends on broader market conditions: years with tighter supplies or colder weather see larger seasonal spikes, whereas milder or well-supplied years see smaller ones. This was evidenced by the wavelet detail coefficients and the range of outcomes in our analogue seasons. Third, beyond the seasonal oscillation, heating oil prices follow multi-year cycles influenced by market fundamentals - price booms and busts that often span 2–4 years. These cycles are irregular in period but clearly present, as seen in both wavelet D_6 components and the low-frequency portion of the spectrum. They can constructively or destructively interfere with the seasonal pattern. Fourth, short-term volatility (weekly-to-monthly noise) is significant but does not show any additional regular periodicity; rather, it represents idiosyncratic fluctuations.

The methodological focus of this paper was on explaining and interpreting these patterns rather than on building a specific forecasting model. However, the insights gained have direct implications for forecasting practice. By separating the time series into interpretable parts, one can build hybrid forecasts: for instance, project the trend using macroeconomic or policy variables, forecast the seasonal component using weather outlooks or historical analogues, and account for multi-year cycle phase perhaps via leading indicators or inventory levels. Our analogue analysis, in particular, demonstrates a practical forecasting approach: if the current season's price evolution is tracking a known historical scenario, that scenario can inform the expected outcome. This kind of retrieval-augmented forecasting can be a powerful addition to quantitative models, marrying data-driven insight with scenario-based reasoning. It is notable that a recent study (Xiao et al., 2025) achieved improved financial time series forecasts by incorporating a retrieval model (FinSeer) to find significant historical sequences – our results suggest that similar benefits could accrue in commodity markets like heating oil, where patterns often repeat under analogous conditions.

From an energy economics standpoint, our findings underscore the importance of seasonality in price formation and the value of accounting for it in both market analysis and policy. The seasonal behavior of heating oil prices reflects the underlying physical reality of fuel demand: consumption spikes in winter and logistical/ storage constraints can lead to price premiums during that period. Policymakers can use this knowledge to time interventions or to communicate effectively with the public. For example, if winter prices soar, it may not solely indicate market dysfunction – it may be partly the normal seasonal effect, albeit perhaps exacerbated by other factors. Conversely, if prices do *not* fall back after winter, that might signal a structural shift that warrants attention. Our multi-scale decomposition would flag such a scenario by showing an unusually large remaining trend component even after the seasonal component subsides. In planning terms, strategic reserve releases or import coordination could be considered ahead of anticipated seasonal crunches in years projected to be tight – essentially smoothing the cycle.

For consumers and businesses, understanding periodic price behavior can lead to cost savings. Many fuels buyers practice timing the market by purchasing off-season; our findings validate that strategy on average, since a predictable seasonal drop occurs most years. Businesses that budget for fuel can incorporate an expected winter increase into their financial plans. Hedging strategies in futures markets also heavily rely on the seasonality – the differential between summer and winter futures is a key indicator. Our analysis provides an empirical confirmation that such seasonal spreads have a basis in actual spot price behavior and are not merely speculative artifacts.

This comprehensive analysis contributes to both methodology – demonstrating the value of combining time-domain and frequency-domain, deterministic and non-parametric techniques – and to substantive energy market insight – confirming the central role of seasonality and characterizing the nature of multi-year fluctuations in heating oil prices. For future research, one could extend this work by integrating exogenous variables into a multivariate wavelet or analogue analysis, to further disentangle causality. Additionally, as markets evolve, continuous monitoring of the periodic structure with these tools can detect if the historical patterns shift.

REFERENCES

Alessio, S. M. (2015). Discrete wavelet transform (DWT). In *Digital signal processing and spectral analysis for scientists: Concepts and applications* (pp. 645–714). Springer International Publishing. DOI: 10.1007/978-3-319-18467-8_17

Bracewell, R. N. (1989). The Fourier transform. *Scientific American, 260*(6), 86–95. DOI: 10.1038/scientificamerican0689-86 PMID: 2727659

Bunrit, S., Kerdprasop, N., & Kerdprasop, K. (2018). Multiresolution analysis based on wavelet transform for commodity prices time series forecasting. *International Journal of Machine Learning and Computing, 8*(2), 175–180. DOI: 10.18178/ijmlc.2018.8.2.683

Chen, H. (2025). *Financial data science with Python: An integrated approach to analysis, modeling, and machine learning*. Business Expert Press.

Harti, A. (1993). Discrete multi-resolution analysis and generalized wavelets. *Applied Numerical Mathematics, 12*(1–3), 153–192. DOI: 10.1016/0168-9274(93)90117-A

Jing, B., Zhang, S., Zhu, Y., Peng, B., Guan, K., Margenot, A., & Tong, H. (2022). *Retrieval based time series forecasting* (arXiv preprint arXiv:2209.13525). arXiv. https://arxiv.org/abs/2209.13525

Kaboudan, M. A. (2001, May). Compumetric forecasting of crude oil prices. In *Proceedings of the 2001 Congress on Evolutionary Computation (IEEE Cat. No. 01TH8546)* (Vol. 1, pp. 283–287). IEEE. DOI: 10.1109/CEC.2001.934402

Khashei, M., Bijari, M., & Hejazi, S. R. (2012). Combining seasonal ARIMA models with computational intelligence techniques for time series forecasting. *Soft Computing, 16*(6), 1091–1105. DOI: 10.1007/s00500-012-0805-9

Lee, D. T., & Yamamoto, A. (1994). Wavelet analysis: Theory and applications. *Hewlett Packard Journal, 45*, 44–44.

Lewis, P., Perez, E., Piktus, A., Petroni, F., Karpukhin, V., Goyal, N., & Kiela, D. (2020). Retrieval-augmented generation for knowledge-intensive NLP tasks. *Advances in Neural Information Processing Systems, 33*, 9459–9474.

Lorenz, E. N. (1969). Atmospheric predictability as revealed by naturally occurring analogues. *Journal of the Atmospheric Sciences, 26*(4), 636–646. DOI: 10.1175/1520-0469(1969)26<636:APARBN>2.0.CO;2

Rigopoulos, G. (2022). Univariate time series forecasting using k-nearest neighbors. *International Journal of Scientific Research and Management, 10*(9), 344–356.

Senin, P. (2008). *Dynamic time warping algorithm review* [Technical report]. Department of Information and Computer Science, University of Hawaii at Manoa. https://seninp.github.io/assets/pubs/senin_dtw_litreview_2008.pdf

U.S. Energy Information Administration. (2023). *Factors affecting heating oil prices.* https://www.eia.gov/energyexplained/heating-oil/factors-affecting-heating-oil-prices.php

Xiao, M., Jiang, Z., Qian, L., ... (2025). Retrieval-augmented large language models for financial time-series forecasting. *arXiv preprint arXiv:2502.05878.* https://arxiv.org/abs/2502.05878

Zamani, H., Diaz, F., Dehghani, M., Metzler, D., & Bendersky, M. (2022, July). Retrieval-enhanced machine learning. In *Proceedings of the 45th International ACM SIGIR Conference on Research and Development in Information Retrieval* (pp. 2875–2886).

Zhao, Z., & Giannakis, D. (2016). Analog forecasting with dynamics-adapted kernels. *Nonlinearity, 29*(9), 2888–2939. DOI: 10.1088/0951-7715/29/9/2888

Compilation of References

Adrian, T., & Mancini Griffoli, T. (2019, Jul 15). The rise of digital money (IMF FinTech Note No. 2019/001). International Monetary Fund. https://www.imf.org/-/media/Files/Publications/FTN063/2019/English/FTNEA2019001.ashx

Aggarwal, D., Brennen, G. K., Lee, T., Santha, M., & Tomamichel, M. (2018). Quantum attacks on Bitcoin, and how to protect against them. *Ledger*, *3*, 67–90. DOI: 10.5195/ledger.2018.127

Ahmed, S., Alshater, M. M., El Ammari, A., & Hammami, H. (2022). Artificial intelligence and machine learning in finance: A bibliometric review. *Research in International Business and Finance*, *61*, 101646. DOI: 10.1016/j.ribaf.2022.101646

Ahnert, T., Hoffmann, P., & Monnet, C. (2022). The digital economy, privacy, and CBDC.

Aidoo, S. AML, I. D., Officer, M. S. A. C., & Certified, I. C. A. (2024, Dec 18). *Cryptocurrency and sanctions evasion: Stablecoins, mixers, and the role of blockchain forensics* [Unpublished manuscript]. ResearchGate. https://www.researchgate.net/publication/393687826_Cryptocurrency_and_Sanctions_Evasion_Stablecoins_Mixers_and_the_Role_of_Blockchain_Forensics

Akbanov, M., Vassilakis, V. G., & Logothetis, M. D. (2019). Ransomware detection and mitigation using software-defined networking: The case of WannaCry. *Computers & Electrical Engineering*, *76*, 111–121. DOI: 10.1016/j.compeleceng.2019.03.012

Akkus, H. T., Gursoy, S., Dogan, M., & Demir, A. B. (2022). Metaverse and metaverse cryptocurrencies (meta coins): Bubbles or future. *Journal of Economics. Finance and Accounting*, *9*(1), 22–29. DOI: 10.17261/Pressacademia.2022.1542

Alessio, S. M. (2015). Discrete wavelet transform (DWT). In *Digital signal processing and spectral analysis for scientists: Concepts and applications* (pp. 645–714). Springer International Publishing. DOI: 10.1007/978-3-319-18467-8_17

Ali, M., Irshad, H., Khan, I., & Hussain, A. (2025). Artificial intelligence in stock market investment: Enhancing decision-making through predictive analytics and behavioral insights. *ACADEMIA International Journal for Social Sciences*, *4*(3), 1039–1056.

Almahdi, S., & Yang, S. Y. (2017). An adaptive portfolio trading system: A risk–return portfolio optimization using recurrent reinforcement learning with expected maximum drawdown. *Expert Systems with Applications*, *87*, 267–279.

Almahdi, S., & Yang, S. Y. (2017). An adaptive portfolio trading system: A risk-return portfolio optimization using recurrent reinforcement learning with expected maximum drawdown. *Expert Systems with Applications*, *87*, 267–279. DOI: 10.1016/j.eswa.2017.06.023

Almgren, R., & Chriss, N. (2000). Optimal execution of portfolio transactions. *The Journal of Risk*, *3*(2), 5–39.

Alsabah, H., Capponi, A., Ruiz Lacedelli, O., & Stern, M. (2021). Robo-advising: Learning investors' risk preferences via portfolio choices. *Journal of Financial Econometrics*, *19*(2), 369–392. https://doi.org/10.1093/jjfinec/nbaa026

Alwashali, A. A. M. A., Abd Rahman, N. A., & Ismail, N. (2021, December). A survey of ransomware as a service (RaaS) and methods to mitigate the attack. In *2021 14th International Conference on Developments in eSystems Engineering (DeSE)* (pp. 92-96). IEEE.

Androulaki, E., Karame, G. O., Roeschlin, M., Scherer, T., & Čapkun, S. (2013). Evaluating user privacy in Bitcoin. In *Financial Cryptography and Data Security* (pp. 34–51). Springer., DOI: 10.1007/978-3-642-39884-1_4

Apostolaki, M., Zohar, A., & Vanbever, L. (2017). Hijacking Bitcoin: Routing Attacks on Cryptocurrencies. In *2017 IEEE Symposium on Security and Privacy* (pp. 375-392). DOI: 10.1109/SP.2017.29

Arner, D. W., Auer, R., & Frost, J. (2020). Stablecoins: Risks, potential and regulation. *Journal of Financial Regulation*, *6*(1), 1–30. DOI: 10.1093/jfr/fjaa004

Assefa, S. A., Dervovic, D., Mahfouz, M., Tillman, R. E., Reddy, P., & Veloso, M. (2020). *Generating synthetic data in finance: Opportunities, challenges and pitfalls*. In *Proceedings of the First ACM International Conference on AI in Finance* (pp. 1–8). DOI: 10.1145/3383455.3422554

Atzei, N., Bartoletti, M., & Cimoli, T. (2017). A survey of attacks on Ethereum smart contracts (SoK). In *Proceedings of the 6th International Conference on Principles of Security and Trust (POST 2017)* (pp. 164-186). Springer. DOI: 10.1007/978-3-662-54455-6_8

Auer, R., & Böhme, R. (2020). The technology of retail central bank digital currency. BIS Quarterly Review, March 2020. https://www.bis.org

Auer, R., Cornelli, G., & Frost, J. (2020). Rise of the central bank digital currencies: Drivers, approaches and technologies. https://papers.ssrn.com/sol3/papers.cfm?abstract_id=3723552

Aysan, A. F., Gozgor, G., & Nanaeva, Z. (2024). Technological perspectives of Metaverse for financial service providers. *Technological Forecasting and Social Change*, *202*, 123323. DOI: 10.1016/j.techfore.2024.123323

Bacry, E., Delattre, S., Hoffmann, M., & Muzy, J.-F. (2013). Modelling microstructure noise with mutually exciting point processes. *Quantitative Finance*, *13*(1), 65–77.

Baele, L., Bekaert, G., & Inghelbrecht, K. (2010). The determinants of stock and bond return comovements. *Review of Financial Studies*, *23*(6), 2374–2428.

Bahamazava, K., & Nanda, R. (2022). The shift of DarkNet illegal drug trade preferences in cryptocurrency: The question of traceability and deterrence. *Forensic Science International Digital Investigation*, *40*, 301377. DOI: 10.1016/j.fsidi.2022.301377

Bai, H., Cong, L. W., Luo, M., & Xie, P. (2025). Adoption of central bank digital currencies: Initial evidence from China. *Journal of Corporate Finance*, *91*, 102735. DOI: 10.1016/j.jcorpfin.2025.102735

Bains, P., Ismail, A., Melo, F., & Sugimoto, N. (2022). *Regulating the crypto ecosystem: The case of stablecoins and arrangements*. International Monetary Fund.

Baisley, T., & Cherrat, Y. (2023). *Cyber threats and engagements in 2022* (Publication No. AD1208002) [Government technical report]. Defense Technical Information Center. https://apps.dtic.mil/sti/html/trecms/AD1208002/

Bai, Y., Gao, Y., Wan, R., Zhang, S., & Song, R. (2025). A review of reinforcement learning in financial applications. *Annual Review of Statistics and Its Application*, *12*(1), 209–232. https://doi.org/10.1146/annurev-statistics-030424-124444

Bakker, B., & Schmidhuber, J. (2004, March). Hierarchical reinforcement learning based on subgoal discovery and subpolicy specialization. In *the 8th Conference on Intelligent Autonomous Systems* (pp. 438-445).

Ball, M. (2020, Jan 13). *The Metaverse: What it is, where to find it, who will build it, and Fortnite*. MatthewBall.vc. https://www.matthewball.co/all/themetaverse

Banaeian Far, S., Imani Rad, A., & Rajabzadeh Asaar, M. (2023). Blockchain and its derived technologies shape the future generation of digital businesses: A focus on decentralized finance and the Metaverse. *Data Science and Management*, *6*(3), 183–197. DOI: 10.1016/j.dsm.2023.06.002

Banerjee, A., Clear, M., & Tewari, H. (2020, Nov). Demystifying the role of zk-SNARKs in Zcash. In *2020 IEEE Conference on Application, Information and Network Security* (pp. 12–19). IEEE. DOI: 10.1109/AINS50155.2020.9315064

Bank for International Settlements. (2022, Jun 21). III. The future monetary system. In BIS Annual Economic Report 2022. https://www.bis.org/publ/arpdf/ar2022e3.htm

Bank of America. (2023). Digital assets: Stablecoins and the US Treasury market. Global Research Report.

Bartoletti, M., Lande, S., Loddo, A., Pompianu, L., & Serusi, S. (2021). Cryptocurrency scams: Analysis and perspectives. *IEEE Access : Practical Innovations, Open Solutions*, *9*, 148353–148373. DOI: 10.1109/ACCESS.2021.3123894

Baur, D. G., & Lucey, B. M. (2010). Is gold a hedge or a safe haven? An analysis of stocks, bonds and gold. *Financial Review*, *45*(2), 217–229. DOI: 10.1111/j.1540-6288.2010.00244.x

Bekaert, G., & Harvey, C. R. (1995). Time-varying world market integration. *the Journal of Finance, 50*(2), 403-444. DOI: 10.1111/j.1540-6261.1995.tb04790.x

Bengesi, S., El-Sayed, H., Sarker, M. K., Houkpati, Y., Irungu, J., & Oladunni, T. (2024). Advancements in Generative AI: A comprehensive review of GANs, GPT, autoencoders, diffusion models, and transformers. *IEEE Access : Practical Innovations, Open Solutions*, *12*, 69812–69837. DOI: 10.1109/ACCESS.2024.3397775

Berrueta, E., Morato, D., Magaña, E., & Izal, M. (2019). A survey on detection techniques for cryptographic ransomware. *IEEE Access : Practical Innovations, Open Solutions*, *7*, 144925–144944. DOI: 10.1109/ACCESS.2019.2945839

Bhargavan, K., Delignat-Lavaud, A., Fournet, C., Gollamudi, A., Gonthier, G., Kobeissi, N., & Zanella-Béguelin, S. (2016, Oct). Formal verification of smart contracts: Short paper. In *Proceedings of the 2016 ACM workshop on programming languages and analysis for security* (pp. 91-96). DOI: 10.1145/2993600.2993611

Biryukov, A., & Tikhomirov, S. (2019). Security and privacy of mobile wallet users in Bitcoin, Dash, Monero, and Zcash. *Pervasive and Mobile Computing*, *59*, 101030. DOI: 10.1016/j.pmcj.2019.101030

Birzoim, A. (2025). Blockchain-driven financial innovation in Hong Kong (2018-2024): Regulations, cross-border payments, and public-private collaboration.

Black, F., & Scholes, M. (1973). The pricing of options and corporate liabilities. *Journal of Political Economy*, *81*(3), 637–654.

Board of Governors of the Federal Reserve System. (2022, Jan 19). Money and payments: The U.S. dollar in the age of digital transformation. https://www.federalreserve.gov/publications/files/money-and-payments-20220120.pdf

Board of Governors of the Federal Reserve. (2022). *Money and payments: The U.S. dollar in the age of digital transformation.* https://www.federalreserve.gov

Böhme, R., Christin, N., Edelman, B., & Moore, T. (2015). Bitcoin: Economics, technology, and governance. *The Journal of Economic Perspectives*, *29*(2), 213–238. DOI: 10.1257/jep.29.2.213

Bollerslev, T. (1986). Generalised autoregressive conditional heteroskedasticity. *Journal of Econometrics*, *31*(3), 307–327. DOI: 10.1016/0304-4076(86)90063-1

Bonneau, J., Miller, A., Clark, J., Narayanan, A., Kroll, J. A., & Felten, E. (2015). SoK: Research perspectives and challenges for Bitcoin and cryptocurrencies. In *2015 IEEE Symposium on Security and Privacy* (pp. 104-121). DOI: 10.1109/SP.2015.14

Bordo, M. D. (2022). *Digital currencies: The US Fed should proceed with caution.* NBER Working Paper 29913. https://www.nber.org

Bordo, M. D., & Levin, A. T. (2023). Central bank digital currency and the future of monetary policy. Hoover Institution Economics Working Paper 21103.

Botte, A., & Bao, D. (2021, October 6). A machine-learning approach to regime modeling. *Two Sigma*. Retrieved August 28, 2025, from https://www.twosigma.com/articles/a-machine-learning-approach-to-regime-modeling/

Bracewell, R. N. (1989). The Fourier transform. *Scientific American*, *260*(6), 86–95. DOI: 10.1038/scientificamerican0689-86 PMID: 2727659

Briola, A., Turiel, J., Marcaccioli, R., Cauderan, A., & Aste, T. (2021). Deep reinforcement learning for active high-frequency trading. *arXiv*. https://arxiv.org/abs/2101.07107

Brownworth, A., Durfee, J., Lee, M. J., & Martin, A. (2024, August). *Regulating decentralized systems: Evidence from sanctions on Tornado Cash* (Staff Report No. 1112). Federal Reserve Bank of New York. DOI: 10.59576/sr.1112

Bryans, D. (2014). Bitcoin and money laundering: Mining for an effective solution. *Industrial Law Journal*, *89*(1), 441–472.

Bühler, H., Gonon, L., Teichmann, J., & Wood, B. (2019). Deep hedging. *Quantitative Finance*, *19*(8), 1271–1291. https://doi.org/10.1080/14697688.2019.1571683

Bullmann, D., Klemm, J., & Pinna, A. (2019). *In search for stability in crypto-assets: Are stablecoins the solution?* ECB Occasional Paper No. 230. https://www.ecb.europa.eu

Bunrit, S., Kerdprasop, N., & Kerdprasop, K. (2018). Multiresolution analysis based on wavelet transform for commodity prices time series forecasting. *International Journal of Machine Learning and Computing*, *8*(2), 175–180. DOI: 10.18178/ijmlc.2018.8.2.683

Burgess, T., & Liu, J. (2025). A tale of two jurisdictions: Contrasting cryptocurrency regulations in Hong Kong and the United Kingdom. Journal of Economic Criminology, 8.

Byrd, D. (2022). Learning not to spoof. In *Proceedings of the Third ACM International Conference on AI in Finance* (pp. 139–147). https://doi.org/10.1145/3533271.3561767

Cai, Q., Yang, Z., & Wang, Z. (2019). Neural temporal-difference and Q-learning provably converge to global optima. *arXiv*. https://arxiv.org/abs/1905.10027

Calomiris, C. W. (2021). Will fractional-reserve stablecoin banking replace Bitcoin and some traditional banking payments? *The Bank of America Journal of Applied Corporate Finance*, *33*(4), 70–75. DOI: 10.1111/jacf.12478

Campbell, J. Y., Sunderam, A., & Viceira, L. M. (2009). *Inflation bets or deflation hedges? The changing risks of nominal bonds (No. w14701)*. National Bureau of Economic Research.

Campbell-Verduyn, M. (2018). Bitcoin, crypto-coins, and global anti-money laundering governance. *Crime, Law, and Social Change*, *69*(2), 283–305. DOI: 10.1007/s10611-017-9756-5

Cao, J., Chen, J., Hull, J., & Poulos, Z. (2021). Deep hedging of derivatives using reinforcement learning. *arXiv*. https://arxiv.org/abs/2103.16409

Cao, L. (2022). Decentralized AI: Edge Intelligence and Smart Blockchain, Metaverse, Web3, and DeSci. *IEEE Intelligent Systems*, *37*(3), 6–19. DOI: 10.1109/MIS.2022.3181504

Capponi, A., Olafsson, S., & Zariphopoulou, T. (2022). Personalized robo-advising: Enhancing investment through client interaction. *Management Science*, *68*(4), 2485–2512.

Carbonneau, A., & Godin, F. (2020). Equal risk pricing of derivatives with deep hedging. *Quantitative Finance*, *20*(12), 1935–1950. https://doi.org/10.1080/14697688.2020.1806343

Carstens, A. (2019). *The future of money and payments.* Speech at the Central Bank of Ireland. https://www.bis.org

Catalini, C., & Gans, J. S. (2018). *Initial coin offerings and the value of crypto tokens* (NBER Working Paper No. 24418). National Bureau of Economic Research. https://www.nber.org/papers/w24418

Chainalysis Team. (2025, Feb 5). *35% year-over-year decrease in ransomware payments, less than half of recorded incidents resulted in victim payments*. Chainalysis Blog. https://www.chainalysis.com/blog/crypto-crime-ransomware-victim-extortion-2025/

Chao, C.-H., Ting, I.-H., Tseng, Y.-J., Wang, B.-W., Wang, S.-H., & Wang, Y.-Q. (2022). The study of DeFi in virtual community and financial supervision. In *Proceedings of the 9th Multidisciplinary International Social Networks Conference (MISNC '22)* (pp. 74–80). Association for Computing Machinery. https://doi.org/ DOI: 10.1145/3561278.3561297

Charpentier, A., Elie, R., & Remlinger, C. (2021). Reinforcement learning in finance. *Annual Review of Financial Economics*, *13*, 383–405. https://doi.org/10.1146/annurev-financial-101820-111754

Chaum, D. (1985). Security without identification: Transaction systems to make Big Brother obsolete. *Communications of the ACM*, *28*(10), 1030–1044. DOI: 10.1145/4372.4373

Chen, H. (2025). Robo-traders and PPO: Advancing grid trading with deep reinforcement learning. In *Machine Learning and Modeling Techniques in Financial Data Science* (pp. 1–20). IGI Global. https://doi.org/10.4018/979-8-3693-6951-7.ch001

Cheng, S. (2023). Metaverse. In *Metaverse: Concept, Content and Context* (pp. 1–23). Springer Nature Switzerland., DOI: 10.1007/978-3-031-24359-2_1

Chen, H. (2025). *Financial data science with Python: An integrated approach to analysis, modeling, and machine learning*. Business Expert Press.

Chen, W., Hussain, W., Cauteruccio, F., & Zhang, X. (2024). Deep learning for financial time series prediction: A state-of-the-art review of standalone and hybrid models. *Computer Modeling in Engineering & Sciences*, *139*(1), 187–224. DOI: 10.32604/cmes.2023.031388

Cho, K., van Merriënboer, B., Gulcehre, C., Bahdanau, D., Bougares, F., Schwenk, H., & Bengio, Y. (2014). *Learning phrase representations using RNN encoder–decoder for statistical machine translation*. EMNLP. DOI: 10.3115/v1/D14-1179

Chou, T.-N. (2019). An explainable hybrid model for bankruptcy prediction based on the decision tree and deep neural network. In *2019 IEEE 2nd International Conference on Knowledge Innovation and Invention (ICKII)* (pp. 122–125). DOI: 10.1109/ICKII46306.2019.9042639

Chow, Y., Ghavamzadeh, M., Janson, L., & Pavone, M. (2018). Risk-constrained reinforcement learning with percentile risk criteria. *Journal of Machine Learning Research*, *18*(167), 1–51.

Christin, N. (2013, May). Traveling the Silk Road: A measurement analysis of a large anonymous online marketplace. In *Proceedings of the 22nd International Conference on World Wide Web* (pp. 213–224). DOI: 10.1145/2488388.2488408

Claessens, S., Frost, J., Turner, G., & Zhu, F. (2021). *Stablecoin risks and prudential regulation*. BIS Papers No 123. https://www.bis.org

Cœuré, B. (2019). *Investigating the impact of global stablecoins*. Bank for International Settlements.

Cohen, L. E., & Felson, M. (1979). Social change and crime rate trends: A routine activity approach. *American Sociological Review*, *44*(4), 588–608. DOI: 10.2307/2094589

CoinMarketCap. (2024). Stablecoin market capitalization. https://coinmarketcap.com

Conti, M., Kumar, E. S., Lal, C., & Ruj, S. (2018). A survey on security and privacy issues of bitcoin. *IEEE Communications Surveys and Tutorials*, *20*(4), 3416–3452. DOI: 10.1109/COMST.2018.2842460

Cont, R. (2001). Empirical properties of asset returns: Stylized facts and statistical issues. *Quantitative Finance*, *1*(2), 223–236. https://doi.org/10.1080/713665670

Creswell, A., White, T., Dumoulin, V., Arulkumaran, K., Sengupta, B., & Bharath, A. A. (2018). Generative adversarial networks: An overview. *IEEE Signal Processing Magazine*, *35*(1), 53–65. DOI: 10.1109/MSP.2017.2765202

Dabney, W., Rowland, M., Bellemare, M., & Munos, R. (2018, April). Distributional reinforcement learning with quantile regression. *Proceedings of the AAAI Conference on Artificial Intelligence*, *32*(1), •••.

Dark, C., Rogerson, E., Rowbotham, N., & Wallis, P. (2022). *Stablecoins: Market developments, risks and regulation*. RBA Bulletin.

Das, R. A., Pahalovi, M. M. S., & Yanhaona, M. N. (2019, Dec). Transaction finality through ledger checkpoints. In *2019 IEEE 25th International Conference on Parallel and Distributed Systems* (pp. 183–192). IEEE.

Dash, A., Ye, J., & Wang, G. (2023). A review of generative adversarial networks (GANs) and its applications in a wide variety of disciplines: From medical to remote sensing. *IEEE Access : Practical Innovations, Open Solutions*.

Dayan, P., & Hinton, G. E. (1992). Feudal reinforcement learning. In *Advances in Neural Information Processing Systems* (Vol. 5, pp. 271-278).

Dempster, M. A., & Leemans, V. (2006). An automated FX trading system using adaptive reinforcement learning. *Expert Systems with Applications*, *30*(3), 543–552. DOI: 10.1016/j.eswa.2005.10.012

Deng, H. (2024). Negotiating currency internationalization: An infrastructural analysis of the digital RMB. *Finance and Stochastics*, *10*(1), 1–17.

Deng, Y., Bao, F., Kong, Y., Ren, Z., & Dai, Q. (2016). Deep direct reinforcement learning for financial signal representation and trading. *IEEE Transactions on Neural Networks and Learning Systems*, *28*(3), 653–664.

Diamond, D. W., & Dybvig, P. H. (1983). Bank runs, deposit insurance, and liquidity. *Journal of Political Economy*, *91*(3), 401–419. DOI: 10.1086/261155

Ding, W., Li, J., Qin, R., Kozma, R., & Wang, F.-Y. (2023). A New Architecture and Mechanism for Decentralized Science MetaMarkets. *IEEE Transactions on Systems, Man, and Cybernetics. Systems*, *53*(9), 5321–5330. DOI: 10.1109/TSMC.2023.3266223

Dixon, M. F., Halperin, I., & Bilokon, P. (2020). *Machine learning in finance* (Vol. 1170). Springer.

Dua, G. K. (2024). Blockchain and its derived technologies. In Kumar, V. (Ed.), *Applications, challenges, and opportunities of blockchain technology in banking and finance* (pp. 41–55). IGI Global., DOI: 10.4018/979-8-3693-6660-8.ch004

Dubey, S. R., & Singh, S. K. (2024). Transformer-based generative adversarial networks in computer vision: A comprehensive survey. *IEEE Transactions on Artificial Intelligence*, *5*(10), 4851–4867. DOI: 10.1109/TAI.2024.3404910

Dubey, V., Mokashi, A., Pradhan, R., Gupta, P., & Walimbe, R. (2022). Metaverse and banking industry – 2023: The year of Metaverse adoption. *Technium*, *4*(10), 62–73. DOI: 10.47577/technium.v4i10.7774

Eichberger, J., & Harper, I. (1997). *Financial Economics*. Oxford University Press., DOI: 10.1093/oso/9780198774051.001.0001

Eichengreen, B. (2019). *Globalizing capital: A history of the international monetary system* (3rd ed.). Princeton University Press.

Elton, E. J., Gruber, M. J., Brown, S. J., & Goetzmann, W. N. (2009). *Modern portfolio theory and investment analysis*. John Wiley & Sons.

Engle III, R. F., & Sheppard, K. (2001). Theoretical and empirical properties of dynamic conditional correlation multivariate GARCH. DOI: 10.3386/w8554

Engle, R. F. (1982). Autoregressive conditional heteroskedasticity with estimates of the variance of United Kingdom inflation. *Econometrica*, *50*(4), 987–1007. https://www.jstor.org/stable/1912773. DOI: 10.2307/1912773

Erb, C. B., & Harvey, C. R. (2006). The strategic and tactical value of commodity futures. *Financial Analysts Journal*, *62*(2), 69–97. DOI: 10.2139/ssrn.650923

Eskandari, S., Clark, J., Barrera, D., & Stobert, E. (2018). A first look at the usability of bitcoin key management. *arXiv preprint arXiv:1802.04351*. https://arxiv.org/abs/1802.04351

European Central Bank (ECB). (2022). *Progress on the investigation phase of a digital euro.* https://www.ecb.europa.eu

Eyal, I., & Sirer, E. G. (2014). Majority is not enough: Bitcoin mining is vulnerable. In *International Conference on Financial Cryptography and Data Security* (pp. 436-454). Springer. DOI: 10.1007/978-3-662-45472-5_28

Falco, G., Thummala, R., & Kubadia, A. (2023, Jul). Wannafly: An approach to satellite ransomware. In *2023 IEEE 9th International Conference on Space Mission Challenges for Information Technology* (pp. 84–93). IEEE.

Fang, Y., Ren, K., Liu, W., Zhou, D., Zhang, W., Bian, J., Yu, Y., & Liu, T. (2021, May). Universal trading for order execution with oracle policy distillation. *Proceedings of the AAAI Conference on Artificial Intelligence*, *35*(1), 107–115.

Fanusie, Y., & Robinson, T. (2018). *Bitcoin laundering: An analysis of illicit flows into digital currency services* [PDF]. Center on Sanctions and Illicit Finance, Foundation for Defense of Democracies. https://www.fdd.org/wp-content/uploads/2018/01/MEMO_Bitcoin_Laundering.pdf

Farhi, E., & Maggiori, M. (2018). A model of the international monetary system. *The Quarterly Journal of Economics*, *133*(1), 295–355. DOI: 10.1093/qje/qjx031

Fenwick, A., & Molnar, G. (2022). The importance of humanizing AI: Using a behavioral lens to bridge the gaps between humans and machines. *Discover Artificial Intelligence*, *2*(1), 14. DOI: 10.1007/s44163-022-00030-8

Financial Action Task Force (FATF). (2021). *Updated guidance for a risk-based approach to virtual assets and VASPs.* https://www.fatf-gafi.org

Financial Stability Board (FSB). (2020). *Regulation, supervision and oversight of "global stablecoin" arrangements.* https://www.fsb.org

Financial Stability Board. (2020, Oct 13). Regulation, supervision and oversight of "global stablecoin" arrangements: Final report and high-level recommendations. https://www.fsb.org/2020/10/regulation-supervision-and-oversight-of-global-stablecoin-arrangements/

Financial Stability Board. (2023). Regulation, supervision and oversight of crypto-asset activities and markets. https://www.fsb.org

Finck, M. (2019). Blockchain and the General Data Protection Regulation: Can distributed ledgers be squared with European data protection law? *European Law Journal*, *25*(6), 574–587. DOI: 10.2139/ssrn.3805647

Finn, C., Abbeel, P., & Levine, S. (2017, July). Model-agnostic meta-learning for fast adaptation of deep networks. In *International Conference on Machine Learning* (pp. 1126–1135). PMLR.

Fischer, T. G. (2018). Reinforcement learning in financial markets—A survey. *FAU Discussion Papers in Economics* (No. 12/2018).

Fischer, T., & Krauss, C. (2018). Deep learning with long short-term memory networks for financial market predictions. *European Journal of Operational Research*, *270*(2), 654–669. DOI: 10.1016/j.ejor.2017.11.054

Fitzgerald, M. (2022). *Tactics, techniques, and procedures (TTPs) of ransomware groups and the threats posed to United States national security* (Master's thesis, Utica University). https://www.proquest.com/openview/a1c2c2ab19921b6dbd43cf2ba343ecba/1?pq-origsite=gscholar&cbl=18750&diss=y

Foley, S., Karlsen, J. R., & Putniņš, T. J. (2019). Sex, drugs, and bitcoin: How much illegal activity is financed through cryptocurrencies? *Review of Financial Studies*, *32*(5), 1798–1853. DOI: 10.1093/rfs/hhz015

Folkinshteyn, D., Lennon, M. M., & Reilly, T. (2015). *The Bitcoin mirage: An oasis of financial remittance* [Manuscript submitted for publication]. *Journal of Strategic and International Studies*.

Force, F. A. T. (2021). *Updated guidance for a risk-based approach to virtual assets and virtual asset service providers*. FATF.

Franck, T. (2018, May 5). *Warren Buffett says bitcoin is 'probably rat poison squared'*. CNBC. https://www.cnbc.com/2018/05/05/warren-buffett-says-bitcoin-is-probably-rat-poison-squared.html

Frank, P., & Rudolf, M. (2024). Is the Metaverse Dead? Insights from Financial Bubble Analysis. *FinTech*, *3*(2), 302–323. DOI: 10.3390/fintech3020017

Fujimoto, S., Van Hoof, H., & Meger, D. (2018). Addressing function approximation error in actor-critic methods. In *Proceedings of the 35th International Conference on Machine Learning* (pp. 1582–1591). PMLR. https://proceedings.mlr.press/v80/fujimoto18a.html

G7 Working Group on Stablecoins. (2019). *Investigating the impact of global stablecoins*. https://www.bis.org

Gandal, N. (2018). Network goods (empirical studies). In *The New Palgrave Dictionary of Economics* (pp. 9432–9436). Palgrave Macmillan. DOI: 10.1057/978-1-349-95189-5_2036

Gandhi, A. K. (2024). AI-powered market risk models: Transforming the future of financial analytics. *International Journal of Artificial Intelligence, Data Science, and Machine Learning*, *5*(1), 57–67. https://doi.org/10.63282/3050-9262.IJAIDSML-V5I1P106

Ganji, V. R., & Chaparala, A. (2024). Wave Hedges distance-based feature fusion and hybrid optimisation-enabled deep learning for cyber credit card fraud detection. *Knowledge and Information Systems*, 1–26.

Garg, R. (2022). Ethereum-based smart contracts for trade and finance. *International Journal of Economics and Management Engineering*, *16*(11), 619–629.

Gaurav, A., Gupta, B. B., Bansal, S., & Psannis, K. E. (2024). *Bankruptcy forecasting in enterprises and its security using hybrid deep learning models.* Cyber Security and Applications., DOI: 10.1016/j.csa.2024.100070

Gervais, A., Karame, G. O., Wüst, K., Glykantzis, V., Ritzdorf, H., & Capkun, S. (2016, October). On the security and performance of proof of work blockchains. In *Proceedings of the 2016 ACM SIGSAC conference on computer and communications security* (pp. 3-16). DOI: 10.1145/2976749.2978341

Geva, B., & Muraj, M. (2023). The digitization of money: Stablecoins and CBDC. *Banking & Finance Law Review*, *40*(1), 115–141.

Ghosh, A., Lavanya, , Hassija, V., Chamola, V., & El Saddik, A. (2024). A Survey on Decentralized Metaverse Using Blockchain and Web 3.0 Technologies, Applications, and More. *IEEE Access : Practical Innovations, Open Solutions*, *12*, 146915–146948. DOI: 10.1109/ACCESS.2024.3469193

Giancarlo, J. C. (2023). The future of digital finance: Why private sector innovation should lead. Cato Institute Policy Analysis No. 942.

Gokhale, G., Karimi Madahi, S. S., Claessens, B., & Develder, C. (2024, June). Distill2Explain: Differentiable decision trees for explainable reinforcement learning in energy application controllers. In *Proceedings of the 15th ACM International Conference on Future and Sustainable Energy Systems* (pp. 55–64).

Goldberg, L., & Lerman, R. (2022). The dollar's global roles: An update. Federal Reserve Bank of New York Liberty Street Economics. https://libertystreeteconomics.newyorkfed.org

Goodell, J. W., Kumar, S., Lim, W. M., & Pattnaik, D. (2021). Artificial intelligence and machine learning in finance: Identifying foundations, themes, and research clusters from bibliometric analysis. *Journal of Behavioral and Experimental Finance*, *32*, 100577. DOI: 10.1016/j.jbef.2021.100577

Goodfellow, I., Pouget-Abadie, J., Mirza, M., Xu, B., Warde-Farley, D., Ozair, S., Courville, A., & Bengio, Y. (2020). Generative adversarial networks. *Communications of the ACM*, *63*(11), 139–144. DOI: 10.1145/3422622

Gopinath, G., & Stein, J. C. (2021). Banking, trade, and the making of a dominant currency. *The Quarterly Journal of Economics*, *136*(2), 783–830. DOI: 10.1093/qje/qjaa036

Gorton, G., & Rouwenhorst, K. G. (2006). Facts and fantasies about commodity futures. *Financial Analysts Journal*, *62*(2), 47–68.

Gorton, G., & Zhang, J. (2021). Taming wildcat stablecoins. *SSRN*, *90*(1), 1–50. DOI: 10.2139/ssrn.3888752

Gronwald, M. (2019). Is Bitcoin a commodity? On price jumps, demand shocks, and certainty of supply. *Journal of International Money and Finance*, *97*, 86–92. DOI: 10.1016/j.jimonfin.2019.06.006

Gunay, S., Sraieb, M. M., & Muhammed, S. (2024). Decrypting Metaverse crypto Market: A nonlinear analysis of investor sentiment. *International Review of Financial Analysis*, *96*, 103714. DOI: 10.1016/j.irfa.2024.103714

Gupta, R., Pandey, A., & Pandey, A. (2025). Can deep reinforcement learning reliably improve dynamic portfolio allocation? *Available at SSRN* 5241923. DOI: 10.2139/ssrn.5241923

Gürses, S., Kundnani, A., & Van Hoboken, J. (2016). Crypto and empire: The contradictions of counter-surveillance advocacy. *Media Culture & Society*, *38*(4), 576–590. DOI: 10.1177/0163443716643006

Haber, S., & Stornetta, W. S. (1991). How to time-stamp a digital document. *Journal of Cryptology*, *3*(2), 99–111. DOI: 10.1007/BF00196791

Haider, A., Hawe, G. I., Wang, H., & Scotney, B. (2021, October). Multi-asset market making via multi-task deep reinforcement learning. In *International Conference on Machine Learning, Optimization, and Data Science* (pp. 353-364). Springer. https://doi.org/10.1007/978-3-030-95470-3_27

Hambly, B., Reisinger, C., & Yang, H. (2023). Recent advances in reinforcement learning in finance. *Mathematical Finance*, *33*(1), 1–30.

Han, W., Huang, J., Xie, Q., Zhang, B., Lai, Y., & Peng, M. (2023). Mastering pair trading with risk-aware recurrent reinforcement learning. *arXiv*. https://arxiv.org/abs/2304.00364

Harti, A. (1993). Discrete multi-resolution analysis and generalized wavelets. *Applied Numerical Mathematics*, *12*(1–3), 153–192. DOI: 10.1016/0168-9274(93)90117-A

Harwick, C. (2016). Cryptocurrency and the problem of intermediation. *The Independent Review, 20*(4), 569–588.

He, D., Leckow, R., Haksar, V., & Jenkinson, N. (2023). *Fintech and financial services: Initial considerations.* IMF Staff Discussion Note SDN/23/02.

Heilman, E., Kendler, A., Zohar, A., & Goldberg, S. (2015). Eclipse attacks on bitcoin's peer-to-peer network. In *24th USENIX Security Symposium* (pp. 129-144).

Hendricks, D., & Wilcox, D. (2014). A reinforcement learning extension to the Almgren–Chriss model for optimal trade execution. *arXiv*. https://arxiv.org/abs/1403.2229

Hileman, G. (2019). State of stablecoins (2019). Available at *SSRN* 3533143.

Hirsa, A., Osterrieder, J., Hadji-Misheva, B., & Posth, J. A. (2021). Deep reinforcement learning on a multi-asset environment for trading. *arXiv*. https://arxiv.org/abs/2106.08437

Hochreiter, S., & Schmidhuber, J. (1997). Long short-term memory. *Neural Computation*, *9*(8), 1735–1780. DOI: 10.1162/neco.1997.9.8.1735 PMID: 9377276

Hong Kong Monetary Authority (HKMA). (2023). *e-HKD: A policy and design perspective.* https://www.hkma.gov.hk

Hong Kong Monetary Authority (HKMA). (2024). *Discussion paper on crypto-assets and stablecoins.* https://www.hkma.gov.hk

Hong Kong Monetary Authority (HKMA). (2024). *Stablecoin regulatory framework.* https://www.hkma.gov.hk

Hong Kong Monetary Authority. (2022, Apr 27). e-HKD: A policy and design perspective. https://www.hkma.gov.hk/media/eng/doc/key-functions/financial-infrastructure/e-HKD_A_Policy_and_Design_Perspective.pdf

Hong, J. (2024). Prospect Analysis for Utilization of Virtual Assets using Blockchain Technology. *Journal of Information and Communication Convergence Engineering*, *22*(1), 64–69. DOI: 10.56977/jicce.2024.22.1.64

Huang, Y., & Luk, P. (2023). De-dollarization in the age of digital currencies. Peterson Institute for International Economics Working Paper 23-5.

Huang, Y., Wan, X., Zhang, L., & Lu, X. (2024). A novel deep reinforcement learning framework with Bilstm-Attention networks for algorithmic trading. *Expert Systems with Applications*, *240*, 122581. DOI: 10.1016/j.eswa.2023.122581

Hughes, S., & Middlebrook, S. T. (2015). Advancing a framework for regulating cryptocurrency and other novel payment products. *Yale Journal of Law & Technology*, *18*, 103–150.

Huynh-The, T., Pham, Q.-V., Pham, X.-Q., Nguyen, T. T., Han, Z., & Kim, D.-S. (2023). Artificial intelligence for the metaverse: A survey. *Engineering Applications of Artificial Intelligence, 117*, 105581. DOI: 10.1016/j.engappai.2022.105581

Hu, Z., Liu, W., Bian, J., Liu, X., & Liu, T.-Y. (2018). Listening to chaotic whispers: A deep learning framework for news-oriented stock trend prediction. In *Proceedings of the 11th ACM International Conference on Web Search and Data Mining* (pp. 261–269).

Ilk, N., Shang, G., Fan, S., & Zhao, J. L. (2021). Stability of transaction fees in Bitcoin: A supply and demand perspective. *Management Information Systems Quarterly*, *45*(2), 563–692. DOI: 10.25300/MISQ/2021/15718

International Monetary Fund (IMF). (2023). *Digital money and central banks' balance sheets.* IMF Working Paper WP/23/105.

International Monetary Fund (IMF). (2024). *Currency composition of official foreign exchange reserves.* https://data.imf.org

International Monetary Fund. (2025, Apr 2). IMF data brief: Currency composition of official foreign exchange reserves – Global FX reserves decreased by 3.0 percent in 2024 Q4. https://data.imf.org/en/news/4225global%20fx%20reserves%20decreased%20by%203%20percent%20in%202024q4

Ismael, R. (2021). Challenges and opportunities cryptocurrency in Iran economy & e-businesses. *Вестник Российского университета дружбы народов. Серия. Ekonomika (Nis)*, *29*(4), 689–698.

Jiang, Z., & Liang, J. (2017). Cryptocurrency portfolio management with deep reinforcement learning. In *2017 Intelligent Systems Conference (IntelliSys)* (pp. 905–913). IEEE. https://doi.org/10.1109/IntelliSys.2017.8324459

Jiang, Z., Xu, D., & Liang, J. (2017). A deep reinforcement learning framework for the financial portfolio management problem. *arXiv preprint*, arXiv:1706.10059. / arXiv.1706.10059DOI: 10.48550

Jiang, Z., Xu, D., & Liang, J. (2017). A deep reinforcement learning framework for the financial portfolio management problem. *arXiv*. https://arxiv.org/abs/1706.10059

Jing, B., Zhang, S., Zhu, Y., Peng, B., Guan, K., Margenot, A., & Tong, H. (2022). *Retrieval based time series forecasting* (arXiv preprint arXiv:2209.13525). arXiv. https://arxiv.org/abs/2209.13525

JPMorgan. (2023). Stablecoins and the US Treasury market outlook. Global Markets Strategy Report.

Jun, A. Y. M., Jinu, B. A., Seng, L. K., Maharaiq, M. H. F. B. Z., Khongsuwan, W., Junn, B. T. K., . . . Sindiramutty, S. R. (2024). *Exploring the Impact of Crypto-Ransomware on Critical Industries: Case Studies and Solutions. Preprint PDF:* https://www.preprints.org/frontend/manuscript/f0bbffef9dcc633cd52819e93336aeda/download_pub

Kaboudan, M. A. (2001, May). Compumetric forecasting of crude oil prices. In *Proceedings of the 2001 Congress on Evolutionary Computation (IEEE Cat. No. 01TH8546)* (Vol. 1, pp. 283–287). IEEE. DOI: 10.1109/CEC.2001.934402

Kalinaki, K. (2024). Ransomware threat mitigation strategies for protecting critical infrastructure assets. In *Ransomware Evolution* (pp. 120–143). CRC Press. DOI: 10.1201/9781003469506-10

Kalra, A., & Brown, D. S. (2022). Interpretable reward learning via differentiable decision trees. In *NeurIPS ML Safety Workshop*.

Kara, H. T. (2023). The relationship between blockchain applications in financial markets and Metaverse. In Paul, P. K., Choudhury, D., Bhuimali, A., & Goyal, A. (Eds.), *Handbook of research on cybersecurity issues and challenges for business and commerce* (pp. 285–304). Springer., DOI: 10.1007/978-981-99-4641-9_20

Karame, G. O., Androulaki, E., & Čapkun, S. (2012). Double-spending fast payments in Bitcoin. In *Proceedings of the 2012 ACM Conference on Computer and Communications Security* (pp. 906-917). DOI: 10.1145/2382196.2382292

Kattenborn, T., Leitloff, J., Schiefer, F., & Hinz, S. (2021). Review on Convolutional Neural Networks (CNN) in vegetation remote sensing. *ISPRS Journal of Photogrammetry and Remote Sensing*, *173*, 24–49. DOI: 10.1016/j.isprsjprs.2020.12.010

Kermitsis, E., Kavallieros, D., Myttas, D., Lissaris, E., & Giataganas, G. (2021). Dark web markets. In *Dark Web Investigation* (pp. 85–118). Springer. DOI: 10.1007/978-3-030-55343-2_4

Ketkar, N., & Moolayil, J. (2021). Convolutional neural networks. In *Deep Learning with Python* (pp. 197–242). Manning. DOI: 10.1007/978-1-4842-5364-9_6

Khantamonthon, N., & Chimmanee, K. (2022, Nov). Digital forensic analysis of ransomware attacks on virtual private networks: A case study in factories. In *2022 6th International Conference on Information Technology (InCIT)* (pp. 410-415). IEEE. DOI: 10.1109/InCIT56086.2022.10067674

Kharraz, A., Robertson, W., Balzarotti, D., Bilge, L., & Kirda, E. (2015, Jun). Cutting the gordian knot: A look under the hood of ransomware attacks. In *International Conference on Detection of Intrusions and Malware, and Vulnerability Assessment* (pp. 3–24). Springer. DOI: 10.1007/978-3-319-20550-2_1

Khashei, M., Bijari, M., & Hejazi, S. R. (2012). Combining seasonal ARIMA models with computational intelligence techniques for time series forecasting. *Soft Computing*, *16*(6), 1091–1105. DOI: 10.1007/s00500-012-0805-9

Kim, H. M., Lee, J., & Paik, R. (2022). *North Korean cryptocurrency operations: An alternative revenue stream*. Belfer Center for Science and International Affairs. https://www.belfercenter.org/publication/north-korean-cryptocurrency-operations-alternative-revenue-stream

Kim, J., & Yang, I. (2020, July). Hamilton–Jacobi–Bellman equations for Q-learning in continuous time. In *Learning for Dynamics and Control* (pp. 739–748). PMLR.

Kim, S., Kim, J., Sul, H. K., & Hong, Y. (2024). An adaptive dual-level reinforcement learning approach for optimal trade execution. *Expert Systems with Applications*, *252*, 124263.

Kiviat, T. I. (2015). Beyond bitcoin: Issues in regulating blockchain transactions. *Duke Law Journal*, *65*(3), 569–608. https://scholarship.law.duke.edu/dlj/vol65/iss3/4

Komalavalli, C., Saxena, D., & Laroiya, C. (2020). Overview of blockchain technology concepts. In *Handbook of Research on Blockchain Technology* (pp. 349–371). Academic Press. DOI: 10.1016/B978-0-12-819816-2.00014-9

Koshiyama, A., Firoozye, N., & Treleaven, P. (2021). Generative adversarial networks for fine-tuning financial trading strategies and their combination. *Quantitative Finance*, *21*(6), 797–813. DOI: 10.1080/14697688.2020.1790635

Koshy, P., Koshy, D., & McDaniel, P. (2014, Mar). An analysis of anonymity in bitcoin using p2p network traffic. In *International conference on financial cryptography and data security* (pp. 469-485). Berlin, Heidelberg: Springer Berlin Heidelberg. DOI: 10.1007/978-3-662-45472-5_30

Krause, D. (2025). *Algorithmic stablecoins: Mechanisms, risks, and lessons from the fall of TerraUSD*. Risks.

Kshetri, N. (2021). Blockchain in Finance: Overcoming Regulatory and Other Challenges in the Era of COVID-19. *Journal of International Management*, *27*(2), 100857. DOI: 10.1016/j.ijinfomgt.2021.102376

Kshetri, N., & Voas, J. (2017). Do crypto-currencies fuel ransomware? *IT Professional*, *19*(5), 11–15. DOI: 10.1109/MITP.2017.3680961

Kumar, A., Mustajab, S., & Sakib, M. (2022). Generative adversarial network (GAN) and enhanced root mean square error (ERMSE): Deep learning for stock price movement prediction. *Multimedia Tools and Applications*, *81*(3), 3995–4013. DOI: 10.1007/s11042-021-11670-w

Kumar, A., Zhou, A., Tucker, G., & Levine, S. (2020). Conservative Q-learning for offline reinforcement learning. *Advances in Neural Information Processing Systems*, *33*, 1179–1191.

Kumar, P. (2023, April). Deep reinforcement learning for high-frequency market making. In *Asian Conference on Machine Learning* (pp. 531–546). PMLR.

Kumar, S., Sureka, R., Lucey, B. M., Dowling, M., Vigne, S., & Lim, W. M. (2024). MetaMoney: Exploring the intersection of financial systems and virtual worlds. *Research in International Business and Finance*, *68*, 102195. DOI: 10.1016/j.ribaf.2023.102195

Lalor, L., & Swishchuk, A. (2025). Deep reinforcement learning in non-Markov market-making. *Risks*, *13*(3), 40.

Lansky, J. (2018). Possible state approaches to cryptocurrencies. *Journal of Systems Integration*, *9*(1), 19–31. DOI: 10.20470/jsi.v9i1.335

Lee, M. (2023). Digital currencies and the future of the dollar standard. Council on Foreign Relations Special Report.

Lee, D. T., & Yamamoto, A. (1994). Wavelet analysis: Theory and applications. *Hewlett Packard Journal*, *45*, 44–44.

Lewis, P., Perez, E., Piktus, A., Petroni, F., Karpukhin, V., Goyal, N., & Kiela, D. (2020). Retrieval-augmented generation for knowledge-intensive NLP tasks. *Advances in Neural Information Processing Systems*, *33*, 9459–9474.

Li, A. W., & Bastos, G. S. (2020). Stock market forecasting using deep learning and technical analysis: A systematic review. *IEEE Access : Practical Innovations, Open Solutions*, *8*, 185232–185242. DOI: 10.1109/ACCESS.2020.3030226

Liang, Z., Chen, H., Zhu, J., Jiang, K., & Li, Y. (2018). Adversarial deep reinforcement learning in portfolio management. *arXiv*. https://arxiv.org/abs/1808.09940

Liang, J., & Li, X. (2018). Generative adversarial networks for financial trading strategies fine-tuning and combination. *Physica A*, *512*, 1057–1071.

Liao, G. Y., & Caramichael, J. (2022). Stablecoins: Growth potential and impact on banking. Board of Governors of the Federal Reserve System. https://www.federalreserve.gov/econres/ifdp/stablecoins-growth-potential-and-impact-on-banking.htm

Lillicrap, T. P., Hunt, J. J., Pritzel, A., Heess, N., Erez, T., Tassa, Y., Silver, D., & Wierstra, D. (2015). Continuous control with deep reinforcement learning. *arXiv*. https://arxiv.org/abs/1509.02971

Lim, B., Zohren, S., & Roberts, S. (2020). Enhancing time series momentum strategies using deep neural networks. *arXiv*. https://arxiv.org/abs/1904.04912

Lin, T., Wang, Y., Liu, X., & Qiu, X. (2022). A survey of transformers. *AI Open*, *3*, 111–132. DOI: 10.1016/j.aiopen.2022.10.001

Liu, X. Y., Xiong, Z., Zhong, S., Yang, H., & Walid, A. (2018). Practical deep reinforcement learning approach for stock trading. *arXiv preprint*, arXiv:1811.07522. https://doi.org/10.48550/arXiv.1811.07522

Liu, H., & Long, Z. (2020). An improved deep learning model for predicting stock market price time series. *Digital Signal Processing*, *102*, 102741. DOI: 10.1016/j.dsp.2020.102741

Liu, X.-Y., Yang, H., Chen, Q., Zhang, R., Yang, L., Xiao, B., & Wang, C.-D. (2020). FinRL: A deep reinforcement learning library for automated stock trading in quantitative finance. *arXiv*. https://arxiv.org/abs/2011.09607

Liu, Z., Nguyen, K., Yang, G., Wang, H., & Wong, D. S. (2019, Sep). A lattice-based linkable ring signature supporting stealth addresses. In *European Symposium on Research in Computer Security* (pp. 726–746). Springer. DOI: 10.1007/978-3-030-29959-0_35

Li, X. (2024). Stablecoin regulation in Hong Kong: Recent developments and critical evaluations. Available at *SSRN* 4870280. DOI: 10.2139/ssrn.4870280

Li, X., Jiang, P., Chen, T., Luo, X., & Wen, Q. (2020). A survey on the security of blockchain systems. *Future Generation Computer Systems*, *107*, 841–853. DOI: 10.1016/j.future.2017.08.020

Li, X., Li, Y., Zhan, Y., & Liu, X.-Y. (2019). Optimistic bull or pessimistic bear: Adaptive deep reinforcement learning for stock portfolio allocation. *arXiv*. https://arxiv.org/abs/1907.01503

Li, Z. H., Yu, Y., Chen, Y., Chen, K., Hu, Z., & Fan, C. (2021). Neural-to-tree policy distillation with policy improvement criterion. *arXiv*. https://arxiv.org/abs/2108.06898

Llmanen, A. (2011). *Expected returns: An investor's guide to harvesting market rewards*. John Wiley & Sons.

Lootsma, Y. (2017). Blockchain as the newest regtech application—The opportunity to reduce the burden of kyc for financial institutions. *Banking & Financial Services Policy Report*, *36*(8), 16–21.

Lorenz, E. N. (1969). Atmospheric predictability as revealed by naturally occurring analogues. *Journal of the Atmospheric Sciences*, *26*(4), 636–646. DOI: 10.1175/1520-0469(1969)26<636:APARBN>2.0.CO;2

Lundberg, S. M., & Lee, S.-I. (2017). A unified approach to interpreting model predictions. *Advances in Neural Information Processing Systems*, 30.

Luu, L., Chu, D. H., Olickel, H., Saxena, P., & Hobor, A. (2016, Oct). Making smart contracts smarter. In *Proceedings of the 2016 ACM SIGSAC conference on computer and communications security* (pp. 254-269). DOI: 10.1145/2976749.2978309

Ly, M. (2014). Coining Bitcoin's "legal bits": Examining the regulatory framework for Bitcoin and virtual currencies. *Harvard Journal of Law & Technology*, *27*(2), 587–608.

MacDonald, C., & Zhao, L. (2022). Stablecoins and their risks to financial stability. Bank of Canada Staff Discussion Paper 2022-20.

Maksymyuk, T., Gazda, J., Bugar, G., Gazda, V., Liyanage, M., & Dohler, M. (2022). Blockchain-Empowered Service Management for the Decentralized Metaverse of Things. *IEEE Access : Practical Innovations, Open Solutions*, *10*, 99025–99037. DOI: 10.1109/ACCESS.2022.3205739

Man Group. (2024, March 21). *AI in asset management: AHL perspective*. https://www.man.com/documents/download/5a8d1-65277-88749-3a182/Man_AHL_Analysis_The_Big_Picture%3A_AI_English_%28United_States%29_21-03-2024.pdf

Markowitz, H. (1952). Portfolio selection. *The Journal of Finance*, *7*(1), 77–91.

Martínez-Miranda, E., McBurney, P., & Howard, M. J. (2016). Learning unfair trading: A market manipulation analysis from the reinforcement learning perspective. In *2016 IEEE Conference on Evolving and Adaptive Intelligent Systems (EAIS)* (pp. 103–109). IEEE.

McDowell, D. (2022). *Bucking the buck: US financial sanctions and the international backlash against the dollar*. Stanford University Press.

McNally, C. A. (2025). Seeking autonomy beyond subordination: Chinese financial statecraft and the e-CNY. In State, Capitalism, and Finance in Emerging Markets (pp. 162-182). Bristol University Press.

Mehtab, S., & Sen, J. (2020, November). Stock price prediction using CNN and LSTM-based deep learning models. In *2020 International Conference on Decision Aid Sciences and Application (DASA)* (pp. 447–453). IEEE.

Meiklejohn, S., Pomarole, M., Jordan, G., Levchenko, K., McCoy, D., Voelker, G. M., & Savage, S. (2013, Oct). A fistful of bitcoins: characterizing payments among men with no names. In *Proceedings of the 2013 conference on Internet measurement conference* (pp. 127-140). DOI: 10.1145/2504730.2504747

Micheler, E., & Whaley, A. (2020). Regulatory technology: Replacing law with computer code. *European Business Organization Law Review*, *21*(2), 349–377. DOI: 10.1007/s40804-019-00151-1

Mienye, I. D., & Jere, N. (2024). Deep Learning for Credit Card Fraud Detection: A Review of Algorithms, Challenges, and Solutions. *IEEE Access : Practical Innovations, Open Solutions*, *12*, 96893–96910. DOI: 10.1109/ACCESS.2024.3426955

Miers, I., Garman, C., Green, M., & Rubin, A. D. (2013, May). Zerocoin: Anonymous distributed e-cash from bitcoin. In *2013 IEEE symposium on security and privacy* (pp. 397-411). IEEE.

Mishev, K., Gjorgjevikj, A., Vodenska, I., Chitkushev, L. T., & Trajanov, D. (2020). Evaluation of sentiment analysis in finance: From lexicons to transformers. *IEEE Access : Practical Innovations, Open Solutions*, *8*, 131662–131682. DOI: 10.1109/ACCESS.2020.3009626

Mnih, V., Kavukcuoglu, K., Silver, D., Rusu, A. A., Veness, J., Bellemare, M. G., Graves, A., Riedmiller, M., Fidjeland, A. K., Ostrovski, G., Petersen, S., Beattie, C., Sadik, A., Antonoglou, L., King, H., Kumaran, D., Wierstra, D., Legg, S., & Hassabis, D. (2015). Human-level control through deep reinforcement learning. *Nature*, *518*(7540), 529–533. https://doi.org/10.1038/nature14236

Moody, J., & Saffell, M. (2001). Learning to trade via direct reinforcement. *IEEE Transactions on Neural Networks*, *12*(4), 875–889.

Möser, M., & Böhme, R. (2017, Apr). Anonymous alone? measuring Bitcoin's second-generation anonymization techniques. In *2017 IEEE European Symposium on Security and Privacy Workshops (EuroS&PW)* (pp. 32-41). IEEE. DOI: 10.1109/EuroSPW.2017.48

Mosic, R. (2017, July 31). Deep reinforcement learning-based trading application at JPMorgan Chase. *Medium*. Retrieved August 28, 2025, from https://ranko-mosic.medium.com/reinforcement-learning-based-trading-application-at-jp-morgan-chase-f829b8ec54f2

Moskovitz, T., Parker-Holder, J., Pacchiano, A., Arbel, M., & Jordan, M. (2021). Tactical optimism and pessimism for deep reinforcement learning. *Advances in Neural Information Processing Systems*, *34*, 12849–12863.

Mystakidis, S. (2022). Metaverse. *Encyclopedia*, *2*(1), 486–497. DOI: 10.3390/encyclopedia2010031

Nakamoto, S. (2008). *Bitcoin: A peer-to-peer electronic cash system* [PDF]. U.S. Sentencing Commission. https://www.ussc.gov/sites/default/files/pdf/training/annual-national-training-seminar/2018/Emerging_Tech_Bitcoin_Crypto.pdf

Nakamoto, S. (2008). *Bitcoin: A peer-to-peer electronic cash system*. https://bitcoin.org/bitcoin.pdf

Namaki, A., Eyvazloo, R., & Ramtinnia, S. (2023). A systematic review of early warning systems in finance [Preprint].

Narayanan, A., Bonneau, J., Felten, E., Miller, A., & Goldfeder, S. (2016). *Bitcoin and cryptocurrency technologies: a comprehensive introduction*. Princeton University Press.

Narayanan, A., Bonneau, J., Felten, E., Miller, A., & Goldfeder, S. (2016). *Bitcoin and cryptocurrency technologies: A comprehensive introduction*. Princeton University Press.

Naylor, R. T. (2004). *Wages of crime: Black markets, illegal finance, and the underworld economy*. Cornell University Press.

Nejadmalayeri, A., Molchanovsky, L., Paleo, B. W., & Prescott, R. W. (2023, May). Stablecoins: Past, present, and future. In International Conference on Financial Cryptography and Data Security (pp. 197-207). Springer Nature Switzerland.

Nevmyvaka, Y., Feng, Y., & Kearns, M. (2006). Reinforcement learning for optimized trade execution. In *Proceedings of the 23rd International Conference on Machine Learning* (pp. 673–680).

Nish, A., Naumann, S., & Muir, J. (2022). *Enduring cyber threats and emerging challenges to the financial sector*. Carnegie Endowment for International Peace.

Niu, H., Li, S., & Li, J. (2022). MetaTrader: A reinforcement learning approach integrating diverse policies for portfolio optimization. In *Proceedings of the 31st ACM International Conference on Information & Knowledge Management* (pp. 1573–1583).

Noether, S., Mackenzie, A., & Research Lab, T. M. (2016). Ring confidential transactions. *Ledger*, *1*, 1–18. DOI: 10.5195/ledger.2016.34

Nwankpa, C., Ijomah, W., Gachagan, A., & Marshall, S. (2018). *Activation functions: Comparison of trends in practice and research for deep learning*.

Ober, M., Katzenbeisser, S., & Hamacher, K. (2013). Structure and anonymity of the Bitcoin transaction graph. *Future Internet*, *5*(2), 237–250. DOI: 10.3390/fi5020237

Ojha, V. K., Abraham, A., & Snášel, V. (2017). Metaheuristic design of feedforward neural networks: A review of two decades of research. *Engineering Applications of Artificial Intelligence*, *60*, 97–116. DOI: 10.1016/j.engappai.2017.01.013

Oranburg, S. (2025). The CLARITY Act: Explaining and analyzing how Congress will transform digital asset markets. Available at *SSRN* 5288934. DOI: 10.2139/ssrn.5288934

Otabek, S., & Choi, M. (2024). Multi-level deep Q-network framework for Bitcoin trading using historical and sentiment data. *Scientific Reports*, *14*(1), 974.

Pandey, D., & Gilmour, P. (2024). Accounting meets metaverse: Navigating the intersection between the real and virtual worlds. *Journal of Financial Reporting and Accounting*, *22*(2), 211–226. DOI: 10.1108/JFRA-03-2023-0157

Pan, F., Zhang, T., Luo, L., He, J., & Liu, S. (2022). Learn continuously, act discretely: Hybrid action-space reinforcement learning for optimal execution. In *Proceedings of the 31st International Joint Conference on Artificial Intelligence* (pp. 3875–3881).

Pantin, L. P. (2023). Financial inclusion, cryptocurrency, and Afrofuturism. *Northwestern University Law Review*, *118*, 621.

Park, H., Sim, M. K., & Choi, D. G. (2019). An intelligent financial portfolio trading strategy using deep Q-learning. *arXiv*. https://arxiv.org/abs/1907.03665

Pavel, M. I., Hu, S., Pratama, M., & Kowalczyk, R. (2025). Onboard optimization and learning: A survey. *arXiv*. https://arxiv.org/abs/2505.08793

Payne, B., & Mienie, E. (2021, Jun). Multiple-extortion ransomware: The case for active cyber threat intelligence. In *ECCWS 2021 20th European Conference on Cyber Warfare and Security* (Vol. 6, pp. 331–336). Academic Conferences Inter Ltd.

Pellegrini, C. (2024). Applicable law in the metaverse: A European international private law perspective. In Corrales, M., Fenwick, M., & Forgó, N. (Eds.), *Research handbook on the metaverse and law* (pp. 375–397). Edward Elgar Publishing. DOI: 10.4337/9781035324866.00033

People's Bank of China (PBOC). (2023). *Progress of research and development of e-CNY in China.* http://www.pbc.gov.cn

People's Bank of China. (2023). Progress of research and development of e-CNY in China. http://www.pbc.gov.cn

Pippas, N., Ludvig, E., & Turkay, C. (2025). The evolution of reinforcement learning in quantitative finance: A survey. *ACM Computing Surveys, 1*(1), 1.

Poon, J., & Dryja, T. (2016). *The Bitcoin Lightning Network: Scalable off-chain instant payments* [PDF]. https://lightning.network/lightning-network-paper.pdf

Prasad, E. (2021). *The future of money: How the digital revolution is transforming currencies and finance.* Harvard University Press.

President's Working Group on Financial Markets (PWG). (2021). *Report on stable-coins.* https://home.treasury.gov

Pricope, T. V. (2021). Deep reinforcement learning in quantitative algorithmic trading. *RE:view.*

Pun, C. S., Wang, L., & Wong, H. Y. (2020). *Financial thought experiment: A GAN-based approach to vast robust portfolio selection.* In *Proceedings of the 29th International Joint Conference on Artificial Intelligence (IJCAI'20).* DOI: 10.24963/ijcai.2020/637

Qin, M., Sun, S., Zhang, W., Xia, H., Wang, X., & An, B. (2024, March). EarnHFT: Efficient hierarchical reinforcement learning for high-frequency trading. *Proceedings of the AAAI Conference on Artificial Intelligence, 38*(13), 14669–14676.

Quantitative modelling frontiers: A literature review on the evolution of mathematical methods in financial risk modelling. (2022). Journal of Risk Modelling.

Radanliev, P. (2024). The rise and fall of cryptocurrencies: Defining the economic and social values of blockchain technologies, assessing the opportunities, and defining the financial and cybersecurity risks of the Metaverse. *Financial Innovation, 10*(1), 1. DOI: 10.1186/s40854-023-00537-8

Reddy, E., & Minnaar, A. (2018). Cryptocurrency: A tool and target for cybercrime. *Acta Criminologica: African Journal of Criminology & Victimology, 31*(3), 71–92.

Redress Compliance. (2023). *AI-powered trading algorithms at Goldman Sachs.* https://redresscompliance.com/ai-case-study-ai-powered-trading-algorithms-at-goldman-sachs

Rega-Jones, N. (2022, May 26). JPMorgan's deep hedging reaches cliquets. *Risk.net.* https://www.risk.net/derivatives/7949306/jp-morgans-deep-hedging-reaches-cliquets

Remolina, N. (2024). DeFi and the metaverse: Legal and regulatory challenges of decentralization of financial services. In Chen, H. Y., Jenweeranon, P., & Alam, N. (Eds.), *Global perspectives in the metaverse* (pp. 223–251). Palgrave Macmillan., DOI: 10.1007/978-3-031-54802-4_11

Research, O. K. G. (2025, May 23). Why stablecoin regulation is speeding up — From D.C. to Hong Kong. The Capital. Medium. https://medium.com/thecapital/why-stablecoin-regulation-is-speeding-up-from-d-c-to-hong-kong-44dcd39f0603

Rettig, R., Mosier, M., & Gilman, K. (2025). Genuine DeFi as critical infrastructure: A conceptual framework for combating illicit finance activity in decentralized finance. Journal of Financial Regulation, fjaf005.

Review of predictive modelling and machine learning applications in financial service analysis. (2024). International Journal of Financial Analytics.

Rigopoulos, G. (2022). Univariate time series forecasting using k-nearest neighbors. *International Journal of Scientific Research and Management*, *10*(9), 344–356.

Riley, J. (2021). The current status of cryptocurrency regulation in China and its effect around the world. *China and WTO Review*, *7*(1), 135–152. DOI: 10.14330/cwr.2021.7.1.06

Risk.net. (2022). *JPMorgan testing deep hedging of exotics*. https://www.risk.net/derivatives/equity-derivatives/7921526/jp-morgan-testing-deep-hedging-of-exotics

Robson, W. (2025). USDX whitepaper. Available at *SSRN* 5267805.

Ryan, J. (2024). China's economic and currency management will make it difficult to dethrone the dollar. Irish Studies in International Affairs.

Saleh, F. (2021). Blockchain without waste: Proof-of-stake. *Review of Financial Studies*, *34*(3), 1156–1190. DOI: 10.1093/rfs/hhaa075

Sanders, A. (2025, May 21). *How do cybercriminals launder cryptocurrency?* Barracuda Networks Blog. https://blog.barracuda.com/2025/05/21/cybercriminals-launder-cryptocurrency

Sapirshtein, A., Sompolinsky, Y., & Zohar, A. (2016, February). Optimal selfish mining strategies in bitcoin. In *International conference on financial cryptography and data security* (pp. 515-532). Berlin, Heidelberg: Springer Berlin Heidelberg.

Schulman, J., Wolski, F., Dhariwal, P., Radford, A., & Klimov, O. (2017). Proximal policy optimization algorithms. *arXiv*. https://arxiv.org/abs/1707.06347

Schwarcz, S. L. (2022). Regulating global stablecoins: A model-law strategy. *Vanderbilt Law Review*, *75*, 1729.

Senin, P. (2008). *Dynamic time warping algorithm review* [Technical report]. Department of Information and Computer Science, University of Hawaii at Manoa. https://seninp.github.io/assets/pubs/senin_dtw_litreview_2008.pdf

Setser, B. (2023). *Stablecoins and the demand for US Treasury securities*. Council on Foreign Relations Blog Post.

Sezer, O. B., Gudelek, M. U., & Ozbayoglu, A. M. (2020). Financial time series forecasting with deep learning: A systematic literature review: 2005–2019. *Applied Soft Computing*, *90*, 106181. DOI: 10.1016/j.asoc.2020.106181

Shanmugam, B., Azam, S., Yeo, K. C., Jose, J., & Kannoorpatti, K. (2017, Jan). A critical review of Bitcoins usage by cybercriminals. In *2017 International Conference on Computer Communication and Informatics (ICCCI)* (pp. 1-7). IEEE. https://ieeexplore.ieee.org/abstract/document/8117693

Sharpe, W. F. (1964). Capital asset prices: A theory of market equilibrium under conditions of risk. *The Journal of Finance*, *19*(3), 425–442. DOI: 10.2307/2977928

Sherstinsky, A. (2020). Fundamentals of recurrent neural network (RNN) and long short-term memory (LSTM) network. *Physica D. Nonlinear Phenomena*, *404*, 132306. DOI: 10.1016/j.physd.2019.132306

Silver, D., Schrittwieser, J., Simonyan, K., Antonoglou, I., Huang, A., Guez, A., & Hassabis, D. (2017). Mastering the game of Go without human knowledge. *Nature*, *550*(7676), 354–359.

Sonkavde, G., Dharrao, D. S., Bongale, A. M., Deokate, S. T., Doreswamy, D., & Bhat, S. K. (2023). Forecasting stock market prices using machine learning and deep learning models: A systematic review, performance analysis and discussion of implications. *International Journal of Financial Studies*, *11*(3), 94. DOI: 10.3390/ijfs11030094

Spooner, T., & Savani, R. (2020). Robust market making via adversarial reinforcement learning. *arXiv*. https://arxiv.org/abs/2003.01820

Sun, R., Xi, Y., Stefanidis, A., Jiang, Z., & Su, J. (2025). A novel multi-agent dynamic portfolio optimization learning system based on hierarchical deep reinforcement learning. *arXiv*. https://arxiv.org/abs/2501.06832

Sutton, R. S., & Barto, A. G. (2018). *Reinforcement learning: An introduction* (2nd ed.). MIT Press.

Sutton, R. S., Precup, D., & Singh, S. (1999). Between MDPs and semi-MDPs: A framework for temporal abstraction in reinforcement learning. *Artificial Intelligence*, *112*(1-2), 181–211. DOI: 10.1016/S0004-3702(99)00052-1

SWIFT. (2023). *RMB tracker: Monthly reporting and statistics on renminbi progress.* https://www.swift.com

Talaat, F. M., Aljadani, A., Badawy, M., & Elhosseini, M. (2024). Toward interpretable credit scoring: Integrating explainable artificial intelligence with deep learning for credit card default prediction. *Neural Computing & Applications*, *36*(9), 4847–4865. DOI: 10.1007/s00521-023-09232-2

Tredinnick, L. (2019). Cryptocurrencies and the blockchain. *Business Information Review*, *36*(1), 39–44. DOI: 10.1177/0266382119836314

Trouble, R. C. I. (2020). *Is the world's reserve currency in trouble? International Economy*. https://williamwhite.ca/wp-content/uploads/2020/04/InternationalEconomyDollarSurvivalWinter2020.pdf

Truong, V. T., Le, L., & Niyato, D. (2023). Blockchain Meets Metaverse and Digital Asset Management: A Comprehensive Survey. *IEEE Access : Practical Innovations, Open Solutions*, *11*, 26258–26288. DOI: 10.1109/ACCESS.2023.3257029

Tsai, Y.-C., & Wang, C.-C. (2019). Deep reinforcement learning for foreign exchange trading. *arXiv*. https://arxiv.org/abs/1908.08036

Tsay, R. S. (2010). *Analysis of financial time series* (3rd ed.). Wiley.

Tschorsch, F., & Scheuermann, B. (2016). Bitcoin and beyond: A technical survey on decentralized digital currencies. *IEEE Communications Surveys and Tutorials*, *18*(3), 2084–2123. DOI: 10.1109/COMST.2016.2535718

Turan, A. C., Kokach, V., Kocacinar, B., Şengel, Ö., & Akbulut, F. (2024). Hybrid deep learning framework for stock price prediction incorporating technical and macroeconomic indicators. In *2024 9th International Conference on Computer Science and Engineering (UBMK)* (pp. 1189–1194). DOI: 10.1109/UBMK63289.2024.10773522

Turi, A. N. (Ed.). (2023). *Financial Technologies and DeFi*. Springer International Publishing., DOI: 10.1007/978-3-031-17998-3

U.S. Department of the Treasury. (2021, Nov 1). President's Working Group on Financial Markets releases report and recommendations on stablecoins. https://home.treasury.gov/news/press-releases/jy0454

U.S. Department of the Treasury. (2025, Apr 30). TBAC Charge 2 Q2 2025. https://home.treasury.gov/system/files/221/TBACCharge2Q22025.pdf

U.S. Energy Information Administration. (2023). *Factors affecting heating oil prices.* https://www.eia.gov/energyexplained/heating-oil/factors-affecting-heating-oil-prices.php

U.S. Senate. (2023). *Stablecoin TRUST Act of 2023.* 118th Congress, 1st Session.

U.S. Senate. (2024). *GENIUS Act of 2024.* 118th Congress, 2nd Session.

U.S. Treasury. (2022). *Illicit finance risk assessment of decentralized finance.* https://home.treasury.gov

U.S. Treasury. (2023). *Report on stablecoins.* https://home.treasury.gov

Vaca, C., Astorgano, M., López-Rivero, A. J., Tejerina, F., & Sahelices, B. (2024). Interpretability of deep learning models in the analysis of Spanish financial text. *Neural Computing & Applications, 36*(13), 7509–7527. DOI: 10.1007/s00521-024-09474-8

Vasek, M., & Moore, T. (2015, January). There's no free lunch, even using Bitcoin: Tracking the popularity and profits of virtual currency scams. In *International conference on financial cryptography and data security* (pp. 44-61). Berlin, Heidelberg: Springer Berlin Heidelberg. DOI: 10.1007/978-3-662-47854-7_4

Vidal-Tomás, D. (2023). The illusion of the metaverse and meta-economy. *International Review of Financial Analysis, 86*, 102560. DOI: 10.1016/j.irfa.2023.102560

Walch, A. (2015). The Bitcoin blockchain as financial market infrastructure: A consideration of operational risk. *New York University Journal of Legislation and Public Policy, 18*, 837–893.

Wang, H., & Yu, S. (2021). Robo-advising: Enhancing investment with inverse optimization and deep reinforcement learning. In *2021 20th IEEE International Conference on Machine Learning and Applications (ICMLA)* (pp. 365–372). IEEE.

Wang, J. X., Kurth-Nelson, Z., Tirumala, D., Soyer, H., Leibo, J. Z., Munos, R., Blundell, C., Kumaran, D., & Botvinick, M. (2016). Learning to reinforcement learn. *arXiv*. https://arxiv.org/abs/1611.05763

Wang, C., Chen, Y., Zhang, S., & Zhang, Q. (2022). Stock market index prediction using a deep Transformer model. *Expert Systems with Applications*, *208*, 118128. DOI: 10.1016/j.eswa.2022.118128

Wang, J., Sun, T., Liu, B., Cao, Y., & Zhu, H. (2021). *CLVSA: A convolutional LSTM-based variational sequence-to-sequence model with attention to predicting trends in financial markets*. arXiv:2104.04041.

Wang, R., Xiao, B., & Liu, X.-Y. (2025). FinRL-Crypto: An open-source framework for deep reinforcement learning in cryptocurrency trading. *Journal of Computational Finance and AI*, *3*(1), 45–62.

Wang, S., & Klabjan, D. (2024). An ensemble method of deep reinforcement learning for automated cryptocurrency trading. In *2024 IEEE International Conference on Blockchain and Cryptocurrency (ICBC)* (pp. 461–463). IEEE.

Wang, Y., Su, Z., Zhang, N., Xing, R., Liu, D., Luan, T. H., & Shen, X. (2023). A Survey on Metaverse: Fundamentals, Security, and Privacy. *IEEE Communications Surveys and Tutorials*, *25*(1), 319–352. DOI: 10.1109/COMST.2022.3202047

Wilmott, P. (2022). *Machine learning: An applied mathematics introduction*. Oxford University Press.

Wolf, T., Debut, L., Sanh, V., Chaumond, J., Delangue, C., & Moi, A.. (2020). *Transformers: State-of-the-art natural language processing*. In *Proceedings of EMNLP System Demonstrations* (pp. 38–45).

Wong, M. C. S., Chan, E. K. H., & Yousaf, I. (2025). CBDCs, regulated stablecoins and tokenized traditional assets under the Basel Committee rules on cryptoassets. *Journal of Financial Regulation and Compliance*, *33*(1), 31–47. DOI: 10.1108/JFRC-03-2024-0050

World Economic Forum. (n.d.). *The Digital Currency Governance Consortium*. https://www.weforum.org/communities/digital-currency-governance-consortium

Xiao, M., Jiang, Z., Qian, L., ... (2025). Retrieval-augmented large language models for financial time-series forecasting. *arXiv preprint arXiv:2502.05878*. https://arxiv.org/abs/2502.05878

Xie, R. (2019). Why China had to ban cryptocurrency but the US did not: A comparative analysis of regulations on crypto-markets between the US and China. *Washington University Global Studies Law Review*, *18*, 457.

Xie, W., & Zheng, X. (2018, November). Research on futures programmed trading based on deep reinforcement learning. In *2018 International Conference on Cloud Computing, Big Data and Blockchain (ICCBB)* (pp. 1–3). IEEE.

Xing, F. Z., Cambria, E., & Welsch, R. E. (2018). Natural language-based financial forecasting: A survey. *Artificial Intelligence Review*, *50*(1), 49–73.

Xu, J., Papangelis, K., Dunham, J., Goncalves, J., LaLone, N. J., Chamberlain, A., Lykourentzou, I., Vinella, F. L., & Schwartz, D. I. (2022). Metaverse: The vision for the future. In *Extended abstracts of the 2022 CHI conference on human factors in computing systems* (Paper No. LBW110). Association for Computing Machinery. DOI: 10.1145/3491101.3516399

Xu, J. (2022). Developments and implications of central bank digital currency: The case of China e-CNY. *Asian Economic Policy Review*, *17*(2), 235–250. DOI: 10.1111/aepr.12396

Xu, M., Guo, Y., Hu, Q., Xiong, Z., Yu, D., & Cheng, X. (2023). A trustless architecture of blockchain-enabled metaverse. *High-Confidence Computing*, *3*(1), 100088. DOI: 10.1016/j.hcc.2022.100088

Xu, Z., Cheng, X., & He, Y. (2022). Performance of deep reinforcement learning for high-frequency market making on actual tick data. In *Proceedings of the 21st International Conference on Autonomous Agents and Multiagent Systems* (pp. 1765–1767).

Yang, H., Liu, X. Y., Zhong, S., & Walid, A. (2020, October). Deep reinforcement learning for automated stock trading: An ensemble strategy. In *Proceedings of the First ACM International Conference on AI in Finance* (pp. 1-8). DOI: 10.1145/3383455.3422540

Yang, H., & Malik, A. (2024). Reinforcement learning pair trading: A dynamic scaling approach. *Journal of Risk and Financial Management*, *17*(12), 555.

Yang, J., & Zhou, G. (2022). A study on the influence mechanism of CBDC on monetary policy: An analysis based on e-CNY. *PLoS One*, *17*(7), e0268471. DOI: 10.1371/journal.pone.0268471 PMID: 35802595

Yang, Q., Zhao, Y., Huang, H., Xiong, Z., Kang, J., & Zheng, Z. (2022). Fusing Blockchain and AI With Metaverse: A Survey. *IEEE Open Journal of the Computer Society*, *3*, 122–136. DOI: 10.1109/OJCS.2022.3188249

Yang, Y., Luo, R., Li, M., Zhou, M., Zhang, W., & Wang, J. (2018, July). Mean field multi-agent reinforcement learning. In *International Conference on Machine Learning* (pp. 5571–5580). PMLR.

Yang, Z., Jin, H., Tang, Y., & Fan, G. (2024). Risk-aware constrained reinforcement learning with non-stationary constraints. In *Proceedings of the 23rd International Conference on Autonomous Agents and Multiagent Systems (AAMAS)* (pp. 2029–2031).

Yeoh, P. (2017). Regulatory issues in blockchain technology. *Journal of Financial Regulation and Compliance*, *25*(2), 196–208. https://econpapers.repec.org/scripts/redir.pf?u=https%3A%2F%2Fdoi.org%2F10.1108%252FJFRC-08-2016-0068;h=repec:eme:jfrcpp:jfrc-08-2016-0068. DOI: 10.1108/JFRC-08-2016-0068

Yermack, D. (2024). Is Bitcoin a real currency? An economic appraisal. In *Handbook of Digital Currency* (pp. 29–40). Academic Press. DOI: 10.1016/B978-0-323-98973-2.00014-9

Ying, C., Zhou, X., Su, H., Yan, D., Chen, N., & Zhu, J. (2022). Towards safe reinforcement learning via constraining conditional value-at-risk. In *Proceedings of the 31st International Joint Conference on Artificial Intelligence (IJCAI)* (pp. 3650–3656).

Yinka-Banjo, C., Akinyemi, M., & Er-rabbany, B. (2023). Stock market prediction using a hybrid of deep learning models. *International Journal of Financial Studies, Economics and Management*. DOI: 10.61549/ijfsem.v2i2.111

Yu, P., Lee, J. S., Kulyatin, I., Shi, Z., & Dasgupta, S. (2019). Model-based deep reinforcement learning for dynamic portfolio optimization. *arXiv*. https://arxiv.org/pdf/1901.08740

Zamani, H., Diaz, F., Dehghani, M., Metzler, D., & Bendersky, M. (2022, July). Retrieval-enhanced machine learning. In *Proceedings of the 45th International ACM SIGIR Conference on Research and Development in Information Retrieval* (pp. 2875–2886).

Zetzsche, D. A., Buckley, R. P., Arner, D. W., & Weber, R. H. (2020). Regulating LIBRA: The transformative potential of Facebook's cryptocurrency and possible regulatory responses. *Oxford Business Law Blog*. https://www.law.ox.ac.uk

Zetzsche, D. A., Arner, D. W., & Buckley, R. P. (2020). Decentralized finance. *Journal of Financial Regulation*, *6*(2), 172–203. DOI: 10.1093/jfr/fjaa010

Zhang, C., Vinyals, O., Munos, R., & Bengio, S. (2018). A study on overfitting in deep reinforcement learning. *arXiv*. https://arxiv.org/abs/1804.06893

Zhang, L., Huang, B., & Wang, Y. (2022). China's digital currency: Design, implications and global impacts. Asian Development Bank Institute Working Paper 1292. ■ Bank of America. (2023). *Digital assets: Stablecoins and the US Treasury market*. Global Research Report.

Zhang, C., Liang, S., Lyu, F., & Fang, L. (2020). Stock-index tracking optimization using auto-encoders. *Frontiers in Physics*, *8*, 388.

Zhang, C., Sjarif, N. N. A., & Ibrahim, R. (2023). Deep learning models for financial time series price forecasting: A review of recent advancements: 2020–2022. *Wiley Interdisciplinary Reviews. Data Mining and Knowledge Discovery*, *13*(2), e1519. DOI: 10.1002/widm.1519

Zhang, X., Guo, Y., Stepputtis, S., Sycara, K., & Campbell, J. (2023). Explaining agent behavior with large language models. *arXiv*. https://arxiv.org/abs/2309.10346

Zhang, Z., Zohren, S., & Roberts, S. (2019). Deep reinforcement learning for trading. *arXiv*. https://arxiv.org/abs/1911.10107

Zhao, Z., & Welsch, R. E. (2024). Hierarchical reinforced trader (HRT): A bi-level approach for optimizing stock selection and execution. *arXiv preprint*, arXiv:2410.14927. https://doi.org/10.48550/arXiv.2410.14927

Zhao, Z., & Giannakis, D. (2016). Analog forecasting with dynamics-adapted kernels. *Nonlinearity*, *29*(9), 2888–2939. DOI: 10.1088/0951-7715/29/9/2888

Zhu, J. Q., Xie, H., Arumugam, D., Wilson, R. C., & Griffiths, T. L. (2025). Using reinforcement learning to train large language models to explain human decisions. *arXiv*. https://arxiv.org/abs/2505.11614

Zimba, A., & Chishimba, M. (2019). On the economic impact of crypto-ransomware attacks: The state of the art on enterprise systems. *European Journal for Security Research*, *4*(1), 3–31. DOI: 10.1007/s41125-019-00039-8

Zou, J., Lou, J., Wang, B., & Liu, S. (2024). A novel deep reinforcement learning-based automated stock trading system using cascaded LSTM networks. *Expert Systems with Applications*, *242*, 122801.

About the Contributors

Haojun Chen holds a Doctorate in Business Administration with a specialization in finance from the University of Manchester Alliance Business School and an MSc in Statistics from Colorado State University. His publications include research articles in prestigious financial journals and several textbooks on financial data science. Dr. Chen has also served as a reviewer and book editor for leading international academic journals and publishers. With extensive experience in hedge funds and the securities industry, Dr. Chen is a founding partner of BlackGold Inc., a global quantitative finance research company. He currently serves as an associate professor of finance at Guangzhou Huali College International School.

***

Laxmana Rao G is a seasoned academician with over 34 years of extensive teaching experience in both undergraduate (UG) and postgraduate (PG) levels. He is currently serving as an Associate Professor in the School of Commerce and Management Studies at Dayananda Sagar University, Bangalore. With a robust academic background and a strong research profile, Dr. Laxmana Rao has made significant contributions to the fields of Finance and Accounts, He obtained M. Com, M.B.A., M. Phil, and PhD degrees from reputed universities, reflecting his deep academic commitment and scholarly excellence. Throughout his career, Dr. Laxmana Rao G has honed his expertise in teaching and research. With 34 years of experience in higher education, he has taught a wide range of subjects related to finance and management. His teaching journey spans various academic levels, including UG and PG programs, where he has mentored and guided students toward achieving academic success. His ability to effectively communicate complex concepts and foster critical thinking has made him a respected figure in the academic community. In addition to his teaching career, Dr. Laxmana Rao has 15 years of dedicated research experience. His research contributions primarily focus on Finance and Accounts, areas in which he continues to explore emerging trends, analyze financial systems, and contribute to the academic discourse. Dr. Laxmana Rao has authored five books on various topics within his field, which have been widely recognized for their academic rigor and practical relevance. His research papers have been published in over 20 journals, including prestigious publications indexed in Scopus. He received the International Research Award from the Institute of Chartered Accountants of India in 2024 for his paper on International Taxation. His work reflects his commitment to advancing knowledge and addressing contemporary challenges in the financial and accounting domains. Dr. Laxmana Rao's primary areas of specialization are Finance and Accounts. His expertise spans financial analysis, corporate finance, accounting principles, financial management, and related subjects. Over the years, he has developed a deep understanding of both theoretical and practical aspects of these subjects, which he integrates into his teaching and research.

V Lava Kumar is an accomplished academician with a diverse educational background and over 13 years of enriching experience in the field of education. Holding an impressive array of qualifications including an MBA, M. Com, PhD in Management, PGDTTM, along with certifications from APSET in Management and APSET in Commerce. His area of specialization is Finance and Accounting. Currently serving as an Assistant Professor at GITAM School of Business, GITAM Deemed to be University, Bengaluru, Dr. Lava Kumar is dedicated to nurturing the minds of future business leaders. His teaching methodology is grounded in both theoretical knowledge and practical insights, ensuring that students receive a holistic understanding of their subjects. Dr. Lava Kumar's contributions extend beyond the classroom, evident through his prolific research endeavours. He has authored numerous research papers, with 3 publications in prestigious Scopus-indexed and ABDC journals, and an impressive tally of 10 research articles in international and peer-reviewed journals. He co-authored a Book which is published in Surana publications. His research interests primarily revolve around contemporary issues in management and finance, where he strives to contribute to the academic discourse with valuable insights and innovative perspectives.

Shawn Li holds an MSc in Statistics from McGill University. He is currently a Senior Research Partner at BlackGold Ins, specializing in statistical arbitrage trading and quantitative strategy development.

Meihua Liu is a researcher at Guangdong University of Foreign Studies. She holds an MBA and has over five years of experience in the private equity industry, specializing in AI technology incubation for IT startups. She is also the founder of QLS Group and several other successful ventures.

Liu Peng is a CFA charter holder and FRM certified professional. He currently serves as a financial analyst at FxPro Financial Services Ltd.

Varanasi Rahul, an Assistant Professor at JAIN University, Bangalore, holds three postgraduate degrees (M.Com in Accounting & Taxation, M.Com in Management, and MA in History) and is a semi-qualified Cost Accountant. He has cleared UGC NET in Commerce twice, AP SET in Commerce, History, and Management, and TS SET in Commerce. With 3 years of teaching experience and 6 months at PwC, he is also a freelance archaeologist, epigraphist, and numismatist. He has authored 3 books, published 6 research articles, contributed 9 book chapters, and written 30+ newspaper articles. Rahul has applied for 11 patents, with 1 granted and 09 published.

N. Sathyanarayana, He has over 15 years of teaching experience at the UG and PG levels. He holds a Master's in Business Administration and Commerce and is pursuing a Ph.D. He currently holds the position of Assistant Professor in the School of Commerce at Jain (Deemed-to-be University), Bangalore. He has published 22 research papers in international journals (2 Scopus Index), 7 research papers in national journals, and presented 14 research papers at international conferences and 11 research papers at national conferences. He has co-authored 2 books at national level and 9 book chapters (Scopus indexed).

Madireddi S S V Sri Kumar is presently associated with Global Business School, Koneru Lakshmaiah Education Foundation (KLEF), Deemed to be university, in Hyderabad. He has done his Masters degree in Commerce, Business administration and he was awarded Ph. D from Acharya Nagarjuna University. He has 27 years of research and Academic experience and has held various positions in leading academic institutions like Jain Deemed to be University, Bangalore, Avanthi's Postgraduate and Research Academy, Hyderabad, Vision P.G. College, Hyderabad, St. Xaviour P.G College Hyderabad etc. as Faculty, Assistant Professor, Associate Professor, Head of the Department and Principal. He is an external project evaluator for different universities. He is guiding two scholars for Ph.D scholars and guiding many projects in different management disciplines and conducted management and faculty development programs in the area of Management. He has attended many national seminars and International conferences and has also published many research papers and his articles got published in leading management international and national journals.

Index

www.ingramcontent.com/pod-product-compliance
Lightning Source LLC
LaVergne TN
LVHW082051011026
849162LV00019B/466
9798337328386